W9-CUC-362

PRESCOTT COLLEGE
LIBRARY

4624

LC
1505
. B5
197

THE IRISH AND CATHOLIC POWER

The Author

PAUL BLANSHARD has written three books on different aspects of the conflict between Roman Catholic policy and modern democracy; *The Irish and Catholic Power* is the third. The earlier two, published in five countries, have attained a distribution of more than 300,000 copies.

Descended from three generations of Protestant clergymen, and trained in both theology and the law, the author is a member of the New York bar. Under Mayor Fiorello LaGuardia, he was head of New York City's Department of Investigations and Accounts. A former associate editor of the *Nation,* he served as a State Department official in Washington and the Caribbean from 1942 to 1946.

The Irish
and Catholic Power

AN AMERICAN INTERPRETATION

With the Supplement and an Introduction to the Reprint Edition

by

Paul Blanshard

GREENWOOD PRESS, PUBLISHERS
WESTPORT, CONNECTICUT

074863

The Library of Congress has catalogued this publication as follows:

Library of Congress Cataloging in Publication Data

Blanshard, Paul, 1892–
    The Irish and Catholic power.

    Original ed. issued in series: Beacon studies in
church and state.
    1. Catholic Church in Ireland. 2. Ireland
—Social conditions. 3. Irish in the United States.
4. Catholic Church—Doctrinal and controversial works
—Protestant authors. I. Title.
[BX1505.B55 1972]   282.415   70-112321
ISBN 0-8371-4708-5

Copyright 1953 by Paul Blanshard

Originally published in 1953
by The Beacon Press, Boston

Reprinted with the permission
of Paul Blanshard

First Greenwood Reprinting 1972

Library of Congress Catalogue Card Number 70-112321

ISBN 0-8371-4708-5

Printed in the United States of America

CIP 3 1 JAN 1972

Contents

Make no mistake about it, my Lord Bishop of Limerick, Democracy is going to rule in these countries.

MICHAEL DAVITT

Introduction to the Reprint Edition

The Catholic-Protestant War in Northern Ireland (1968-71)

The western world was startled in 1968 when a new religious war broke out in Northern Ireland between Catholics and Protestants. Men wondered how such a thing could happen in the twentieth century. The new conflict seemed doubly incredible after the Second Vatican Council of 1962-65 where so many thousand words of amity about the ecumenical future had been poured out by both Protestants and Catholics.

The causes of the new war were not new. In fact, almost all of the basic factors behind the new conflict are described in detail in Chapter 9 of this book, "Northern Ireland and Partition," and that chapter should be read in conjunction with this Introduction. When Northern Ireland was created fifty years ago, the people of the Irish Republic to the South did not accept its right to exist. And the people of the Protestant majority in the North have never ceased to live in fear that their country might be taken away from them by joint action of Northern and Southern Catholics.

The new troubles came to a head on October 5, 1968 with riots in Derry (Londonderry). Demonstrating civil rights advocates, nearly all Catholic, were arrayed against Protestant Unionists. These riots were described as religious disturbances, and there was some truth in this description because nearly all the Catholics in Northern Ireland were on one side and nearly all the Protestants on the other. But the motivation on both sides was as much political as religious. These riots were also nationalist riots, and probably two-thirds of the animosity was based on political loyalties. The Catholics were loyal to the Irish Republic which they openly acknowledged as "their" government, while the Protestants were loyal to Stormont (the Northern Parliament) and to the United Kingdom, of which Northern Ireland is a part. Both sides regarded their opponents as subversives and, in a sense, both were correct because they were loyal to different countries.

On both sides of the dispute extremists brought pressure to bear upon political leaders who dared to talk about compromise and concessions. Captain Terence O'Neill, who served as Northern prime minister from 1963 to 1969, proposed reforms that would have eliminated most of the anti-Catholic discrimination in local governments in the North, but he was virtually forced out of office because the die-hard Unionists in the right wing of his own party thought that he was becoming too soft in dealing with the enemy. He was succeeded by a slightly more intransigent prime minister, James Chichester-Clark, who in turn was succeeded by a hopeful moderate, Brian Faulkner.

In the beginning of the new disturbances the Catholic drive was headed by the Northern Ireland Civil Rights Association, founded in 1967. Ostensibly it stood for legal justice to be achieved without violence. It centered its attack on discrimination against Catholics in housing, employment, and local elections. In this respect its indictment was about sixty per cent correct since there is no doubt that, at the *local* level, as we have made clear in Chapter 9, Catholics suffered real discrimination. The discrimination was particularly evident in places like the city of Derry, where the majority of the people were Catholics governed by a privileged Protestant minority.

The leader of the new civil rights drive was one of the most colorful figures in political history, the young Bernadette Devlin, a product of the Bogside slum of Derry who was elected and reelected to the British House of Commons as a representative of a new party called the People's Democracy, an organization which denounced both the government of Northern Ireland and the government of the Irish Republic as instruments of capitalist imperialism. Although she was a practicing Catholic and nearly all her followers were Catholic, this mini-skirted, nonstop talker of twenty-two, the youngest person to sit in the British Parliament since the days of William Pitt, tried to turn the Northern civil rights movement into a revolutionary socialist movement. Participating in the riots, she was sentenced to six months in jail for "riotous behavior." The Catholic hierarchy of Ireland was profoundly embarrassed by her leadership, especially after she produced a baby in 1971 without benefit of husband. When she came to America in 1969 to raise $1,000,000 for her cause, the American hierarchy treated her with frosty skepticism, and she returned to Ireland with less than one-tenth of her quota achieved. Nevertheless, the Catholic hierarchy of both Northern Ireland and the Irish Republic stood solidly against the Stormont regime in the struggles and helped to make the conflict a Catholic-Protestant war.

On the Protestant side the dominant Unionist Party, representing two-thirds of the Northern people and holding a clear majority in the Northern Parliament at all times, encountered great difficulty in working out a policy on which all factions could agree. The violence and extremism on the Catholic side strengthened the extremists among the Unionists. A new leader of the right wing Protestant forces arose with a program which threatened every politician who favored constructive compromise. He was the eloquent fundamentalist preacher, Ian Paisley, who formed a string of independent Free Presbyterian churches, not affiliated with the major Presbyterian church of the North. The slogan of his campaign was "No surrender to the Pope," and after scoring several political triumphs he claimed at least 100,000 militant followers. He even organized a parade to protest against the "romanizing tendencies" of the general assembly of Northern Ireland's regular Presbyterian church.

The situation worsened in 1970 and 1971 partly because the leadership of the Catholic forces was taken over by the extremist faction of the old Irish Republican Army, which specialized in sniper attacks and the planting of bombs. This faction, called "the provisionals," made no pretense of nonviolence. It turned the struggle into guerrilla warfare. Although the I.R.A. was nominally outlawed on both sides of the border, the enforcement of the law in the South was farcical. No jury in the Irish Republic would convict an Irishman for I.R.A. activity, and as a result, the three hundred mile border became a sieve through which I.R.A. terrorists filtered to the South after planting bombs in the North. When one of the most famous gunmen of the I.R.A., Joe Cahill, tried to come to the United States in 1971 to raise money for more I.R.A. guns, and was denied entrance by American customs, he returned to the Irish Republic and was promptly freed as a legal patriot.

One of the most bitter complaints of the Northern Catholics was that Stormont had organized the Ulster Special Constabulary, an auxiliary police force composed largely of determined Protestants who, it was alleged, were extremely partisan in their activities. Under British pressure the Northern government disbanded this special police force, and the Wilson government finally sent in British troops to attempt to restore order impartially. But order was not restored. In fact, the arrival of the British troops gave the Catholic opposition the opportunity to describe the whole "peace" operation as a revival of old style British imperialism.

As the conflict became more bitter, the I.R.A. assumed leadership and turned sniper's bullets and bombs on British soldiers. In the conflict women and children were caught in the cross fire, adding to the religious-nationalist frenzy. After a particularly prolonged riot in August 1971, with twelve dead and hundreds of homes destroyed by fire, the Northern government invoked emergency powers of preventive detention and interned, after a night raid, more then three hundred alleged leaders of the I.R.A. Although many of these leaders were later released, the majority were held without trial. Although this new policy of internment increased the fury of the Catholics, the Northern government justified it as a necessary war measure, arguing that the I.R.A. was a military force which must be met with military strategy.

This was the position late in 1971, after Harold Wilson's Labor government in Britain had been supplanted by the Conservatives and Edward Heath. British Labor was slightly more friendly to the Northern Catholics than Heath's Conservatives, but both parties stood by the British pledge that Northern Ireland "should not cease to be a part of the United Kingdom without the consent of the people of Northern Ireland," and both parties reasserted the blunt warning that the parliament of Northern Ireland was the only agency authorized to give consent to any change of status. In spite of this pledge there was considerable agitation in Britain for a complete take-over of Northern Ireland by the British government and its rule from London in the manner of British rule over Scotland and Wales.

During the three-year conflict there was much pressure for compromise solutions. Yielding to British influence, the Northern government appointed the Cameron Commission, headed by a Scottish High Court judge, Lord Cameron, with power to make a thorough investigation of causes. Reporting in 1969, the Cameron Commission declared that there were many features of Northern government policy which discriminated against Catholics. The report listed six areas where Unionists have controlled local elections by gerrymandering boundary lines and by limiting the local franchise. As to government employment at the local level, the Commission said: "We are satisfied that all these Unionist-controlled councils have used their power to make appointments in a way which benefitted Protestants." The Commission, incidentally, scored Bernadette Devlin by name and Ian Paisley by implication. In its report there was one sentence which deserved the attention of every student of Irish policy: "Segregated education—insisted upon by the Roman Catholic Church—also plays its part in initiating and maintaining divisions and differences among the young."

Some of the most important local reforms demanded by the Catholics of the North have already been granted by Stormont and approved by Britain, but the mutual murder still goes on. Three solutions are being proposed: reform of the Northern regime to eliminate discrimination in housing, jobs, and franchise; a complete take-over by Great Britain; and the partial absorption of Northern Ireland into an all-island regime with major power in Dublin but considerable local autonomy for Northern Ireland.

The last of these solutions, called the "reunification of Ireland" is that championed by Prime Minister John Lynch of the Irish Republic and, unofficially, by the hierarchy of the Catholic Church. It is the solution which the majority in the North reject unequivocally on the ground that a Catholic majority in an all-Irish regime could not be trusted to keep any promise favoring Protestants. Protestant propaganda emphasizes the fact that the Southern regime is still a priest-ridden regime with no birth control and no divorce, and a declaration in Article 44 of the Republic's Constitution that "The State recognizes the special position of the Holy Catholic Apostolic and Roman Church as the guardian of the Faith professed by the great majority of the citizens." The Protestant opposition to reunification is strengthened by the fact that the Irish hierarchy, even since the Vatican Council, has been consistently reactionary, supporting the papal opposition to birth control and divorce, and scorning nearly all movements toward ecumenism.

The immediate future seems to favor the first solution I have listed, the reform of the worst discriminatory features of the Northern regime without destroying the framework of Northern government. But it would be a rash prophet who attempted any confident prophecy about so complex and troubled a problem. Hate and bigotry and nationalism and racial prejudice have poisoned the atmosphere. My own gloomy prediction is that "the troubles" will go on for a long time no matter what framework of power is adopted. Perhaps the Irish people of North and South will never be brought together in genuine friendship until Irish children, both Catholic and Protestant, go to school together. At present their separatism is promoted and exaggerated by both religion and nationalism. If they could grow up in neutral, nonsectarian classrooms, and learn to accept the separation of church and state, they might find a permanent solution.

Fortunately, some Irishmen, both in the North and the South, are beginning to see the wisdom in such a policy. A recent opinion poll of a Belfast newspaper showed that a majority of both Protestants and Catholics wanted a school system in which Catholic and Protestant children could be brought up together, and in 1970 the Unionist Party passed a resolution in favor of the "integration of all schools."

PAUL BLANSHARD

Foreword

In 1951, a Jesuit scholar, reviewing my *American Freedom and Catholic Power* in the leading Jesuit magazine of Dublin, challenged me in effect to take the Irish Republic as a "pilot model" for a future Catholic America. I have accepted this suggestion, and here is my answer.

Appropriately enough, the answer was commenced in Dublin, continued in London, and finished in Boston. It is a book not only about Ireland but about Irish Catholicism as a social and political force throughout the English-speaking world. It is the product of a year's study outside of Ireland, and more than six months in Ireland between May 1952 and February 1953. With Dublin as headquarters, and a small car as transportation, my wife and I visited every corner of the island. At our Dublin flat on Fitzwilliam Place we entertained a varied and delightful assortment of Ireland's most charming and brilliant citizens, and we talked and listened. I interviewed at length the most important Catholic and Protestant leaders from Prime Minister Eamon de Valera in the South to Lord Brookeborough in the North, including such diverse personalities as Sean MacBride, the Republic's former Minister for External Affairs; Harry Midgley, present Minister of Education in the North; William Norton, head of the Irish Labor Party; and Cahir Healy and Edward McAteer, chief nationalist militants of Derry and Enniskillen. I spoke with distinguished churchmen of all faiths, with editors, with labor leaders, with noted writers, with Orangemen, with veterans of the I.R.A., with veterans of the British occupation, with priests and preachers, with Protestant and Catholic professors, and with hundreds of people in villages, cities, and schools. I attended debates in the Dail, Sinn Fein conferences, Orangemen's rallies, anti-Partition mass meetings, and great gatherings of Catholicism's right-wing organization, Maria Duce.

Although I am deeply grateful to the many Catholic and non-Catholic friends who helped me so generously, I shall not thank them by name. Under the circumstances it is best to respect and preserve their anonymity. Ireland, as this book will make clear, is not a place where men can express frank and unorthodox opinions on church and state without penalty. Many of the men who gave me the most significant information are

Catholics or non-Catholics living in an atmosphere approximating genteel terror in which any association with an outspoken critic of the hierarchy's policies might lead to the termination of professional careers.

In addition to the standard works on Irish history and the Dublin newspapers, my primary documentary sources have been the approved Irish Catholic journals, particularly the learned journals of the priests which are produced under official Imprimatur; and the Irish Catholic journals of England, Scotland, and the United States. At the end of this book in the Notes the reader will find a running, page-by-page listing and discussion of sources, indicating where — in the months of research in the British Museum, the Central Catholic Library of Dublin, the National Library of Ireland, and Trinity College Library — I was able to find facts buttressed by documentation. Frequently the reference will be entirely unnecessary, because the fact will be as obvious as daylight; but since the field of Catholic policy is probably the most controversial field in modern dialectics, I have chosen to err on the side of caution.

To Jeannette Hopkins of the Beacon Press, I am especially indebted for searching analysis and sound advice in the final stages of the preparation of the manuscript.

Samuel Johnson once said: "The Irish are a fair people; they never speak well of one another." They also, I have discovered, never speak well of any non-Irish writer who writes a book about Ireland. Nobody, in fact, can write a book about Ireland which the Irish will like. Having thoughtfully provided my ego with this shield against the slings and arrows of Celtic wrath, I hasten to explain that this is not primarily a book for Irishmen in Ireland — although I hope that some of them will read it, if the censors permit. It is a book about something larger and more significant than Ireland, a world-wide cultural and political force which began with Saint Patrick but which spread to London, to Glasgow, to Boston, to Toronto, to Melbourne, and to the whole English-speaking world. It is a force which may change the future of Western democracy, particularly if it is not properly understood. My primary purpose is to help the non-Irish world to understand it.

PAUL BLANSHARD

THE IRISH AND CATHOLIC POWER

1

Perspective and Purpose

"Ireland," says Bishop Fulton J. Sheen, "is the last bastion of Christian civilization in Western Europe."

"Ireland," says Jesuit Robert I. Gannon, former president of Fordham University, "is a lesson in true democracy."

"Ireland," according to the Rt. Rev. Monsignor James H. Cotter, "standing majestically among the wrecks of earth . . . is still brilliant apostle among the nations, still model of principle before those governments that ignore and disregard all principle."*

From an Irish Catholic point of view, these eulogies of the home country by Irish-American priests are only slightly extravagant. The Irish Catholic story is the great success story of Catholic power in our time. It is a story of astounding clerical achievement in the face of stupendous odds. The Irish Republic is the No. 1 exhibit of Roman Catholicism in the English-speaking world — in fact, the *only* Roman Catholic country in the English-speaking world. In practice it is the world's most devoutly Catholic country, not even excepting Portugal and Spain. If its overseas missionaries of Irish stock are included in the reckoning, it produces more priests and nuns per capita than any country in the world. It is so confident of its exalted mission in modern society that it sends out to non-Catholic countries, including Great Britain and the United States, more than three-fourths of all its young priests, instructed to win them to the Irish Catholic way of life. In terms of Catholic policy it is triumphantly unique. It is the only modern democracy with no

_____
* See Notes (beginning on page 340) for all sources and for supplementary material.

3

divorce, no legal birth control, and no comprehensive public-school system.

As an exhibit of church-state relations, the Irish Republic is a paradox. Although the nation's schools, libraries, newspapers, and publishing firms are almost completely dominated by the Catholic outlook, and although that outlook is imposed by a hierarchy chosen in Rome, the majority of the Irish people do not resent this domination. They accept it as an organic and established part of Irish life. They permit ecclesiastical dictatorship and political democracy to live side by side without any sense of incongruity. Although they cherish their official political freedom with fierce jealousy, they are more loyal to Rome than the people of any other nation, far more devoted and obedient than the natives of the Vatican's home country. "Ireland," says Dr. James Devane, one of Dublin's noted champions of the Church, "is the most Catholic country in the world. Perhaps the Republic of Ireland, as it is constituted today, is the only integral Catholic State in the world; a Catholic culture as it existed in the Middle Ages."

This Irish Catholic culture is spreading outward from Ireland to every corner of the world. Nominally it is a thoroughly Roman culture, subservient to the Vatican and accurately representing the Vatican; but in practice it is something more than Roman Catholicism. It is a super-zealous and distinctive form of the original faith, more pugnacious, more self-centered, and more dogmatic than the spirit of Rome itself. It has captured the leadership of Catholicism throughout the West and in many sections of Africa and the Orient.

In the English-speaking world, Roman Catholic power is essentially Irish Catholic power, inspired by the dynamic energy of Irish leadership and in many places organized in nationalist-religious-political blocs designed to promote Irish and Catholic interests simultaneously. In many English-speaking regions outside of Ireland, the Roman Catholic Church *is* Irish, unashamedly and completely Irish. In other regions the Church works and expands under the complete control of an Irish hierarchy which keeps the clerics and laymen of Italian, German, and Polish stock in subordination. The Roman Catholic Church in England, Scotland, Northern Ireland, the United States, western Canada, and Australia is ruled in each case by cardinals and bishops of Irish descent, and in each case the great majority of the active members are of Irish stock. There are six times as many Irish Catholics outside of Ireland as there are at home, and their hold on the machinery of Catholic power has never been more impregnable. The United States probably has five times as many Catholics of Irish descent as the Irish Republic itself, the Boston area claims more Catholics than Dublin, and the New York City region has two-thirds as many as the whole of the Republic. Not only is the Irish-dominated Roman Catholic Church much the largest church in America, but its people have become by far the most distinctive foreign segment in American life.

The whole Catholic power system of the West is, as the *Irish World* puts it, "Ireland's spiritual empire." And, as the editor asserts, that "spiritual empire is world-wide. . . . So when fools and ignoramuses try to belittle Ireland and sneer at it and its people, we can call attention to Ireland's Empire of the soul where bread, beauty and brotherhood and all that goes with charity, kindness and toleration are enthroned for all to enjoy without preference or favoritism of any kind."

A Political Phenomenon

The extent of Irish Catholic power would be of little concern to the non-Catholic world if Irish Catholicism happened to be a purely devotional phenomenon. The prevailing conviction of the English-speaking peoples is that all men of every faith should be left alone to worship God, or not to worship God, in their own way, without interference or direct public criticism. Not only is religion free in the English-speaking democracies but it is protected by a heavy traditional shield of tolerance and good will which usually saves it from direct attack. In a sense, religion in Western society occupies a kind of special cultural reservation, where the standards of combat and criticism are softer and more genteel than they are in the world of politics and commerce. It is considered bad taste to criticize purely religious institutions for their devotional activity, and most men who do not share a particular faith with their friends elect to remain silent about those features which they consider unacceptable.

What takes Irish Catholicism out of this protected reservation and makes it a fair subject for political analysis is that it has become a great political as well as devotional phenomenon in Western life. I use the word "political" here in its broadest sense to include all those matters of citizenship which are not denominational. The Irish priests have no political party of their own in any English-speaking country. But they have something very much more important politically: a program for the control of great areas of modern life which belong to democracy, such general areas as elementary education, freedom of thought, domestic-relations law, and medical hygiene; and such specific political areas as Irish Partition, Franco's fascism, Jerusalem's independence, and Tito's collaboration with the West. On all these issues Irish bishops and priests are boldly political in the sense that they carry their moral authority over into the world of citizenship and tell their people what they should and should not do.

Irish Catholicism is also important in the West because in Catholic propaganda Ireland is being constantly used as a model for church-state relations in Christian society. Whenever a public disagreement arises in the United States or a British commonwealth concerning such moral-legislative problems as censorship, the use of public money for religious schools, the right of divorce, government medical service, or the right to practice birth control, some protagonist of the Roman Catholic point of view is certain to suggest that the Irish way of solving these problems of church and state is the superior way, more godly, more democratic, and more moral than the "pagan" methods of non-Catholic society. Ireland is represented by these Catholic champions not only as the last bastion of Christian civilization in Europe but also as the last bastion of a system of church-state relations which democracy needs for its moral welfare.

I propose to examine these representations and claims in some detail, and to build my discussion of Ireland and Irish Catholic power around the church-state issue. Such a method of analysis has both advantages and disadvantages. The arbitrary limitation of scope means that many significant aspects of Irish life must be passed over lightly. Ireland is a land of fascinating perplexities which are worthy of far more extensive treatment than this book can attempt. The non-Irish writer is almost overwhelmed with the richness of Irish life and the variety of its appealing features. He may consider the island as an orphan of British imperialism, as a delightful haven for ubiquitous tourists, as a land of charming and warm-hearted friends, as an isolated backwater of Celtic culture, or as a larder for British beef-eaters.

Ireland as a Political Yardstick

I am interested in Ireland primarily as a yardstick for the measurement and appraisal of Catholic political policy in the West. For that purpose it is the best yardstick in the world, far better than Spain or Portugal. Spain and Portugal are Latin and totalitarian; Northern Ireland and the Irish Republic are politically democratic. If we wish to ask how Catholic power might function in the future in an English-speaking democracy which became 95 per cent Catholic, we can turn to the Irish Republic for one answer. If we wish to know how Catholic power might function in an English-speaking democracy which became one-third Catholic, we can turn to Northern Ireland. Perhaps from these two pilot studies we can extract lessons of real significance for the shaping of church-state policy in such non-Catholic nations as the United States, Great Britain, Canada, and Australia.

Irish Catholicism is particularly important for the West because its compromise with democracy in the Republic is the most advanced form of church-state adjustment in any completely Catholic country. It represents the utmost compromise which the Papacy can make with Western society and still be true to its principles. In a sense, the Irish Republic is the world's best showpiece of Catholic tolerance in a Catholic society, and that is one of the reasons why the Vatican permits a demonstration of liberalism in Ireland. Catholic champions are justified in pointing to the Republic as a model for Catholic-democratic relations within a Catholic order. Their model, as we shall see later, lacks many of the basic ingredients of freedom, but it is the best model which Catholicism can offer to its critics.

Since Irish Catholicism abroad is actually much more important than Irish Catholicism at home, this study would be incomplete without some discussion of Irish Catholic power as it has developed in the United States, Great Britain, Canada, and Australia. The Catholic power pattern in each of these countries has a definite relationship to the pattern of church-state policy. If all the English-speaking countries of the world could be arranged on a chart in respect to their church-state adjustments, the United States would occupy one end of the spectrum and the Irish Republic the other, with the British Commonwealths between. The United States stands for the complete separation of church and state, with an almost absolute prohibition against public expenditures for religious institutions. Its clean-cut policy of church-state separation is America's most distinctive contribution to modern statecraft. In the Irish Republic, on the other hand, there is a system of church-state cooperation in which Catholicism is almost identified with the national spirit, and clerical power is absorbed into the structure of the country. Religion and politics are interwoven in a unity which is as much Catholic as Irish.

Between these two contrasting samples of church-state policy come the British Commonwealths, each with its own peculiar brand of church-state mixture, and each disposed to give religion a more official place in political life than it is given under the American Constitution. All these English-speaking countries have one thing in common in respect to Catholic power. They are all engaged in a desperate struggle to protect their present areas of community control from further encroachments by the Irish Catholic bishops. The struggle with these bishops is virtually world-wide, and its outcome is, I believe, of immense importance for the survival of a free culture in the West. The facts which I develop in these pages will, I hope, demonstrate the truth of this conclusion.

I have called this analysis "An American Interpretation." American interpretations of anything are not very popular in Europe today, especially if they become eulogies of American policy. We Americans in recent years have sent so many immature nationalists overseas to promote our way of life that one cannot blame Europe for discounting our claims. But if we have been too boastful of many second-rate American contributions to civilization, we have been too modest about the one feature of our political life which might be of more value to the outside world than all our other ideological exports combined — our policy of separation of church and state. That policy is relatively unknown and unappreciated in Europe, even by Protestants and Jews. Spokesmen for European Catholicism denounce it violently and neglect its virtues.

I confess that I am writing this analysis of Irish Catholicism partly to remedy that neglect. I believe that America has a lesson for the West in the field of church-state adjustment, a lesson of tolerance and good will derived from the practice of separating church and state, and that this lesson is flatly contrary to the gospel of church and state which is preached by Irish Catholicism. The two philosophies cannot both be right for the democratic world, and I believe that by analyzing one in terms of the other, the weakness and the strength of both will be revealed.

Such an analysis would be worse than useless if it were made from a purely partisan point of view, Catholic, Protestant, or Jewish. Most Protestant and Jewish policies in the English-speaking world today happen to be more tolerant and co-operative than the corresponding policies of Irish Catholicism, but no religion has a right to boast of the purity of its record. All denominational critics must *ipso facto* hurl their stones from glass houses, because the balance sheet of every great religion is stained with some disgraceful record of intolerance. Moreover the danger of hidden prejudice is always present in the human mind.

Bigotry and Sentimentalism

In discussing Irish Catholic power in the United States, the writer is confronted with very special dangers. First, there is the danger that any adverse comment concerning clerical policy will play into the hands of such anti-Catholic and anti-Semitic merchants of hate as Gerald L. K. Smith and the leaders of the Ku Klux Klan. Second, there is the danger that any comment reflecting upon the Irish as a group in American society will be seized upon by those provincial-minded citizens who exploit all anti-foreign sentiments in behalf of reaction. Third, there is the opposite danger of treating Irish Catholicism with such bland sentimentality that all its basic evils will be overlooked.

My own conviction is that this third danger is by far the greatest. The first two dangers are very slight. America has comparatively few people who hate Catholics as Catholics or Irishmen as Irishmen, and who desire to see them suppressed or discriminated against in any way. Even the most hostile critics of Catholic policy do not want a single right taken away from the Catholic Church or the Catholic people, and most anti-Irish sentiment in America died in the last century. Catholicism in the American environment has complete freedom to teach, to proselyte, to establish its own school system, and to expand its power without any legal obstacles — and no decent American would have it otherwise.

But a great many decent citizens of the United States want to run away from the twin challenges of Irish separatism and Catholic intolerance in American life out of cowardice or indolence or just plain lack of information. They are afraid of acquiring a reputation for intolerance if they criticize anything which has a religious label. An Irish bishop has only to say "bigot" and they dissolve in panic — forgetting their obligation as Americans to fight intolerance and bigotry in any form, whether inside or outside the churches. Many Americans are actually deceived by the old verbal trick of calling any critic of Catholic policy an enemy of the Catholic people. The tendency of liberals to beat a cowardly retreat in the face of any noisy clerical offensive has led to an astonishing situation in America. Although the United States has the most advanced and successful policy on church-state relations in the world, non-Catholic Americans are actually on the defensive today in maintaining that policy against an adroit and continuous attack by the Irish Catholic bishops. I believe that it is time to meet that attack with counter-attack if our American traditions of religious freedom and church-state separation are to endure.

As I see it, the three most important expressions of bigotry and separatism in American life today, after racial segregation, are: (1) the Catholic rule that Catholic children must not attend public schools with the children of other faiths; (2) the Catholic rule that Catholics must not marry non-Catholics on a basis of equality; and (3) the Catholic rule that Catholics may not read books directly critical of Catholic policy. (The text of these three rules is given in the Notes.) Although all three of these supreme examples of bigotry are made in Rome, they are enforced and executed in America primarily by the Irish priests, and it is fair to describe them as the most distinctive features of Irish Catholic power in America. They are all expressions of priestly power, not peoples' power, imposed upon the genial and kindly and patriotic Irish people by the Irish priests as part of a partisan battle plan which was originally developed in Ireland in the days when Catholicism had to be pugnacious to survive, and which was imported into this country with the great wave of Irish immigration. They have nothing to do with the devotional aspects of Catholicism or with the worship of God. They are weapons of clerical power in a non-Catholic society, and their ultimate effect, as we shall see in this book, will be to break down the American policy of separation of church and state.

Perhaps the American policy of church-state separation *should* be destroyed, and succeeded by the Irish Catholic policy of partial church-state union under a democratic government. That question will be for the reader to decide when he has finished this book. As I see it, the separation of church and state is desirable in view of its ultimate purpose. It is not an end in itself but only a means to an end — a genuinely free and tolerant society. It is worth fighting for because it tends simultaneously to preserve religious freedom and to destroy religious bigotry. In the United States it is being challenged by the largest and most powerful church — and that Church is controlled by an Irish clerical bloc. But if the challenge came from a Swedish Lutheran or Chinese Buddhist or Russian Jewish clerical bloc in our society, believers in the separation of church and state would have the same obligation to resist. And their resistance would not mean that they were anti-Swedish, anti-Lutheran, anti-Chinese, anti-Buddhist, anti-Russian, or anti-Semitic, so long as they could say with a clear conscience that they were opposed to all bigotry and to all denominational special privilege.

The one who has a right to be heard as a champion of the separation of church and state is one whose aim is a society of tolerance and good will where men of different faiths can live together as equals, educate their children together, marry across religious boundaries without discrimination, and refuse to use sectarian advantage for political power. This kind of society, it seems to me, should be the ultimate aim of all discussion and analysis in this field. Certainly no one has a right to discuss the tragedy of religious partisanship in Ireland — and religious partisanship *is* the major tragedy of Irish life — unless his outlook is that of denominational non-partisanship.

Neutrality may seem impossible for me, since I was born in a Protestant parsonage and I am descended from a Protestant grandfather of County Down. But no one can write fairly about Ireland unless he is ready to recognize that the Irish tragedy goes back to Protestant as well as to Catholic bigotry. In the eighteenth and nineteenth centuries, English Protestants taught Irish Catholics to hate and to fear because they used Protestantism as an auxiliary weapon of oppression. They created the conditions under which Irish Catholicism became the world's leading symbol of separatism and religious aggression. On many occasions, particularly in the nineteenth century, English Protestantism could have taken the sting of bitterness from the Irish Catholic opposition by renouncing its own special privilege and by inaugurating a policy of denominational fair play.

Now it is too late for reconciliation, and Irish Protestants have no choice but to defend themselves against the most thoroughly regimented and most persistently aggressive religious oligarchy in the world. In their struggle the Irish Protestants have the best wishes of most believers in democracy and freedom — but even their devoted friends cannot help murmuring with T. S. Eliot: "Of all that was done in the past you eat the fruit, either rotten or ripe."

2

Past and Present

"Religion," says the noted Catholic convert, Sir Shane Leslie, "has been the underlying inspiration, consolation, and it must be said the smouldering poison in Irish life." Without a religious cleavage, it is probable that there would have been no Irish revolution in the first place and no Irish Partition today. The Irish struggle against England, as Dr. James Devane has said, "was not less political than religious — the conflict of two cultures, the Catholic and a Protestant culture. . . . It is not bigotry to recite such an obvious fact." And it is not bigotry to speak frankly of the North-South division of Ireland today as primarily a product of the arrogance of creeds. In Ireland, geography and economics are important, but religious conflict is even more important. The meandering 200-mile border which divides the island into two parts is as much a product of faith and morals as the Mohammedan-Hindu border between Pakistan and India. It is a Protestant-Catholic border; it is a British-Irish border; it is a barrier in time between the spirit of the modern democratic state and the medieval spirit of Rome.

The present political division of the island is very recent: Northern Ireland in its present form dates only from 1921, and the Irish Republic did not become completely independent until 1949. But the forces that created the present division are very ancient. Sometimes they are described as racial. But they are not primarily racial — or linguistic. The people of the whole Irish island, and the people of Britain, English or Irish, are essentially the same kind of people — speaking the same tongue, belonging to the same race, loyal to the same moral values. I am

13

sure that they would like to live together with mutual trust and affection, but they are caught in the tragic interplay of two emotional forces, nationalism and faith. This, however, is getting ahead of our story. It is one of the purposes of this book to show in detail how nationalism and faith have worked together in Ireland to serve and extend Catholic power. The demonstration calls for a brief survey of Irish history.

Saint Patrick and His Mission

Saint Patrick, it seems, was a Roman Catholic. For brevity's sake, I shall begin with Saint Patrick, although there is a little authentic Irish history before Saint Patrick. (For those who want a running historical outline, I have included in the Appendix a section called "Names and Dates in Irish History.")

Or was Saint Patrick a Roman Catholic? Some Protestants are not willing to concede either his bones or his loyalties to Rome. They have allegedly located his alleged bones in a Protestant cemetery in County Down; but they do not treat the bones too respectfully, because they doubt the authenticity of the bones and because they question the use to which the image of Saint Patrick has been put in Catholic propaganda. Saint Patrick, they contend, was not a Roman partisan at all, and if he had lived in the sixteenth century, they say, he might have joined the Protestant revolt. They argue that in his famous *Confessions* he did not make one verbal gesture of loyalty toward papal power. He functioned in Ireland long before any great division in the early Church, and he landed on Irish shores in 432 A.D., before the Roman bishops had won universal recognition. He was a pre-papal Christian, not concerned with schisms, rather crude and unlettered, a great organizer of men and monks, but certainly no philosopher. He was successful in making Ireland into a Christian country largely because he had the good sense to combine Christian doctrine with native legend. The surviving traces of the old Druid magic were absorbed into Irish Christianity, and the whole Catholic amalgam of faith and magic came down through the centuries with a distinctive local flavor.

Saint Patrick found in Ireland in 432 an island which was not yet a nation, ruled over by dissident chieftains and divided into tribal states. Its people, the historians tell us, were Celts. No one is sure exactly what a Celt is, and it is known that there were people in Ireland long before the Celts arrived; so Ireland is not purely Celtic. Some of the pre-Celts were probably wanderers from the Mediterranean. There was a sprawling Celtic empire on the continent long before Saint Patrick came to the West, and among its warriors there were some who found their way to Ireland about a century before Saint Patrick arrived. It is certain that there was not only one spot on the European continent from which a single body of people emigrated across the waters and the intervening British land to Ireland. The people from the continent and from Britain dribbled into Ireland over a period of several centuries, and they did not come from a single region or a single biological stock. Some were blond and came from northern Europe. Some were black-haired and came from southern Europe, perhaps from the Iberian peninsula. Undoubtedly a large number came across the narrow waters from the lands which are now known as Scotland and England — it is only thirty-five miles from Stranraer to Larne.

Some Celts certainly came from the territory that is now called France; there are traces of French words in early Irish. They mixed with and married the primitive Irish, and ruled over them by virtue of superior knowledge and tempered iron. Thus Ireland became a Celtic nation — "the only Celtic State left in the world," according to the great Irish historian Edmund Curtis, whose classic narrative is the best guide for casual readers in this field. But in spite of Professor Curtis, there are a great many people who are inclined to brush aside all ethnic verbalisms in describing the Irish and to agree with Bernard Shaw that "There is no Irish race any more than there is an English race or a Yankee race."

Saint Patrick spoke a kind of Latin, but he also spoke old Gaelic, since he had spent six years of his youth as a swineherd in Ireland, after he had been captured and carried off from his Welsh home by a great Irish High King, Niall, in one of those successful Irish raids on the eastern island. When he returned to Ireland in 432 as a young missionary bishop, with headquarters in the north, he did not meet much organized resistance.

The almost illiterate countryside was ready for a wider culture, and Saint Patrick supplied the foundation for it along with his Latin brand of Christianity. As his churches grew and prospered, they took on the role of building an Irish culture.

Strangely enough, in this development the abbot with his monastery became more important than the bishop with his cathedral. In fact, there was hardly anything in early Irish church history which could be called a cathedral. The church was poor, and the monks lived with the people. The celibacy, the poverty, the security, and the leisure of the monks set the tone and purpose of Irish moral life. The monks brought the people to the monasteries, which became their schools, libraries, and even trading centers. In many cases, the monasteries were the creators and centers of the towns, the only towns that the people had in those days. The Irish monks not only Christianized Ireland and taught the people how to write their own language, but also sent back to Britain and the Continent earnest and able missionaries of the new faith to rescue the Scots and the Lombards from paganism. Thus, the monk Columba (Saint Columcille) went from Ireland to Iona in 563 and ultimately became the Saint Patrick of Scotland; and an even greater Irish missionary, Saint Columbanus, a few years later carried the Gospel to those regions which are now called France. Thirteen hundred years later he became the patron saint of the Knights of Columbanus — the super-zealous Irish counterpart of America's Knights of Columbus.

This early history of Irish monastic Christianity is important to keep in mind for a number of reasons. Too often Americans and Englishmen tend to rate Irish culture as derivative and secondary. They think of Ireland as tucked off in isolation on the periphery of the European world, immature in development and lagging behind the great nations of the West. The Irish themselves know that they are spiritual descendants of pioneers of Christian expansion, a source-nation of Western culture. No matter how far they may have fallen from their earlier glory, they remember that their forebears once helped to civilize Europe. Moreover, it should be remembered that in those earlier and formative years of Irish life, the priest assumed a role in community affairs which was much more important than the priest's role in other lands. He was in many ways the political as well as the intellectual and moral leader of his people. Also, a special type of holy person rose to moral and cultural ascendancy in Ireland, the celibate and self-abnegating monk; and his leadership placed a special stamp — some would say a scar — upon Irish culture and politics. The monks were simultaneously men of action and men of reflection, soldiers and celibates, statesmen and hermits. They were men of God, but they were also men of battle. They did not hesitate to join in combat for their country, and it is said that eight hundred of them, monks of Ferns, died in a single battle in 816.

The reasonably placid course of Irish development was rudely interrupted about 795 by the landing of the Norsemen, coming mostly from territory which is now Norway, and later by others from territory which is now Denmark. Between 800 and 1000 A.D., they remade the map of Ireland, and in their last century of conquest they almost succeeded in subduing the whole island. They founded the great cities of Southern Ireland, including Dublin, Cork, Waterford, and Limerick. For a long time they had their own way in overrunning the seaboard areas, partly because they craftily divided the local kings, and enlisted Irishman against Irishman. For a time Ireland had High Kings with a seat at Tara, but they were little more than arbitrators for local quarrels. The Norsemen took Irish women to wife and bred Irish heirs who thought in terms of Norse-Irish rule instead of exclusive Irish sovereignty. Finally, in 1014 at Clontarf, now in the outskirts of Dublin, the Norsemen met their master in Brian Boru, a High King, who unified most of Southern Ireland under his rule. Although Brian himself was killed with an axe by a stray Norse warrior in the last stage of the fighting, the battle of Clontarf marked the end of the threat of total Norse conquest.

The Norsemen disturbed and weakened Irish Christianity, but they did not destroy it. During the two centuries of their occupation, the local tribal nations continued to have priest-kings and bishop-kings who combined the sword and the spirit with no sense of unfitness. For more than a hundred years afterwards, up to 1169, Christianity in its monastic form, and in new diocesan forms, continued to grow and to control the fragments of national culture. That culture became Roman culture, for

Rome recognized the Irish Church and granted Ireland four archbishops, all duly blessed by the Pope.

The Normans Win for England

Then came the Normans. They were Norman-English and Norman-Welsh, for they had ruled much of England for about a century before they crossed the Irish Sea. Their conquest of Ireland was destined to make Ireland a British dependency for more than 750 years. The local Irish kings fought back energetically against the Norman armies, but the Normans won because they were professional, full-time soldiers, trained for continuous war, and because they were equipped with the new gadgets of warfare — mail shirts, iron helmets, and movable wooden towers. Even at that, the Normans did not conquer Ireland except in alliance with Irish chieftains and a Catholic Pope. Henry II of England became ruler of Ireland in 1170 partly because he came with the blessing of the Papacy, and because he was encouraged by a large section of the clergy.

It should be explained that by this time four great regions of Ireland had assumed definite form and were later to become the four modern provinces. They were: in the South, Munster, which included Cork, Waterford, and Limerick; in the middle East, Leinster, which included Dublin, Tara, and Drogheda; in the West, Connaught, which included Galway and Sligo; and in the North, Ulster, which included the territory now known as Northern Ireland in addition to Donegal. (See the map of Ireland, page 330.) It actually took several hundred years for the English to subdue the Irish — and there are some Irishmen who contend that the feat has not yet been accomplished.

At first the English kings did not try to Anglicize Irish culture or establish a strong central government. They were busy dividing up the island among their gentlemen buccaneers and suppressing almost continuous revolts. Norman conquest was a slow, piecemeal affair, and Ulster was not subdued until long after a subject Irish parliament had learned to obey English commands. The process of conquest included the suppression or attempted suppression of almost everything Irish.

The suppression took notorious form in 1366 under Edward III in the Statutes of Kilkenny, which were railroaded through an Anglo-Irish Dublin parliament whose only Irish "representatives" were hand-picked abbots and bishops. They represented England's desperate defense against the rising power of a hostile Irish majority. J. C. Beckett in his comprehensive little book, *A Short History of Ireland,* says of these Kilkenny Statutes:

. . . by far the most important were those which aimed at setting a permanent barrier between the two races in Ireland, for it was recognised that wherever they mingled it was the Gaelic influence which predominated. So, alliance between them by marriage or concubinage or by fostering of children was forbidden; neither the English (i.e. the Anglo-Norman settlers) nor "the Irish living amongst the English" were to use the Irish language; the English were not to use Irish names, Irish dress, Irish law, nor to ride without saddles after the fashion of the Irish.

The Kilkenny Statutes covered only about one-third of Ireland, and they were not markedly effective; but they remained on the books for more than two hundred years, embittering the relations between English and Irish, and identifying English Christianity with the grossest forms of oppression. When the Reformation came, the stored-up hatred of English Christianity was transferred to Protestantism. The restrictions and discriminations were modified gradually in the fifteenth century, but the philosophy of Irish inferiority and English supremacy inspired all English rule in Ireland from the days of the Kilkenny Statutes until the twentieth century.

Before the Reformation, the Irish Church was not conspicuously nationalist in character. It was either passive on Irish rights or strongly allied with the British masters. It did not rise to the defense of its oppressed Irish members until its own interests became inextricably bound up with Irish nationalism. The three archbishops and five bishops present at the Kilkenny Parliament in 1366 blessed the discriminatory laws by solemnly publishing sentences of excommunication against all those who should break them, and the Papacy for a long time afterwards was far from being pro-Irish or even neutral. It did nothing to protect its faithful followers against injustice, and it seemed to care no more for the common people than the English overlords had.

Then came Henry VIII and the English Reformation. Out of Henry's conflict with the Papacy emerged the Church of England, with the king as head, claiming full apostolic succession. Since Henry's aim was not so much theological as selfish and national, his Reformation had a much more political cast than the Lutheran Reformation on the Continent. To Henry VIII, a bishop was more an auxiliary nobleman than a representative of God. His forces moved into Ireland in 1534 to accomplish the same type of sweeping reform in his Irish colony that he had accomplished in England. Through a small and unrepresentative Reformation parliament, he dissolved the Irish monasteries, took over their lands for himself and his henchmen, and declared himself the head of the Anglican Church of Ireland as against "the usurped authority of the Bishop of Rome." He won considerable support among the Irish nobles, and many of the Irish bishops took the new oath of allegiance to their Protestant king; but the bulk of the Irish people and the Irish clergy never accepted Henry and the Reformation. In England the majority went along with their king against their Pope; in Ireland the process was reversed. So Anglican Protestantism in Ireland became an Anglo-Irish phenomenon imposed on a resentful Catholic majority.

While the fortunes of the new Protestantism were going up and down in England, the variations in fortune in Ireland followed a similar but less violent pattern. The quick changes in England from Catholicism to Protestantism and back to Catholicism were doubly embarrassing to Irish churchmen. They could never be sure in which camp their heads would be safer. When England swung back to Catholicism under Bloody Mary, Ireland swung back also, with considerable alacrity. In the reversion, no Protestants were beheaded or burned, because they were not numerous and outspoken enough to cause much trouble. When England turned again — and finally — to Protestantism under Elizabeth, it was too late to reconcile the new faith with the Irish masses, especially after 1570 when Pius V excommunicated Elizabeth and released her subjects from obedience to her. "Irish history," as Trevelyan puts it, "till then fluid, ran into the mould where it hardened for three hundred years. The native population conceived a novel enthusiasm for the Roman religion, which they identified with a passionate hatred of the English. On the other hand the new colonists, as distinguished from the old Anglo-Irish nobility, identified

Protestantism with their own racial ascendency, to maintain which they regarded as a solemn duty to England and to God."

Religion as War

The important thing to note about these early conflicts of English and Irish power is that religion became part of the warp and woof of the national antagonism. English force was labeled the "Protestant Ascendancy" and the "Garrison," interchangeably. It was not so much that the Papacy was always on the side of the Irish, but that the basic differences in religion were fused with the basic national animosities, each set of emotions strengthening the other. The English overlords stole the Irish land by force, exploited it as absentee owners with great recklessness, and divided it up into Protestant plantations for their favorites. Then they added salt to the Irish wounds by claiming sanction for their robbery from a conveniently docile English God.

The Protestant Reformation in Ireland never got far down among the people of the South. They remained reasonably faithful to the old Church, in part because the English did not bother to do a good missionary job among them. The English prelates were too arrogant to explain the new Protestantism in terms that the Irish peasants could understand. By 1600 the Jesuits had already won the battle for the Irish soul, partly because of what Edmund Spenser called "the zeal of Popish priests," as against "our idle ministers" who "will neither for . . . any love of God nor zeal of religion be drawn forth from their warm nests."

Meanwhile a new type of Protestantism, made not by kings but by the people, was arising in England and Scotland. It was destined to conquer both Scotland and the new British colonies across the sea. The English Civil War of the seventeenth century, which cost Charles I his head and made Cromwell supreme in the British Isles, cut Protestantism in two but did not strengthen Roman power either in England or in Ireland. There was one subject on which Puritan and Anglican could always agree — fear of the Pope. Catholic prestige fell with Charles's head, since Catholics had supported him in the Civil War. For a time the English Parliament became anti-Anglican and pro-Presbyterian; but after the restoration of Charles II, the Church of England soon came back into power. By that time the new Presbyterian Dissenters had gained a firm foothold in Scotland and in Ulster; and this is the main reason why Scotland today is Presbyterian, and why the Presbyterian Church today is the largest Protestant church in Northern Ireland. In Scotland, Presbyterianism became almost as much a national faith as Catholicism was to become in Southern Ireland.

Cromwell visited upon the Catholics of Ireland a terrible vengeance for their support of Charles I, and today the Catholic children are taught in their schools to regard his march through their island and his sack of Drogheda with the same horror that the children of Georgia regard the march of Sherman from Atlanta to the sea. That is why millions of good Irish-Americans were horrified when, during the American presidential campaign of 1952, Dwight Eisenhower untactfully hailed Cromwell as a personal hero.

The cruelties on both sides during this period of the English Civil War are difficult to comprehend today. After his victory, Cromwell penalized the Irish Catholics and their Protestant allies by appropriating for his soldiers 11,000,000 out of Ireland's 20,000,000 acres. The Catholics were the main sufferers, and anti-Catholicism was written into English law so firmly that it was not entirely eliminated until the twentieth century. The whole island of Ireland was penalized, and commercial penalties were added to political and religious ones. Ireland was forbidden after 1663 to send goods directly to the British colonies or to receive colonial goods except through England.

The Irish Catholics were to make one more stand against non-Catholic England when England's last Catholic monarch, James II, was deposed and succeeded by William III in the "Glorious Revolution." The Irish Catholics fought vainly for James at the Battle of the Boyne in 1690. They lost to England and to the Protestants, and after that came the Penal Laws and the Protestant Ascendancy. From 1691 to 1829, under the Penal Laws, Catholics could not sit in either an English or an Irish parliament because all parliament members had to renounce the Mass, transubstantiation, and the Pope. Anglican Protestantism was written into the law of the land; Roman Catholic worship was permitted by law, but Roman Catholics as individuals were deprived of many of the vital rights of citizenship. They could not hold office or serve as grand jurors, and for a time they could not vote. They could not operate public schools or send their children to schools abroad; they could not own a horse which was worth more than five pounds; they could not bear arms; they could not practice law without renouncing the Pope; and they could not go for advanced study to Trinity College. All the Roman Catholic bishops were, for a time, banished from Ireland, and a £50 reward was offered for their capture within the country. If a Protestant woman married a Catholic, she forfeited her estates. Anyone attending a Catholic pilgrimage was subject to a fine of ten shillings and a public whipping.

This policy of discrimination was fostered and developed largely by the established Church of Ireland, which also visited upon the Presbyterians and other Dissenters similar punishments and disabilities. The Dissenters could own land and vote, but their preachers could not legally perform the marriage ceremony, and their people, like the suppressed Catholics, were compelled to pay tithes for the support of the dominant Anglican clergy. One result of this policy was that when the Dissenters streamed across the Atlantic to New England, Pennsylvania, and the southern colonies, they carried with them a bitter hostility to English religious policy; and this hostility later played an important part in the establishment of the American policy of separation of church and state.

Grattan to O'Connell

After a dreary eighteenth century in which an irresponsible "Irish" parliament met every second year in Dublin to rubber-stamp the policy of an English Lord Lieutenant, the Anglo-Irish upper classes demanded the right to govern Ireland. Their new leader was the great liberal Protestant, Henry Grattan, and for about eighteen years — from 1782 to 1800 — the country was partially ruled by "Grattan's Parliament" under George III. Liberty was in the air in those days, and Britain was too busy with other foreign troubles to spend much time or money in subduing the Anglo-Irish. It was inevitable that the American and French revolutions should have some effect upon the Irish masses. Irish Protestant leaders began to question English Protestant tyranny as vigorously as the Catholics had questioned it. Earlier, Jonathan Swift, for thirty-two years dean of Saint Patrick's Protestant Cathedral in Dublin, had been ridiculing the political corruption of the English Protestant Ascendancy and suggesting that everything "be burnt that comes from England except the people and the coals." The Volunteer Patriot army, raised by Irish Protestants, threatened English control and made demands upon England which resembled the demands by the American colonists. On the defensive, the English Protestant aristocracy abandoned some of the worst anti-Catholic features of the Penal Laws, but it was too short-sighted to realize its full danger. As Matthew Arnold said, the concessions by England "were given too late . . . and they seemed to be given not from a desire to do justice, but from the apprehension of danger." When Henry Grattan called for full Catholic emancipation, he called in vain. With Anglo-Irish support in Ireland, the same stiff-necked George III who had driven the American colonists to rebellion stood by his outdated coronation oath to keep Catholicism in a state of subjection throughout his realm.

Ireland in the Grattan period won self-government of a sort, but it was a corrupt and "rotten-borough" kind of self-government, operated by Protestant aristocrats under the veto of an English king. Its aim was to benefit the Protestant Ascendancy, which owned about 85 per cent of the Irish land. The masses of the Catholic people were dispossessed peasants, usually tenants of large Protestant estates, desperate and embittered in their poverty. When they threatened insurrection in the North, the Protestants of Ulster replied by organizing the semi-military Orange Order, which was later to become the advance guard of non-Catholic power in Northern Ireland. This Order in the beginning was Anglican, but it was soon broadened to include the Free Church Dissenters.

On the Irish side there arose a new revolutionary movement, the United Irishmen, led by a young non-Catholic lawyer, Theobald Wolfe Tone. The followers of Wolfe Tone, with Presbyterian help in the North and some abortive aid from France, staged the pathetic little rebellion of 1798 against England. It ended in quick disaster, and Wolfe Tone, when he learned that he was to be hanged in prison, committed suicide. Now he is one of Ireland's immortals — in spite of the fact that he was a freethinker who described the Irish priests as "men of low birth, low feelings, low habits and no education." Pitt, fearing an anti-English majority of Catholics and Dissenters in any Dublin parliament, forced through that parliament by patronage and bribery an Act of Union which made Ireland an organic part of the United Kingdom for 120 years. Ireland was given 100 members in the British House of Commons and 32 members in the House of Lords — but not a single Catholic.

Although England finally granted to all Catholics new political rights in the Emancipation Law of 1829, the gift was so slow in arriving that the Irish did not recognize it as a gift. They saw it as a victory won in the hard way by their new national leader, Daniel O'Connell, still to this day the South's greatest hero. (O'Connell's statue on Lower O'Connell Street, Dublin, is still for all nationalist Irishmen the counterpart of the Washington Monument in America; and at the other end of O'Connell Street stands the monument of Ireland's second greatest hero, Charles Stewart Parnell, the Protestant leader of Ireland's later fight for self-rule. Between them is the tallest monument in Ireland, the Nelson Pillar, which, surprisingly, has been allowed to stand unmolested.)

O'Connell was a great orator in the grand manner, a natural spokesman for Irish nationalism, and a sincere Catholic in spite of the fact that — as Yeats pointed out — you could hardly throw a stick in Dublin without hitting an illegitimate child of his. By suasion, manipulation, and blackmail, with the help of his Catholic Association, he had broken down the opposition of the English aristocracy and the reluctance of Wellington and Peel, and had finally won emancipation for Catholics in 1829. Then he began the great repeal movement for Irish self-government. Before he died, on his way to see the Pope in 1847, he directed that his body be sent back for burial to Ireland, and that his heart be buried in Rome.

The next great champions of Irish freedom were the Young Irelanders, whose most distinguished leaders were Thomas Davis and John Mitchel. These new rebels, largely Protestant, resented the Catholic emphasis in O'Connell's campaign, and pointed out that with all his eminence he had not been able to win the right to hold independence mass meetings in his own country. They wanted swifter and more direct action. But before they could make much headway, all aspirations for self-government were suddenly submerged in the great potato famine of 1845-47. That historic famine, caused by a potato blight, was the worst famine in the West in modern times, and before its effects had ended, a half-million Irishmen had died and four million more had migrated to the United States and other countries in desperate flight.

Exploitation — British and Protestant

Ireland, throughout the whole period of union with Britain (1800-1921), was in a more or less continuous state of discontent — political, religious, and economic. Probably the economic discontent was the most important, and if the Catholic peasants had received some economic fair play perhaps the other grievances would have taken care of themselves. As it was, these peasants had almost no land, and at the same time they were compelled until 1837 to pay tithes directly or indirectly to a Protestant denomination which represented only one-eighth of the population. This Anglican Church of Ireland became identified in their minds with everything that was cruel and repressive. Its members were wealthy and powerful; its churches received, along with the Presbyterian Church, state subventions, while the churches of the Catholic majority received nothing, except a small grant to Maynooth for the training of priests. In other words, the great masses of the people paid for the religious special privilege of the few.

Sydney Smith, once canon of St. Paul's, described the cause of Irish Catholic dissatisfaction: "On an Irish Sabbath morning the bell of a neat [Anglican] parish church often summons to worship only the parson and an occasional conforming clerk, while two hundred yards off a thousand Catholics are huddled together in a miserable hovel, and pelted by all the storms of heaven." Daniel O'Connell, fighting the tithe system in 1832, read in the House of Commons the following figures of Catholic and Protestant membership in certain districts at a time when the established Protestant church alone was receiving tithes:

No. 1. Eight parishes in which there were 18,129 Catholics, 0 Protestants.
No. 2. Eight parishes in which there were 16,077 Catholics, 6 Protestants.
No. 3. Ten parishes in which there were 41,274 Catholics, 70 Protestants.
No. 4. Sixteen parishes in which there were 66,635 Catholics, 245 Protestants.

The Anglican Church of Ireland was not disestablished until 1869, when it received in partial satisfaction of its claim a property settlement in cash, and was made into the self-governing Church of Ireland "in communion with the Church of England." In the final financial settlement, the Catholic institutions received some money also, but by that time the long record of prejudice and discrimination had made reconciliation between Protestants and Catholics virtually impossible. The Irish peasants who had been compelled for so long to support the church of the English aristocracy could not or would not forget. They had lived as peasants on a daily wage hardly sufficient to feed a dog, and their tenure on the land had been so uncertain that they could be evicted without appeal if they could not pay an exorbitant rent. For them Protestant Christianity and economic oppression had become twin evils in a hideous pattern of injustice.

These economic factors in Irish discontent assumed even greater significance after the famine. An organization called the Tenant Right League sent many representatives to the British Parliament to fight for improved conditions. After a long struggle, the land fight was won by a series of boycotts and rent strikes, resulting in the Land Acts passed by the British Parliament which finally made the Ireland of the twentieth century into a country of small landowners, working under fairly reasonable conditions of land ownership. But twice Home Rule bills sponsored by Gladstone and his Liberals were defeated by the English Tories and the English House of Lords. In fact, if it had not been for the House of Lords, the whole Irish problem might have been amicably settled in the 1880's within the framework of the British Empire. The representatives of Ireland in the British House of Commons held the balance of power between the chief political parties, and they used their strategic position with great shrewdness. But a short-sighted English aristocracy would not offer the Irish an honorable compromise.

Even Charles Stewart Parnell, an aristocrat and landowner of the Irish Protestant Ascendancy who spoke the language of aristocracy with great power, could not dissuade the English Protestants from their stubborn arrogance in treating Ireland like a colony. Parnell, backed by Irish-American money and sympathy, led a brief and brilliant fight for Home Rule; but he died in 1891 at the age of forty-five, the victim of a great divorce scandal which caused both Catholic bishops and leading Dissenters to turn against him. He was succeeded in 1900 by a devout and conventional Catholic, John Redmond, who believed in obtaining Home Rule by peaceful methods. But history had already destroyed the hope for peace. Arthur Griffith, a young Irish journalist, had already started a new direct-action movement called Sinn Fein, which was destined to hold the center of the Irish stage for many years.

Although Sinn Fein began as a movement for Irish self-government under a British king, it soon became a movement for an Irish republic, with a powerful military wing urging open rebellion. Its policy was partly determined by the policy of its opponents. For at this moment Irish bitterness was intensified by the rise among the Protestants of the North of an anti-Home Rule movement in opposition to Sinn Fein. The Orangemen of Ulster declared that Home Rule would be "Rome Rule." They united the non-Catholic elements of the North under a new leader from the South, Sir Edward Carson, with an Irish Unionist party which was just as loyal to the British nation as the Sinn Feiners were to Dublin. Soon the Orange movement matched that of the Sinn Feiners in militancy. There is still a bitter dispute as to which movement first threatened force. Both sides played freely upon religious as well as political emotions. The Northern Unionists declared that they would rather die than live in a Catholic nation under Roman control, and millions of Englishmen expressed sympathy with them. "Ulster will fight," they chanted, "and Ulster will be right." When the Asquith government proposed a Home Rule bill, some 200,000 Northern Unionists, on September 28, 1912, signed a "solemn covenant" to resist Dublin rule to the death. To show that they meant business, they organized the Citizens' Army, ran guns to Ulster, and mobbed Winston Churchill when he came to Belfast as a representative of compromise. They raised a force of 100,000 loyal men and dared the British Parliament to launch a war against British subjects who wanted to remain part of the British nation.

The Easter Rebellion

World War I prevented an open break between the North and the South by suspending the application of a new Home Rule bill, which had finally been passed by the British Parliament. But the Irish Republican Volunteers in the South were not content to wait for peace in order to gain their demands. On Easter Monday of 1916, about a thousand of them staged the most momentous rebellion of Irish history by seizing the Dublin post office and other important buildings, and by proclaiming a republic. Their forlorn and valiant force was divided into two sections working together — the Citizens Army, led by the Dublin socialist James Connolly; and the Irish Volunteers, led by the young intellectual Padraic Pearse. After fighting desperately for a week, the rebels, overwhelmed, surrendered unconditionally. In their brief struggle for nationhood about five hundred people were killed and eleven hundred wounded. Their insurrection was war of a sort, desperate and unofficial war, but the English government, threatened at that very moment with defeat by Germany, was not in a mood to treat the Irish rebels as honorable soldiers. Instead, they were treated as traitors to their country in time of war.

Whatever may have been the technical correctness of this policy, it was one of the most tragic blunders of British history, and the method of carrying out the harsh policy was even worse than its principle. One after one, after brief courts-martial, the young Irish rebels were led out and shot. If the shooting had taken place all at once on the morning after the surrender, the reaction might have been relatively slight; the majority of the Irish people were only mildly sympathetic with the rebels, and regarded their desperate rebellion as juvenile melodrama. But when the British military authorities executed their victims one by one over a period of ten days, the repercussions produced national hysteria. When the echo of the last volley had died away, the fifteen young Irishmen had become national martyrs.

Today their names are at the top of Ireland's honor roll, and in Irish Catholic schools the children repeat them over and over with an almost religious reverence, in the order in which they were shot — Padraic Pearse, Thomas MacDonagh, Thomas J. Clarke, Joseph Plunkett, Edward Daly, Michael O'Hanrahan, William Pearse, John MacBride, Cornelius Colbert, Edmund Kent, Michael Mall, J. J. Heuston, Thomas Kent, James Connolly, and Sean McDermott. James Connolly, the next to the last to die, was carried from an ambulance to his execution, having been wounded early in the shooting, and then having directed the fighting from his bed. A little later Roger Casement, who had tried to enlist German support for the rebellion, was hanged in London.

One name which might well have been close to the top of the list to be executed was that of a young professor of mathematics at Blackrock College, Eamon de Valera. One reason why he was spared was that he had been born in Brooklyn, of an Irish mother and a Spanish father. The telephone message which saved him came from Prime Minister Asquith at 11 o'clock the night before he was to die. In those trying days of the First World War, the British did not wish to strain American relations by shooting any man who might be considered an American citizen.

The guerrilla warfare between Irish Volunteers and British Black and Tans which began after World War I was an unofficial war, fought by Irish rebels in Ireland with Irish-American money and with the sympathetic support of the overwhelming majority of Irish and non-Irish people in the United States. Lloyd George recognized that something had to be done about Ireland, but there was no easy solution, no reasonable compromise that all parties could agree upon. Self-determination for subject peoples had been one of the major war aims of the Allies, and thousands of Irish Catholics had fought on the Allied side in the belief that victory would bring freedom for them too. But what did "freedom" include? With Carson's volunteers ready to die for freedom from Dublin control, no British statesman of first rank dared to throw the Northern Protestants to the Southern Papist rebels. Self-determination, some argued, was a two-way road. The North argued that self-determination inside British democracy was just as real a democratic value as self-determination in a new Irish republic. The Northerners voted for British democracy in spite of Dublin's description of it as British imperialism; and they stuck to their old slogan, which had become the battle cry of the North: "Home Rule Is Rome Rule."

Sinn Fein had risen to majority status in the South even during the time of the official union with Britain. The leaders had formed their own clandestine parliament, the Dail Eireann, in 1919, in defiance of Westminster, with Eamon de Valera as president. In the British general election of December 1918, although 47 of the 73 Irish Republican candidates were in jail, Sinn Fein captured 73 of the 105 seats in all of Ireland, and Home Rule nationalists captured 6 more. The Unionists polled a majority only in the four Ulster counties of Antrim, Derry, Down, and Armagh.

Ireland Is Divided

The British government was faced with a dilemma. Undoubtedly the majority of the Irish people wanted independence from British rule, and both sides in Ireland were willing to engage in civil war. Civil war actually began in the form of guerrilla warfare against England and guerrilla defense by the British forces. It lasted for two terrible years of repression and terror. Finally Lloyd George — recognizing that the North would not go along with the South in any solution acceptable to the South — in 1920 granted separate status to the North within the British nation. The grant included a Northern parliament for local affairs, which began to function at Stormont, the Belfast capital, in 1921. The new semi-dominion commonwealth of the North embraced only six of the island's thirty-two counties — Antrim, Down, Armagh, Tyrone, Derry, and Fermanagh — plus two county boroughs. Strictly speaking, it was a commonwealth of northeastern, rather than of northern, Ireland. Donegal, in the northwest, remained with Dublin, as did Monaghan and Cavan, the other two counties of Ulster.

Officially it was a three-party settlement that Lloyd George worked out with Irish leaders. In December 1921 he offered Arthur Griffith and Michael Collins, as negotiators for the De Valera regime, a choice between "immediate and terrible war" and a treaty which granted the Irish people of the South a status of independence and dignity approximately equal to that of Canada. Griffith and Collins — later the Sinn Fein parliament by 64 votes to 57, and the people of the South in a general election which amounted to a referendum — accepted the new agreement with a sigh of relief. The Catholic hierarchy threw its weight on the side of compromise and the treaty. But De Valera and a number of his friends held out. De Valera charged that his own trusted negotiators had double-crossed him by signing an agreement to take the detested oath of loyalty to the British king without consulting him. Five years later, De Valera was to concede this point about the oath temporarily in order to capture the new Irish parliament and abolish the oath.

In the meantime came tragedy — the outbreak of one of the bloodiest, most fratricidal wars in Irish history. Partisan critics of De Valera still like to count the numbers of Irish dead who would not have died if he had accepted the oath in 1922 instead of 1927. Today most Irishmen would like to forget what happened to their country in 1922 and 1923, before Britain finally withdrew from Dublin Castle and turned its power over to the new Irish Free State government. Irishmen turned against one another. The bitter-end Republicans, defying their own Free State regime even after it had won approval at the polls, killed many of their old comrades. Griffith died in the first year of the struggle, and Michael Collins was murdered in ambush shortly afterward. Constant murder and ambush destroyed some of the country's finest leaders, and divided families and communities. In the long guerrilla warfare, rules of gentlemanly combat were not observed on either side. When the rebels seized the Dublin law courts, the Free State government shelled them out with terrific slaughter. When the Free State regime saw its leaders being picked off and murdered, it seized Republican hostages in reprisal and shot them in cold blood. Altogether, in this fratricidal struggle, the Irish executed almost twice as many of their own number as the British had executed between 1916 and 1921. Irish schoolbooks tend to treat this period with nervous haste, and today the pictures of the great heroes of the Free State government who were killed by De Valera's rebels are hung in obscure corners of government buildings. Irish textbooks also tend to pass over lightly the fact that remnants of the Irish Republican Army continued to murder and terrorize until 1939, climaxing their campaign with the slaughter of innocent English men, women, and children by means of bombs placed in mailboxes.

The Free State government was headed for ten troubled years by William T. Cosgrave, who gave the country solid and efficient administration. But his regime was always on the defensive against the threat of republican revolution.

De Valera ended the military phase of the guerrilla warfare in 1923, but he continued the political campaign outside of parliament until 1927. Then he reversed himself, entered parliament, and, with obvious mental reservations, took the oath to the British king. Five years later, in 1932, he won a majority in the Dail Eireann and continued in power for sixteen years until 1948 — acknowledged master of the nation he had done so much to create. He lost control of the government in 1948 to an Inter-Party regime. But in 1951 De Valera was returned to power by a slender margin. Now in his seventies and partially blind — he underwent six eye operations in Utrecht in 1952 — De Valera still symbolizes for most Southern Irishmen the successful battle for national freedom. His austerity, his almost fanatical devotion to the cause of Irish freedom, and his long service to his country have made him, while still living, one of Ireland's immortals. "Dev," as he is affectionately known in Ireland, almost single-handed wrote the nation's new Constitution in 1937. His handiwork is evident in almost every aspect of Irish life.

It was by a strange irony of history that on Easter Monday, April 18, 1949, it was not the regime of De Valera but the government of his critic, Costello, which captured the ultimate honor of severing the ties with Britain by declaring Ireland a completely independent republic. This final severance was a bitter pill for British public opinion, but the Attlee government, recognizing an accomplished fact, gracefully accepted the verdict and passed the Ireland Act of 1949, giving Irish voters new legal status in British law. The one affirmative item in that act worthy of mention here is that it sealed the future status of Northern Ireland as a distinct commonwealth separate from the South. We shall see later that this Partition has become the great political issue of Irish life.

3

Progress and Poverty

The divided island which has emerged from this long struggle for freedom is not one of the most prosperous or happy or secure territories of the globe. It is about the size of Maine, and it has in all less than four and one-half million people. British-ruled Northern Ireland — the Six Counties — has about 1,371,000 people living on one-sixth of the island. The Irish Republic of the South — the Twenty-six Counties — has about 3,000,000 people living on the rest of the island. The one great city in the South is Dublin; the one great city in the North is Belfast; and each is the cultural and economic as well as the political capital of its region. Of the two, Dublin has always been the larger and the more important; it is a city of character, of beauty, of tradition, and of decay. Belfast is modern, dour, gaunt, bustling, industrialized, a hybrid Manchester on Scotch-Irish soil.

The three most distinctive features of the Republic which emerged from this long struggle for freedom are its religion, its politics, and its climate.

About 95 per cent of the Republic's people are Roman Catholic. Of the non-Catholics, the great majority are Church of Ireland Episcopalians. There are a few congregations of Presbyterians, Methodists, Baptists, and Friends, and about four thousand Jews; but, aside from the survival of two great Anglican cathedrals in Dublin, the non-Catholic congregations of the South are not conspicuous for activity or power. Their rosters include many men of substance from the old Anglo-Irish aristocracy, but their numbers are declining year by year and the average age level of their congregations is rising. In

34

the Twenty-six Counties in 1871, there were 108 non-Catholics per 1,000 of the population; in the corresponding territory of the Republic in 1946, there were 57; today there are even fewer. In the South, the Catholic Church is the church of the Irish masses, and its hold upon those masses appears at this moment to be beyond challenge. As one of the characters in Bernard Shaw's *John Bull's Other Island* says boastfully, "in Ireland the people is the Church and the Church is the people."

The Political Whirlpool

The political whirlpool in the new Republic is as confused as the political whirlpool of an American presidential campaign, and even more personal. All the political parties are, in actual fact, Catholic parties, and no politician or party could survive a single month with an "anti-Catholic" label. But none of these Irish parties is affiliated with any Catholic international political body; nor is any party officially called a Catholic party. This may be because political power in the Republic is so completely Catholic that there is no need of such labeling.

All the parties of the Republic are unanimously anti-British, anti-Partition, and anti-Communist. They are also anti-socialist in theory — although they frequently carry out socialistic measures in the name of the Catholic moral law. In fact, Ireland, while loudly disclaiming any Marxist influences, has become more socialistic than most Protestant countries. Its railroads, electricity supply, telegraph system, radio, telephone service, sugar manufacture, and transportation are all publicly or semi-publicly owned; and the government participates very actively in a national system of economic controls. When a team of United States economic experts made a survey of the Irish economy in 1952, one of their rather startling conclusions was that, "despite a general assumption of opposition to the socialist credo, the state has assumed a far larger role in the channeling of investment funds than in England under a Labor government."

This statement made the Irish Catholic politicians quite red-faced, because they are almost as reluctant to follow British Labor as they are to follow Moscow. In both cases, their hostility is passionate and noisy. Communism is condemned in a loud chorus which is even more emotional than the corresponding anti-Communist chorus in the United States; and anti-Communism is closely identified with Catholic loyalty.

In Ireland, speech is so free that it easily passes over into physical violence. In the single session of the Irish Parliament which ended in August 1952, there were five physical assaults by deputies upon one another in the parliament building. Irishmen love an argument, and their new Constitution gives them the kind of government in which political controversy tends to be magnified. It is a party government founded on that noble but questionable device, proportional representation, which tends to keep politics in a turmoil by creating splinter parties. At the top of the present Irish government is a small gentleman of no great importance, President Sean O'Kelly, elected by popular vote for a seven-year term, and supposedly non-partisan. His function is chiefly ceremonial, and he seems to divide his public appearances between Catholic and civil ceremonies in about equal proportion.

The real power of Irish political life lies in the Dail Eireann, the lower house of parliament, elected by all citizens over twenty-one. Broadly speaking, this Dail takes the place in Irish life occupied in Britain by the House of Commons; the nation's Prime Minister, the Taoiseach (pronounced "Thee-shock"), draws his cabinet from its elected members. The upper house of parliament is the Seanad (Senate), partly appointed and partly elected, which usually discusses political issues with less heated partisanship than the Dail. It has the power to delay but not to veto or indefinitely hold up legislation.

One political party, De Valera's Fianna Fail, has topped most of the polls since 1932, and it still leads all other parties in membership and elected representatives in the Dail. But its hold on power is very precarious. It polled less than half of the votes at the 1951 general election; after losing several by-elections in 1953, it continued to control the government only with the uncertain support of a few independents.

Ireland is far from being a one-party state, and without the enormous personal prestige of De Valera the nation could easily become a country of minute political factions engaged in personal quarrels. Some observers would apply that description to Irish politics today. The opposition to De Valera, by forming a motley political coalition on negative principles, actually captured a majority in the Dail in 1948, and held it until 1951. In that three-year coalition, the political party known as Fine Gael, led by General Richard Mulcahy, played the leading role. It is still the second party in the state, but it is much smaller than Fianna Fail and uncertain of its own political philosophy.

For its three-year period of rule, Fine Gael put an independent barrister, John A. Costello, in De Valera's place as head of the Republic; but the coalition he headed was a rickety and incongruous affair. Associated with Fine Gael were the Irish Labor Party, headed by the traditional trade-union leader, William Norton; and a new reform party slightly left of center, Clann na Poblachta, headed by the fiery and aggressive Sean MacBride. MacBride was an able Minister for External Affairs, but most of his initial following faded away when he appeared to compromise with political and economic reaction, and his party is now virtually non-existent.

Perhaps unfortunately for the reality of Irish politics, the Labor Party, which might be expected to represent the Irish masses with a comprehensive program, is not to be compared in strength or purpose to its counterpart in Great Britain. A small party, standing cautiously for functional and piecemeal reform, it has not been sufficiently dynamic to capture much of the labor vote from De Valera. After joining the conservative coalition under Costello in order to defeat De Valera, it became a "floating" independent party in 1952, not formally allied either with the government or with the opposition. It seems to be waiting for an advantageous political deal in order to get the highest possible price for its support.

As to which of Ireland's parties is most capitalistic or socialistic or imperialistic or Catholic or Communist or chauvinistic, it would be difficult to say. The parties themselves do not know the answer. By tradition, Fine Gael is conservative — at least it is more conservative than Fianna Fail. But when it is out of power its leaders adopt the language of dissent as enthusiastically as if they were Communists. Political opportunism rules the Irish roost, and the politicians tend to speak out for the principles and policies that will capture the most votes. The leaders are for all the people all the time — and also for national unity, adequate defense, increased social services, lower taxes, the Irish language, and the Church. Within this orbit of traditional beliefs and purposes, all the political parties quarrel with terrifying public passion over trivial differences. On the major divergencies of politics and economics, they appear to be about equally conservative — and equally adroit in adjusting principle to popular support.

If this sounds like a cynical description of modern democracy in general, it only goes to show that the Irish people are quite typical. What makes Irish political posturing seem at times a trifle unheroic is that the Irish stage is distressingly small. As the crow flies, the Republic is only about 100 miles wide from Dublin to Galway and 300 miles long from the tip of County Cork to the tip of County Donegal, and its population is less than that of Chicago.

The Irish Climate

It is possible that the climate has had an even more serious effect on Irish character than British imperialism or Catholic faith.

Ireland has a heavy rainfall. Rain is good for grass, and grass is good for livestock, and so Ireland breeds thousands of good horses, good cows, and good sheep. But there seems to be so much moisture in the air that it devitalizes human beings. There are a great many people who think that the rainy Irish climate keeps the Irish people from attaining their full stature as creative and productive human beings. There is no sure way to prove this theory — it may be true and it may not. The Irish people who go abroad seem to display a type of physical persistence and hardihood that win them steady employment at the most difficult types of labor. Clearly the Irish do not possess so much energy at home — and this deficiency is quite generally admitted. Is this difference in productivity due to a change in psychological climate or in physical climate? A scientific answer is scarcely possible. The figures show that Irish rainfall is excessive by comparison with Britain, but not the highest in the world. The interference with sunshine is more important than the total rainfall. Farming is hazardous when dry weather is so uncertain. "The weather of Ireland," says T. W. Freeman, the best authority on this subject, "is commonly described as 'mild, moist and changeable' . . . Ireland is not so much a country of perpetual rain as one in which frequent showers alternate with sunny periods." This statement may be described as a model of restraint. The climate of Ireland might well be summarized in a sentence in the *Irish Times* of December 22, 1952: "The weather will be dull, with outbreaks of rain and drizzle in all districts."

"Of the Irish climate," says Shane Leslie, "it suffices to say that nothing is dry in Ireland except some fly fishing and a few canals . . . the Irish climate produces a slow mental and moral change . . . Space ceases to be a diagram and Time is no longer referred to a dial." "There *is* an Irish climate," says Bernard Shaw, "which will stamp an immigrant more deeply and durably in two years, apparently, than the English climate will in two hundred." Perhaps that is one reason why Bernard Shaw and almost every other great writer of modern Ireland have chosen to escape from the climate of their native land.

The Heritage of Poverty

As to the economic condition of Ireland, such a modest country was never meant for complete independence in the modern economic world. It has almost no coal or iron; its forests will not supply its own needs; in fact, it has the lowest proportion of wooded land of any country in Europe. Water power exists, but it is strictly limited, and the electricity boards are constantly finding difficulty in supplying local needs.

Poverty does not make for beauty. Irish standards of dress are slovenly, and the cities have conspicuous slum areas. The countryside is, with few exceptions, a depressed area. Those whitewashed Irish cottages which have been so consistently sentimentalized in song and story are not always fit places for healthy human beings to live. More than three-fourths of them do not have even a privy or a dry closet, and less than half enjoy any kind of piped water supply. There is much child labor in both country and city, because children are allowed to quit school and go to work at fourteen. Approximately 12 per cent of the working force is unemployed. In food, the average calory intake per person is one of the highest in the world, but averages may be deceptive in a small country with a relatively large tourist trade. The Irish diet is sadly unbalanced in favor of cereals and potatoes, and from 40 to 50 per cent of the total meals consist of bread and butter with tea.

The Irish people are better off in terms of real income than the peoples of eastern Europe, but they fall somewhat below the standards of western Europe, and far below the standards of the United States. In 1951 the average weekly earnings of employees in all industries covered by the government's census of industrial production was less than $15. In buying power the average Irishman's income is about one-third that of the average American, and one-half that of the average Englishman. Political independence has not brought the Republic's citizens economic equality with the rest of the English-speaking peoples. In that respect independence has been a bitter disillusionment — but in fairness it should be pointed out that before the separation Ireland was similarly underprivileged in relation to England. The fact that the Irish have the lowest per-capita real income of any white English-speaking country is not entirely the fault of the Republic's politicians. Irish poverty is partly an accident of geography and partly a result of the imperialism of the past.

Industrially Ireland is making great strides toward a self-sustaining position behind high tariff walls, but it is far from being a prosperous nation. In comparison with other European countries Irish agriculture is a relative failure, and this failure is the new nation's greatest tragedy, since the Republic is still primarily an agricultural country. "The volume of our agricultural production has remained almost static for one hundred years," says Michael Costello, "and since the end of the war tends to decline." This is a startling fact in a world of increasing soil production, and it makes Ireland almost unique among the nations. On an acreage basis, Holland out-produces the Republic by 5 to 1, and Denmark by 3½ to 1. Gross agricultural output has actually declined 4 per cent since 1939, and livestock 7 per cent. This decline can no longer be blamed upon British landlordism or the land monopoly of great estate owners. The present land laws in Ireland favor the small Irish owner in many ways. From De Valera down, the leaders of the nation are now calling upon the Irish to face the facts. De Valera has declared that the disastrous decline in the amount of tillage is a primary cause of failure, and that only 15 per cent of Ireland's agricultural land today is tilled as compared to 40 per cent in the Netherlands.

There are a great many Irish critics who place the responsibility for this decline of the land on the indolence and shiftlessness of the farm workers themselves. The country folk, they say, lack a will to work, and they ruefully contrast the easy-going ways of the Irish countryside with the intense energy and industry of the Germans after World War II. Too often the Irish farmer "divides his time between opening and closing gates and looking at the jobs he means to do next year." "We are thought to suffer from no indiscreet enthusiasm," says the *Irish Rosary* in an editorial. " 'Sure now, won't it do well enough?' used to be the suggestion of a certain professor if ever discussion arose about a national motto for our country." "Rural Ireland," says Cornelius Lucey, Bishop of Cork, "is stricken and dying, and the will to marry and live on the land is almost gone."

Unwilling Satellite

Brave new programs of economic expansion have been inaugurated in recent years by competing regimes, but Ireland is still in many particulars an economic dependency of Great Britain, living as a poor relation within the orbit of the British economy. Its money is still tied to the British pound at par, and it still belongs to the sterling bloc. Its trade treaties with Great Britain, chiefly for the sale of beef, mutton, and pork, are necessary to save the nation from economic ruin. Fortunately, enlightened self-interest on both sides has led to very friendly trade relations. Even during World War II, when British-Irish tensions were greatest, Britain appreciated having a safe agricultural hinterland for food supply, and British resentment was further abated by the sight of over 200,000 Southern Irish men and women crossing the Irish Sea to work in war industries, or to join the British forces as volunteers. The Irish economy has also gained some generous support from the United States in recent years — an outright gift of $18,000,000 and a Marshall Plan loan of $126,000,000.

Aside from the bitter controversy over Partition, British political policy in dealing with the new Republic has been recognized by the Irish as reasonable. Britain grants to Irish immigrants the full voting rights of British citizens, just as if the nation had not broken away from its British connection; and the Irish immigrants are exempt from British military service for the first two years of their British residence. Britain recognizes Irish medical and educational degrees for professional appointments. Prime Minister Attlee, in discussing the Ireland Act in the British House of Commons in 1949, said: "I am aware that hitherto . . . one has recognized people as either belonging or foreign, but international law is made for men, not men for international law."

The Irish receive this British generosity with a kind of uneasy suspicion. Hostility to Britain is still one of the dominant emotions of Irish Catholic life, and over-friendliness to Britain still means political suicide for any Irish statesman. The Dublin Catholic press continually regurgitates the most sanguinary tales of past British crimes, and indulges in retrospective self-pity. Even the Irish labor movement is divided into two factions largely because one faction contains some unions affiliated with head offices in London, and the other does not; but probably this situation will change as all unions become more distinctively Irish.

The North as Rival and Prize

The Southern Irish will never allow the British to forget that Northern Ireland stands between them as a perpetual issue. That is one reason why Northern Ireland has lived for three stormy decades in never-ceasing tension. Its whole political life revolves around the "border question," and because of the threat of increasing Catholic power, every Northern election is a crisis in which the very existence of the small Northern state is at stake. With one-third of the people of Northern Ireland as Catholics, their Church is the largest single church in the state. Although there are a few exceptions to the rule, the Catholic in the North is almost invariably a nationalist and the non-Catholic a Unionist. Religion and politics are inextricably mixed. In the chapter on Northern Ireland and Partition, it will be shown how this identification of religion with political conflict has made Northern Ireland into a militant Protestant state.

But in spite of religious and political animosities, the Irish Republic, Northern Ireland, and Britain must live together in a state of more or less unwilling economic interdependence. Britain, quite naturally, treats the North somewhat better than the South, since the North is part of the British nation. This double standard is a constant source of Southern jealousy. Many citizens of the South regard the "mutilation" of the island by Partition as the central cause of Southern poverty, and they regard the superior industrial development of the North as a reward for the North's "treason" toward Irish freedom. They covet for the Republic the great shipyards and linen mills which have made the Belfast area the most highly industrialized area of Ireland.

There is no doubt that the standard of living is slightly higher in the North, particularly on the farms, and that the social services supplied by the Northern government as part of the British system of social security are distinctly superior to the welfare services of the South. The Northern Irelanders pay Britain's higher taxes and reap the harvest in better wages and services. A Northern farmer's weekly income is about £1 higher than the corresponding income in the South. In regularity of employment, the North is less fortunate except during a war; but over a period of years the worker's real income is likely to be higher in the North than in the South.

This relative prosperity, of course, is due to Northern Ireland's British connection. The statesmen of the South, in spite of their Sinn Fein background, recognize the value of this connection, and dare not cut their nation off from the British economic empire. They even recognize some political affinity with British interests. At international conferences such as the Council of Europe, Irish statesmen, after collaborating behind the scenes with the Catholic parties of the Continent, usually vote with Britain at the most critical moments. In spite of their traditional hostility to Britain, their natural friendship for Catholic governments, and their burning desire for the acquisition of Northern Ireland, they know that their future is inextricably bound up with the future of Britain.

A Lucky, Lucky Church

In surveying the development of modern institutions in both North and South, it is impossible to escape the conviction that the Roman Catholic Church in Ireland has been extraordinarily lucky. It gained the advantages of scientific progress in the British tradition without being compelled to adapt its strategy and tactics to modern concepts. It rose to power along with the anti-British masses on a wave of irrepressible Irish nationalism. It won the fruits of democracy without being compelled to submit to the tests of democracy. At no point in the process was its foreign and undemocratic control by Rome challenged by its own followers — partly because the opposition power of English Protestantism was even more tangibly associated with foreign despotism.

The good fortune of Rome seems doubly clear when it is realized that the Church has supported the Irish masses only spasmodically. Again and again throughout Irish history, the hierarchy has sought compromise bargains with the Protestant Ascendancy at the expense of the Irish people. "Internationally," says the Irish Catholic leader Sir Shane Leslie, "the Papacy has stood steadily against Ireland's policy to be a nation since Tudor times." The head bishops of Ireland have sometimes been nationalists at heart, but they have uniformly followed Roman orders when Rome favored peace and compromise with the British throne. In the nineteenth century a Catholic bishop declared: "Hell is not hot enough, nor eternity long enough to punish the Fenians." The Irish bishops did not approve of the great revolt which reached a climax in the Easter Monday uprising of 1916, and they condemned the rebels of 1922 so vigorously that thousands of them were excommunicated, after being refused absolution in the confessional. Earlier, as Sean O'Faolain has pointed out, "right up to the union of Britain and Ireland in 1800, the terminus of the century, the constant policy of the hierarchy was to proclaim its loyalty to the Throne in the hope of winning at least some relief from the Penal Laws. . . . The coldly disapproving attitude of the clergy to rebellion, let alone disloyalty, fostered by the Gallicanism of Maynooth, persisted into the nineteenth century." As Francis Sheehy Skeffington put it in summarizing the conclusions of Michael Davitt, "the ecclesiastical power, taken as a whole, was ranged on the side of England," and "with the overthrow of the landlord garrison England was building up for herself a new garrison in the Catholic hierarchy."

Throughout the long struggle for independence, in spite of many acts of anti-nationalist sabotage, the Catholic hierarchy gained credit for supporting the Irish masses, because its priests were closer to those masses than were the clergymen of the established Anglican Church. This Church of Ireland, speaking with the voice of England, became identified in the minds of the people with English oppression. The voices of the Catholic priests were, on the whole, only spasmodically revolutionary and rarely progressive, but they sounded to the Irish masses like the voices of Ireland. So, paradoxically enough, loyalty to authoritarian Rome and loyalty to Irish freedom were fused in the Irish Catholic mind as one emotional value.

If the Church has been lucky, the Irish people have been unlucky. In the whole course of the Irish fight for freedom, the people of the island have never had a reasonable chance to build a nation which would be neutral in matters of religious power. Britain had an established church before and after the Reformation, and it made no attempt to temper its policy of religious favoritism to suit the Irish people until it was forced to do so. It did not force a complete financial separation between church and state, and to this day Britain's Queen is by legal requirement a Protestant monarch. The British conception of education permitted — and still permits — the use of public money for religious schools. The British tradition of the partial union of church and state was carried over into the life of Ireland where it became an instrument for dividing the people into creedal categories, with a policy of discriminatory treatment by the state. The opportunity of establishing a neutral and impartial policy in matters of religion, which was the great achievement of the American people in their first century of independence, was denied to the Irish people. Their nation rose to independence in an atmosphere of intense religious partisanship, and the people never succeeded in shaking off that partisanship. The very notion that churches should be non-political and governments non-denominational never had a fair chance to develop.

It is not surprising, then, that in the whole course of Irish history there has never been a substantial movement for the separation of church and state. Or perhaps it would be more accurate to say that in all Irish history the movements for separation have not been genuine attempts at clean-cut separation of church and state so much as partisan movements against the particular privileges of a particular sect at a given moment. At only one period in the long Irish struggle for self-government did the leadership of the movement for freedom fall into the hands of sincere believers in a non-clerical state. That was in the 1840's, when the Young Irelanders boldly declared for real public schools and a non-denominational government policy. Thomas Davis, the foremost leader of the Young Irelanders, said of his country: "To mingle politics and religion in such a country is to blind men to their common secular interests, to render political union impossible, and national independence hopeless." But the Church was hostile to this "indifferentism," and under clerical pressure the Young Irelanders would probably have died a natural death if the great famine had not come along at that particular moment and extinguished them by starvation. In 1906, Michael Davitt, Parnell's chief lieutenant and brilliant founder of the Land League, challenged the domination of the priests and the doctrine of church-state union; but he was not strong enough to defeat the priests.

Since then, religion and politics have always been completely intermingled in the Irish story, and no one in the present generation can remember a time in which the commingling has not been taken for granted. The Irish bishop, Anglican or Roman, had always been a power in the state, and it seemed natural to the people after they gained independence that their Catholic bishops should assume the authority once exercised by the bishops of the Protestant Ascendancy. It has also seemed natural to the Irish that every successful politician should be either a good Catholic or a good Protestant — never religiously neutral. The Irish people never had a fair chance to get away from this denominational conception of statesmanship. The Dissenters who emigrated to America from England and Ireland escaped from the conception only because they had an opportunity to develop and expand in a new continent where ecclesiastical and political privilege were not traditionally bound up together.

It is true that in both Northern and Southern Ireland today modern liberalism has brought about the technical disestablishment of all churches. The government in Ireland pays no salaries of priests or preachers directly. But, as we shall see later, this freedom from the burden of direct church taxes does not mean real disestablishment or genuine separation of church and state. The entire educational structure of Irish life is a privileged and protected form of ecclesiastical culture, endowed by the state. In the twentieth century, while other modern nations have been breaking away from the concept of church-state union, Ireland has moved nearer to the medieval tradition of Spain and Portugal.

4

The Clerical Republic

The Irish Republic is a clerical state.

Any writer who makes such a statement must define his terms carefully. The Republic is not a clerical state in the sense that Spain and Portugal are clerical states. Its political democracy is genuine, and it grants complete official freedom to opposition political parties and opposition religious groups. In Ireland, the Catholic Church has no official share in government, which is officially democratic.

Portugal, by contrast, has an extra-constitutional alliance between a Catholic dictator and the Church, in which a Catholic layman, Oliveira Salazar, as "the little priest," operates a one-party semi-fascist machine, with the Church as an organic part of that machine. The Church co-operates with the political dictatorship in suppressing democracy and in promoting loyalty among the masses. The dictatorship repays the Church by giving it supreme authority over such areas as education, marriage, and missionary expansion. The arrangement is regarded by the Vatican as one of the most satisfactory forms of church-state co-operation ever devised, and Portugal is constantly praised in Catholic journals — in Ireland and elsewhere — as a model of Christian policy.

Spain has an even closer union of church and state than Portugal. Franco is a complete Catholic totalitarian in philosophy and practice. The Church supports his fascist dictatorship by including in its catechism in the elementary schools a definite commitment to that dictatorship and a definite renunciation of freedom of thought and political democracy. In return, Franco recognizes the Church as an organic part of his government, and co-operates in the partial suppression of Protestant sects. The Vatican-Spanish Concordat of August 1953 gave Franco primary power in the selection of all Spanish bishops.

The church-state alliance in Ireland is unofficial and much more informal than the alliance in either Portugal or Spain. Ireland is not a police state, and it is not fascist. No Catholic bishops sit in its government councils. The Irish Republic combines the continental and medieval ecclesiastical monarchy of Rome with a modern, streamlined parliamentary system in a unique mixture, and the two organizations live in genuine amity most of the time because the state does not venture to challenge clerical authority directly and because the Church is usually discreet enough to assert its power unobtrusively.

Catholic power is so great in Irish political life that the Vatican has never attempted to bind the Republic by a concordat; a formal treaty is considered unnecessary. Nor has the Vatican ever found it necessary to threaten Irish Catholic politicians with excommunication for deviation from Catholic legislative principles. This is in sharp contrast to the Church's policy in Latin countries. In August 1953, Cardinal Vasconcelos of Brazil threatened armed rebellion "should any Brazilian government dare to institute divorce in Brazil." In Italy, with its powerful anti-clerical movement, the Vatican considered it necessary to write into the 1929 Lateran Treaty a rule for the compulsory teaching of Catholic faith in all public schools and a rule eliminating divorce — thus depriving the Italian parliament of freedom of action in these matters. In the Salvador Concordat (typical of many Latin American concordats) the right of the Catholic bishops to censor books was specifically recognized. All of these precautions are unnecessary in Ireland.

The Irish state treats the Church with public adulation, and the Church replies with audible appreciation of the state. The Very Rev. Canon Boylan expressed the appreciation of clergymen when, speaking at St. Patrick's College, Maynooth, at the time the new Irish Constitution was announced in 1937, he boasted: "The Catholic Church is more favourably placed in Ireland than it is in even the most Catholic countries of the continent."

Protestant Apprehensions

Before the Irish Free State was formed in 1922, there was a great deal of apprehension among Protestants about the future of their liberties, particularly in those isolated sections of the South where the small Protestant "Garrison" was surrounded by a huge and menacing Catholic majority. Would the Catholic majority in an independent Ireland take revenge for centuries of oppression? Would a Catholic state outlaw Protestantism either directly or by economic discrimination? Certainly the Irish Catholics could find in history many excuses for reprisals and many precedents for suppression. Perhaps, if they had won independence directly in a full-dress civil war, Protestantism would have been ruthlessly suppressed.

As it was, when the British government finally decided to yield to Irish guerrilla warfare and world liberal opinion, it took the precaution of writing certain guarantees of continuing religious liberty into law. In the treaty of December 1921 between the new Irish Free State and the British government, one section said:

Neither the Parliament of the Irish Free State nor the Parliament of Northern Ireland shall make any law so as either directly or indirectly to endow any religion or prohibit or restrict the free exercise thereof or give any preference or impose any disability on account of religious belief or religious status or affect prejudicially the right of any child to attend a school receiving public money without attending the religious instruction at the school or make any discrimination as respects state aid between schools.

The apprehensions of Irish and English Protestants about formal religious liberty were scarcely justified. The Catholics of Ireland had demanded religious liberty for themselves under a Protestant state for so long that they had come to think of it as a Catholic fundamental. To that extent they had been influenced by the best English liberal tradition of those Protestants who had so often fought by their side for Catholic emancipation. They had also become accustomed to living with substantial non-Catholic blocs in the community, and — unlike their fellow Catholics in Spain and Portugal — they had come to accept the right of non-Catholics to proselyte.

Accordingly, when the 1922 Constitution of the Irish Free

State was written, the Catholic majority in the South was quite happy to include all the major guarantees desired by the Protestants. Article 8 of this first Constitution used the language of the Anglo-Irish treaty in prohibiting religious endowments and preferences, and it proclaimed the sacredness of religious liberty in phrases which would have satisfied any anxious minority. "Freedom of conscience," said the Constitution, "and the free profession and practice of religion are, subject to public order and morality, guaranteed to every citizen." There were only a few skeptics who wondered about the phrase "subject to public order and morality." The "public order" condition seemed perfectly natural and harmless. Did not any state have a right to prevent disorder? It was conceivable that religious demonstrations in certain places at certain times might transgress public order; if so, the state would have the duty to restore public order by curtailing certain religious practices. At least the critics decided that they could afford to wait and see whether such phrases carried with them any real limitation upon religious freedom.

The words "subject to . . . morality" caused a little more misgiving. If the "free profession and practice of religion" was to be established only on condition that the profession and practice were moral, who would be authorized to define "morality"? Would a discussion of birth control in a Protestant parish hall be "moral" in an Irish Catholic Republic? If not, who should decide the question — the Protestant bishop, the Catholic bishop, or the Catholic-dominated state? Would a lecture on the right of divorce be protected under the Constitution if it championed that right for Catholics as well as Protestants? Could a public attack on the authority of the Pope be considered "immoral" within the meaning of the Constitution?

The answers to these hypothetical questions were not forthcoming, and those who had misgivings did not express them openly. The religious provisions of the 1922 Constitution excited very little argument, and the Constitution was promptly accepted. The Protestants were pleased because the new document continued the distribution of public money to their schools, as well as the Catholic schools, without discrimination. It also gave full freedom to Protestant parents to withdraw their children from the catechism classes of Catholic schools if they cared to send their children to such schools. By British standards these religious provisions of the 1922 Constitution were quite traditional. There was no mention of any claim for a special position for the Catholic Church in matters of education, marriage, birth control, censorship, or divorce.

Catholic Power Emerges

Then, in the 1937 Constitution — the present Constitution of the Republic — Catholic power emerged with more definitely partisan policies. Up to that point, while the Free State had still been attached to the British Crown under a special treaty agreement, nothing had been said in its Constitution or laws which granted a special status to any particular faith. The 1922 Constitution even declared that all the powers of government "are derived from the people of Ireland" — a theory flatly contrary to Catholic teaching. It is true that this democratic heresy was partially contradicted in a phrase in the preamble to the effect that "all lawful authority comes from God to the people." Catholics could read the preamble, and Protestants could read Article 2.

The new Constitution of 1937 expressed a more specifically Catholic philosophy of government. It began:

> In the name of the Most Holy Trinity, from Whom is all authority and to Whom, as our final end, all actions of both men and States must be referred,
> We, the people of Eire,
> Humbly acknowledging all our obligation to our Divine Lord, Jesus Christ, Who sustained our fathers through centuries of trial . . .

This was a little difficult for Irish Jews and agnostics to appreciate; but there were very few Jews and agnostics in Ireland, and such devout phrases could easily be classed as introductory fanfare. They were not considered unduly discriminatory in a nation which was so overwhelmingly Catholic.

The other new religious features of the 1937 Constitution were more substantial. "All powers of government," said Article 6, "legislative, executive and judicial, derive under God from the people." The sovereignty of the Irish people had been lowered one degree since the 1922 Constitution, in agreement with the philosophy of Leo XIII, who preached that all sovereignty comes from God and not the people. Most of the readers of this article probably dismissed it as a pious and not very meaningful salute to the Deity. They did not realize that in Catholic theory the phrase "under God" means in practice "under the Church," since the Church is the only authentic voice of God on earth. Hence, when the new Constitution put the government — legislative, executive, and judicial — "under God," it obliquely acknowledged the Church's supremacy over any area of democracy which the Church cared to claim as its own. This interpretation was strengthened by the phraseology of the reference to the Most Holy Trinity, which acknowledged the duty of the State to refer all its actions to this Trinity.

This oblique acknowledgment of clerical authority was made more specific in Article 44 of the new Constitution, headed "Religion." It began:

1. The State acknowledges that the homage of public worship is due to Almighty God. It shall hold His Name in reverence, and shall respect and honour religion.
2. The State recognizes the special position of the Holy Catholic Apostolic and Roman Church as the guardian of the Faith professed by the great majority of the citizens.
3. The State also recognizes the Church of Ireland, the Presbyterian Church in Ireland, the Methodist Church in Ireland, the Religious Society of Friends of Ireland, as well as the Jewish congregations and the other religious denominations existing in Ireland at the date of the coming into operation of this Constitution.

What did the phrase "special position of the Holy Catholic Apostolic and Roman Church" mean? To this day the courts of the Republic have not interpreted the words fully. Do they give the government the right to discriminate between sects in various ways? If so, the Constitution does not indicate what kinds of discrimination are intended, and in several particulars it specifically prohibits discrimination.

The guarantees of religious freedom in the 1922 Constitution were repeated in the 1937 Constitution almost word for word. The new Constitution provided that laws regulating the right of free assembly should "contain no political, religious or class discrimination," and that the state should impose no religious disabilities on any person. It guaranteed "not to endow any religion."

All these provisions for religious liberty and fair play reassured the outside world. They were hailed in America and Britain by both Catholics and Protestants as refreshing evidence that Catholic policy on church and state, even in a Catholic nation, could be reasonable and fair. The Protestant scholar M. Searle Bates, in his study *Religious Liberty,* said: "The Eire Constitution of 1937, generally approved in its working, deserves close study as an independent reconcilement of Roman Catholic concepts with a free society, under special conditions of history and political needs." Under this new Constitution, the phrase "special position of the Holy Catholic Apostolic and Roman Church" was considered by many observers to be merely a harmless devotional and rhetorical tribute to the faith of the majority.

The religious presuppositions of the new Irish commonwealth were not all embodied in the Constitution's article on religion. The Catholic point of view crept into several other articles of the new charter. Certain provisions about marriage and censorship raised some disquieting doubts as to what the Constitution actually meant by giving the Catholic Church a "special position." We shall discuss these clauses in the chapter on "Sex, Chastity, and Population."

Article 40 of the new Constitution set forth a Catholic interpretation of the right of freedom of speech which watchful critics recognized as the potential basis for clerical censorship. It said that "the State shall endeavour to ensure that organs of public opinion, such as the radio, the press, the cinema, while preserving their rightful liberty of expression, including criticism of government policy, shall not be used to undermine public order or morality or the authority of the State. The publication or utterance of blasphemous, seditious, or indecent matter is an offence which shall be punishable in accordance with law."

The key word in this article, of course, is "morality." The citizens of the new Republic are given the right to express their opinions freely if they do not thereby "undermine . . . morality." What does "undermine" mean? What is "morality"? Almost any public statement against Catholic policy on sex, medical hygiene, indulgences, celibacy, gambling, nudity, divorce, or atheism could be interpreted by Catholic officials as "undermining morality." We shall see in the chapter on censorship how these words and the corresponding word "indecent" can be stretched by public officials under clerical domination to cover many acts of cultural suppression.

In practice, the Irish Constitution does not curtail the ordinary rights of worship or religious activity in any way. Protestant churches are permitted to function in every corner of the Republic without legal restriction. Protestant voters have exactly the same rights as Catholic voters; and in theory Protestant officeholders have the same opportunities for public service. There were, early in 1953, four Protestants serving as elected members of the Dail, and one Protestant member of the cabinet in De Valera's government. The first President of the Irish Republic, Douglas Hyde, was a Protestant leader in the Irish-language movement.

Today, aside from the few special instances to be discussed later, all religious organizations are allowed freely to worship, to proselyte, and to publish their own journals and books. Even the agents of Jehovah's Witnesses are permitted to hawk their inflammatory magazines on the streets of Dublin without let or hindrance. Non-Catholic schools may include their own religious concepts in their teaching while continuing to receive full public support from the taxpayers on the same proportionate basis as the Catholic schools. The Catholic Church never endorses any political party as such, and it never permits its priests to serve as members of parliament.

All these facts can be offered to the world as evidence that the Irish Republic is technically free from clerical control.

The Browne Incident

How much power *does* the Catholic hierarchy actually exercise over Irish democracy? In a sense the greater part of this book is an answer to that question. It will be seen that an unofficial Catholic clerical state may be just as effective an instrument of Catholic power as an official one. This was demonstrated dramatically in 1952 by the famous "Browne incident." As a result of that incident, an Irish political struggle involving the Church reached the front pages of some of Britain's and America's leading newspapers for the first time in many years.

Noel Browne is a brilliant, though somewhat temperamental,

Irish Catholic physician. In 1948, while still in his early thirties, he was made Minister for Health under the Inter-Party (Costello) government. A burning dynamo of energy and idealism, the young cabinet minister set out to eliminate the major disgrace of Irish life, the nation's high infant-mortality rate — one of the worst in Europe. In public speeches early in 1948 he revealed that the deaths of Irish infants during the first year of life in the previous five-year period had been 55 per cent higher in the Republic than in England and Wales. He showed that the government had failed to improve conditions as rapidly as other governments had. Since the beginning of the century, he demonstrated, infant mortality in Southern Ireland had declined 25 per cent; in England and Wales 67 per cent; and in New York State 71 per cent. He pointed out that the record of Southern Ireland was distinctly worse than that of the North.

Dr. Browne's study of the situation convinced him that one reason for the appalling infant-mortality rate was the absence of a national system of maternity education and care for all mothers. Needy mothers could get public charity with some inconvenience — but they were often too proud to apply for it. Dr. Browne announced a mother-and-child health plan which would undertake to give free maternity care to every mother, plus child care to the age of sixteen. Included in the plan was a general scheme for education in maternity problems.

Although the financial provisions of Dr. Browne's scheme were over-ambitious, there was nothing particularly revolutionary in the principles of his scheme. Its main concepts had been endorsed by a previous government, and across the Irish Sea at the same time a similar plan was being successfully operated by the British National Health Service. Irish politics in the South had been seething for years with demands for improved government health services on the British model, and the political coalition to which Dr. Browne belonged had won many votes by making urgent demands upon the government for better health services for all the people.

In his idealistic — and somewhat ill-digested — plans for a medical revolution, the Minister for Health had two formidable enemies: the conservative Irish Medical Association, and the hierarchy of his own Church. This hierarchy, directly or through religious orders, controls a large proportion of the hospitals of the Republic, and indirectly controls nearly all the private hospitals as well, through its power over Catholic directors, doctors, and nurses. It is jealous of this power, especially in any area where its traditional medical code might be challenged by modern science. Under this code, every precaution must be taken by every institution under Catholic control to ensure that no non-Catholic concept or practice shall be allowed.

In layman's language, the particular rules which the Catholic hierarchy is most anxious to protect in every hospital are two: (1) No woman must ever learn about birth control as an incidental feature of maternity education. (2) No physician may recommend or carry out a therapeutic abortion even if this is the only remedy by which he can save the life of a mother. These well-known rules are embodied in Catholic canon law and the public declarations of Pius XII and other Popes.

There was nothing whatever in Dr. Browne's plans to contravene these traditional provisions of Catholic law. His scheme was to be administered almost wholly by Catholic physicians and nurses, inasmuch as there are very few non-Catholic physicians and nurses remaining in the Republic. No physicians were to be asked to do or to say anything contrary to their hierarchy's teachings. No indication had ever been given in the literature used to promote Dr. Browne's scheme that there would be any opposition or challenge to Catholic teaching on sex. It is true that the scheme, as Dr. Browne publicly admitted, was calculated to include non-Catholic as well as Catholic doctors, nurses, and patients. Under the Constitution the rule could hardly be otherwise, since the law obliges the government to refrain from public discrimination on the ground of denominational status.

Although the Irish hierarchy had privately objected to similar principles in a projected health scheme drawn up by the De Valera regime in 1947, Dr. Browne had not been reminded by his cabinet colleagues of this private opposition. So he boldly put forth in 1951 his own comprehensive scheme for a mother-and-child health service designed to be absolutely free. Apparently the idealistic young doctor believed that his scheme was in full accord with Catholic moral teaching, and that the hier-

archy of his own Church could not consistently take exception
to it. In a letter sent to Prime Minister Costello, his superior
officer in the government, in the midst of the controversy which
later developed over his plan, the Minister for Health made his
own allegiance to Catholicism quite clear. "I should have
thought it unnecessary," he wrote, "to point out that from the
beginning it has been my concern to see that the Mother and
Child Scheme contained nothing contrary to Catholic moral
teaching. I hope I need not assure you that as a Catholic I will
unhesitatingly and immediately accept any pronouncement
from the Hierarchy as to what is Catholic moral teaching in
reference to this matter."

The Irish hierarchy insisted that it should have the opportunity
to approve or disapprove of any government medical program in
advance of its submission to the people. On October 10, 1950,
after a meeting at Maynooth, Ireland's most famous Catholic
theological seminary, the hierarchy sent to Prime Minister Costello the following letter. It is such a classic declaration of
Catholic clerical authority in a modern state that I shall quote it
in full:

Dear Taoiseach:
The Archbishops and Bishops of Ireland, at their meeting on October
10th, had under consideration the proposal for Mother and Child health
service and other kindred medical services. They recognize that these
proposals are motivated by a sincere desire to improve public health but
they feel bound by their office to consider whether the proposals are in
accordance with Catholic moral teaching.
In their opinion, the powers taken by the State in the proposed
Mother and Child health service are in direct opposition to the rights of
the family and of the individual and are liable to very great abuse. Their
character is such that no assurance that they would be used in modera-
tion could justify their enactment. If adopted in law they would constitute a ready-made instrument for future totalitarian aggression.
The right to provide for the health of children belongs to parents, not
the State. The State has the right to intervene only in a subsidiary
capacity, to supplement not to supplant.
It may help indigent or neglectful parents; it may not deprive 90
per cent of parents of their rights because of 10 per cent necessitous or
negligent parents.
It is not sound social policy to impose State medical service on the
whole community on the pretext of relieving the necessitous 10 per cent
from the so-called indignity of the means test.

The right to provide for the physical education of children belongs to the family and not to the State. Experience has shown that physical or health education is closely interwoven with important moral questions on which the Catholic Church has definite teaching.

Education in regard to motherhood includes instruction in regard to sex relations, chastity and marriage. The State has no competence to give instruction in such matters. We regard with the greatest apprehension the proposal to give to local medical officers the right to tell Catholic girls and women how they should behave in regard to this sphere of conduct, at once so delicate and sacred.

Gynaecological care may be, and in some other countries is, interpreted to include provision for birth limitation and abortion. We have no guarantee that State officials will respect Catholic principles in regard to these matters. Doctors trained in institutions in which we have no confidence may be appointed as medical officers under the proposed services, and may give gynaecological care not in accordance with Catholic principles.

The proposed service also destroys the confidential relation between doctor and patient and regards all cases of illnesses as matter for public records and research without regard to the individual's right to privacy.

The elimination of private medical practitioners by a state-paid service has not been shown to be necessary or even advantageous to the patient, the public in general, or the medical profession.

The Bishops are most favourable to measures which would benefit public health, but they consider that instead of imposing a costly bureaucratic scheme of nationalized medical service the State might well consider the advisability of providing the maternity hospitals and other institutional facilities, which are at present lacking, and should give adequate maternity benefits and taxation relief for large families.

The Bishops desire that your Government should give careful consideration to the dangers inherent in the present proposals before they are adopted by the Government for legislative enactment, and, therefore, they feel it their duty to submit their views on this subject to you privately and at the earliest opportunity, since they regard the issues involved as of the greatest moral and religious importance.

I remain, dear Taoiseach,

Yours very sincerely,

/s/ JAMES STAUNTON
Bishop of Ferns,
Secretary to the Hierarchy.

John A. Costello, T.D., Taoiseach.

It should be noted that this letter contained two general objections to Dr. Browne's proposals. The hierarchy expressed specific apprehensions about the dangers of non-Catholic moral teaching on such matters as sex, birth control, and abortion; and it also expressed philosophical opposition to any extension of the welfare state. The first objections could be interpreted, even by those who considered them unjustified, as coming within the rightful domain of Catholic moral judgment; the second had nothing to do with Catholicism, Mohammedanism, or any other religion. When, for example, the bishops declared that the "elimination of private medical practitioners by a state-paid service has not been shown to be necessary or even advantageous to the patient, the public in general, or the medical profession," they were delivering an economic and political opinion that had nothing to do with their normal orbit of activity. The judgment may or may not have been true. In this case it was an obvious echo of the judgment of the Irish Medical Association, which had launched a powerful drive against the Browne scheme resembling in scope and bias the similar drives against health insurance by medical organizations in the United States.

The beleaguered Minister for Health, when he was finally given an opportunity to reply to the bishops' letter, easily disposed of all the objections raised. In respect to sex education, he guaranteed that he would "provide such safeguards in matters of health education as would meet the requirements of the Hierarchy . . . the Minister is prepared to submit to the Hierarchy for their approval the draft, when available, of that part of the regulations which will deal with these matters."

By this time even such sweeping gestures of submission could not appease the bishops. The issue had become one of prestige and power as between the Catholic Church and the Irish state. "The Hierarchy," replied the bishops in a letter to the Prime Minister dated April 5, 1951, "cannot approve of any scheme, which in its general tendency, must foster undue control by the State in a sphere so delicate and so intimately concerned with morals as that which deals with gynaecology or obstetrics and with the relations between doctors and patients." By the time the story had reached the American Catholic press, the Irish Catholic hierarchy was represented in the Denver *Register* as fighting against a "proposal to give local medical officers the right to tell girls how they should behave in the matter of sex relations."

It is one of the proofs of the iron control of Irish culture by Catholic power that no newspaper in the Republic dared to suggest that unmarried bishops might be treading rashly on delicate ground when they made judgments in the field of gynaecology without consulting any of those poverty-stricken Catholic mothers who are the beneficiaries.

When the Minister for Health refused to yield on the central issue involved — free care for all mothers — he was publicly ordered to resign by Sean MacBride, fiery leader of his party, Clann na Poblachta, who was at that time the nation's Minister for External Affairs. Browne had no alternative but to comply. He was immediately subjected to a whispering campaign of fact and fancy. One of the "charges" against him — and quite true — was that he had allowed himself to be "photographed with the Protestant Archbishop of Dublin"; another was that he had married a Protestant. Moreover, he had taken a medical degree from the Republic's only non-denominational university, Trinity College. These facts were enough to damn most men of political ambition in the Republic, and it was a tribute to the moral character of Dr. Browne that he had been able to rise in spite of such handicaps. He was a Catholic — and a product of the schools of the Christian Brothers and the Jesuits, and these things counted in his favor in the battle of vilification which followed.

"The Effective Government"

As soon as Dr. Browne was forced to resign, virtually every minister in the government — all members of the Church — rushed to repudiate him, proclaiming heartfelt loyalty to Catholic "moral principles." De Valera, then leader of the Opposition, remained astutely silent. Already, as the *Irish Times* pointed out, Browne had been "left to fight a single-handed battle when once the Church entered the arena." Concerning Dr. Browne's forced resignation the *Times* added: "This is a sad day for Ireland. It is not so important that the Mother and Child Scheme has been withdrawn, to be replaced by an alternative project embodying a means test. What matters more is that an honest, far-sighted and energetic man has been driven out of active politics. The most serious revelation, however, is that the Roman

Catholic Church would seem to be the effective government of this country."

This interpretation of the Browne incident was borne out by the submissive statements made by government leaders in the Dail, and by the official correspondence of the government in this case. In a letter to Dr. Browne dated March 15, 1951, the Prime Minister had written: "I have no doubt that all my colleagues and, in particular, yourself, would not be party to any proposals affecting moral questions which would or might come into conflict with the definite teaching of the Catholic Church." In a letter of March 21, 1951, addressed to Dr. Browne, Prime Minister Costello had said: "My withholding of approval of the scheme is due to the objections set forth in the letter to me from the secretary to the Hierarchy, written on behalf of the Hierarchy, and to the reiteration of their objections by His Grace the Archbishop of Dublin, as Archbishop of Dublin." The repetition of the official titles of the Church revealed the Prime Minister's conviction that he was yielding not to the incidental reasonableness of any bishop's objection but to the superior power of the official Church itself. Lest there be any doubt about the nature of the submission, the Prime Minister had written to Dr. Browne on the same day: "Accordingly, you are not entitled to describe your scheme as Government policy and you must not so describe it hereafter unless and until you have satisfied the Hierarchy that in respect of the matters relating to faith and morals your scheme is unobjectionable."

So the Prime Minister of the Irish Republic acknowledged the veto power of the Catholic hierarchy over a plan which, apparently, he considered acceptable otherwise. To make his point of view doubly clear, he wrote Dr. Browne on the following day, March 22: ". . . it is for the Hierarchy alone to say whether or no the scheme contained anything contrary to Catholic moral teaching." On March 27 he wrote to the secretary of the hierarchy: "His Grace of Dublin has . . . kindly agreed to inform the Standing Committee that the Government would readily and immediately acquiesce in a decision of the Hierarchy concerning faith and morals."

In concluding a long summary of his case before the Dail, Prime Minister Costello gave a final public pledge that his government would accept "advice or warnings by the authoritative people in the Catholic Church on matters strictly confined to faith and morals," and would give to such "directions" "our complete obedience and allegiance." "I, as a Catholic," he said, "obey my Church authorities and will continue to do so."

Several significant points about this Browne incident should be emphasized. The first is that the mother-and-child health scheme was, theologically, a border-line case. The general policy advocated was not a self-evident violation of Catholic moral law on which all Catholics could instantly agree. The hierarchy, if it had been able to overcome its conservative bias against the expansion of the welfare state, could just as easily have found authority for accepting the scheme. Liberal Catholics could quote many passages in papal encyclicals favorable to its underlying principles — and they could also cite the Catholic acceptance of the British National Health Service. It seemed clear that, if the Irish hierarchy could win obedience so easily in a border-line area where the moral principles involved were only remotely connected with Catholic law, any more positive assault upon Catholic discipline would meet an even swifter fate.

The incident also revealed how meaningless the religious-liberty guarantees of the Constitution could be when the hierarchy chose to sidestep them. The hierarchy in this case carved out from the domain of the state a special territory which it labeled "moral." Sean O'Faolain, Catholic biographer of Cardinal Newman and one of Ireland's foremost writers, stated the case against this political intervention of his Church in terms that were at once courageous and authoritative:

The issue is that no country can be ruled "democratically" by two parliaments; or at least not as the world understands that word.

Here in the Republic, as this crisis has revealed to us, we have two parliaments; a parliament at Maynooth and a parliament in Dublin. . . .

Nobody, so far as I have observed, has denied the right of the Catholic bishops to "comment"; or to give "advice" on proposed legislation; or to enunciate the official attitude of the Roman Catholic Church to proposed legislation. That principle is fully and wholeheartedly admitted. I believe that not even the most ashen-jawed, beetle-browed, black-bowler-hatted Orangeman in Portadown could reasonably object to that principle. I doubt if anybody, north or south, could even object to the Hierarchy publicly condemning any proposed piece of legislation, provided that, in the end, it is the Parliament which freely decides. I doubt if there is a single bishop in the Republic or in all Christendom, who would wish to contravert this. In practice, the Hierarchy does much more than "comment" or "advise." It commands. . . .

The Maynooth Parliament holds a weapon which none of the other institutions mentioned holds: the weapon of the Sacraments. The Church of England cannot wield the power of the Catholic Church because it does not hold this weapon. If a Prime Minister in England were informed by the Archbishop of Canterbury that a proposed law would be condemned by the Church of England, he would deplore it, but he would not be afraid of any effects other than political effects. If our Taoiseach were informed thus by the Protestant Archbishop of Dublin he would measure the effects in the same way. And likewise with most other institutions religious or secular. But when the Catholic Church, through its representatives, speaks, he realizes, and the Roman Catholic public realizes, that if they disobey they may draw on themselves this weapon whose touch means death. (Most of us feel, I think, that it is unfair to use this weapon on political occasions: and that is putting it mildly.)

There is, therefore, no use in talking blandly about "comment," or "advice." The lightest word from this quarter is tantamount to the raising of the sword. That is why it is just to speak of two parliaments. The Dail proposes; Maynooth disposes. The Dail had, when up against the Second Parliament, only one right of decision: the right to surrender.

That is what made the Browne affair so interesting and so dramatic. It revealed to the people of the Republic that if this is a Democracy it is a form of Democracy unlike any other in the world. That is to say: the supreme power is not here, in practice — which is what matters — vested in the people's Parliament.

The Aftermath

To what extent did the Browne incident indicate the power of the Catholic hierarchy over the Irish people? There are some in Dublin today who declare that the political results of the incident proved that the power of the Church can sometimes be successfully challenged. The events following Dr. Browne's forced resignation indicate that some incipient rebellion is in the air. Although all the heads of government departments and political parties promptly deserted Dr. Browne, some of his colleagues remained loyal; and because they held the balance of power in the Dail they forced the government in 1951 to go to the country in a spectacular general election. In spite of the fact that Dr. Browne had been read out of his party and forced to run as an independent, he was returned to his seat in the Dail by a majority larger than his former one, and by a margin considerably larger proportionately than the margin given to his former political leader, Sean MacBride, who barely escaped defeat. And when the votes had been counted, the party totals were so close that the small company of Dr. Browne's friends again held the balance of power in the Dail. They took a sweet revenge on their former political chieftains by voting the Inter-Party government out of power, and returning De Valera as Prime Minister.

It would be reassuring to interpret this victory as proof of a great and vigorous spirit of independence among the Irish voters. But I could not find in Ireland any evidence that the rebellion was more than a temporary expression of pique against clerical tactlessness combined with sincere admiration for the bravery of a young Catholic doctor. The opposition to the Church engendered by the public discussion did not seem to be well reasoned. The newspapers of Catholic persuasion completely failed to face the fundamental issue of clerical power. Among the newspapers only the *Irish Times* dared to discuss the issue frankly. The two Dublin dailies of greatest circulation, the *Irish Independent* and the *Irish Press,* either avoided the issue altogether or gave a completely partisan and pro-clerical twist to the news. Most of the Irish people in the countryside were scarcely aware that their country had passed through a significant moral and political crisis.

The resultant return of De Valera to office in the 1951 election — without an over-all majority — could not, under the circumstances, be described as an important moral victory over the bishops. De Valera had played a most ignoble role in the whole Browne affair. He and his party associates remained adroitly silent while the government punished Dr. Browne. Then, after De Valera had returned to power, his new Minister for Health, Dr. James Ryan, presented in 1953 a health plan which the *Irish Times* described as "a pathetic compromise." Even this bill met so much opposition from the Catholic hierarchy that it was revised under their direction before being passed by the Dail in the summer of 1953. The government, surrendering to the hierarchy on the main issue of the whole dispute, included official and unofficial means tests in the new health plan. This time the hierarchy's letter of instruction was not officially made

public, but it was circulated among legislators and editors —
and it produced immediate submission. On August 7, 1953, Dr.
Ryan declared in the Dail that De Valera and he, having "several times" consulted with the Catholic hierarchy on the new
bill, "had met objections they put forward by Amendments."

Etiquette in a Clerical State

Sometimes the etiquette and protocol of a government reveal
its spirit even more clearly than its formal laws. A gesture of
homage or contempt may be more expressive than a concordat
or a constitution. In the case of the Irish government, the man-
ners of the state's leaders in dealing with Catholic dignitaries
are definitely "colonial": the leaders of the Church are treated
with that conspicuous deference which the subject peoples
showed to British imperial dignitaries a century ago. A bishop
is usually called "Your Lordship," although some Irishmen use
the more correct "My Lord." An archbishop is treated with the
adulation that might have been accorded to a medieval prince;
and a cardinal is honored like a king. Papal titles are treated
so respectfully that if an Irishman is made a Papal Count, he
actually is known thereafter in Ireland by that title. When President O'Kelly went to Rome during the Holy Year of 1950, he
went as a humble pilgrim; but he was not content with the
general proclamation of loyalty made by individual pilgrims.
He announced on his arrival in Rome: "I come as President of
the free people of Ireland and as President of the Irish Republic,
a pilgrim of this Holy Year, to place my personal homage, and
that of my people, at the feet of His Holiness Pope Pius XII."
When, on his return to Dublin after the pilgrimage, the Archbishop of Dublin met him at the airport, the President knelt to
kiss the archbishop's ring.

Foreign Minister Sean MacBride had already flown to Rome
to represent his government at the ceremony of the opening
of the Holy Door. The Dublin Corporation — its city council
— unanimously passed a Holy Year resolution, not merely con-
gratulating the Pope but also pledging "filial homage and devotion." The Fermoy District Council called upon the government
to incorporate a cross into the Irish flag. A movement was
launched to erect a statue at the Port of Dublin in honor of

"Our Blessed Lady, the Virgin Mary, who is Queen of Ireland" in the style of the Statue of Liberty in New York Harbor. Later, in 1951, the armed forces of the Republic were placed under "the protection of the Virgin Mary" in a public ceremony.

The highest officials of the Irish state commonly kneel before the Church's bishops at public celebrations. They go obediently to the headquarters of the bishops when they are summoned, instead of inviting the bishops to their public offices. The army regularly participates in this homage, and its officers publicly join in the kneeling process. Military organizations frequently give bishops the honors of formal salute. When Archbishop John D'Alton of Armagh was made a cardinal in January 1953, and passed through Dublin on his way to Rome, Prime Minister De Valera met him at the airport and twice genuflected before him for the benefit of the newsreel cameras, kissing his ring. Just before the ball is tossed out at the great national finals of Ireland's distinctive game of hurling, in Croke Park, the competing captains kneel and kiss the ring of the Papal Nuncio to the Republic. The Nuncio, of course, is the dean of the diplomatic corps, and chief spokesman in all public ceremonials for all foreign diplomats accredited to the country. When he arrives from Rome he is met at the airport by the Republic's Minister for Foreign Affairs, who kneels in homage. His palatial residence is in Phoenix Park, Dublin, where only three political residences are privileged to stand: his own, the residence of the President, and that of the American ambassador.

One of the significant features of the government's conduct during the Browne incident was its ecclesiastical etiquette. During the entire negotiations, the Archbishop of Dublin only once came to the headquarters of the Prime Minister, and then it was to formalize a decision on policy which had already been made at the Archbishop's house. When the bishops originally decided to broach the matter of mother-and-child policy to the Prime Minister, they summoned *him*. When they wished to discuss the problem with the Minister for Health, they did not go to the Minister's office — he came to *them*. In describing this incident, Dr. Browne said: "I was informed that His Grace the Archbishop of Dublin wished to see me in connection with the proposed scheme. I attended at the Archbishop's House on the following day." When the Prime Minister referred to this interview between the Minister for Health and the bishops, he stated that the Minister for Health had asked for an early *decision* — not an opinion — by the hierarchy. When the bishops replied to Dr. Browne in a formal memorandum, they referred to the "principle which *must* be amended, and it is the principle which *must* be set forth correctly, in a legally binding manner and in an enactment of the Oireachtas [Parliament]." This was a very specific legislative order to a national cabinet chief and his fellow legislators; it was not to be considered a mere tender of clerical opinion or advice.

Usually such directives by a clerical pressure group are carefully concealed or disguised, since it is the settled policy of the Vatican to avoid the appearance of interference in politics. In the Browne case the bishops had become somewhat careless because of long and successful practice in controlling Irish policy from behind the scenes; but Dr. Browne and the *Irish Times* stripped them of their anonymity.

The "Second Parliament"

What of the "second parliament" itself? Is there no democracy, no restless urge for Irish self-determination, among the priests and bishops? In an astute study of Catholic influence in Ireland, *The Pope's Green Island,* published in 1912, W. P. Ryan declared that the priests of that period were quite anti-Roman in their private attitudes and that they distrusted and disliked domination of their Church from abroad. The Irish bishops voted against papal infallibility in 1870 despite tremendous clerical pressure. But today there is no sign of an Irish spirit of independence among the clergy. There is no modernist movement among the priests, and no anti-clerical movement among the laymen. The Roman machinery of power still rules the Irish Church from a distance without any vestige of local democracy and without any Irish representative assembly. Only those priests who are thoroughly docile before the absolute power of Rome have any chance of promotion to the rank of bishop. In accordance with world-wide practice, all the Irish bishops are appointed in Rome and all the Irish priests are chosen and controlled by those bishops.

Occasionally in clerical journals one can find among the writings of the younger priests a few faint intimations of the love of freedom, a few oblique suggestions that they are suffering pain and humiliation because they have been asked in an age of democracy to dedicate their lives to a system of power in which they have no voice or vote. But their protests are mild, and apparently their voices can be easily hushed. It is true that the Pope permits the Irish bishops to hold plenary councils, and he appoints a Primate of Ireland — two rights which are denied to Catholicism in the United States. But beyond these minor privileges there is no self-government for the Irish in their own Church. The Maynooth Synod of Irish bishops, the controlling body of Irish Catholicism, has not held a plenary session since 1927. When it does meet, it serves only as a committee of Roman-appointed prelates whose every decree must be approved by Rome before official announcement. The Synod is extremely careful to give no legislative or even advisory rights to mere priests, and it gives no recognition to laymen except as ecclesiastical wards of the priests. The decrees of the Synod are binding on both priests and laymen without recourse. Below the Maynooth Synod come the Diocesan Synods, which are completely subordinate in each case to a local bishop. The individual bishops have power to appoint, remove, and transfer their priests; they can even order a young priest to become a teacher instead of a priest, and he has no right to refuse the teaching assignment. "It is an old joke among Irish curates," says Sean O'Faolain, "that 'the Irish bishop stands on ceremony and sits on everybody.' "

It is almost thirty years since the system of clerical autocracy has been even faintly challenged from within. In 1923 a young priest, signing himself "A Voice in the Wilderness," asked in the columns of the *Irish Ecclesiastical Record,* "whether priests in the Diocesan Synod had the right to ask questions appertaining to Diocesan affairs." "It does not seem just or in harmony with the spirit of the new Code," he wrote, "that priests should be compelled to live under laws in the making of which they have no voice." The official answer of the hierarchy was kindly in tone but stern in content. It said:

. . . it is in harmony with the spirit not merely of the Code, but even of the Divine foundation itself of the Church, that priests must live under laws in the making of which they have no voice. By Divine institution, legislative as well as every other jurisdiction is reserved to the Pope and the Bishops; and in the actual discipline of the Church, as represented by the Code, the general body of the clergy have not even a consultative voice in the making of general, national, or provincial laws, and their participation in diocesan legislation is . . . dependent altogether on the will of the Bishop.

While some priests have a traditional right to attend certain Synods, "curates, as a body, and the great majority of parish priests, have not a strict right to intervention in the Diocesan Synod at all." If they attend and vote, it is by courtesy. The priests' voice, continued the *Record,* is

. . . merely consultative, not deliberative; the Code expressly confirms the old discipline that the Bishop himself is the sole legislator. . . . As for the justice of being compelled to live in subjection to laws, clearly all that is required is that the laws proceed from a competent authority and that they be good in themselves; and nobody, we think, will seriously maintain that a law cannot promote the welfare of a community unless the community as a body has had a voice in its making.

Earlier, one of Ireland's ablest priests, Father Walter Mc-Donald, professor of theology at Maynooth, staged a courageous personal revolt against the arbitrary rule of the Irish hierarchy, and was ruthlessly suppressed — along with his books. Sean O'Casey has made his story famous in *Inishfallen Fare Thee Well.* McDonald had the supreme audacity to suggest that the Catholic Church in Ireland should publish a detailed financial budget telling the people where their contributions went; and he said in 1908 that the Church should endorse "the principle that the people had a right to control State-endowed schools: that if priests wished to retain their present position of sole managers, they should do so as delegates of the people."

Anti-clerical voices among laymen are almost never heard except in a small intellectual circle in Dublin. In all of Southern Ireland there are only two small independent journals edited by Catholics, the *Leader* and the *Bell,* which ever venture to challenge Church policy; and they do not reach any large section of the population. The *Bell* is the more outspoken, and it has served as a welcome vehicle for the forthright comments of Sean O'Faolain. There is one progressive civil-liberties association, led by sincere Catholics, but its valiant efforts meet with resistance and indifference. There is in the whole Republic no anti-clerical society or political party or cultural movement which directly challenges the Church — nothing resembling the spirited and saucy anti-clericalism of France and Italy. Almost all the newspapers are, as the *Catholic Encyclopedia* puts it, "wholeheartedly Catholic in their presentation of news." The independence of the *Irish Times* represents not so much any leftist tendency as the last stand of the Anglo-Irish Protestant Ascendancy in behalf of freedom. In the Catholic press — which includes virtually all of the press except the *Irish Times* — no sign of anti-clerical liberalism is ever allowed to creep into editorial comment. The Catholic press is the press which reaches more than 90 per cent of the newspaper readers; the two leading Catholic dailies of Dublin, the *Irish Independent* and the *Irish Press,* have a combined circulation of more than 400,000, as against the 36,000 circulation of the *Irish Times.*

Meanwhile — as we shall see in the chapter on "Fanaticism and Moral Childhood" — there is among the more conservative Catholics an ominous movement to the right, exalting all that is Spanish and Portuguese, and promoting anti-Semitism. These right-wing Catholics are not content with the present clerical state — they consider it too liberal and too lenient to Protestants. Some of the priests are teaching their people a conditional and lukewarm loyalty to the Irish Constitution, and so creating an attitude which could easily be transformed into hostility to the Irish state if it decided to move in an anti-clerical direction. It is too early to say that there is any clerical fascism in Ireland today; but the material for a clerical fascist state is ready for use by a dictator if the Church needs a dictator to maintain its position.

5

Censorship, Official and Unofficial

Like Spain's Inquisition under Torquemada, the Irish book censorship is not so much famous as infamous. Because of its infamy, it is probably the best-known feature of the Irish clerical republic. At one time or another, the censorship has victimized almost every distinguished writer of fiction in the non-Irish world, and it has brought under its blight Ireland's greatest poets, dramatists, and scholars. Its black list, as a Catholic writer in the *Irish Times* has suggested, might almost be considered "a concise index to modern literature."

William Butler Yeats once said in the Free State Senate, during a debate on censorship: "I think you can leave the arts, superior or inferior, to the general conscience of mankind." As an Irishman who came from the Protestant Ascendancy but who was at the same time a sincere advocate of Irish independence, Yeats puzzled and embarrassed the Irish hierarchy. In the world of culture he stood for everything which the bishops feared and distrusted. He attacked their restrictive notions on literature and the arts with the directness of one who could speak the truth because he had no political ambitions. He was so eminent that they did not dare to challenge him directly. It is one of the ironies of Irish history that the leaders of the Church, who hated and feared him when he was alive, have learned to speak of him after his death with carefully modulated respect.

On the fundamental question of the restraint of the human mind, the philosophy of Yeats and the philosophy of Irish Catholicism are at opposite ends of the critical spectrum. Yeats believed that the mind should be free from external restrictions in order to grow to maturity. He thought that adults should be trusted to work out their own standards of literary fitness. The Catholic Church, on the other hand, has no confidence in "the general conscience of mankind," and insists that even educated men should be subject to a priestly apparatus of censorship. A noted Irish Jesuit, Father Stephen J. Brown, has put the Church's doctrine into a one-sentence mandate for Ireland: "As for the rights of art and literature, neither has any rights against God."

The meaning of the mandate is made clear in Canon 1399 of the Church's law, and in the official commentaries on that Canon. All books "against God" are without rights, no matter whether they are published under a democracy or under a dictatorship. If they are allowed to exist in a Catholic state, it is not because of the Church but in spite of it. Books "against God" include all books "which of set purpose treat of, tell or teach obscene or impure topics"; "which impugn or deride any Catholic dogmas"; "which attempt to overthrow ecclesiastical discipline"; "which declare that duelling, suicide or divorce are licit"; "which avowedly aim to defame the hierarchy or the clerical or religious state"; "which defend heresy or schism"; "which avowedly attack religion or good morals."

Because Cosgrave and other leaders of the Free State government in 1929 were sensitive to foreign criticism, the Irish Republic did not embody in its original censorship laws the full Catholic proscriptions — although some members of the Dail wanted such proscriptions. To have included the whole Catholic censorship code in Irish law would have destroyed religious freedom too obviously. In fact, Spain is the only country in Europe today which prevents the publication of works on the Catholic *Index of Prohibited Books* (*Index Librorum Probitorum*) simply because they are listed there. In the theological sense Ireland today has anti-religious as well as religious liberty in the publication and sale of books. That is, anti-Catholic and anti-Christian literature can legally be bought and sold — if a courageous bookseller can be located who cares to risk the discrimination and boycott which such liberties invite. Free thought is not legally prohibited, and atheism may be advocated without official penalties. It is even possible for a Protestant canon to say in a letter in the *Irish Times* that "the Papacy is the father and mother of totalitarianism, and that Hitler merely transferred to the political and social spheres the principles which Rome has developed through centuries of autocracy." Probably there is not a large newspaper in the United States today which would venture to print such an opinion.

Two decades before complete independence was declared, the Irish Free State had passed, in 1929, a censorship law which gave to a Censorship of Publications Board comprehensive powers over books and magazines. In the new Constitution of 1937, Article 40 went farther and gave the government power to suppress published material which was considered obscene or sacrilegious. This new Article provided that the "publication or utterance of blasphemous, seditious, or indecent matter is an offence which shall be punishable in accordance with law." Interpreted strictly, this constitutional provision could be used to ban any work hostile to Catholic theology or discipline as "blasphemous"; but since the word "blasphemous" is ambiguous, the Irish bishops were not completely satisfied. When the Constitution was being discussed in 1937, some of them demanded a more stringent and more theological censorship. In an important article, "The Freedom of the Press," in the *Irish Ecclesiastical Record,* Dr. Cornelius Lucey, now Bishop of Cork, said of Article 40:

> Were the word "anti-religious" inserted after the word "blasphemous" in the last sentence, this article would be as perfect as we could expect it to be. We would like the addition of this word "anti-religious" simply because we are not sure that the publication of anti-God or atheistic propaganda would be accounted blasphemous in law. . . . There is good reason in this country why the State should tolerate all religions and allow them all freedom of expression. But there is no reason why it should tolerate unbelief or, at any rate, open propaganda on behalf of unbelief.

The Catholic Theory of Suppression

This theory — that it is justifiable to suppress unbelief and anti-Catholicism, even when it is not feasible to suppress non-Catholic worship — has long been blessed and sanctioned by the Vatican in Spain; but it was a little shocking to hear it expressed in a Western democracy. The theory is based upon the well-known Catholic principle of limited freedom of the press. Bishop

Lucey set forth so clearly this doctrine of limited freedom that a few representative sentences should be quoted:

> The journalist, like any other human being, has the right to propound what is true or what is at least possibly true. But he has not the right to defend what is false, or to induce people to do what is wrong. . . . Opinions and convictions clash on many important issues. . . . Who is to decide in such circumstances what views are fit for publication? The answer is that the Church is entitled to decide when the views are views on faith and morals. . . . However, in all such cases, the State as the guardian of the social order, is entitled to interfere and ban news or views likely to injure the common good. . . .
>
> A free Press is a good thing. And by a free Press is meant, first of all, a Press that is legally free to print whatever it is morally justified in printing. Hence any restrictions on the publishing of falsehoods, indecent or pornographic matter, seditious articles, etc. are not restrictions on the freedom of the Press. They are rather restrictions on the abuse of that freedom by pressmen.

To any student of Catholic law this is familiar doctrine. It can be used to justify the suppression of almost any hostile criticism of a Catholic dictator, since the dictator can construe the offending comments as "likely to injure the common good"; and it can likewise be used to justify almost any suppression of criticism directed against the Church, because such criticism can be construed as not "morally justified."

The government, in spite of Catholic pressure, decided to put a broadly moral rather than a narrowly theological interpretation on the censorship phrases in the 1937 Constitution. Perhaps De Valera feared the ridicule of Irish, English, and American intellectuals. He made no attempt to legalize the suppression of heresy, and when, on the day after the adoption of the new Constitution by the Dail, he hailed the "liberty of speech, assembly and associations subject to the moral law," which was provided by the new charter, the Catholic hierarchy did not protest. It was evident that, although intellectual freedom in Ireland would always be definitely subordinate to Catholic moral law, the people did not wish to incorporate the Spanish laws of cultural suppression, and the bishops were not prepared to force them upon Ireland.

From the beginning, the censorship has infuriated Irish intellectuals. They have objected, as one critic has put it, to being "watched, nurtured, disciplined, superintended, protected from all literature except pious tripe and racing tips." They had not been accustomed under the Protestant Ascendancy to such discipline, and they resented it doubly when it came from their own countrymen. England at that time had no statutory system of literary censorship for Ireland, but only the general rules of local police supervision under which particular complaints could be filed against particular books. Today England and Northern Ireland still have that same unofficial and very limited censorship, and in practice few books and magazines are ever banned in British territory. Even when a powerful newspaper attempts to suppress a very frankly written novel, British prosecutors rarely attempt to stop the circulation of a book if it is a serious work of art. Norman Mailer's *The Naked and the Dead* survived such an attempt at suppression in England, without a prosecution; James Jones's *From Here to Eternity,* one of the frankest books ever published, was not suppressed in England. Both works were suppressed in the Irish Republic.

Technically speaking, the only books which can now be suppressed under Irish law (Censorship of Publications Act of 1946) are those which a five-man Censorship Board condemns as: (1) indecent or obscene; (2) devoted primarily to matters of crime; (3) advocating "the unnatural prevention of conception or the procurement of abortion or miscarriage or the use of any method, treatment or appliance for the purpose of such prevention or procurement." If two of the five members consider the work printable, it is saved from condemnation; perhaps this is one reason why the Board has never at any one time had more than one non-Catholic member. It is typical of official Catholic policies on sexual questions that the statute lumps together without any separating commas the harmless forms of contraception and the deadly forms of criminal abortion.

The Censorship Board began to make Ireland notorious as early as 1929, and its methods have not substantially changed since those days. An Appeal Board was added in 1946, chiefly to correct the Censorship Board's worst blunders; but the principles of proscription have remained unchanged. The Censorship Board itself might be considered a literary court of first instance, if it were really a court. It is a politically appointed committee which examines all books in secret and passes judgment in secret without giving the accused any opportunity to be heard, and without publishing detailed reasons for its action. At present it is a wholly Catholic institution, appointed by a Catholic Minister for Justice, composed entirely of Catholics, and headed by a Catholic priest. All its employees are Catholic.

The task of the Censorship Board is prodigious and its output of prohibitions is formidable. It must protect all the people of the Republic against a menace which the priests describe as "a flood of indecent literature" coming from "foreign centers of corruption." Its work in sifting out obscenity from Irish books is negligible, partly because publishing in Ireland is a very minor industry. Almost all books published in the Republic are strictly Catholic, and the publishers rarely include many fiction titles in their modest output of about 100 titles a year. Great Britain publishes over 17,000 titles a year, and the Irish people buy most of their books from Britain.

To protect the people from "foreign filth," the Censorship Board still uses an old British act which gives customs officers the power to capture and hold for inquiry any literature which in their opinion "ought to be examined." For a time, even copies of the *New Statesman and Nation* containing advertisements for birth control were confiscated from astonished travelers as they arrived in Ireland. Today the individual tourist coming to Ireland with a single copy of a forbidden book or magazine is rarely molested.

How the Censorship Works

Complaints against books usually come into the Censorship Board from small semi-fanatical Catholic groups accompanied by copies of the challenged works with marked passages. It is the task of the five members of the Board to read all the suspected works and to weigh them judiciously. Since there may be hundreds of such books each month, it is a task which no human being could perform conscientiously while carrying on an independent profession. But the unpaid members of the Board are in fact busy professional persons who are compelled to make their judgments after a hasty glance through the great masses of literature which they are asked to judge. It is not surprising, therefore, that the procedure of the Board has been reduced to the level of a farce. When the condemnations are announced, the lowest types of pornography are lumped together in the public verdict with the highest forms of literary art. The result is moral confusion and public ridicule. The process has become such a perpetual source of jest that banned authors of distinction proudly wear their badges of exclusion as tokens of fellowship in what one critic has called "The Order of the Marked Passage."

In 1948, one member of the Censorship Board, Professor J. D. Smyth of Trinity College resigned in protest against its hurried and superficial judgments. Lynn Doyle, a Protestant writer, had earlier resigned for the same reason. For four months Professor Smyth attended the Board's meetings and protested against its procedures. In the course of his labors he discovered that the five busy members of the Board were faced with a virtual *fait accompli* when they arrived at each session and saw huge piles of suspected books before them, containing heavily marked passages which had already been appraised by Catholic underlings. The sessions of the Board, presided over by a priest, were technically free for frank discussion but in practice the Catholic members did not dare to express "anti-Catholic" opinions in the presence of the priest. The members, nearly all old men, overwhelmed with the numbers of books they were expected to examine, tended to judge the books on the basis of hints and suggestions without a thorough perusal.

Since Dr. Smyth's resignation, the government has been unable to persuade any Protestant professors of Trinity College to co-operate in such proceedings.

It is true that authors and publishers, by depositing £5, may appeal from an adverse decision of the Censorship Board to the five-man Appeal Board, also appointed by the Minister for Justice; at present this Appeal Board contains one distinguished non-Catholic professor of literature from Trinity College. Because of the high caliber of this Board, serious and frank works of art usually receive intelligent analysis on appeal. But the process of appeal takes time and money, including the deposit of six copies of the condemned work, and few foreign publishers care to risk the money and time when the sales of any work in the Irish Republic are so small. Moreover, many authors feel, with Ireland's famous storyteller Frank O'Connor, that even the Appeal Board "can never be anything but an instrument of autocracy"; and they share with him the view that as a matter of principle "writers should never accept the onus of proving publicly that their work is not harmful."

That is one reason why the appeals of authors and publishers to the Appeal Board have been so few, representing a very small proportion of the total works banned by the Censorship Board. Only eight reversals were granted in 1951. In spite of the superior quality of its practices, the Appeal Board is only a little less peremptory than the Censorship Board. It does not guarantee to any publisher the right to appear either in person or through counsel to defend a condemned book. Its proceedings are in secret, and the basis of its final judgment is secret. It never explains either in writing or orally the reasons for any ruling; nor does the Censorship Board itself ever give to any harassed author or publisher any specific finding, beyond the bare report of exclusion. The offending passages in a condemned work are not brought to the author's attention, so that they could be eliminated in a later edition. The public is never given an opportunity to see the workings of the censorial mind. In the whole procedure there is no public hearing, no court trial, no detailed written finding, no bill of particulars of the charges, no examination of experts, no questioning of the Board members, no cross-examination of the employees.

In the course of twenty-three years — up to February 1953 — 4,057 books and 376 periodicals have been banned by this procedure. Some of these works were so pornographic that they would have been banned by any responsible government. Here is a partial list of banned publications, most of them popular books written by authors who have achieved some success. All of them can be legally bought and sold in the United States, Great Britain, and Northern Ireland — but not in the Irish Republic. The titles marked with asterisks, after being banned by the Censorship Board, have been "unbanned" by the Appeal Board. The banned list is compiled as of June 1953, the reversals as of February 1953.

Hervey Allen	*Bedford Village* *Anthony Adverse* *The Forest and the Fort*
Sherwood Anderson	*Horses and Men*
Sholem Asch	*The Mother* *The Thief Mottke* *The Cities*
Tallulah Bankhead	*Tallulah*
H. E. Bates	*Dear Life*
Vicki Baum	*Falling Star** *Grand Hotel* *Helen* *Hotel Berlin*
Henry Bellamann	*Kings Row*
Leon Blum	*Marriage*
Phyllis Bottome	*Under the Skin*
Kay Boyle	*My Next Bride* *The Crazy Hunter* *1939*
Robert Briffault	*Europa in Limbo*
British Government	*Report of Royal Commission on Population**
Louis Bromfield	*Wild Is the River* *Twenty-four Hours* *Until the Day Break* *The Rains Came* *A Modern Hero* *Night in Bombay*
Pearl S. Buck	*Portrait of a Marriage* *Dragon Seed** *Pavilion of Women* *The Patriot*
Niven Busch	*Duel in the Sun*
James Branch Cabell	*Jurgen* *The Devil's Own Dear Son*

Erskine Caldwell	*Tobacco Road* *God's Little Acre*
Taylor Caldwell	*The Wide House* *The Arm and the Darkness* *The Earth is the Lord's* *This Side of Innocence*
Truman Capote	*Other Voices, Other Rooms*
Joyce Cary	*Castle Corner* *Charles Is My Darling* *A Fearful Joy* *Herself Surprised* *A Certain Rich Man* *The Horse's Mouth* *The Moonlight* *Prisoner of Grace*
Ilka Chase	*In Bed We Cry*
Church of England	*Threshold of Marriage**
Noel Coward	*To Step Aside**
James Gould Cozzens	*Guard of Honor* *Men and Brethren*
Marcia Davenport	*East Side, West Side* *The Valley of Decision*
Warwick Deeping	*I Live Again* *Reprieve*
Paul de Kruif	*Life Among the Doctors*
Bernard De Voto	*Mountain Time*
Pietro Di Donato	*Christ in Concrete*
John Dos Passos	*Adventures of a Young Man* *The Forty-second Parallel*
Theodore Dreiser	*Dawn*
Daphne du Maurier	*I'll Never Be Young Again*
Havelock Ellis	*Psychology of Sex*
James T. Farrell	*A World I Never Made* *Ellen Rogers* *A Father and His Son*

William Faulkner	*Soldier's Pay*
	Sanctuary
	The Hamlet
	The Wild Palms
	Pylon
	Light in August
F. Scott Fitzgerald	*This Side of Paradise*
	Tender Is the Night
C. S. Forester	*The African Queen*
Anatole France	*A Mummer's Tale*
Sigmund Freud	*Collected Papers**
Martha Gellhorn	*The Wine of Astonishment*
André Gide	*If It Die*
Oliver St. John Gogarty	*Going Native*
	Mr. Petunia
Louis Golding	*Five Silver Daughters*
Maxim Gorki	*Bystander*
A. Herbert Gray	*Men, Women and God**
	Successful Marriage
Henry Green	*Doting*
Graham Greene	*The Heart of the Matter**
	The End of the Affair*
	Stamboul Train*
Ernest R. Groves and Gladys H. Groves	*Sex in Marriage*
A. B. Guthrie, Jr.	*The Big Sky*
	The Way West
J. B. S. Haldane	*The Inequality of Man*
Knut Hamsun	*Hunger*
Thomas Heggen	*Mister Roberts*
Ernest Hemingway	*The Sun Also Rises*
	For Whom the Bell Tolls*
	Across the River and into the Trees
Stefan Heym	*Hostages*
	Of Smiling Peace

Hedda Hopper	*From Under My Hat*
Rev. Norman S. Hough	*Letters on Marriage*
Fannie Hurst	*Anywoman*
	Great Laughter
	Hallelujah
	The Hands of Veronica
Aldous Huxley	*Eyeless in Gaza**
	Point Counter Point
	Ape and Essence
	Time Must Have A Stop*
Christopher Isherwood	*Goodbye to Berlin*
Charles Jackson	*The Fall of Valor*
	The Outer Edges
Naomi Jacob	*Fade Out*
Storm Jameson	*Company Parade*
	Delicate Monster
	Here Comes a Candle
	The Single Heart
James Jones	*From Here to Eternity*
James Joyce	*Stephen Hero**
Frances Parkinson Keyes	*Fielding's Folly*
Alfred C. Kinsey, *et al.*	*Sexual Behavior in the Human Male*
Arthur Koestler	*Thieves in the Night*
	Arrival and Departure*
	Arrow in the Blue
Sir W. Arbuthnot Lane	*The Modern Woman's Home Doctor*
Maura Laverty	*Lift Up Your Gates*
Sinclair Lewis	*Ann Vickers*
	Cass Timberlane
	Elmer Gantry
Eric Linklater	*The Crusader's Key*
	Magnus Merriman
Richard Llewellyn	*How Green Was My Valley*
Ross Lockridge	*Raintree County*

Walter Macken	*I Am Alone* *The Moon Quench* *The Bogman*
Compton Mackenzie	*The East Wind of Love*
Salvador de Madariaga	*The Heart of Jade*
Norman Mailer	*The Naked and the Dead* *Barbary Shore*
Thomas Mann	*The Holy Sinner* *The Transposed Heads**
F. Van Wyck Mason	*Cutlass Empire* *Eagle in the Sky* *Rivers of Glory* *Proud New Flags*
W. Somerset Maugham	*The Razor's Edge** *Christmas Holiday* *Creatures of Circumstance* *The Maugham Reader* *Up at the Villa* *Theatre* *The Painted Veil*
Joseph McCabe	*The Popes and Their Church*
Claude McKay	*Home to Harlem*
Margaret Mead	*Coming of Age in Samoa* *Growing up in New Guinea* *Male and Female*
Medical Adviser (London Sunday *Chronicle*)	*One Thousand Medical Hints*
Bryan Merriman	*The Midnight Court* (translated by Frank O'Connor)
James A. Michener	*Tales of the South Pacific* *Return to Paradise*
Nicholas Monsarrat	*The Cruel Sea**
Alberto Moravia	*Disobedience* *The Fancy Dress Party* *Wheel of Fortune*

Charles Morgan	*The Fountain*
	*The Frontier**
	*The Voyage**
Christopher Morley	*The Trojan Horse*
	*Kitty Foyle**
Lee Mortimer and Jack Lait	*Washington Confidential*
	Chicago Confidential
Charles G. Norris	*Seed*
	Zest
Kate O'Brien	*The Land of Spices**
Sean O'Casey	*Windfalls*
	*Pictures in the Hallway**
Frank O'Connor	*The Common Chord*
	*Dutch Interior**
	Traveller's Samples
Sean O'Faolain	*Midsummer Night Madness*
	*Bird Alone**
Liam O'Flaherty	*Land*
	The Martyr
	Shame the Devil
John O'Hara	*Appointment in Samarra*
	A Rage to Live
	Hellbox
George Orwell	*Nineteen Eighty-Four*
Fulton Oursler	*Joshua Todd*
Elliot Paul	*Ghost Town on the Yellowstone*
	My Old Kentucky Home
	A Narrow Street
Robert Payne	*David and Anna*
	The Great Mogul
Frederick Prokosch	*The Asiatics*
	The Conspirators
Marcel Proust	*Remembrance of Things Past*
Eric Remarque	*The Road Back*
	Arch of Triumph
	Flotsam
	Three Comrades

Quentin Reynolds	*Courtroom*
Henry Morton Robinson	*The Great Snow**
Jules Romains	*Men of Good Will*
Maude Royden	*Sex and Common Sense*
Bertrand Russell	*Marriage and Morals*
J. D. Salinger	*The Catcher in the Rye*
Margaret Sanger	*Happiness in Marriage*
	My Fight for Birth Control
William Saroyan	*Dear Baby*
Jean-Paul Sartre	*Iron in the Soul*
	The Reprieve
Budd Schulberg	*The Harder They Fall*
	What Makes Sammy Run
	The Disenchanted
Ramon J. Sender	*The Dark Wedding*
	The King and the Queen
Bernard Shaw	*The Black Girl in Her Search for God**
Vincent Sheean	*A Certain Rich Man*
Ignazio Silone	*Fontamara*
	The Seed Beneath the Snow*
Upton Sinclair	*Wide Is the Gate*
Betty Smith	*The Tree in the Yard*
Lillian Smith	*Strange Fruit*
Stephen Spender	*The Burning Cactus*
Howard Spring	*Oh Absalom*
Wallace Stegner	*Second Growth*
John Steinbeck	*Grapes of Wrath**
	Cannery Row*
	To a God Unknown
	The Wayward Bus
	East of Eden
Marie C. Stopes	*Birth Control To-day*
	Married Love
	Roman Catholic Methods of Birth Control

Rex Stout	*How Like a God*
	Seed on the Wind
Halliday Sutherland	*The Laws of Life*
Frank Swinnerton	*The Fortunate Lady*
	Thankless Child
Harry Sylvester	*Dayspring*
James Ramsey Ullman	*The White Tower*
Jan Valtin	*Out of the Night*
William Vogt	*Road to Survival*
Frederick Wakeman	*The Saxon Charm*
Hugh Walpole	*The Blind Man's House*
	The Sea Town
Robert Penn Warren	*All the King's Men*
	At Heaven's Gate
Ethel Waters	*His Eye Is on the Sparrow*
Alec Waugh	*No Truce With Time*
H. G. Wells	*Babes in the Darkling Wood*
	You Can't Be Too Careful
	The Bulpington of Blup
	The Work, Wealth and Happiness of Mankind
Edward Westermarck	*The Future of Marriage in Western Civilization*
Angus Wilson	*Hemlock and After*
Kathleen Winsor	*Forever Amber*
	The Lovers
Thomas Wolfe	*Of Time and the River*
	The Web and the Rock
Herman Wouk	*The Caine Mutiny*
Richard Wright	*Black Boy*
Frank Yerby	*The Foxes of Harrow*
	The Golden Hawk
	Pride's Castle
	The Vixens
	A Woman Called Fancy

Honorable Dishonor

It will be seen that this list includes at least four winners of
Nobel prizes in literature, and many of the outstanding novels of
the Book-of-the-Month Club, the Literary Guild, and the British
book clubs. It includes virtually every living Irish author whose
fame has spread beyond the borders of Ireland — Sean O'Faolain, Frank O'Connor, Sean O'Casey, Liam O'Flaherty, Oliver
St. John Gogarty, Maura Laverty, and others. (Elizabeth
Bowen has surprisingly escaped.) It includes many well-known
Catholic authors, living and dead, such as Graham Greene,
Frances Parkinson Keyes, Fulton Oursler, Salvador de Madari-
aga, Halliday Sutherland, Henry Morton Robinson, Harry
Sylvester; and several writers like Taylor Caldwell who have
been ardent defenders of Catholic policy.

Even when a book is released from the ban imposed by the
Censorship Board, the acquittal may come too late to save the
publishers from financial loss. Nicholas Monsarrat's *The Cruel
Sea,* choice of the American Book-of-the-Month Club, was "mis-
takenly" banned in October 1951, and not released until the
following July — when the peak of the sales boom had passed.
Somerset Maugham's *The Razor's Edge* was banned for more
than two years before its release; the *Collected Papers* of Sig-
mund Freud for more than three years; Pearl Buck's *Dragon
Seed* for six years; Arthur Koestler's *Arrival and Departure* for
four years; James Joyce's *Stephen Hero* for seven years. The
record for refurbished reputations was achieved by Bernard
Shaw's *The Black Girl in Her Search for God,* which was banned
for sixteen years before redemption.

It is evident that age, dignity, and popular approval have
something to do with the release of a work from detention.
James Joyce's *Ulysses* might be considered as unconventional
enough in some of its passages to earn Catholic censorship, but
recent printings have been ignored — apparently because the
world has acclaimed the book as great literature. Similarly,
Ernest Hemingway's *For Whom the Bell Tolls* and John Stein-
beck's *Grapes of Wrath* have been released to the Irish public
after winning international approval. These books, and such
other literary successes as Richard Llewellyn's *How Green Was*

My Valley, Irving Stone's *Lust for Life,* and Aldous Huxley's *Eyeless in Gaza,* have probably been rescued because some members of the Appeal Board are sensitive to ridicule. It is likely that Ireland's three greatest writers of the recent past, Shaw, Joyce, and Yeats — all violent opponents of the censorship — would turn over in their graves if they knew that they had been finally released from the censor's ban while other Irish authors were still being victimized.

The relative liberalism of the Appeal Board enrages the Censorship Board, and on at least two occasions the Censorship Board has sent furious letters to the press condemning the "unbanning" of a book by the Appeal Board, and reasserting its own judgment that the work should be untouchable. Although the two boards have the same paid secretary, there is no affection in their relationship. The tension between the two boards contributes to the contemptuous amusement with which the whole censorial apparatus of the law is regarded by almost all educated persons.

Sometimes a doomed book published in England reaches the Irish market in large quantities ahead of the censorship ban. If the advance reviews indicate a likelihood that it will be suppressed, Dublin readers rush to the bookstores to beat the literary executioners. Tallulah Bankhead's *Tallulah* was stacked high on the counters of Dublin's bookstores for several weeks during the Christmas rush of 1952 before its sale was finally interrupted by a stop order.

Such good fortune, however, never comes to Dublin publishers. Their primary profits come from textbooks sold to Catholic schools and from works of devotion sold to priests, nuns, and laymen, and because of their subjection to the priests they dare not risk the boycott and condemnation of any of their published works. That is one reason why nearly all Irish authors who attempt to deal candidly with modern life go abroad in search of a publisher.

Some Dublin Catholic intellectuals have joined with the Protestants in bitter denunciation of the censorship, because they realize that it is destroying the reputation of Irish Catholic culture throughout the world. Benedict Kiely, a Catholic critic of some note, and an ardent defender of Irish Republican policy, was quoted with approval in 1950 by Ireland's chief Catholic weekly, the Dublin *Standard,* when he said: "The Dublin literary censorship has been, since its foundation, a group of men sitting in the clouds and responding to spasmodic Puritan appeals on behalf of decency. The main results of the labors of this remarkable body have been to penalize serious readers in Ireland, to make the country look ludicrous to the eyes of any interested foreigners, to label the majority of Irish writers as lecherous and improper persons." Sean O'Faolain, in a critical letter to the *Irish Times,* charged that the censorship system clearly violates "the supremacy of the rule of law," and that it uses "the good old technique of absolute monarchy and veiled tyranny." "It is a Star Chamber," he said. "It works through the delegated power of the Minister. The Appeal Board is a Star Chamber of a Star Chamber. All are immune from the power of the Courts." He predicted that, "when Ireland becomes adult," the strictures of the Censorship Board will be wiped out.

Perhaps the most notable storm of criticism in recent years raged over the 1949 report of Great Britain's Royal Commission on Population. This report, one of the great social documents of modern times, was prepared under the Labor government by a commission of British scholars and national leaders, headed by Viscount Simon. The Catholic Church was hostile to the commission from the beginning, because the British government had decided to omit Catholic leaders from membership in order to get an unbiased verdict on birth control. When the final report in fact recommended birth control as a natural and necessary regulator of population growth, it was violently denounced by the Catholic authorities. In a great public meeting in London, Catholic leaders attacked it as "a dreadful example of the way in which the mind of England has gone pagan." The *Irish Catholic* — referring to it as "A Nasty Document" — said: "The principle of the stud farm rather than the morals of a Christian home informed the Report." Actually, the main report did not contain specific descriptions of birth-control techniques, but it did warmly recommend the dissemination of birth-control information to those married couples whose religious scruples did not prevent them from requesting it.

Several months after its publication, and after it had received the almost unanimous acclaim of the learned world, it was suddenly banned in Ireland by the Censorship Board. The announcement of the Board lumped it together in blanket condemnation with works which advocated "the unnatural prevention of conception or procurement of abortion or miscarriage or the use of any method, treatment or appliance for the purpose of such prevention or procurement." Even Ireland was shocked by such treatment of a distinguished government report — this was the first British government publication ever to be suppressed by the Board. The *Irish Press,* unofficial organ of De Valera's Fianna Fail, questioned the wisdom of the ban and expressed surprise that such a document should be "associated with tawdry pornography." The report was promptly taken to the Appeal Board and released by unanimous vote. The Catholic members of that Board could not deny that the report might come under the prohibitions of the law — since it advocated the right of married persons to acquire knowledge of contraception — but they also pointed out that the law obliged them to consider the scientific merits and general tenor of a work; on these counts the virtues of the report outweighed the incidental dangers. Perhaps one reason it was released was that it was too heavily scientific to become a work of general circulation: The Catholic bishops could rest content in the knowledge that it would never reach the Irish masses. William Vogt's *Road to Survival,* which discussed population and birth control in more popular terms, was permanently banned because it was capable of reaching those masses.

Thus, the potential success of a book may be a factor in its suppression, and the wealthy raconteur may garner tidbits from a limited edition which would condemn a paper-backed book to oblivion. This philosophy of the double standard for the masses and the classes is inherent in the censorship law itself, which tells the Censorship Board, in deciding for or against suppression, to consider "the nature and extent of the circulation" of a book, and "the class of reader which . . . may reasonably be expected to read it."

Catholic Victims of Catholic Censorship

Another ban which produced some embarrassment among

educated Catholics was the suppression of *The Heart of the Matter* by the famous English Catholic convert Graham Greene. Greene's writing has occasionally been used by the Church as the basis for earnest denominational propaganda on the screen, and his reputation as a Catholic author has been much exploited in the American diocesan press. In 1948, Father Harold C. Gardiner, literary editor of *America*, called *The Heart of the Matter* "a noble achievement." In 1949, after the book had been banned in Ireland, Greene, together with Evelyn Waugh and François Mauriac, was elected to the American Catholic "Academy of Forty Contemporary Immortals." The Irish ban on *The Heart of the Matter* thus came at an awkward moment. The Dublin *Standard* thought the action brought "little credit to us as Catholics and intelligent humans." The Appeal Board undid the damage after three months, but there were a number of Catholic protests from the right. Irish Catholic leaders are still uneasy about Graham Greene's Catholicism, since he is suspected of heresy in matters of sex. "Never once," said W. Gore Allen mournfully in the *Irish Ecclesiastical Record,* "has he [Greene] described a woman happily married and fulfilled in bringing up her children. The women in Greene's novels are essentially infertile. . . . The priest in *The Power and the Glory* sees his illegitimate daughter for a few minutes — on a dung hill. . . . Never was an author more enamoured of the sterile, the aseptic, the unripe."

The Greene incident and the final release of the British population report proved that the priests are not always able to hold the Irish intellectuals in line on matters of sex. This is particularly true when the works of non-Catholic authors win the support of leading Protestants. In several direct conflicts between the Anglican and the Catholic conceptions of marriage, the Anglican interpretation has won the right to be heard in Ireland, after temporary suppression by the Censorship Board. This was true in the case of a famous marriage manual, *Threshold of Marriage,* prepared by the Church of England and issued by its Moral Welfare Council, with a foreword by the Lord Bishop of Bath and Wells. This manual does not specifically advocate birth control or give detailed information about contraceptives, but it contains a special appendix discussing three possible views of birth control: that contraception is contrary to Christianity; that it is acceptable; and that "self-control" is the only Christian method of planned parenthood. The argument in the manual is slightly weighted against contraception, but it is, on the whole, studiously impartial in its tone.

At first the Irish Censorship Board rejected even this temperate presentation of three differing views on birth control as a violation of the law; but one year later, in June 1947, the Appeal Board released the work. At the same time it also released from ban another noted Protestant manual on marriage, *Men, Women and God,* by A. Herbert Gray, D.D. Perhaps one reason for the release of such Protestant manuals on marriage is that the Irish priests are very vulnerable in their own ecclesiastical glass houses. Their manuals on sex, designed to prepare young celibates for giving advice on marriage practice in the confessional, contain some of the frankest details on copulation and sodomy which have ever been recorded in print. The descriptions, of course, are embalmed in Latin, and presumably the Censorship Board does not believe that Latin words can be "indecent or obscene."

Today the prohibition continues against nearly all marriage manuals which do not have a specifically Catholic approach. Serious works issued by the highly reputable National Marriage Guidance Council of London have been consistently banned, including such works as *Sex Difficulties in the Wife* and *Sex in Marriage.* The Censorship Board banned not only the Kinsey report, *Sexual Behavior in the Human Male,* but also two books about the Kinsey report. It has banned such serious works on the anthropology of marriage as Westermarck's *The Future of Marriage in Western Civilization* and Margaret Mead's *Coming of Age in Samoa* and *Growing up in New Guinea.* Included in the ban is *Sex and Common Sense* by the noted British Protestant evangelist Maude Royden, and *Sex in Marriage* by Ernest R. Groves and Gladys H. Groves, two of America's most sober and conservative commentators on marital matters. The famous British birth-control advocate, Dr. Marie Stopes, is still not permitted to circulate her earlier work, *Roman Catholic Methods of Birth Control,* in which she shows that Catholic bishops before 1930 were by no means unanimous in their opposition to contraception. Nor is Margaret Sanger permitted to tell the Irish people the story of her heroic struggle for planned parenthood.

Great glee was created among the intellectuals of the Republic in 1941 when the Censorship Board banned a book, *The Laws of Life*, written by England's most famous Catholic opponent of birth control, Dr. Halliday Sutherland, and published by the great Catholic publishing firm of Sheed and Ward. The book had been successfully sold to English Catholics for six years before it was challenged in Ireland. Then an Irish Catholic father complained to the Censorship Board that in dealing with sexual matters it was too frank for his adolescent daughter. The Board obligingly examined the work through adolescent eyes and suppressed it. For twenty-five years in England, Sutherland had advocated the doctrine that birth-control propaganda should be made a criminal offense, and his condemnation by the Irish Board came as a considerable shock to him and to many prominent English Catholics. The ban was warmly debated in the Irish Senate, and the book's defenders pointed out that the author and publisher had obtained the official Catholic *Permissu Superiorum* of the Westminster Diocesan Council of Censorship. But English Catholic approval did not produce Irish Catholic approval, and the work is still banned in the Republic as "in its general tendency indecent." Sutherland was moved to protest in the London Catholic *Tablet* that "in Ireland there are too many adults who regard ignorance and purity as synonymous. These . . . should ask our Commissioner of Police how many Irish girls, ignorant of the physiology of sex, have come to London and are now known to the police as prostitutes."

Minister for Justice Boland, when challenged in the Irish Senate to justify such a ban, blandly shifted the responsibility to the hierarchy by saying: "I am not a theologian but, on the Board that made that recommendation, was a very eminent Catholic ecclesiastic, and I am sure he was able to tell the Board all about the position." It was in the Dail debate on Halliday Sutherland's *The Laws of Life* that the Minister for Justice revealed how the government's vague interpretations of the law may be stretched to cover many extraneous types of unpopular thought. When challenged to explain why the book was banned, he refused to "go into the law of the State," but he said: "If it were widely circulated, it would do untold harm. Whether the Board was technically and legally correct, whether the book in its general tendency was indecent or obscene, may be open to question, but, on the ground that it was calculated to do untold harm, I was perfectly satisfied that it should be banned." This test — "calculated to do untold harm" — is so broad that almost any unpopular book could be brought within its all-encompassing terms.

The Irish censors seize with special relish upon any British newspaper or magazine which transgresses the censorship laws. The Sunday *Chronicle* of London was compelled to stop the circulation in Ireland of its *One Thousand Medical Hints,* by its Medical Adviser, because the book suggested contraceptive possibilities. The great London co-operative Sunday paper, *Reynold's News,* has been banned and reinstated several times for printing material about crime and birth control. In August 1931, the Censorship Board swooped with obvious satisfaction upon the London Communist *Daily Worker* on the ground that it had violated the ban against birth-control information; the luckless journal was not reinstated for eight years. More respectable periodicals usually win reinstatement more swiftly. That model American journal, *The Woman's Home Companion,* was given a six-month sentence in June 1950, apparently because it carried a perfectly harmless and conventional article, "Why I Oppose Mercy Killings." The magazine was actually reinstated within four months.

The attempted banning of current magazines for printing favorable judgments on birth control has recently been reduced to an absurdity because of the flood of such favorable comments in popular periodicals. In a single month of 1952 — October — the New York *Times, Time,* and London's *Eugenics Review* all arrived in the Republic with excellent articles specifically describing new birth-control discoveries. None of these publications was confiscated or banned.

The Unofficial Censorship

We have seen how the De Valera government decided not to include in the 1937 Constitution any specific ban against anti-religious or anti-Catholic books. In a Catholic state this omission must be rectified by somebody; in the Republic this purpose is accomplished through an unofficial Catholic censorship of all libraries, publishers, and booksellers by informal committees of Catholic laymen or by the priests themselves. Since very few people in the Irish Republic buy books, the important feature of the unofficial censorship is the Catholic surveillance over all public libraries. This process of surveillance is described euphemistically by Father Stephen Brown, leading Dublin Jesuit, in his *Libraries and Literature From a Catholic Standpoint:*

> The task of the public librarian has been further lightened in Ireland by the formation, under the auspices of the Library Association of Ireland, of an Advisory Committee on Book Selection. This Committee draws up lists of books which are rated very good . . . and also those that are definitely objectionable from the standpoint of Christian morality. Books outside those two categories it leaves outside, to be dealt with by individual librarians. . . . As we know in English speaking countries, Ireland not excluded, Catholics have to live in a mental climate that is far from being Catholic. . . . We must be inoculated against it, we must take measures so that the climatic conditions may not offset our spiritual health.

This unofficial censorship of the librarians, which is duplicated in the publishing world, is in practice far more important than the official censorship of the Censorship Board — because it covers a wider range of taboos than the government apparatus, and because the people accept it as the priests have schooled them to do. The Church makes a special point of seeing that no Protestant is chosen as a supervising public librarian; and Catholic librarians are, of course, subject to theological penalties for disobeying their priests. Perhaps this surveillance is one of the reasons why most public libraries in Ireland are pitiful travesties of the name — under-equipped, under-staffed, and under-supplied with good books and magazines.

The right of the Church to bar any Protestant as a librarian was successfully asserted in a famous public controversy in County Mayo, in the west of Ireland, in 1931, and the details are worth recording. Miss Letitia Dunbar-Harrison, a Protestant graduate of Trinity College, was appointed in that year to be the county librarian of the Carnegie Library in Castlebar, with certain advisory functions for the whole of County Mayo.

No one questioned her intellectual fitness, her professional training, or the legality of her appointment. But the local branch of Catholic Action immediately began a bitter campaign against her on denominational and patriotic grounds.

Although she was a native of Dublin and had been educated entirely in Ireland, it was claimed that her knowledge of the Irish language was limited. The Catholic Church, it was said, had certain definite rules about books, rules which a non-Catholic librarian might not interpret correctly or enforce rigidly. The Mayo County library committee, headed by a Catholic bishop, voted against her appointment, two dissenting votes being cast by Protestants. The overwhelmingly Catholic Mayo County Council, supporting its library committee, refused to take the necessary steps to install Miss Dunbar-Harrison as librarian. Since the power to appoint a county librarian lay with the national government, headed at that time by William Cosgrave, the responsibility for action rested with the Dublin authorities. They bravely and promptly abolished the Mayo County Council — as they had the right to do — "for its failure to carry out an order of the Ministry." This courageous gesture received the warm praise of the *Irish Times* for a "bold stand for fair play"; but bravery was totally unavailing against the campaign of intolerance which was then inaugurated by the local leaders of Catholic Action, headed by the district archbishop.

The expelled Council members met and advised a tax strike. From all over the country came resolutions by other county councils backing up the threatened tax rebellion. In some cases Catholic parades of protest were organized, headed by bands and banners. In Ballina the Rev. Denis O'Connor, chairman of the library committee, said: "A Protestant young lady . . . has been appointed as our library adviser. Her culture and philosophy are, on many vital questions, diametrically opposed to Catholic principles and Catholic ideas, and therefore we, as Catholics, cannot be guided by her in selecting the literature that we need." From many parts of County Mayo bundles of books were shipped back to the Carnegie Library in protest against Miss Dunbar-Harrison's appointment. If the people could not have a Catholic librarian, they made clear, they would not have a library at all. The Catholic archbishop, Dr. Gilmartin, encouraged the rebels and made the principle behind the boycott quite clear. In the *Irish Times* he said:

> It is gratifying to see how the representatives of our Catholic people are unwilling to subsidize libraries not under Catholic control. Not to speak of those who are alien to our faith, it is not every Catholic who is fit to be in charge of a public library for Catholic readers. Such an onerous position should be assigned to an educated Catholic who would be as remarkable for his loyalty to his religion as for his literary and intellectual attainments.

De Valera, then the leader of the Opposition, seized the opportunity to make political capital out of Catholic indignation. He encouraged the critics of Miss Dunbar-Harrison by raising the question whether it was logical to have a non-Catholic librarian in a county which was 98 per cent Catholic. The *Catholic Bulletin* jumped into the fray and elaborated the philosophy behind Archbishop Gilmartin's pronouncement. It said:

> To levy a compulsory Library rate on Mayo, as long as this iniquitous situation lasts, is tyrannically to trade on the previous excellent work of Catholic Action through the County Library centres all over Mayo. Dr. Gilmartin's words make the radical injustice of this bullying tyranny quite plain. A librarian alien to our Faith is not fit for the onerous position. It is one necessarily involving the use of moral and educational influence. . . . Only a thoroughly educated Catholic man or woman, loyal to and energetic in the cause of Catholic Action, can be deemed fit for the highly reasonable and influential post of County Librarian.

After that, the government was compelled to surrender as gracefully as possible, and Miss Dunbar-Harrison was finally transferred to a good position elsewhere. The inevitable happened, and today the Irish Republic does not have a single Protestant county librarian.

Since then, the Church has co-operated in creating various organs of preventive local censorship, sometimes in the form of Catholic library committees and sometimes in the form of informal advisory services. For a time almost all Irish localities had special library panels or committees which graded books as "Suitable" and "Unsuitable" before they were permitted to reach the public. In order to protect the Church as far as possible from hostile criticism, the lists were kept confidential, and they were carefully described as purely advisory lists, not black lists. But in practice the county librarians almost never dare to purchase books after they have been put on an "Unsuitable" list. They are not free to follow their own inclinations in book selection because of the danger to their future careers involved in any unorthodox choice. They become automatically super-censors of an extra-legal censorship. "Every individual librarian," says Sean O'Faolain in discussing Irish censorship, "also exercises over and above, and even counter to the decisions of our official censorship, a private censorship of his own."

One county librarian in a report several years ago frankly analyzed all the practices of repression to which he was subjected in a western county, and expressed the judgment that there were seven cultural filters between any serious book and the average Irish reader. Nearly all of these filters are controlled by Church power. In practice the members of every panel of critics are effectually controlled by their priests. Even when a book has been "unbanned" by the government's censorship Appeal Board, the mere fact that it has once been officially frowned upon is enough to destroy the possibility of its approval by a group of Catholic Action devotees organized as a library committee. It is not surprising that a distinguished Dublin professor has described the continuing mental state of a sensitive Irish librarian as "near neurosis."

The Catholic Supplementary Lists

Almost all works on the Catholic *Index of Prohibited Books* are quietly and effectively excluded from all Irish libraries and from all Catholic bookstores. These works on the Vatican's own Index, about 5,000 in number, are rarely covered by the official government censorship because they consist largely of foreign-language books or out-of-print classics. They include all the original and translated works of Zola, Anatole France, André Gide and Jean-Paul Sartre, as well as the most famous works of Voltaire, Kant, Bergson, Gibbon, Paine, Hugo, and Balzac.

In addition hundreds of recent works of fiction are excluded each year from Irish public libraries by Catholic library committees or librarians on the ground that they are too realistic or heretical. The exact form of this exclusion varies from year to year, but the principle remains the same.

I have before me as I write three "secret" typewritten boycott lists put out by Catholic library committees a few years ago in Dublin, in Cork, and in County Kilkenny, containing altogether the titles of some 630 books which were graded "Unsuitable." The lists are devoted almost entirely to fiction; if they included non-fiction, the list would be much longer. As it is, the lists include many of the finest novels written during the past century by both Catholic and non-Catholic writers. These books are *not* banned by Ireland's Censorship Board; they are acceptable under Irish law, but unacceptable under the extra-legal Catholic censorship. They include Willa Cather's *Death Comes for the Archbishop,* and *The Professor's House;* Dorothy Canfield's *The Bent Twig;* Dostoevski's *The Brothers Karamazov;* Arnold Bennett's *Imperial Palace;* Marie Corelli's *Holy Orders;* Norman Douglas' *South Wind;* Edgar Rice Burroughs' *Tarzan, Lord of the Jungle;* all the works of John Galsworthy; Knut Hamsun's *Growth of the Soil;* all the works of Sheila Kaye-Smith (who was elected an "immortal" of the American Catholic Academy of Living Authors in 1936); Gogol's *Dead Souls;* Ernest Poole's *The Harbor;* Sterne's *Tristram Shandy;* Tolstoy's *Anna Karenina;* Sigrid Undset's *The Axe* and *In the Wilderness* (she is another Catholic "immortal" among living authors); Edith Wharton's *Glimpses of the Moon;* Christopher Morley's *Thunder on the Left;* Thomas Mann's *Buddenbrooks;* Thomas Hardy's *Tess of the D'Urbervilles;* A. A. Milne's *The Sunny Side;* Dumas' *Count of Monte Cristo;* Theodore Dreiser's *Jennie Gerhardt;* Hans Fallada's *Little Man, What Now?;* Robert Nathan's *One More Spring;* Franz Werfel's *The Forty Days;* and so on, and so on.

Some of these books have since been readmitted to respectable circles and are being circulated in Ireland's public libraries, but the general system of unofficial bannings is almost as strict today as it was when these lists were circulated. The tendency is to accept the suggestion of the local priest on all questionable volumes. ("We haven't got any committee to read the books now," the sweet-faced young library attendant told me in Tralee, "but we always ask the priest if there is any question, and of course we do what he says.") The unofficial lists are significant chiefly because they reveal how the Church goes beyond the statutory censorship to bar fiction and history with a non-Catholic flavor. The unofficial censorship list includes, in addition to the above works, several books which have obviously been banned for doctrinal reasons. That mildly modernist novel, *The Inside of the Cup*, by the late American novelist Winston Churchill, is on the list apparently because it discusses theological difficulties faced by a clergyman in search of truth. Upton Sinclair's *They Call Me Carpenter* must certainly have been excluded for the same general reason. And it is impossible to find any excuse except anti-Protestant bias for the exclusion of Harold Bell Wright's *That Printer of Udell's* and *God and the Grocery Man*. The ban includes Francis Hackett's *Henry VIII*, Croce's *History of Europe in the Nineteenth Century*, and H. L. Mencken's *Selected Prejudices*. Appropriately enough, it includes also *Hold Your Tongue* — a brisk exposure of the follies of censorship by Morris Ernst and Alexander Lindey.

It is not surprising that the *Irish Times* complained editorially: "The twin oppressions of official and unofficial censorship suggest mawkishness rather than high moral standards." And it added that "this unofficial form of censorship is more effective, and more insidious, than the official form." Unfortunately, the librarians of the Republic are completely fear-bound before the power of the priests, and they accept without a murmur acts of clerical interference which American and British librarians in parallel circumstances would reject with indignant scorn.

My own two previous books on Catholic policy, *American Freedom and Catholic Power* and *Communism, Democracy, and Catholic Power*, have not, so far as I know, been acquired by a single public library in the Irish Republic, although they have been published in British editions by two of England's most reputable publishing firms, and neither book has been banned by the government's Censorship Board. The second of these books could not under any circumstances be construed as contrary to censorship regulations; and the frank discussions of birth control and priestly medical standards in the first are probably protected by the fact that the most revealing paragraphs are directly quoted from Catholic sources. A Catholic government can scarcely describe priestly sexual teachings as obscene.

Only two bookstores in the Republic have ventured to sell either of the books openly, and one of these is an official Protestant distributing agency. One non-Catholic bookseller in Dublin dared to put *American Freedom and Catholic Power* in his window for one day. A priest saw it and directed its removal; it was removed. The Irish Catholic daily press, of course, has refused to review these books, and Irish Catholics are not permitted under canon law to read them. *American Freedom and Catholic Power* has been "analyzed" by Catholic professors in Maynooth in their classroom discussions, but the seminary students have no way to get the offending volume unless they commit a mortal sin by purchasing it at a non-Catholic bookstore.

One reason why the Catholic organizations find little difficulty in imposing their extra-legal censorship is that the priests in their censorial propaganda very skillfully combine hostility to sin in print with an appeal to anti-foreign prejudice. Since nearly all banned books are published abroad, the native suspicion of anything foreign can re-enforce high moral "principle." Printed matter coming from England is especially suspect, and English Sunday newspapers are favorite targets. Many Catholic organizations in recent years have demanded that the circulation of English Sunday newspapers be entirely prohibited. Early in 1953 huge posters were affixed to public walls in all parts of Dublin, declaring in heavy black type: "THE FOREIGN PRESS IS A NATIONAL MENACE." These posters represented far more than the temporary propaganda of a lunatic fringe of the Church. Many campaigns against the "corruption" of the foreign press are launched officially from Irish parish pulpits, with the blessing of the hierarchy. Here is an account of a Catholic boycott, taken verbatim from the *Irish Catholic* of July 20, 1950:

ANNAGRY REJECTS ENGLISH SUNDAY NEWSPAPERS

The Irish-speaking parish of Annagry, Co. Donegal, has given a lead to the rest of Ireland in an important matter. Not one English Sunday newspaper is now sold there. . . .

"You cannot expect pure water from a tainted source," said Most Rev. Dr. McNeely [Bishop of Raphoe] when he warned the people against the dangers of a pagan imported press and urged that parents should be very circumspect in admitting such papers to their homes, in the course of his exhortation at Confirmations in the parish in May.

Following His Lordship's visit, several prominent parishioners intimated their willingness to assist Rev. Vincent Chambers, Annagry, in a campaign to secure the exclusion of English Sunday newspapers from the area.

Newsagents were approached and consulted, and in every case co-operation was willingly and enthusiastically given. Within a week the whole parish had been made aware of the effort to stamp out the importation to the parish of newspapers that are undesirable for Irish readers and that contain much that is not fit for the young to read.

In frequent addresses to the congregation on Sundays, Father Chambers stressed the importance of heeding the warning given by their beloved Bishop and announced that the newsagents, conscious of their loyalty to their Church and Bishop, had decided to refuse to accept English Sunday papers in future. On June 26 when the newspapers arrived in the parish and commenced distribution, the agents informed the carriers that they were not accepting delivery.

It should be noted that not a single fact was produced in this campaign to show that any particular English newspaper had published any item which was morally or legally objectionable. In such campaigns in Ireland it is usually enough to identify the publication as foreign and non-Catholic. At a Dublin mass meeting in 1950, a famous Jesuit, Father R. S. Devane, asked: "Can we call ourselves a free people and a sovereign state when we are so dependent for our reading matter on papers whose ideals are not our own?" Elsewhere Father Devane had warned that "the alien pen will accomplish in a few decades what the alien sword failed to achieve in centuries." The president of the Gaelic League, one of Ireland's most powerful organizations, echoed this sentiment when he declared: "Ireland cannot retain her separate national identity, cannot attain her full national aspirations, while English publications swamp our book shops and our homes." Deploring the fact that eight times as many British-produced books and five times as many British-produced magazines were sold in the Republic as Irish-produced publications, he said: "As a people we Irish have an inordinate fear of being labelled intolerant or narrow-minded by the foreigners. . . . I submit that tolerance should begin at home, and that it is time we got down to the task of developing our nation in accordance with God's precepts and our people's distinctive national genius . . . our objective cannot be achieved as long as British publications hold their present dominant position on the Irish reading market. . . . The power of the British Press in Ireland must be broken."

In fact, however, the power of the British press in Ireland has not been broken, and the London Sunday newspapers continue to pour into the Republic in large quantities in spite of the priests.

Censorship of Radio and Films

In the Irish radio and film world, Catholic control is complete but not scandalous. Perhaps one reason for this condition is that in both the film and radio firmaments Ireland tends to be a satellite of Great Britain, and Irish critical judgments are usually subordinated to those of London and Hollywood. "In Cinema matters," mourns the film critic of the *Irish Catholic,* "we have as a nation even lower than Dominion Status."

The Republic has its own small Radio Eireann, a semi-independent unit under government patronage, which observes both Catholic and Protestant taboos quite conscientiously; but it is not unduly partisan in view of the overwhelming preponderance of Catholics in the population. It avoids direct denominational controversy whenever possible. In Ireland such avoidance means that many of the most vital and important controversies in Irish life must be eliminated from the air waves. But of course this policy is not unique in the radio world; it is also the general rule for American air waves and, to a less extent, for Britain's great broadcasting monopoly, the British Broadcasting Corporation. Probably more Irishmen listen to the B.B.C. than to their own Irish stations — a fact which has saddened and annoyed Irish patriots, especially when the B.B.C. described the coronation of a British queen for 455 consecutive minutes. The B.B.C. is a little more outspoken on some Catholic issues than the American networks, and it occasionally permits quite frank discussions of Vatican political policy. Such discussions naturally cause discomfort in Irish Catholic circles, and Ireland's own radio broadcasting corporation observes the Catholic amenities more carefully.

The Catholic Church in both England and Ireland fights strenuously against any radio program which smacks of "maintaining the common element in all religious bodies." The quoted phrase comes from the 1951 report of a committee, headed by

Lord Beveridge, on B.B.C. religious broadcasting; the report drew prompt fire from Catholic authorities. The hierarchy wants no suggestion of religious compromise on the air, no appeal for mutual adjustment among the sects as against separatism. Its B.B.C. adviser, Father Agnellus Andrew, O.F.M., has declared that the suggested Beveridge policy of common-element religion is "quite unacceptable to Catholics." Thus far there has been no definite settlement between Catholics and the British government on matters of radio religious policy. Both the English and the Irish priests continue to promote a narrow orthodoxy when they are given time on the air, and no one challenges them directly. In both England and Ireland it is the independent critics of all orthodoxy who suffer. In neither country is there a fair opportunity to criticize the outstanding policies of any church, while adulation for all forms of orthodoxy is accepted as permissible.

Film censorship in Ireland is slightly more tolerable and somewhat less fanatical than book censorship. Although it protects the population completely from any specifically anti-clerical ideas, it has never attained the reputation for fanaticism enjoyed by the book censorship. Dublin has no counterpart of the American Legion of Decency, because it would be superfluous to have a separate priestly film organization under a government which is itself so devoutly Catholic. The Irish government's Film Censor is a good Catholic, and he has power to ban any film in the Republic, subject only to the right of appeal to a Censorship of Films Appeal Board. This Appeal Board, composed of seven Catholics and two Protestants, occasionally reverses an over-strict decision of the Censor, and exercises a restraining influence upon denominational fanatics. In 1952 it reversed the Film Censor's ban five times.

Not many imported films — and virtually all films exhibited in Ireland *are* imported — are completely banned; in 1951 the Censor completely prohibited only 27 offerings out of 2,187. But the cutting of films is quite common, and over 265 were excised. In 1952, 19 films were banned and 196 cut. Such cutting is indicative of very severe standards, since most of the films exhibited in Ireland are sifted by three fine-screened filters before they reach Dublin: the Production Code authority of Hollywood, the American Catholic Legion of Decency, and the British Film Censorship. About nine-tenths of Ireland's films come from Hollywood via London, and after the triple filtering there is not much sin left — and sometimes not much sense. *A Streetcar Named Desire* was so badly mutilated by the compulsory cutting of its seduction scene that Dublin customers in December 1952 were quite mystified by the jerky and disconnected sequence they saw on the screen.

The Film Censor will not, of course, tolerate any anti-Catholic nonsense. When the March of Time's brisk documentary *Tito* reached Ireland in 1951, it was withheld from circulation on the grounds that it glamorized the Yugoslav Communist dictator too much, and that such glamorization would be "offensive to Catholics when there is so much persecution going on in Yugoslavia." When the Italian film *The Miracle* arrived in Ireland in 1950, it was promptly banned. This sober work of art — which was denounced as sacrilegious by the American Cardinal Spellman because it suggested a parallel to the story of the Virgin Birth — could be legally suppressed in Ireland as blasphemous, because the theory of the Irish Constitution on blasphemy is strikingly different from the theory of American law on sacrilege. "It is not the business of government in our nation," said the United States Supreme Court in finally permitting the showing of *The Miracle* in America, "to suppress real or imagined attacks upon a particular religious doctrine, whether they appear in publications, speeches or motion pictures."

In practice almost no film is ever imported into Ireland which might be directly offensive to the Catholic hierarchy. Films which seem to approve or condone divorce, suicide, adultery, or abortion are subject to severe trimming. *Sunset Boulevard* was heavily cut because it contained a suggestion that He was living with Her. *Detective Story,* hailed by many critics as a masterpiece, was banned because there was a suggestion that somebody had resorted to abortion.

Sometimes Catholic Action groups prevent the exhibition of a film, even after it has been approved by the government's Censor. This is most likely to happen in those rare cases when a film reaches Ireland via London after being condemned by America's Legion of Decency. The general assumption in

Ireland is that Irish Catholics could not possibly tolerate any product considered too obscene for "pagan America." "Last year," boasted the film critic of the *Irish Catholic* in 1949, "through the active intervention of this newspaper and its readers and through the splendid co-operation of the cinema owners throughout the country, Ireland rejected even purged and censored versions of *Forever Amber* and *Duel in the Sun,* both of which had been condemned by the American Legion of Decency . . . the fact that we are a Catholic nation, and therefore a useful barometer indicating Catholic reactions, makes our decisions important to Hollywood's and Britain's careful observers."

Occasionally, however, the more liberal Catholics of Dublin successfully resist an attempt to boycott a serious work of cinema art. In spite of priestly support, a special right-wing censorship body, the Catholic Cinema and Theatre Patrons Association, of Dublin, has not won enthusiastic and general Catholic approval. In September 1952 it tried to suppress Arthur Miller's notable *Death of a Salesman,* alleging among other things that the author had "Communist-front connections." The Catholic *Standard* refused to join the amateur crusade, and the picture was saved.

The Irish priests are rightly jealous of the influence of American films on the younger generation. They blame these films for a constant "flow of Paganism," and for enticing young people away from Ireland. The cinema, they contend, is "a school of worldliness, produced by people who know not God . . . our Christian spirit is being slowly corroded by the spirit of Hollywood." From the point of view of their own professional interests, these complaints by the priests are quite justified. The foreign cinema is helping to break down the Catholic isolation promoted by the priests and to give the common people glimpses of a world in which moral values do not necessarily center in the Catholic Church. Hollywood, with all its nauseating adolescence, can still be credited with this important intellectual achievement, and the Irish people are almost hysterically devoted to Hollywood films. In all of Ireland's cities and towns they can be seen standing in long queues, even in the driving rain, waiting to crowd into local theaters to see American pictures. They are learning in the cinema that attitude of broad tolerance

toward all faiths, Catholic and non-Catholic, which is characteristic of the moral climate of Great Britain and the United States
and which is commonly described by the Irish priests as "paganism."

The Irish drama is somewhat more free than publishing and
cinema, because there is no formal government censorship of
the theater. The plays of Paul Vincent Carroll, which contain
pointed criticism of priestly power, are still popular in Ireland
today, and Carroll is still considered a worthy Irish playwright.
The Abbey Theatre, although it has declined from the supreme
position in Irish culture which it occupied in the days of Yeats
and Lady Gregory, is still an institution of great importance in
Irish life. Many of its productions contain anti-clerical implications, and the anti-clerical material is usually greeted with pleased
recognition by Dublin audiences. The Abbey is less rebellious
in mood than it was in earlier days, perhaps because it now
receives a government subsidy for some of its work; but it is
still a center of independent criticism of the nation's social life.

Other theaters besides the Abbey Theatre help to keep alive
the spirit of independence in Dublin. The Longford players
presented in 1952 a historical drama, *Witch Hunt,* which contained a pointed attack upon clerical tyranny in Ireland — in
the fourteenth century. The villain was an English, not an Irish,
bishop — but the mere fact that in Dublin in 1952 a Catholic
bishop could be portrayed on a Dublin stage as a thoroughly
obnoxious person proved that the playwright in the Republic is
not completely muzzled. Occasionally disrespectful references
to priestly power creep into a Dublin play which even a New
York producer would not dare to permit. The legitimate stage
is the one place left in cultural life in the Republic where an
Irish intellectual may thumb his nose at the Church and still
continue to write.

While the educated Catholic people of the Republic hate the
censorship, and sing the praises of condemned books, the candid
critic is bound to point out that, to use a radio term, the wave-
band of modern cultural and mental maturity seems to exist only
at the top of Irish society. The masses of the people in the
country districts rarely read anything that the priests do not want
them to read. They live in a carefully insulated cultural world.

Because of this condition, the total cultural climate of Ireland is not much above that of Portugal, whose dictator, Dr. Oliveira Salazar, has set forth the standard principle of Catholic thought control: "Literature is the mental pabulum of the people. Like other foods the food of the mind must be protected by the State from poison and adulteration."

6

Segregated Education

In *Gulliver's Travels,* Jonathan Swift pictured a land called Laputa, a floating island in the sky, whose inhabitants had many of their physical features transposed or distorted in some way — heads inclined to the right or left, one eye turned inward, one "up to the Zenith." The American who studies the Irish Republic's school system feels as if he had come to an educational Laputa.

Americans are proud of the *public* nature of their school system. Their schools are owned by the people, managed by boards of education chosen by the people, and paid for by the people. They are open without cost to children of all creeds from the kindergarten through the twelfth year of study. In some states like California and some cities like New York, young men and women residents may receive part or all of their university training at public expense as a matter of right. No public schools in the United States are owned or controlled by churches, and no formal religion is taught as part of the school curriculum. The American people are proud of their public schools and proud of the fact that they spend more money on them per capita than the people of any other nation.

One of the distinctive achievements of American democracy is that under the American public-school system the children of all creeds are educated together. Churches are permitted to organize their own school systems at their own expense, but these private denominational systems do not serve more than 11 per cent of the nation's elementary-school pupils. The public school is regarded by the overwhelming majority of the American

110

people as the people's own school, the place where the children of all religious groups can learn to live together in friendship and mutual tolerance. The American people also believe in coeducation, and do not segregate children by sex in their school system.

In Ireland all these values are reversed. The Irish Republic, like Quebec, has no public-school system. Its so-called national schools, Catholic and Protestant, are in fact denominational schools. About 97 per cent of the pupils attend Catholic denominational schools; nearly all the rest attend Protestant denominational schools. The Catholic schools are managed by priests, the Protestant schools by parsons; and in each case the clergy appoint the teachers.

The Catholic schools are conducted virtually as organic parts of the Church. Although the Irish taxpayers provide at least 99 per cent of the running expenses and a large share of the construction costs of the Catholic elementary schools, the titles to school property and the detailed management remain in the hands of the priests and bishops. The nation has no free high schools, and less than one-fourth of the children ever enter the only alternative schools — the fee-charging secondary schools, operated for the most part by Catholic religious orders. These schools segregate the children by sex according to the papal law on coeducation. They prepare the elite among the Irish children for the universities — but only about 3 per cent of the children ever enter a university. (The corresponding figure in the United States is 22 per cent.) Some 65 per cent of the children drop out of school at fourteen; and most of the others take only a very brief supplementary course of technical training. An American child has at least three times as good a chance of going beyond the sixth grade in school as an Irish child.

In 1949, the Irish people spent on each child in the primary schools about $35. The corresponding figure for the United States was $226. Since cash comparisons between Ireland and the United States are generally unfair, the comparison with Great Britain is more significant. *Teachers' Work* of Dublin, a reputable teachers' magazine, has estimated that in 1945 the English taxpayers were spending at least three times as much per child on primary schools as the Irish taxpayers.

These facts will seem quite startling to most Americans. They have been trained to think of education as a natural function of local government, and they have learned to take for granted the American program of compulsory education up to the age of sixteen, with free tuition for high-school training.

The Church Condemns the Public School

Perhaps the most striking fact about Catholic education in Ireland from an American point of view is the open and unanimous hostility of the priests to a public-school system. Although Irish Catholic leaders in America frequently make friendly statements about public schools, the Church's leaders in Ireland make no attempt to disguise their enmity to "godless" schools as a source of corruption and decadence in modern civilization. Any school which does not officially teach religion is considered "godless"; education is considered the function of the Church rather than the state. I have heard a leading priest declare at a Dublin meeting, with the apparently unanimous support of his audience: "Lay education is poison. The government should stay away as far as possible from education."

This suggestion that the government "stay away" from education does not mean that the Church refuses public money for Catholic schools, or rejects any incidental service which the state is willing to offer. In accordance with papal encyclicals and canon law, all Church leaders in the Republic teach that the state owes the Church full financial support for the Church's educational enterprise, and that the state should "interfere" in the schools only to the extent of underwriting the educational enterprise and of guaranteeing that certain minimum standards are enforced.

In the Irish Catholic educational world, the national government through its Ministry for Education inspects all elementary schools, except the classes in religious instruction; prescribes a list of textbooks from which the school managers may make their choices; enforces the truancy laws; and sets the minimum standards for teacher training. But all the schools in the Republic for young children, with the exception of a few vocational and completely private schools, are operated by religious organizations and managed by religious officers. Since the teachers are chosen by religious managers, the whole spirit and tone of Irish elementary education is set by religion. The Catholic people think of "their" schools as belonging to their Church, and they think of the priest as the natural ruler over the training of their children. Even those few incidental decisions concerning textbooks and teacher training which nominally belong to the Irish state are in practice usually made by the priests. The state only brings up the rear of the educational procession as a kind of combination treasurer and policeman. The secondary schools of the religious orders are even more completely Catholic than the primary schools.

In this respect the Irish national school system embodies the letter and the spirit of papal doctrine on education. The Church's canon law and Pius XI's encyclical *Christian Education of Youth* lay down two essentials of Catholic education: that "Catholic children must not attend non-Catholic, neutral, or mixed schools . . . open to non-Catholics," and that every "subject taught [must] be permeated with Christian piety." Thus it is clear that the segregation of Catholic children in Ireland is not merely an Irish policy but, technically, is enforced against all Catholic people everywhere as a matter of moral law. Parents are taught that no school can be a Catholic school unless it meets the priestly requirement that its atmosphere be wholly Catholic.

And the atmosphere of the Irish Catholic schools *is* wholly Catholic. "I think I am justified in saying," declared the Minister for Education in a public address at Carlow in 1938, "that in no country in the world does a national system of education approach the Catholic ideal system as in the Free State." The Minister might have added that in this respect the Church's position in Ireland is far more favorable than in the Vatican's home country, Italy.

Having secured this unique position, the Irish Catholic Church is proud of its achievement, and its leaders are very frank in describing their triumph over any possibility of a public, nondenominational school system. They contradict any statement to the effect that their schools are national schools simply because they are labeled "national." "What, then, is the educational system of Ireland?" asks Father M. Brennan, Professor of Education at St. Patrick's College, Maynooth. "Our schools, both of the primary and the secondary grade, are in the strictest sense

Catholic schools. . . . They are all private Catholic institutions, founded by diocesan or other religious bodies for the education of our people. . . it is very wrong to speak of the national schools as if they were State institutions." "The Irish National School system," says the Catholic Education Council for England and Wales, in a propaganda booklet on behalf of such schools, "is undenominational in theory but denominational in practice." When, in 1952, a rumor was spread through Dublin by an afternoon newspaper that the Irish National Teachers' Organization, the chief teachers' union, was beginning to think about the possibility of a public-school system for Ireland, the general secretary of that organization published an anxious denial, which the *Irish Times* embodied in a headline worthy of the *New Yorker:* "NO SUGGESTION OF NATIONALISING NATIONAL SCHOOLS." (The only adequate parallel I know is a banner displayed in a Dublin street during the 1932 Eucharistic Congress: "GOD BLESS THE TRINITY.")

It was quite understandable that D. J. Kelleher — the Irish teachers' leader involved in this incident — should hasten to deny the rumor that he favored public as against Church education. Any Catholic educational leader in Ireland today who openly advocated a public system of education would be disowned, disgraced, and discharged. The spokesmen for *national* education go out of their way to disclaim interest in *public* education at every opportunity. The Irish Minister for Education, Sean Moylan, in an address before the Irish National Teachers' Organization in April 1953, referred to public control of education as a kind of penalty to be resorted to only if religious control should fail. He regarded state control of education, he said, as "wholly undesirable"; but if "the public were not prepared to meet their responsibilities and were not prepared to take a greater interest in primary education it was evidently paving the way to complete State control of education."

"The managerial system," as it is politely called, is apparently favored by all Irish Catholics and by nearly all Irish Protestants. Protestant support is at least partially based upon class feeling and snobbishness: the Protestant denominational school keeps Protestant children away from the social contamination of a "lower" element in Irish society, and permits them to live in

Catholic Ireland without being submerged in the Catholic masses. The support of the Protestant clergy has been secured by giving them control over the education of the 3 per cent of the country's children who are Protestants.

The Protestant method of operation of Protestant elementary schools is not quite identical with the Catholic method, but the general process of supervision is essentially the same, and both systems are completely denominational. The taxpayers, local or national, pay all the salaries of all the teachers by public grants, supply the necessary equipment, and usually construct and repair the buildings. The religious institutions themselves must supply for their elementary schools only a portion of the charge for cleaning and heating the buildings. The educational arm of Irish Catholicism, under this system, receives from the taxpayers a contribution of more than $25,000,000 a year, and the contribution to Protestant schools is proportionate. The chief technical difference between the role of the parson in the Protestant school and the role of the priest in the Catholic school is that in the Catholic school system the priest is more subordinate to his bishop. The Catholic bishop has the right to step into any school in his diocese in order to hire or fire any teacher, regardless of the decision of the local priest-manager. In the Protestant school system the local parson-manager, rather than the bishop or the moderator, has final authority over the hiring and firing of teachers. The right of Catholic bishops over national school teachers is written into the law of the Republic, and against that right no teacher has any appeal, or any claim to permanent tenure.

Academic Freedom, Limited

In neither the Catholic nor the Protestant school system is a teacher free to be an open skeptic about religious doctrine — and often political beliefs are covered by religious taboos. A teacher in a Catholic school in Waterford was fired by the school's priest-manager during the Spanish Civil War simply because he spoke out against Franco. He was finally taken in by a Jewish national school in Dublin.

The teacher's acceptance of orthodoxy is assumed when he takes his place in the teaching profession. Agnosticism has no rights, and orthodoxy is a necessary ingredient of "character and fitness," as required for entrance into the profession. The Irish Catholic teacher, under the law as it now operates, has less freedom in matters of religious conviction than the Irish pupil; the Constitution grants exemption from religious teaching to every pupil whose parents request such exemption, but the teacher has no such protection. His competence is no defense against any charge of heresy — and one of the worst forms of heresy is disbelief in denominational schools. If he suggests that a modern democracy has the same obligation to control its schools as its post offices, its roads, and its fire companies, he is likely to be confronted with Pius XI's denunciation of such principles as socialistic. In Ireland today the taint of alleged Communism is even more fatal than it is in the United States. Usually it is sufficient to guarantee the prompt termination of any teaching career.

Perhaps that is one reason why leaders of the teachers' union try to outdo one another in attacks on public education. "State control of the aims and machinery of education," said the president of the Irish National Teachers' Organization in 1948, "is a first principle of totalitarianism." And he went on to cite "proof" that Nazism, fascism, and Communism all sprang from secular education under state control.

"In thirty years' experience in the Irish school system," a leader of this organization said to me, "I have yet to find a teacher who objects to the system of religious education which we have, or to the system of managerial control by the priests. We are unique and we are proud of it. After all, religion is essential for education, and the priest is likely to be the best-educated man in his community. Who is better equipped to choose teachers on a basis of fitness?"

This praise of the system is echoed, somewhat less enthusiastically, by some Protestant leaders. On the whole, Southern Irish Protestantism is satisfied with the present system of school control. In its financial operations the scheme is administered with scrupulous impartiality, and the government has carried out the pledges of the Constitution not to discriminate against the children of non-Catholic faiths. No child is compelled to receive religious instruction to which his parents object; and if a school cannot be found which fits the theological outlook of the parents, the child cannot be compelled to attend *any* school.

In practice, almost no Irish parents ever ask for the exemption of their children from religious instruction. This is largely because the parents are permitted to choose denominational schools which suit their theological outlook even when their choice involves the transporting of their children over considerable distances. One Protestant canon boasted in 1937 that government-supported school buses carried Protestant children free of charge "past 3 or 4 or 5 schools to the school of their own denomination." He was publicly grateful for this service. He was not disturbed by the fact that the practice guaranteed the social isolation of the Protestant children from the children of the community in which they lived.

In this respect he was not unique. The assumption behind both the Protestant and the Catholic theories of education in Ireland is that Protestant and Catholic children will remain culturally segregated for their whole lives. The theory of segregation applies also to Jews. A few Jewish schools are provided in Dublin and Cork for the small Jewish communities in those cities, and they are financed by public funds in the same manner as Catholic and Protestant schools.

Not the least astonishing feature of the Irish school situation is the fact that its denominational character is maintained behind a legal fiction of church-state separation. Perhaps the existence of this Irish fiction is one of the reasons why Irish Catholic leaders in the United States discuss education and church-state separation in words of such hopeless ambiguity: their Irish precedents are drawn from a world of semantic confusion. Many leaders in Ireland actually believe that their nation has written the separation of church and state into its organic law, and they have no conception of the meaning of the phrase "separation of church and state" as it has been developed in the United States.

Article 44 of the Irish Constitution provides: "The State guarantees not to endow any religion. The State shall not impose any disabilities or make any discrimination on the ground of religious profession, belief or status." Such phrases, if they appeared in the Constitution of the United States, would be construed by the American Supreme Court as outlawing all appropriations to denominational schools, since the payment of public money to an important arm of the Church, the parochial school, would be interpreted as a religious "endowment." But the payment of more than $25,000,000 a year to Irish Catholic schools is not treated under the Irish Constitution as an effort "to endow any religion," although everyone admits that the Catholic school in Ireland is an organic part of the Catholic parish, and perhaps more essential in the development of Catholicism than the Church itself. (In this particular the Protestant schools have less organic connection with their church than the Catholic schools.) The catechism classes in the Catholic schools systematically prepare the children for the confirmation classes in the churches, and the auxiliary expenses of school activity are raised directly by the parish priest in his regular appeals from the pulpit. The attendance of Catholic children at these schools is interpreted as morally obligatory, and any refusal of the obligation may be punished by denial of the sacraments. Protestant emphasis in the Protestant schools is more restrained and voluntary, and Protestant textbooks, although pro-English in tone, are less partisan.

The Irish courts, of course, follow the English rather than the American precedent on church-state separation, since the practice of supporting denominational schools with public money was established in Ireland in the days of British occupation, and the tradition was continued when the new Republic won its independence. When the Irish Constitution says that the state shall not endow any religion, it is interpreted to mean only that the state shall not endow any church *directly* by paying the salaries of priests as priests. Priests, nuns, and laymen who serve as Catholic teachers in Catholic schools are not covered by the prohibition, nor are preachers.

Similarily, in their schools, both the Catholic and Protestant churches evade the prohibition of the Irish Constitution that "the State shall not impose any disabilities or make any discrimination on the ground of religious profession, belief or status." The Republic permits the spirit of this clause to be constantly violated in the schools — where the discrimination against skeptical teachers is practiced by the priests and preachers and not directly by the government. In practice, the religious status of a teacher is usually the first requisite of employment, and the recommendation of his parish priest the most important endorsement.

The British Heritage

This close identification of public education with religion in Ireland is partly a product of the British tradition. Denominational education developed in England and Ireland simultaneously, and to this day there is nothing in the British constitution which prohibits the expenditure of public funds for even the most dogmatic denominational schools. Until 1870, practically all the elementary schools of England, Wales, Ireland, and Scotland were church schools which imparted denominational viewpoints as a matter of course; and it was not until 1944 that Britain adopted its first comprehensive state-supported scheme of free education. Today, although nearly three-fourths of England's children attend purely public or council schools, the government continues to support "aided" and "controlled" church schools by paying their teachers' salaries and almost all their running expenses. In the "controlled" schools — which receive almost as large a proportion of their costs from the taxpayers as the public schools — a broad general course in religious education is taught from an inter-faith syllabus, but the teachers are appointed without a religious test by public educational authorities. In the "aided" schools, the religious teaching is more denominational and the teachers are chosen by church representatives. These "aided" schools receive a slightly smaller proportion of public funds.

The Catholic hierarchy in England and Scotland will not allow its children to attend any but strictly Catholic denominational schools, although this decision costs the Church a substantial loss in government appropriations. This intransigence is largely Irish intransigence, and one result is that the Catholic schools in England are Irish schools. "The Catholic primary schools all over England," boasted the Dublin *Catholic Bulletin* in 1939, "are, and have been, ours by population, by teachers and by priests, and by their costs and upkeep, Irish by at least 90 per cent, as against 10 per cent from all other sources, personal and otherwise." The *Bulletin* was in error in one respect — its claim that the "costs and upkeep" are Irish contributions. It is the English taxpayer who foots more than 95 per cent of the costs of the English Catholic schools.

The extreme denominational partisanship of the Catholic schools in Ireland is a natural product of the nation's history and goes back to the days of British control. Education was regarded by the Protestant Ascendancy as an instrument for making Irish children pro-English. For instance, they were taught to sing:

> I thank the goodness and the grace
> That on my birth have smiled
> And made me, in these Christian days,
> A happy English child.

When the British government set up an educational system for Ireland through a National Board of Education in 1831, it tried to bring the Catholic and Protestant children together in the same schools, with religious instruction in separate classes. But the clergy of both faiths would have none of such co-operation. They insisted that the schools be strictly denominational, and they have remained strictly denominational ever since. Today the Protestants would probably welcome more co-operation, but the Catholic bishops would not. The parish priest as the head of each Catholic school undertakes to see that the religion taught is militantly Roman as well as militantly Irish. In many of the popular Christian Brothers' schools, there is a brief prayer every hour on the hour. Usually Catholic instruction is given to the students daily for at least half an hour by a lay member of the regular teaching staff. (Proportionately, there are not so many nuns teaching in the elementary schools of the Republic as in the Catholic schools of the United States because so many nuns are used for the operation of the higher schools and for the management of Irish missions overseas.)

Although the parish priest does not draw a salary from his national school, or teach regular classes, he is the professional master of the school. He personally supervises the school's religious training and at least once a week lectures to the students on Catholicism. He and his assistants round up the children at regular intervals, and take them to confession in groups — I have seen this process in operation in Irish school grounds. The children learn to think of the priest as the central figure in their moral universe, and in the whole course of their schooling they never encounter anyone who questions his supremacy. "From their first yell at birth," says Liam O'Flaherty, "until the sod falls on them in their grave, their actions and thoughts are under his [the priest's] direction." O'Flaherty, in his inimitable *Tourist's Guide to Ireland,* describes some of the characteristics of the village priest in his capacity as supervisor of the schools: "He is, almost invariably, himself of peasant abstraction and almost invariably he is just about as well informed as a well-informed peasant. . . . He has an idea that Ireland is the only moral country in the world. . . . The parish priest himself has had no education worth speaking of, so he dislikes others receiving one."

Priests have improved since O'Flaherty wrote this indictment, but most observers doubt whether the relative intellectual position of the priest in Irish life has changed. Too often the parish priest is a man past fifty when he reaches a position of authority over the village school, and his mind is set in provincial ways. His vigorous years may have been spent as a poorly paid curate in the cultural isolation of the Irish countryside. The supervising priests in the Irish cities are likely to be more intelligent, but their intelligence is often outbalanced by overwork and by the overcrowding and wretched physical conditions in city schools. "In the cities and large towns," says the Irish National Teachers' Organization, "the proportion of teachers to pupils is very often abnormal, sixty or seventy children per teacher being not uncommon. In such circumstances effective teaching is difficult if not impossible."

Church Control of Secondary Schools

The government does not completely finance the Irish secondary schools but it gives them money grants when they conform to its standards, and these grants serve as endowments for the teaching orders of the Church. In general, the grants are miserably inadequate and teachers' salaries scandalously low. Advertisements appear in Irish newspapers for secondary-school teachers with "Honors M.A." — at salaries of less than $500 per year. The government does not build secondary schools, and for twenty-five years it has not increased the capitation grants to religious orders for the students in such schools. Nevertheless, because there is no other choice for Catholics, parents generally accept the assumption of the priests that the best secondary education for both boys and girls is given by the religious orders. This control of high-school education helps to explain the great success of the Church in recruiting priests and nuns. In their sensitive adolescent years, the best of the Republic's young men and women are subjected to a rigorous devotional routine under the supervision of Sisters of Mercy, Jesuits, Christian Brothers, and other celibate devotees. Here is the devotional schedule used in one of the best Jesuit secondary schools in Ireland, taken down in rough notes from the comments of one of its graduates. (It may not be typical of all such schools.)

Rise at 7:00, and rush to the chapel for Mass and communion. (Some of the boys are so devout that they are reluctant to go to breakfast at all.)

After breakfast, fifteen minutes of praying, before the Blessed Sacrament.

Some spend the next thirty-five minutes, before a 9:10 class, in praying.

Classes, lunch, football, and dinner until 4:30. The class subjects include religious instruction.

Fifteen minutes of the Rosary before 5:00.

Five minutes of prayers at bedtime.

Of these items, three are absolutely obligatory — morning Mass, the Rosary before 5:00, and bedtime prayers. Junior and senior retreats are held during the year, and there is constantly a favorable portrayal of the celibate priestly life. There is no correspondingly favorable presentation of lay life. It is not surprising that about half of the boys in this school finally become priests. James Joyce in *A Portrait of the Artist as a Young Man* has described the way in which the priest in such a school exploits the adolescent sense of sexual guilt on behalf of Catholic vocations.

Religious orders also control the primary education of more than one-third of the Catholic pupils in the Republic, and they naturally tend to favor the devout teachers of their own orders above laymen. Their motives in this connection are not without a color of financial design. Members of religious orders, when they receive teaching salaries from the state, are obliged by their oaths to turn over to the treasuries of their orders all funds in excess of living expenses. Curiously enough, they do not, as in the United States, escape income taxes on these salaries.

In both elementary and secondary Catholic schools, the full, dogmatic message of Catholic theology is impressed upon the students as a necessary part of Christianity. The religious textbooks are chosen by the priests, the secular textbooks by the Catholic Minister for Education, acting under the veto power of the Catholic hierarchy. Under such circumstances, the censorship of textbooks after publication is rarely necessary. The writing, publication, sale, and use of these books are all exclusively in Catholic hands. All history, science, and art are given a Catholic flavor. The atmosphere of such education has not changed since 1904, when Bernard Shaw in his preface to *John Bull's Other Island* burst out in indignation: "Imagine trying to get a modern education in a seminary of priests, where every modern book worth reading is on the index, and the earth is still regarded, not perhaps as absolutely flat, yet as being far from spherical as Protestants allege!"

Shaw's anger seems especially justified after an examination of history books in the Irish schools. They are not all flagrant examples of partisanship — but the tone and spirit are distinctly partisan. There is a tendency throughout to represent all modern, non-Catholic progress as decadence. French lay education is held responsible for the collapse of France in World War II. The past of Catholic nations is painted in rosy colors wherever possible. In a typical article called "The Catholic View of History" in the *Irish Ecclesiastical Record* in 1937, the Very Rev. John Johnson summed up the point of view taught in Catholic textbooks:

The awful sixteenth century closed with the ruin of united Christendom. . . . Protestantism was therefore directly responsible for the reintroduction of spiritual slavery, and even temporal slavery — disguised as serfdom — took on a new lease of life. The poor and the lowly were the real victims of the "Reformation." Germany, the hope of the "Reformation," took the lead in exploiting the poor. . . . It all ended in the French Revolution. The 19th century lived up to the revolutionary expectations. Everywhere the rights of God came to be regarded as an anachronism, and the State took over more and more from the Church. That was Liberalism, and its fitting sequel is the spiritual chaos of today.

In Catholic textbooks both religious and secular subjects are presented, as far as possible, in a theological setting. A priest, reviewing a sociology textbook in the *Irish Ecclesiastical Record,* once said ruefully: "Just half of the book is taken up with explaining and proving God's existence, the Divinity of Christ, Man's Free-Will, his Supernatural Destiny, the Fundamental Human Rights and Duties, and the error of Evolution." Very tentatively he implied that a social scientist might deal with the present world a little more directly. In many textbooks there is a tendency to make the world a papocentric globe, revolving about Rome as planets revolve about the sun. Even famous Biblical passages are tailored to suit priestly convictions. The standard *Catechism of Catholic Doctrine* used in Irish Catholic schools — "approved by the Archbishops and Bishops of Ireland" — entirely omits the second of the Ten Commandments, because it conflicts with some of the practices of the Church. ("Thou shalt not make unto thee a graven image, nor any likeness of any thing that is in heaven above, or that is in the earth beneath. . . .") The version of the Ten Commandments used in Irish Catholic schools covers up this deficiency by splitting the tenth commandment in two — thus making two separate sins of coveting one's neighbor's wife and one's neighbor's goods.

The Priestly Versions of Literature

In 1952 *A Guide for Catholic Teachers* appeared, with a foreword by the Archbishop of Dublin, which told the teachers in very frank terms of their duty to use textbook material for the greater glory of the Church. The guide's instructions for a Catholic teacher of literature offer a striking parallel to the instructions given teachers in the Soviet Union concerning the injection of Marxism into every subject:

One may ask: What is the Church's function in literature? The Catholic Church does not exercise a merely divine function in literature. She claims to control, nay, to own by unquestionable title all that is good in art, in literature, in life. She places the stamp of her approval not only upon the works of those who are in visible communion with her, but also upon the works of those who are unconsciously in visible communion with her through the good that is in their work. And more than that, she claims to understand their final purport better than even those who have created them. For the firm possession of Catholic truth, while it is no guarantee of merely executive skill, is a real guarantee of power to comprehend the ultimate drift of a work of literature, or a work of art, and hence its influence upon conduct.

In the hands of the Catholic educator the teaching of literature can become a very powerful ally in fortifying the minds of the young against the widening and multiform attacks on Catholic truth. The teacher must seek to Catholicize the class-room treatment of the subject, and to press out of it the fullest yield of intellectual support to the faith. . . .

The ideal instrument of literary training, then, is a graduated series of texts, so planned that the cumulative effect of the reading, and of the instruction on the reading, may be that the mind of the pupil becomes saturated with those fundamental ideas that give a true Catholic outlook on human life as planned by God.

Literature teachers are told in this official guide how to "reconstruct" standard works of literature which may contain "streaks of false philosophy" in such a way that they become "interpenetrated with the vein of Catholicism." As an example of the way in which non-Catholic literature can profitably be revised for this purpose, the author uses W. E. Henley's famous poem "Invictus," and then appends a "superior" Catholic version of the type that students should be encouraged to produce. Here are both of the poems:

INVICTUS

by W. E. Henley

Out of the night that covers me,
    Black as the Pit from pole to pole,
I thank whatever gods may be
    For my unconquerable soul.

In the fell clutch of circumstance
    I have not winced nor cried aloud.
Under the bludgeonings of chance
    My head is bloody, but unbowed.

Beyond this place of wrath and tears
    Looms but the Horror of the shade,
And yet the menace of the years
    Finds, and shall find me, unafraid.

It matters not how strait the gate,
    How charged with punishment the scroll,
I am the master of my fate;
    I am the captain of my soul.

Variation on Henley's "Invictus"

Out of the night that looms above,
    Shadowing all-e'en Life's grand Goal,
I thank Thee, Lord of Light and Love,
    For my redeemed Soul.

'Mid painful trials and misery
    I do not wince nor cry aloud:
Sharing Thy Cross to Calvary
    I go, with bleeding head unbowed.

Though past this vale of sighs and tears
    Looms dark the menace of Death's shade,
Thy love gleams bright across the years,
    I face the future unafraid.

It matters not how strait the gate,
    How charged with punishment the scroll,
For Thou, the Guardian of my Fate,
    Art with me, Captain of my Soul.

The textbooks for specifically religious classes are even more distinctly partisan. The standard *History of the Catholic Church for Schools* by Father J. Mahony, S. J., justifies the Spanish Inquisition in this manner:

Suppression of Protestantism in Spain

The defence of the Faith throughout his dominions was regarded by Philip as one of his principal duties as sovereign. At his command the Spanish Inquisition adopted vigorous measures for the suppression of heresy. It was soon discovered that Seville and Valladolid were active centres for Protestantism. Numerous arrests were made; and the culprits received their sentences at five great Autos de Fé held at Toledo, Valladolid and Seville (1559-60).

According to a modern non-Catholic historian, hardly more than a score of Spanish Protestants suffered death at the stake. "It is worthy of notice," says Fr. Guggenberger, "that Spain owes to the Inquisition the preservation of the Catholic faith, the acquisition of national and civil unity, and an unbroken internal peace at the time when, in consequence of the Protestant Revolution, nearly all the countries of Europe were suffering and bleeding under the curse of civil and religious wars."

Even in the primary schools the priests in their religion classes stress the full Church opposition to marriage with non-Catholics.

"A Catholic cannot validly contract marriage with an unbaptised person, e.g., a Jew or a Mohammedan," says the *Handbook of Religious Knowledge for Primary Schools,* written by Father Michael Murphy. As to marriage with Protestants, the text says: "The Church *most severely* forbids the marriage of Catholics to baptised non-Catholics, e.g., Protestants. Generally, such bring loss of faith, great unhappiness, conflicts in the home, and grave danger to the faith of the children."

In the textbooks for higher schools, the full Catholic gospel on church and state is developed as a necessary part of Christianity. Archbishop Sheehan's *Apologetics and Catholic Doctrine,* the most popular religious textbook in both English and Irish Catholic schools, states the Catholic philosophy on this subject quite frankly. While "matters spiritual" belong exclusively to the Church and "matters temporal" to the state, he says, "Matters of a mixed character which affect both societies alike should be dealt with by mutual agreement, but in case of conflict, the State, inasmuch as it pursues the less important end, must yield to the Church." Among the more important duties of the state is "to protect the Church, to promote her interests, and in general, to act in perfect harmony with her." The students are told: "She [the Church] has expressly declared that the separation of Church from State is an evil, and that she admits it only with a view to avoid greater evil."

Having gone this far, the Church does not forget to include in its school teaching its own specific claim to control the schools and to receive public funds for their operation. The American notion of community schools is anathema, especially because in the United States public money is denied to Catholic schools. Says Archbishop Sheehan: "If, therefore — as happens in some English speaking countries where a strong Protestant sentiment predominates — the State builds and finances schools acceptable to the majority, and at the same time refuses proportional assistance to the type of school which alone can satisfy the conscience of the Catholic minority, it is guilty of a grave offense against natural justice." The claim behind this theory is stated thus: "The authority given to the Church by Christ includes the right to conduct schools herself, to safeguard the faith of her children in the schools under the control of others, to supervise the election of teachers and of the matter taught, and to condemn any school or educational system which she considers to be hostile or dangerous to holy religion."

Catholic Power in the Universities

For the tiny minority of Catholic young people who reach the level of university education — about 3 per cent of those who start school — there are only two choices within the Republic. One is Trinity College (Dublin University), an old and distinguished university which has always existed under Protestant or undenominational control. The other is the National University of Ireland — unofficially Catholic — which has three branches: University College Dublin, University College Cork, and University College Galway. But for good Catholics the choice is not a real one. Each year the Archbishop of Dublin, the unpopular and reactionary John Charles McQuaid, issues in his Lenten pastoral a flat prohibition against attendance at Trinity, and a warning that "any Catholic who deliberately disobeys this law is guilty of a mortal sin and while he persists in disobedience is unworthy to receive the Sacraments." Friends of Trinity have replied with a slightly irreverent verse:

> Our young men may loot,
> Perjure and shoot,
>   And even have carnal knowledge;
> But however depraved
> Their souls will be saved
>   If they don't go to Trinity College.

Archbishop Kinane summarized the prohibition against Trinity in a formal speech in June 1952:

I deem it my duty to warn them [students] that attendance at Trinity College, Dublin, is forbidden under pain of grave sin to Catholics. This prohibition arises not only from a decree of the Maynooth Council, which mentions Trinity College explicitly, but also from the general law of the Church, which forbids attendance at all non-Catholic schools. . . .

The need for and wisdom of the prohibition against attendance at Trinity College has recently been strongly emphasized. Certain Catholic graduates of Trinity College, whilst openly parading their Catholicity, have, at the same time, publicly set themselves up in opposition to a fundamental part of the Catholic religion, namely the teaching authority of Bishops.

The Archbishop's reference was to the famous case of Dr. Noel Browne, a Trinity graduate, who — as shown in Chapter 4 — had dared to defy the hierarchy. It is part of the hierarchy's campaign of attrition against Trinity that the possession of a degree from that institution may be used against any Catholic who wishes the favor of the Church. Part of the animosity against Trinity is historical, since the institution was once closed to Catholics. Today Trinity manages to survive in spite of the bishops and in spite of attacks upon it as "the Academic Fortress of the Protestants" and the "English State of Trinity College." It has some 2,500 students, of whom about 500 are Catholic. The educated Catholics of the South recognize its value as an outpost of freedom in a controlled culture, and the De Valera government continues a fairly generous allowance to it. In spite of stern public denunciations by the Archbishop of Dublin, strong-minded Catholic parents frequently obtain dispensations from him to send their sons and daughters to the institution.

Those Catholic Irishmen who do not attend Trinity can secure in the larger National University an unofficial Catholic education. Although the bishops permit Catholic students to attend, they describe the institution as unsatisfactory because it is not "wholly Catholic," and they apparently consider themselves very generous to permit as much liberalism as now exists there. The National University has many brilliant scholars and lovers of intellectual freedom who are fighting to keep their university free, but the outcome of the struggle is still in doubt. The atmosphere of the institution is intensely Catholic, with a student body and faculty almost exclusively Catholic, and an administrative policy dominated by the bishops. In the arts department a very large percentage of the students are priests and nuns. Although the University's professional schools have high standards, the students are completely insulated against modern influences in philosophy, sociology, and economics that might challenge the Catholic outlook. Each professor takes an oath that in carrying out his duties he will not "make any statement or use any language that would be disrespectful to the religious opinions of any of his class." In practice this means the censorship of anything critical of Catholic policy. The entire philosophy department is staffed by priests, and its teaching, in accordance with papal edict, exalts St. Thomas Aquinas as the greatest philosopher of all time. A university program of night study for the working classes aims, in the words of the *Irish Catholic*, "to educate the future leaders of the workers in this country in Catholic social principles and their practical application." The lecturers in sociology in this adult-education program are priests nominated by regional bishops.

The intellectual activities of students in the National University are conducted under special surveillance. In 1949, a long-established student group in University College Dublin, the Literary and Historical Society, attempted to stage a public debate on the 1848 *Communist Manifesto*. The list of speakers included a distinguished Trinity liberal, Dr. Owen Sheehy Skeffington; a Catholic priest; and a noted Catholic convert, the Earl of Wicklow, as chairman. After the speakers had accepted the students' invitation, university authorities forbade the debate. "At the present time," said the *Standard* in defending the university's ruling, "when civilisation is facing the threat of extinction, it is sheer flippancy to pretend that Communism is a suitable topic to be debated (in the usual style) and voted upon by young Catholic undergraduates." To which an anonymous university student replied in the *Irish Times:* "The University is becoming an intellectual nursery in which the students are allowed to play with soft toys only."

Indeed, the National University appears to be repeating the mistakes of English university education in the seventeenth century, when first the Puritans and then the Anglicans proscribed their critics as university teachers and used higher education to promote orthodoxy. Sir George Trevelyan, in describing the failure of that earlier policy, wrote a sentence which might well serve as a warning for present-day Ireland: "The enforcement of questioning orthodoxy in politics and religion is incompatible with the true life of a University." Even Cardinal Newman found in 1852, during his ill-fated attempt to found a Catholic university in Dublin, that the Irish bishops were so jealous of their power that they would not give due authority to lay scholars. He abandoned his scheme largely because he found Irish culture too priest-ridden. I doubt that he would alter his verdict today.

The "Green Elephant"

Next to Catholicism the most important force in the segregation and isolation of Irish culture is the Irish-language "revival." This venture in cultural nationalism, which Arland Ussher has called a "Green Elephant," is embarrassing to most Irishmen and is the subject of furious under-cover controversy. The controversy has become especially bitter in recent years with the introduction of compulsory Irish into both Catholic and Protestant national classrooms.

The Irish Constitution makes Irish "the first official language" of the Republic and describes English as merely "a second official language." Then the Constitution adds: "Provision may, however, be made by law for the exclusive use of either of the said languages for any one or more official purposes, either throughout the State or in any part thereof." The leaders of the language movement visualize a day when Ireland will adopt a program dispensing altogether with English as an official tongue. Their campaign for the language is coupled with violent attacks on English culture and fervent appeals to "the Irish soul." "When a nation like the Irish loses the language that has been spoken in Ireland for well over 2,000 years, without one day of intermission, that nation loses in greater part her heart and soul," says Dr. James Devane in the *Irish Rosary*. "It is true that the nation may live on, but its present, its past and its future change. It breathes a different air, lives under different skies, looks back on an alien past and forward to a changed horizon. It thinks in the language of the people whose tongue it now speaks. It talks with the larynx of a gramophone, and thinks with a papier mache mind formed out of the pulp of a foreign printing press."

The movement for Irish was started in the days when it did not seem likely that Ireland could win independence from a superior military power by political agitation alone. Cultural independence seemed a feasible alternative, and it was recognized that agitation for the revival of a native Irish language could be used as a supplementary weapon against British rule. Although Daniel O'Connell was quite unenthusiastic about the revival of Irish, his successors who captured the nationalist movement after he was dead made it into a Gaelic movement. With Thomas

Davis and the Young Irelanders of a century ago, the language revival was a mixture of starry-eyed nativism with shrewd political propaganda, designed to foster simultaneously hatred of the British and respect for all things Irish. The advocates of Gaelic did not stop to think that if their movement actually succeeded it would cut Ireland off from many of the world's richest cultural sources. The language reformers produced extravagant eulogies of the literary treasures waiting for the Irish people if they would return to their ancient tongue.

Actually, there is almost no literature worthy of serious study in modern Irish, the language which the reformers are still attempting to revive. There *is* an Irish language with a considerable treasury, old Irish, which was the tongue of the Irish people of the countryside for a thousand years — but nobody has spoken it for centuries. In order to appreciate the treasures which still exist in that tongue, a scholar would have to master material as different from modern Irish as ancient Anglo-Saxon is different from modern English.

Modern Irish is a living, native tongue in only six tiny and remote sections of Ireland's west coast and in one tiny area in the extreme south. The Gaeltacht — the section where the language is indigenous — is not only small, but largely unlettered and desperately poor. Although its language is rich in local idiom, the region is nothing more than a backward cultural pocket whose survival as a language pool is entirely accidental. The region is too small to be used for the promotion of a general revival. Even its own newspapers are printed in English, and its business dealings with the outside world are conducted chiefly in English. Its young people, who are brought up to speak Irish exclusively in their schools and homes, listen enviously to the English language of the radio, and attend the English-language cinema. They are anxious to master the only linguistic tool which will help them to secure work in the outside world, and few of them share the sentimental notions about their language which the professional revivalists attempt to spread. They are leaving their Gaeltacht homes at a more rapid rate than the young people of any other section of the country.

In spite of these unpleasant facts, many Irish enthusiasts have adopted the concept of the national language as a barrier to cut

off the Irish people from non-Catholic culture. The Irish politicians, during the struggle for independence, seized upon the
language concept as a political weapon, and after 1921 the Free
State wrote a drastic bilingual program into law. Under this,
nearly all government documents must be bilingual, and nearly
all public placards and notices must be either bilingual or exclusively in Irish. Every employee of national or local governments must pass an examination in Irish to secure a civil-service
post, and every student in the national schools must study Irish
for several years. In practice this means that the language is
used as a tool of discrimination against all foreign-born appli-
cants for government posts and, to a certain extent, against native
Protestants who are less enthusiastic than the Catholics about
mastering Irish.

The most important, and most disturbing, fact connected with
the language revival is that hundreds of schools in many sections
of the country teach all of their subjects in Irish. By this practice
the whole tempo and quality of Irish education are adversely
affected. Every recognized teacher in a secondary school must
show fitness to teach in Irish. Thousands of elementary students
and one-fourth of all secondary students attend schools where
the rule of the *exclusive* use of Irish is in force. In Dublin some
of these schools have actually attempted to hold Greek classes in
Irish for children who speak English exclusively in their homes.
In the lower grades of Dublin's primary schools the infants are
given "learning" only in the native tongue. Even in the Abbey
Theatre, the younger actors whose contracts have been written in
recent years must have their names printed on the program exclusively in Irish. On the streets of Dublin the street signs and
government office titles must be in both Irish and English, and
occasionally the English is omitted.

The government spends huge sums in subsidizing and promoting Irish, particularly in the schools. National University students who choose Irish as the medium for the study of a subject in
the classroom are required to pay only half of the standard tuition
fee. Secondary schools which choose Irish as their medium of
instruction are also favored with special government grants. I
have visited normal schools, taught wholly in Irish, where virtually all the students came from English-speaking homes and

were being trained to teach English-speaking children in a tongue which was as unnatural to the teacher as to the children.

The language revival, as a frank Irish Catholic critic once declared in the Dail, tends to make Ireland "illiterate in two languages." This critic, Deputy Frank MacDermott, denounced the language policy of the government as "90 per cent eyewash," and pointed out that to require young children to learn their basic school lessons in a language with which they are not familiar is "to tie a millstone educationally around the necks of those unfortunate children, to befog them, to close their minds, to put a premium upon what is vague and slipshod." The influential Jesuit *Irish Monthly* spoke out in 1949, denouncing Irish primary education in the cities as "a dull, dreary round of memory tests and monotonous repetitions that kill all interest and initiative. . . . The majority think and try to think in the language of their homes, and have to parrot all day in a tongue never heard anywhere save within what they soon evaluate as the prison walls of a school. . . . This is not education . . . the dreary day is often terminated by the escapism of juvenile delinquency." G. A. Olden, writing in the *Irish Times,* has been even more frank:

The revival of Irish has led to more boredom, bad blood and nauseating hypocrisy than any of our national aspirations. Let it be spoken "consciously and for pleasure" and we may yet live to see the day when it will cease to be the bane of the Civil Service, the sneaking embarrassment of innumerable T.D.'s [members of the Dail], and the innocent cause of more sullen antipathy than the other subjects of the school curriculum put together.

I am convinced that 90 per cent of the educated people of the Irish Republic secretly agree with these quoted opinions, but they dare not speak out for fear of being branded anti-Irish and anti-Catholic. The official proponents of the language are a little like the losing presidential candidate in the hour before he admits defeat in an election: all the candidate's friends know that he has been beaten, but no one is permitted to acknowledge the fact openly until the candidate himself accepts defeat.

It is the compulsory aspect of the government's program in the schools and the civil service which has aroused the deepest resentment. Although a great many people now read some

Irish, and about one person in five in the Republic speaks it a little, it has not gained in popularity in recent years, and the proportion of the people who actually speak it has increased only slightly since 1921. To an American ear it seems harsh and unmusical. Although I have heard many speeches in Irish, I have never heard anything in the native tongue which sounded easy and natural, except one well-rehearsed play at the Abbey Theatre. The politicians who learn enough Irish to make short and stumbling speeches in the language never seem to enjoy the painful performance, and the audiences enjoy the experience even less. The children who study Irish in the schools soon revert to English as the working language of their lives, and in the Dublin area about one-third of them forget it almost completely. This is quite understandable, since their books and newspapers are almost entirely in English, and since their conversation is in English. The small Irish sections in the daily newspapers are maintained only as a matter of form, and the books published in Irish constitute a very small and unattractive library.

In spite of the tremendous campaign of government promotion and the financial favoritism granted to schools that adopt Irish, the inescapable truth is that the language is rapidly dying, and this fact is almost universally admitted privately by the leaders of both church and state. There is, as Arland Ussher says, "no thought whatever being produced in Irish." No one, of course, would oppose the study of Irish as a special language of culture like Latin; but its use as an exclusive or major medium of reflection and communication seems to be doomed. The leaders of the Church seem almost ready to accept this basic fact, and it is generally admitted that they are cooling off in their championship of the language. There are many good reasons why they, as Catholics, should cease to advocate Irish. Catholic education in the Republic is already completely segregated education, and the Catholic children do not need an additional linguistic barrier to protect them from English Protestant "paganism." In the meantime Ireland, as the Catholic missionary center of the English-speaking world, must use English in its program of missionary expansion, and English happens to be the language of the United States, where Irish priests and nuns are finding fertile fields of employment. Accordingly, although the priests continue to pay lip service to the Irish language and to denounce English literature, they preach their sermons and write their books in the language of the Protestant enemy. No one is quite ready to admit that the language revival has become a national farce, but the Church is foresighted enough to adopt a realistic policy in private.

Balance Sheet of Values

In perspective the segregated schools of the Irish Republic can be rated good or bad according to the observer's attitude towards denominational aims in education. There is no doubt that these schools tend to preserve the faith of the children, and many parents regard this preservation as the most important factor in education. Irish Protestants want segregated education for social reasons, even when they deplore denominational culture as such. Protestant children do not suffer so much as Catholic children from rigid and antiquated methods in education, because Protestant training is less mechanical and dogmatic — although, strangely enough, corporal punishment still persists in both Protestant and Catholic national schools.

It would be difficult to measure the cultural effect of the Catholic schools apart from the total Catholic environment. All the Catholic people of Ireland tend to live in cultural isolation because of the priestly fear of non-Catholic books and newspapers. No independent studies of the quality of education in the Catholic schools have ever been made, and it is likely that any candid and impartial survey would meet with immediate clerical opposition. Without such a survey it is impossible to say with any accuracy whether Catholic education is much worse than non-Catholic education. A 1911 test of illiteracy showed that in the Dublin area the rate of illiteracy among Catholics was more than six times that among Protestants; and in Ulster the disparity was almost as great. But no one knows how much of this disparity was due to inequality of opportunity for education.

The priests regard their school system as their own business, and it is impossible to find in the educational literature of Ireland any frank and searching criticism. For them the system has justified itself in keeping the Irish people loyal to the faith. They point with pride to the fact that in Ireland the young people who remain in the country do not desert the Church as often as do those in the United States and Great Britain; in "pagan England," the priests estimate, 50 per cent of their youth drift away from the Church shortly after leaving school.

Certain professional aspects of the school system are worthy of some praise. Although the school buildings are often wretchedly dirty, overcrowded, and cold, the Irish government maintains a reasonably high standard of school inspection and teacher training. The over-supply of teachers is so great that only the highest-ranking students in the lower schools are admitted to professional training. The sincere and devoted nuns and brothers who staff so many of the Catholic schools have a permanent life interest in education which gives them some advantages over those lay teachers who regard their profession as temporary. On the whole, the Catholic parents of Ireland seem to be well satisfied with their system of priest-controlled schools, and the Protestant parents are only a little less enthusiastic. For both classes of parents, the concept of religious segregation is so traditional that it is never questioned. Nor is the control of the schools of 97 per cent of the children by a hierarchy appointed in Rome ever publicly questioned on patriotic grounds. During my entire stay in Ireland, I never heard an Irish parent, Catholic or Protestant, voice the elementary question: Why should bishops appointed in Rome determine the educational policies and choose the educational personnel of an Irish school system?

When all the favorable factors have been added up, it cannot be said that the picture of segregated education in Ireland is pleasing. Catholic education is not only dogmatic and partisan; it is also education in which large areas of modern thought are excluded from consideration. Laboratory science tends to be neglected in favor of subjects more congenial to the priests. There is no emphasis on freedom of thought or upon scientific curiosity. In the secondary schools the students are not now required to study any science at all. On the political side, the children are taught that democracy is worthy of respect only when it accords with Catholic principles. This doctrine of conditional loyalty to democracy permeates all the teaching about the modern world in the Catholic schools. No suggestion is ever permitted to enter the curriculum that the Church itself should adopt democracy. Catholic Ireland is represented as the moral exemplar among the nations because it is faithful to Catholic Rome. Spain, Portugal, and Italy are exalted because they are "Christian" nations, more worthy of imitation than any of the Protestant and "materialistic" nations of the West. The priests and nuns are profoundly ignorant of non-Catholic values because they are never given an opportunity to read the literature of Western liberalism; and they drill their narrow outlook into their pupils. Few of the children ever go to school beyond the age of fourteen, and of those enrolled in the elementary schools about 17 per cent are absent at any one time. The absence of free high schools handicaps the poor and tends to make education a privilege of the well-to-do. The prodigious amount of time spent in learning Irish and in attempting to learn other subjects in Irish deadens the whole educational process.

The American Catholic *Register* of Denver declared in a leading article in 1951: "The school systems of Ireland, Holland and Scotland are examples of how the state and the church integrate their resources to produce first, good men, and second, good citizens." Against this judgment can be balanced the more frank opinion of Ireland's present Minister for Education, Sean Moylan, a Catholic, who declared in 1952: "I do not think there is any interest in education amongst the people of this country."

7

Sex, Chastity, and Population

If the control of schools is the first great source of Irish priestly power, the control of sex is the second. In Ireland, everything connected with marriage and sex comes within the scope of the Church's power. Courtship is the business of the Irish priest, and petting is the business of the Irish priest, and even the etiquette of the marriage bed is the business of the Irish priest — as well as birth control, abortion, mixed marriage, illegitimacy, sodomy, masturbation, divorce, separation, sex education, and "keeping company." Every Irish Catholic is trained to accept the rule of his Church in all these areas as a matter of course, and in practice he accepts such supervision of personal conduct with far more docility than his fellow Catholics in Latin countries.

Priestly control of family relations is written into the Irish Constitution in somewhat ambiguous phrases. These phrases may be read either as a charter of personal power for all parents or as a declaration of dependence upon the Church. Article 41 of the Constitution leads off with a general declaration:

> The State recognises the Family as the natural primary and fundamental unit group of Society, and as a moral institution possessing inalienable and imprescriptible rights, antecedent and superior to all positive law.
>
> The State, therefore, guarantees to protect the Family in its constitution and authority, as the necessary basis of social order and as indispensable to the welfare of the Nation and the State.

The phrase "antecedent and superior to all positive law" means, in a Catholic country, that no democratic legislative body has the moral right to pass any law which, in the opinion of the Catholic bishops, encroaches upon moral essentials. The Constitution pledges the nation "to protect the Family in its constitution and authority, as the necessary basis of social order," and to prevent the breaking up of families through neglect on the part of working mothers employed outside the home. Then it pledges the government to support the Catholic conception of marriage, and it prohibits divorce:

The State pledges itself to guard with special care the institution of Marriage, on which the Family is founded, and to protect it against attack.

No law shall be enacted providing for the grant of a dissolution of marriage.

No person whose marriage has been dissolved under the civil law of any other State but is a subsisting valid marriage under the law for the time being in force within the jurisdiction of the Government and Parliament established by this Constitution shall be capable of contracting a valid marriage within that jurisdiction during the lifetime of the other party to the marriage so dissolved.

It is not strange that a Catholic country like the Republic should prohibit divorce, since this policy is universally advocated by the Church. What makes the Irish policy on marriage unique is that Ireland is probably the only place of any considerable size in the world today where the entire Catholic sexual code is accepted at face value. The Irish priests and nuns are sincere celibates who accept virginity with sober enthusiasm. Irish married couples rarely divorce each other, and Irish cities have no licensed prostitution. The mere statement of these facts distinguishes the Irish Republic from other Catholic countries, particularly from Latin countries like Spain and Italy, where the Catholic sexual code is more honored in the breach than in the observance. In Italy, for example, there are seven hundred licensed brothels, some of them almost in the shadow of St. Peter's, tolerated by a Christian Democratic government which received the unofficial support of the Church for many years. In Italy also, there are literally millions of "good" Catholics living together without benefit of clergy because the Catholic law will not permit divorce and remarriage when a legal union has failed.

In Ireland this typically Latin situation is reversed. Outwardly and officially at least, the Irish Catholics accept their Church's

standard of sexual conduct. If there is some rebellion against
that standard — and there is not much doubt that Irish young
people feel rebellious — it is an unsuccessful rebellion which
rarely reaches the level of public protest. The Irish priests have
been so triumphant in imposing their sexual standards upon the
people that they are now somewhat embarrassed by their own
success. They have exalted virginity to the point where it is
almost a national catastrophe: they have surrounded the sins
of the flesh with such a poignant sense of guilt that they have
weakened the Irish mating instinct.

An Unsuccessful Laboratory of Love

Today the Irish Republic is the least successful laboratory
of love in the whole world. The Irish girl of 22 has less chance
of marriage in Ireland than a girl of the same age in any other
country. This is an astonishing fact in a country whose priests
constantly preach the virtues of marital bliss, and it is a fact
which the priests themselves admit rather ruefully. Sometimes
they blame the failure of Irish family life on economic factors,
and there is no doubt that economic causes play a major part in
delaying and preventing marriage; but the anti-sexual attitude
of the priests and nuns themselves also plays a substantial part.
Ireland's failure as an exhibit of Catholic family life is in part
due to the triumph of celibacy over sex.

The present sorry condition of the Irish family as a reproductive unit has been described by many orthodox writers in the
United States and Ireland. One of America's best-known priests,
Father John A. O'Brien of Notre Dame, writing in *St. Joseph's
Magazine* after a tour of Ireland, said that "Ireland is rapidly
becoming a nation of bachelors and spinsters; the Irish people
will soon become extinct if they do not increase the marriage
rate." Father O'Brien described the Republic as a country which
is "rapidly becoming a land of foreigners, where the extinct Irish
will be found only in mausoleums, tombs and graves." Kevin
Devlin, writing in one of Ireland's most orthodox priestly journals, *Christus Rex,* deplored Father O'Brien's "apocalyptic
rhetoric," but admitted that his facts "are correct as far as they
go," and that Ireland is suffering from a "hardening of the national arteries." He pointed out that "only 2 out of every 5 Irish-

men between 30 and 34 are married, the lowest proportion in the world"; that "65 per cent of the population is single, and only 28 per cent married"; and that "Ireland has the highest recorded marriage age in the world." Continued Devlin:

> In England and Wales, the marriage rate for 1949 was 8.5: in Scotland it was 8.1: in Ireland it was 5.45. The 1946 census showed that of all those over thirty-five years of age, 46.6 per cent of the men and 29.5 per cent of the women in rural areas were unmarried; and 33.7 per cent of the men and 34.8 per cent of the women in urban areas. In the whole country more than two-thirds of the men between the ages of 20 and 44 were still single. The average marriage age for men is 35, and for women 29. About one-fourth of the population never marries at all, about one-tenth in England.

Devlin's analysis is quite unassailable, and the evidence to support his statements is apparent everywhere in Ireland today. The 1951 census showed that the percentage of the unmarried is still the highest in the world. The Irish towns and the Irish countryside have an astonishing number of bachelors and old maids. The frequent photographs in the Dublin newspapers of "young" married couples, with their balding grooms and their aging brides, look like extracts from the albums of the middle-aged. Whatever may be the cause, it is obvious that marriage in Ireland is surrounded with such anxieties, hesitations, and fears that only the brave, the foolish, and the well-to-do dare to undertake it at the age which is common in other countries.

Some Irish Catholic writers and priests have tried to explain the national marriage debacle in moral terms. "How have we betrayed the family?" asks Sean de Cleir in *Christus Rex*:

> We have betrayed it largely by sins of omission. . . . In the rural areas clearly defined classes of men are for all practical purposes totally celibate. . . . Non-marrying and late marrying force the young women to forsake the countryside. . . . Here there can be no question of alien influence. . . . There is here a disregard for the duties and the privileges of parenthood which ill becomes Catholic men. . . . Our fields are lonely of children. . . . If our people will not marry, let us remember that they are a Catholic people and preach to them the Vocation of Matrimony.

Preaching, however, has not thus far had much tonic effect on the Republic's marital situation. Neither Protestant nor Catholic marriage can be described as very successful in the

Republic. The Protestant birth rate is even lower than the Catholic, but this condition is largely due to the greater age of the Protestant segment in the population. The left-overs of the Protestant Ascendancy are relatively old, and no one expects them to reproduce as rapidly as the Catholics; in 1936, 38 per cent of the Protestants were more than 45 years of age as against 29 per cent of the Catholics. For the Irish Catholics there is no logical alibi for the failure to maintain the Irish population. The country now is theirs, and the future belongs to them, but they are running away from their new Republic by the thousands, so that the country is compelled to announce year by year that its net population is decreasing. The situation is worsened by the fact that it is the marriageable young women who are running away in the greatest numbers and thus reducing the possibility of marriage for the men who are left behind. "What is to become of a country whose women leave it?" asks B. J. P. F. Waters, head of the Irish guild of Catholic doctors. "What is the future of a nation where young women, the potential and irreplaceable mothers of the race, stream out of it? Already the women of Ireland are much fewer than the men."

The drift away from the Irish land and the Irish family is not, of course, a new thing; it began more than a century ago, and it has never stopped. It is a two-stage drift — from the country to the city, and from the city to England, Australia, Canada or the United States. Today the whole island has less than half as many people as it had in 1840; Southern Ireland was the only national region in the world which recorded a smaller population in 1950 than in 1900.

At the beginning of this drift away from Ireland two adverse forces united to produce the tragedy — the great potato famine of 1845, and the absence of opportunity for farm workers to own enough land to support a normal family. The great Irish estates were for many generations parceled out by royal grant to faithful subjects of the English Crown, and the farm workers were left to suffer continuing poverty as landless peasants. While these conditions have now been remedied and the Irish Land Acts have brought about a considerable redistribution in ownership of the once-great plantations, the life of the Irish peasant is still very difficult. The average Irish farmer does not own enough land to justify division among several sons, and the sons who do not inherit have no safe future. Nor do the sons who inherit land in their late middle age have a much happier time, since their fathers in the new day of preventive medicine tend to live so long that they do not give their sons economic independence until "the boys" have reached 50 or 60 years of age.

But when all these economic and biological difficulties are taken into account, there is a puzzling failure of Irish marriage as a social institution, and honest critics admit their inability to explain the failure wholly in economic terms. There is a failure of marriage entirely apart from the failure of reproduction. The nation, with all its rural poverty, does not offer to its small farmers less opportunity than many continental Catholic countries where the marriage rate and the birth rate are both quite high. The Irish countryman refuses marriage in his youthful years even when his economic anxieties are relieved. This conclusion is supported by the fact that the government's efforts to stimulate early marriage by the granting of economic rewards and bonuses have not met with much success. Extra inducement has not produced a birth rate which compensates the nation for the loss from migration. A national family-allowance system, encouraged by the Church and costing the taxpayers $14,000,000 a year, has also failed to lift the birth rate high enough to outbalance migration.

Mortal Migration

The failure of early marriage, however, would not seriously handicap the growth of the Republic if the nation could halt the flow of migration. It is migration which is striking the mortal blow at Irish family life. Year by year, when Irish men and women marry, they reproduce as rapidly thereafter as other married people in other nations. The reproductive rate is only a little lower in the Republic than it is in Northern Ireland; the crude birth rate is almost as high as that of the United States, because the fertility rate *after* the late Irish marriages is high. But the Irish natural increase is all drained off in migration, and as a result year by year the number of children of school age declines. In many rural districts, once-crowded classrooms are being abandoned. In western Ireland there are ghost towns where nearly all the young people have left to go to England and

America. Early in 1953 the government announced with evident relief that the latest 5-year population census, dated April 8, 1951, for the first time in a hundred years revealed not an actual loss in total population, but rather an increase of two-tenths of 1 per cent. The basis for optimism, however, was very slight. Southern Ireland has actually lost in numbers since independence came; its population is 0.4 per cent less than in 1926, while the Northern population is 2.4 per cent higher. The net emigration is continuing to rise, and it has risen steadily ever since the war. The nation now has the lowest proportion of the "young active" age group of any nation in the world for which figures are available.

Many reasons have been advanced to explain why the Irish people leave home. The opportunities for employment are greater in other English-speaking countries, and those countries do not raise barriers against the Irish newcomer. The Irish immigrant communities in Britain, Australia, Canada, and the United States have been so successfully organized as Irish social units that they are often more attractive than the Irish communities at home. Also, the Irish in both Britain and the United States have been willing to shoulder certain onerous types of labor which British and American workers prefer to avoid. Britain needs servants and nurses, and the Irish girls are willing; Britain needs unskilled factory work and unskilled laborers in the heavy industries, and the Irish boys from the farms are willing. So Britain admits Irish young men and women without formality, and usually gives them, in cities like Liverpool, London, and Glasgow, steadier employment at higher wages than they could earn at home. Australia also has welcomed many Irish workers, and encouraged them with travel grants. Canada absorbs some, and guarantees them unemployment benefits. The United States immigration quota for the Republic, about 17,000 a year, is still large enough to accommodate all the Irish who desire an American future, but only about one-fourth of the quota has been filled in recent years. At present the first preference of the Irish emigrant is England, partly because it is easy to return home when the occasion arises.

When all these reasons for a flight from Ireland have been mentioned, there still remains a suspicion that Irish young people are leaving their nation largely because it is a poor place in which to be happy and free. Have the priests created a civilization in which the chief values of youth and love are subordinate to Catholic discipline? This is the question which many observers have asked, especially in analyzing the failure of the Irish countryside. The majority of the Irish still live in the country, and it is the countryside which is being deserted most swiftly by the young people. Also, it is in the countryside that the priest reigns most completely. It was Blake in his *Proverbs of Hell* who said, "As the caterpillar chooses the fairest leaves to lay her eggs on, so the priest lays his curse on the fairest joys."

Many Irish writers have written about the effect of the anti-sexual philosophy of the priests upon Irish country life. In his play *The White Steed,* Paul Vincent Carroll describes the priest-led witch-hunt directed against a decent Catholic girl in an Irish village because she has gone walking with her boy friend in a dark lane to escape from the only place she can call home — "a white-washed hovel with two rooms." The intolerant young priest discharges her as village librarian, and simultaneously discharges a Catholic schoolteacher for keeping company with "a girl of alien faith" — a Protestant.

W. P. Ryan, after serving as editor of an Irish rural paper for many years, described in *The Pope's Green Island* the tyranny of the Irish priest over the love life and amusements of his people, blaming the English occupation for conniving to permit priestly dominance in Irish life as a support for British rule. Then he went on to tell how often, in the Irish countryside,

. . . the heart and spirit gave way in a sort of terrorism before the priest. In his [the priest's] day of dominance he did much to make Irish local life a dreary desert. He urged war on the favorite cross-roads dances — with exceptions here and there — and on other gatherings where young men and women congregated, even in the company of their older relations and friends. Indeed there were cases where the priest, whip in hand, entered private houses and dispersed social parties. . . . After several changes theologians had fixed the number of Deadly Sins as seven; Irish parish priests in practice made courtship an eighth. For lovers to walk the roadside in Ireland when the average priest was abroad was a perilous adventure. He challenged engaged couples, on occasions he challenged married people. . . . Their [the priests'] sere and shortsighted teaching on the subject of love, or rather their denunciation of it, has done much to blight and mar and materialize humanity in a deal of rural Ireland. It is largely, though not wholly, responsible for the fact that marriages in the Irish farming class — to a goodly extent their own class — are often repellently materialistic, the outcome of "match-making," which is human buying and selling.

Ryan's indictment needs to be modified only slightly to be applicable today. There is still a surprising amount of arranged and commercially managed marriage in Ireland, and the village priests co-operate in maintaining the tradition of management. The practice of the cash dowry from the family of the bride is almost universal in the countryside — in this respect the recent film *The Quiet Man* is scarcely an exaggeration. Sometimes commercialism is so dominant in the match that men and women are brought to the altar as virtual strangers. Usually the rural Irish match is arranged formally through a "speaker," who bargains and haggles over the girl's dowry and the groom's cattle with all the romantic delicacy of a horse-trader. The girl's fortune in the deal goes to the groom's father, and the father in turn makes over to his marrying son the major interest in his farm to start the new couple on the road to security. It would be difficult to imagine a tradition which is less romantic or less likely to endear Irish village life to young people who have glimpsed the headstrong independence of love à la Hollywood.

The Priest as Moral Policeman

The power of the priest as a moral policeman in rural life has steadily declined since the days when Ryan wrote *The Pope's Green Island*. But the celibate priests are still anti-sexual in their emphasis, and they have softened their puritanical code, not because of any change of heart, but only because of new cultural competition. They are being challenged not only by cinema, radio, and television, but even more successfully by the increased opportunity afforded to young Irish people of going abroad. In some regions they are in full retreat before these modern tendencies and are less the masters than the alarmed chaperons of young Ireland. But they still have the power to make rural life miserable for young people, and if their power has declined it is largely because the young people have discovered that their counterparts in other countries have much more freedom from priestly control.

The effect of the teaching of the priests in matters of sex is still evident in the recruitment of thousands of young Irish people into the lifelong celibacy of the religious orders. Ireland still honors the priest and the nun as the highest exemplars of professional status. Almost one-third of all the professional people of the Republic are in the direct service of the Church, about 20,000 priests, nuns, and brothers; and they occupy dominant positions in the schools, universities, hospitals, and allied institutions. "The Irish in modern times," says Arland Ussher, "have had no native upper caste except the priesthood, with the consequence that the typical Irishman is a little like a priest." Automatically, by their example, the priests serve as perpetual propagandists for chastity. In their public pronouncements they exalt the virgin state and, implicitly at least, condemn sexual intercourse. Naturally, they stress the superior holiness of virginity in their campaigns for vocations.

"Chastity," says Father Sean MacGuire, in an important article on "Keeping Company," in the *Irish Ecclesiastical Record*, "is not a mystic virtue, a virtue of the cloister and the initiated; it is a moral and social virtue, a virtue necessary to the life of the human race. Without it, life withers in its sources, beauty is effaced from the visage, kindness withdraws itself from the heart. . . . All evils, in fine, enter by that door." The priestly propaganda on sex relations is strikingly unrealistic. The Church's pamphlets on sex education, nearly all written by celibates, scarcely mention sexual intercourse, and the moral textbooks used in the schools treat of matrimony, at arm's length, as a solemn ecclesiastical problem. The teaching of the priests on sexual matters is as heavy and ominous as a funeral march. "Is Temptation Ever Irresistible?" asks Father David Barry in an entirely non-humorous article in the *Irish Ecclesiastical Record*. His judiciously negative answer is highlighted with a quotation from Genesis 4:7, "But the lust thereof shall be under thee, and thou shalt have dominion over it."

The antagonistic attitude toward sex as an impediment to moral excellence pervades the whole educational system. Co-education is avoided in Irish higher schools wherever possible. The emphasis on virginity in all recruitment campaigns turns the impulses of many Irish young women away from natural sex

desires at a time when young women in other countries are thinking of marriage. The recruitment of priests and brothers takes
out of circulation thousands of Ireland's natural husbands. Dublin theater audiences laughed appreciatively in 1952 during the
performance of a theatrical hit by Maura Laverty when an
Irish spinster, despairing of acquiring a husband, lashed out at
the Christian Brothers for destroying the desires of the young
men of Ireland by their attacks on the sins of the flesh. In the
famous banned poem *The Midnight Court,* by Bryan Merriman,
as translated by Frank O'Connor, an Irish maid hurls this accusation at the Irish priests:

> Has the Catholic Church a glimmer of sense
> That the priests won't marry like anyone else?
> Is it any wonder the way I am,
> Out of my mind for the want of a man,
> When there's men by the score with looks and leisure,
> Walking the roads and scorning pleasure?
> The full of a fair of primest beef,
> Warranted to afford relief,
> Cherry-red cheeks and bull-like voices,
> And bellies dripping with fat in slices,
> Backs erect and heavy hind quarters,
> Hot-blooded men, the best of partners,
> Freshness and charm, youth and good looks
> And nothing to ease their mind but books! . . .
> It passes the wit of mortal man
> What Ireland has lost by this stupid ban.

And the fairy queen replies:

> In the matter of priests a change is due,
> And I think I may say that it's coming too,
> For any day now it may come to their knowledge
> That the case has been judged by the cardinal's college,
> And we'll hear no more of the ban on marriage.

This cheerful prophecy of the end of celibacy for the priesthood
has nothing to support it except a lady's wish; and even if 99
per cent of all Irish Catholics wanted their priests to marry, the
release would have to come from a celibate hierarchy in Rome.

Irish priests are frequently taken into the seminaries at the
age of 17 or earlier, but ordination usually comes at about 23.
Most young men are mature enough at that age to understand

the full sacrifice which they make by sexual renunciation. In fact, the realization of the unnaturalness of male chastity is probably one of the most important factors in reducing the number of priestly students at Maynooth; about one-third of them drop out during the course of the seven-year routine. Although the school does not compel students to continue in the priesthood when they decide to change their profession, their very isolation from all normal adolescent recreation with members of the opposite sex from the age 17 onwards conditions them toward celibacy. At Maynooth and in other seminaries, they receive intensive training in Catholic anti-sexual discipline.

The religious orders advertise in the Irish Catholic press for boys and girls of tender years as recruits; when they are once drawn into the routine of the orders, their whole thoughts are turned away from marriage as something to be shunned. The Marist Brothers receive "juniorates" at the age of 13; the Franciscan Brothers at "over 13"; the Presentation Brothers at "about 14." The postulants of the Brothers of St. Patrick begin at 14. In the words of Father Francis Cassilly, S.J., "the tender sprout must be carefully tended, and shielded from wind and storm until it grows into maturity. In like manner, a young person who desires to serve God, should be placed in an atmosphere favourable to the development of his design, and guarded from sinister influence, until he has acquired stability of purpose and strength of virtue."

In England the recruiting of nuns has almost stopped, except for the Irish girls who come across the Irish Sea, because among modern English girls the notion that a life of service is necessarily based on sexual denial is rapidly disappearing. But in Ireland itself chastity, poverty, and obedience are still firmly and successfully linked, and the convents continue to secure much of the best blood of the younger generation. Recruiting of girls as postulants takes place at 16, and thereafter only a miracle can return them to the world of marriage and motherhood. Since the cradle and the convent cannot both be victorious, the cradle tends to lose. The conflict has become so acute that occasionally the priestly journals recognize it and endorse marriage, at least obliquely, as a reasonable alternative to virginity. But the endorsement of marriage for *other* people by a celibate caste of

20,000 Irish men and women scarcely balances the force of the living example of renunciation offered to Catholic young people.

Celibacy has a prestige in Ireland which it cannot claim in any other country, and that prestige serves to lower the social standing of marriage. The priests, ambitious for their own clerical institutions, exploit the alleged superiority of chastity over marriage in order to fortify those institutions against decline. In October 1952 the Very Rev. John D'Elbee, Superior General of the Congregation of the Sacred Heart, arrived in Ireland to work for the benefit of his order, which recruits boys for service as priests and brothers. "YOUNG MARRIED COUPLE ENTERED ORDERS" was the headline of greeting to Father D'Elbee in the Dublin *Standard*. The feature story described the French priest as a moral hero because, though "happily married," he had renounced marriage in his middle years and had become a celibate, while his wife had simultaneously renounced wedlock and entered a cloistered Carmelite convent in Louvain. The two "spiritually divorced" spouses were offered to the Irish Catholic public as examples worthy of emulation.

The Catholic young people of Ireland suffer from the sexual ignorance and narrowness of their priests and nuns in many ways. The priests will not countenance any frank teaching on sex in the Catholic schools, and they are themselves unable to give such teaching in their churches. (Sean O'Faolain, in his brilliant story "Sinners," has described the stumbling embarrassment of an Irish canon groping for usable words about sex while hearing the confession of an adolescent girl.) Even that liberal and independent Catholic, Dr. Noel Browne, when publicly asked about sex education in Irish schools in 1949 while he was Minister for Health, replied: "In general it is considered that, in view of the moral integrity and strong family life which results from the moral and religious teaching so readily and widely available in this country, it is neither necessary or desirable to risk the doubtful consequences of sex-education of youth."

The Effect of Sexual Taboos

In such an atmosphere, the subjects of prostitution and venereal disease are almost universally taboo. When the *Irish*

Times had the courage to print a series of articles on venereal disease in Ireland, its careful factual discussion was greeted with dismay in higher Catholic circles, and the subject was almost completely boycotted by the Catholic press. One of the unfortunate effects of this evasive habit of mind in dealing with the subject, as the *Times* discovered, is that Irish V.D. patients who report to medical agencies for cures do not usually complete them. The stigma which Catholic propaganda has attached to the whole subject of sex has greatly impeded the government in fighting the "secret" diseases.

Actually, although the head of the Irish guild of Catholic doctors in 1938 warned the nation against venereal disease, as well as sexual misconduct, there is no reason to believe that the sexual standards in the Republic today are lower than in other nations, or that the venereal disease rate is higher. Judgments in this area are necessarily tentative and subject to revision, but it is clear that the Irish Republic is quite free from licensed prostitution and that the public opinion of the country is genuinely hostile to departures from the Christian monogamous ideal. Especially in the countryside, adultery is socially disgraceful and, when exposed, usually a cause for social ostracism. As for the standards of the priests themselves, I heard of only one illegitimate child of a priest during my entire stay in the country. It is apparent that the priests practice what they preach, and the people respect their abnegation.

Nevertheless, the paradox and the riddle of Irish sexual life persist. Irish men and women in England and America are obviously persons of normal vigor. What makes their sexual conduct so abnormal in the old country? Men do not wait until the age of 35 and women to the age of 29 to marry unless there are some unusual sexual factors involved. Even poverty and the browbeating of the priests seem inadequate to explain such abstinence. Men do not give up one of life's basic sources of happiness without some compensation. The priests and nuns are fortified and rewarded for their renunciation by many social compensations; they are given a special dignity and veneration in return for their sacrifice. What do the ordinary young people of Ireland do to compensate themselves for the frustrations of delayed marriage?

There are many answers to that question, some of them in print and many more circulating in the underworld of Dublin gossip. I can only record here the conclusions given in private conversation by a score or more of Ireland's leading physicians, writers, and social workers. Some say that masturbation is the answer, and that Irish men, particularly, from adolescence to marriage masturbate very frequently — James Joyce discussed this factor in *Stephen Hero*. Some say that the moist climate damps down sexual ardor in both men and women to the point where it is less persistent and demanding than it is in other countries. Some say that there is a great deal of extra-marital and pre-marital intercourse, especially in the cities, and that the unfortunate results are concealed by the fact that pregnant girls escape to England for the delivery of their illegitimate children. Some say that unofficial and unlicensed prostitution is much more extensive than is commonly supposed.

Perhaps there is some truth in all of these theories. My own inclination is to believe that, whatever the explanation, the total sexual expression of the Irish people is much less than it is in other countries, and that the Catholic crusade against normal sexual life has actually created a nation of men and women who try to drown their fundamental instincts. This explanation has some slight historical support. Ireland was, in the age of monasticism, one of the world's most ascetic countries, and the monastic ideal has undoubtedly left a deep mark on the Irish mind. Although Irish priests were permitted to have wives as late as the eighth century, sexual renunciation came to be identified with virtue and distinction in the community, and thousands of the best men and women lived apart from each other. Kevin Devlin in his *Christus Rex* article on "Single and Selfish," to which I have already referred, says of the ancient Irish that "when they 'fell in love with Christianity' . . . they took to the ideal of virginity with a Pauline enthusiasm unknown elsewhere. St. Patrick himself noted this with an inflection of surprise in the *Confession:* 'The sons of Irishmen and daughters of their chieftains desire to become monks and virgins of Christ.' "

The charge that Irish young men and women produce an unusually large number of illegitimate children in the long years preceding marriage is impossible to prove or disprove. The prohibition of birth control would naturally tend to produce such a result, but the generally high standards of the people would militate against such a deduction. One thing is certain: Irish Catholics, regarding illegitimacy as supremely disgraceful, make desperate attempts to conceal it. Frequently they send unmarried girls to English hospitals for deliveries. In a single year recently, one English hospital near London had 290 illegitimate babies born to young Irish mothers. This extra-territorial activity explains why there is in England a great surplus of illegitimate Catholic children for adoption, while there is a long waiting list for the relatively small number of Protestant foundlings. "The Catholic surplus of babies," says Margaret Kornitzer in her *Child Adoption in the Modern World,* "is due to the influx of foreign and Irish Catholic girls, not domiciled in this country, whose babies have to be absorbed by the domiciled Catholic population."

Irish girls in Ireland rarely resort to criminal abortion, because the law against criminal abortion is so strictly enforced, and because Church taboos against abortion are so strong. Even therapeutic abortion, when indicated as the sole remedy required to save the life of a mother, is allowed in only one hospital of the Republic. When Pius XII, in October 1951, reaffirmed the papal doctrine of the equality of mother and fetus in childbirth — under which a Catholic mother is permitted to die even if therapeutic abortion is the only means of saving her — the announcement was accepted without demur by the Irish press, while the storm of criticism in London could be heard across the Atlantic. The birth of so many illegitimate Irish Catholic babies abroad, of course, makes all government statistics on illegitimacy in Ireland quite useless. The official illegitimacy rate is not at all alarming — about 2,500 babies a year, less than 1 in 25 births. The rate in the United States is about 1 in 42 births.

One of the reasons for late marriage is undoubtedly the official prohibition of birth control. Contraception is illegal under all circumstances, and even a non-Catholic doctor is liable to imprisonment for giving a contraceptive device to his own non-Catholic patient. Oddly enough, an Irish doctor who merely gives contraceptive *advice* to his patient is not penalized in the Republic; in this respect the statute is less severe than the law in Massachusetts, where a non-Catholic doctor may be jailed for merely advising contraceptives for a non-Catholic patient.

A Nation Without Birth Control

The Irish Republic is probably the only nation in the world today which takes the Catholic strictures on birth control with full seriousness. The chemists refuse to sell contraceptive goods even when labeled "For the prevention of disease only" — a rule which distinguishes them from Catholic-owned drugstores in both Boston and Rome. No medical or economic necessity is permitted to alter this rule. Recently a prominent Protestant physician of Dublin privately tested the government's policy on this point in the case of two of his patients, a husband and wife both of whom were suffering from advanced tuberculosis. Pregnancy might have meant death to the wife, and it would have imposed on the husband a crippling economic burden. This Protestant physician and a leading Protestant chemist petitioned the government for permission to bring into the Republic a small supply of contraceptives for this tubercular couple alone. The petition was rejected in a blunt, one-sentence letter of refusal.

The well-to-do, of course, can evade this priestly prohibition by going to Belfast or Liverpool, where British freedom and British frankness on the subject result in window displays of approved devices for family planning. It is the Irish poor who suffer. They are told by the priests that absolute continence and the rhythm method of birth control are the only two moral means for family limitation. Usually the rhythm method is not mentioned as acceptable. The Irish hierarchy's position on the subject of birth control was summed up in the pamphlet *The Young Husband*, published under the Imprimatur of the Archbishop of Dublin:

> Keep your young married life unstained by this crime. Let there be no speculation, but live in accordance with God's Holy Will. The one who desires to limit the number of his children will come under God's anger. There may be very serious reasons for limiting the number of children — illness, great danger to health, and so on. In such a case the married pair must use their willpower and prudence, and live as brother and sister. Such abstinence is difficult, but possible. And there is no other way.

Under such a rule, young Irish couples naturally hesitate to marry until they are able to support a number of children, and this inhibition undoubtedly helps to explain the advanced age of Irish brides and grooms. In America and England the young people of comparable age and social status marry early and continue working, after agreeing to plan their families.

The Irish priests take such an extreme position on this subject that they will not permit an Irish wife to co-operate in sexual intercourse even passively if the husband uses contraceptives — a prohibition more severe than the present Catholic rule in the United States. In such circumstances, according to the Irish priests, "the woman's obligation of resistance is precisely the same as that of a virgin threatened with rape." The priest-editors of the *Irish Ecclesiastical Record* were asked in March 1948 whether a wife whose husband threatened to send their children to a Protestant school unless she passively accepted intercourse with a contraceptive device should yield to her husband's ultimatum. The editors replied, citing the Sacred Penitentiary, that "it is perfectly clear that a woman is bound positively to resist her husband who attempts condomistic intercourse. She may not remain passive . . . this means active, forceful resistance which may be discontinued only in the face of the greatest actual danger." The threat of sending children to a Protestant school, although recognized as a great evil, was "not a sufficiently grave cause to justify the wife's passivity." Since this rule applies to all Protestant husbands in mixed marriages, it is evident that the Protestant who marries a Catholic before a priest in Ireland not only must surrender the religion of his children to the priest, but also must submit to priestly regulation of the marriage bed.

For a number of years the Irish priests, acting in collaboration with the English hierarchy, succeeded in banning absorbent vaginal tampons for feminine hygiene from sale in Ireland. In a very solemn article in 1949, "The Morality of the Use of Tampons," the Reverend J. McCarthy, D.D., D.C.L., of Maynooth, personally deplored the use of tampons by Irish Catholic women, since they "can easily be a grave source of temptation, especially to those who have strong physical desires." He said that they were "definitely unlawful" in the absence of necessity. He did not cite any feminine authority for this judgment, but he did cite the ruling of the hierarchy of England and Wales in an official 1940 statement, which "disapproved of the use of internal tampons instead of sanitary towels, and asked the Union of Catholic Women to make their decision known to all Catholic Women's Societies." For a time one popular tampon was not sold in Ireland because of this ruling. But now it may be purchased universally. The priestly ruling on the subject broke down, after a great deal of subdued laughter.

The attack on birth control is similar to the bitter and uninformed campaigns in the United States, and Catholic doctors' associations dare not resist or expose the ignorance of the priests. Nowhere in the Republic could any young Irish person discover for himself that his nation stands alone among English-speaking countries in its position on birth control, and that the overwhelming majority of the people of the West accept contraception as a respectable practice. The branches of the National University do not present to their students a candid analysis of the world population problem, nor would any Catholic medical school dare to discuss the subject scientifically. In the excellent Catholic Central Library of Dublin, even the books *against* birth control are kept under lock and key, lest the mere statement of the arguments which the priests must demolish might corrupt the Catholic young.

As a Catholic state, the Republic also carries this attitude on birth control into international bodies on which it is represented. (The Republic is not a member of the United Nations, but it belongs to auxiliary agencies of the U.N.) In May 1952, the battle on birth control in the assembly of the World Health Organization in Geneva came to a climax when Dr. Karl Evang of Norway proposed a study of the "health aspects" of the population problem, including birth control. "The Catholic representatives present," boasted the London *Tablet,* "were united in the condemnation of the proposal, and its rejection seems to have been mainly due to their combined efforts." It was Ireland's representative to the W.H.O. who backed up the Catholic leader of the opposition, Dr. J. J. van de Claseyde of Belgium, by threatening that the proposed study might "lead immediately to the resignation of a large number of States." The non-Catholic powers promptly surrendered.

Irish Catholic pressure was not so successful twenty years

earlier when the League of Nations issued a report by its Committee on Maternal Welfare endorsing birth control under specified circumstances. The Irish Free State delegation, acting under Vatican directives, then attempted to block the issuance of the report — but succeeded only in getting a slight modification.

One of the most ominous features of the Irish Catholic war on birth control is the exportation to Africa and the Orient of the Irish taboos on the subject via the Irish priests and nuns who go there as missionaries. (The same, of course, is true of Catholic missionaries from other nations.) Irish Catholicism is strong in some parts of Asia, and it is probably the most important missionary force in Africa today. Everywhere the priests and nuns teach the non-white races that even the most elementary efforts at family limitation are sinful. British medical officers in such colonies as the Gold Coast find their attempts to teach the concept of smaller families to hungry natives completely defeated by the Irish priests.

A Nation Without Divorce

The late Bishop of Cork, Dr. Daniel Cohalan, in a letter read at all Masses in his diocese on October 1, 1950, declared: "We thank God for our Christian understanding of marriage; for the deep regard for the sanctity of marriage which exists in our country. We thank the Irish Government that banned divorce in the Irish Free State. We should be glad if divorced persons remained away from us."

The bishop's suggestion that divorced persons should accept voluntary exile from Ireland was scarcely necessary. The whole marital atmosphere of the Republic is so overwhelmingly Catholic that a divorced person could not feel at home except in the small Anglo-Irish segment of the cities. He may even encounter some hostility in these Anglican communities. Any Catholic in the Republic who goes abroad to secure a divorce, in order to return with a new spouse, is likely to receive a very frosty welcome. If his name has been clouded with scandal, his professional or business future may be destroyed. The priests may even hold him up to public scorn from the pulpit.

When the Irish Catholic bishops succeeded in getting an absolute prohibition of divorce written into the 1937 Constitution, they probably spoke for the great majority of their people. The people themselves, trained in the atmosphere of Catholic tradition, tend to regard divorce as unnecessary, the product of pagan civilization. The question of the right of divorce is never raised in public, and no one dares to suggest an impartial survey to discover what are the actual facts concerning marital discord in the country. Any Catholic legislator voting for divorce would be subject to excommunication under the canon law of his Church, and there is no doubt that the Irish hierarchy would promptly resort to this penalty if any movement for divorce-reform appeared.

When the British Medical Association met in Dublin in July 1952, it was confronted with a typical Catholic protest movement on the subject of divorce, led by the British guild of Catholic doctors. A special committee of the Association had dared to recommend to a royal commission a more liberal divorce law for Great Britain. In Dublin the large Catholic bloc of doctors attacked the recommendation as especially insulting to their Church when presented in a convention meeting on Irish soil. The Catholic doctors won, and the carefully reasoned report in favor of a more liberal divorce law was withdrawn. In their next annual report, the Catholic doctors boasted of their victory.

The hierarchy feels that in a Catholic country divorce should be made impossible for Protestants and Jews as well as for Catholics, and in this doctrine it sees no fundamental threat to the liberty of non-Catholics. In Catholic theory, Protestants are as much subject to divine law as Catholics — and the rule against divorce is divine law. This theory was applied to divorce legislation in 1953 in a public statement by the Most Rev. Dr. O'Callaghan, Bishop of Clogher:

If the bishops see any law passed or any harm about to come upon the individual, the family or the Church, they will speak out and even give up their lives rather than allow God's law to be violated. Even Protestants as Christians must observe the natural law, which is the law of God. No State has any right to pass legislation contrary to the Ten Commandments of God or the Divine natural law. British law has legalized divorce. We will speak against that as long as there is life in us. Let them know that we are prepared to lay down our lives rather than be traitors to Almighty God or His Divine law.

This theory — that Catholics have a right to impose Catholic standards on the non-Catholic population — has aroused the opposition of the intellectual leaders of Protestant Ireland more than any other one Church policy. William Butler Yeats, in a great debate on divorce in the Free State Senate in 1925, challenged the Catholic position directly. He asked the hierarchy, in effect, whether it was creating a state where non-Catholics were to be treated as second-class citizens in matters of marriage. Up to this time in Irish history, citizens had been given the legal right, under the divorce laws of England, to secure divorce on grounds of adultery. When the Free State Constitution of 1922 was written, the drafting committee refused to incorporate a provision against divorce, because this would have destroyed a right that the Protestant community had long enjoyed. But the Catholic hierarchy, in accordance with papal tradition, marshaled its full power against the granting of the right of divorce to any Irish citizen. It asserted its authority to establish rules concerning the marriage and divorce of all baptized persons, Protestant or Catholic. Said Archbishop O'Donnell:

No power on earth can break the marriage bond until death. . . . That is true of all baptized persons no matter what the denomination may be. To be sure, we hear that a section of our fellow-countrymen favor divorces. Well, with nothing but respect and sympathy for all our neighbours, we have to say that we place the marriages of such people higher than they do themselves. Their marriages are unbreakable before God and we cannot disobey God by helping to break them.

Father Peter Finlay put the case of the Catholic right to prohibit non-Catholic divorce even more specifically. He compared divorce to polygamy, robbery, and murder:

The refusal to legalise divorce is no denial of justice to any section of our people; it is no infringement of the fullest civil and religious liberty which our Constitution guarantees to all. As well say that prohibition of suttee is a denial of justice to the Hindu widow. The Hindu widow had a far clearer right to do herself to death on her husband's funeral pyre — her religion imposed it upon her as a duty — than any member of a Christian community can have to put away his wife and enter into a state of public legalised adultery. England acted justly, and in fulfilment of a plain and grave moral obligation, when she forbade suttee in India. The Irish Free State will act justly, and in fulfilment of a plain and grave moral obligation, in refusing to legalise absolute divorce and re-marriage among ourselves.

Yeats's reply to Archbishop O'Donnell and Father Finlay was historic. He began by pointing out that, if the Catholic and Protestant members of the Irish parliament could be let alone to work out a reciprocal compromise on common-sense lines, all the difficulties might be ironed out. The Protestants could pass a divorce law for Protestants only, and the Catholics could pass a law covering the rights of Catholics. Both groups could be reasonably happy in the application of their own standards. Instead, as he said to the Catholics,

. . . you are to legislate on purely theological grounds and you are to force your theology upon persons who are not of your religion. . . . If you legislate upon such grounds, there is no reason why you should stop there. There is no reason why you should not forbid civil marriages altogether, seeing that civil marriage is not marriage in the eyes of the Church. . . . Once you attempt legislation upon religious grounds you open the way for every kind of intolerance and for every kind of religious persecution. . . .
It is one of the glories of the Church in which I was born that we have put our Bishops in their places in discussions requiring legislation. Even in those discussions involving legislation on matters of religion they count only according to their individual intelligence and knowledge. The rights of divorce, and many other rights, were won by the Protestant communities in the teeth of the most bitter opposition from their clergy. The living, changing, advancing human mind, sooner or later refuses to accept this legislation from men who base their ideas on the interpretation of doubtful texts in the Gospels.

Yeats knew that he had already been defeated by the priests, and that under the Catholic code no Irish legislator who listened to him was free to vote in favor of divorce. But he also knew that in his protest he represented the forces of modern freedom which would some day assert their supremacy in Ireland. So he went down with colors flying, and uttered one last battle cry for the Protestant Ascendancy

I think it is tragic that within three years of this country gaining its independence we should be discussing a measure which a minority of this nation considers to be grossly oppressive. I am proud to consider myself a typical man of that minority. We against whom you have done this thing, are not petty people. We are one of the great stocks of Europe.

We are the people of Burke; we are the people of Grattan; we are the people of Swift, the people of Emmet, the people of Parnell. We have created the most of the modern literature of this country. We have created the best of its political intelligence. Yet I do not altogether regret what has happened. I shall be able to find out, if not I, my children will be able to find out, whether we have lost our stamina or not. You have defined our position and have given us a popular following. If we have not lost our stamina then your victory will be brief, and your defeat final, and when it comes this nation may be transformed.

The Control of Marriage

Yeats had suggested that if the Catholic code on divorce was to be given official sanction the government could just as logically prohibit civil marriage in Ireland altogether, and turn the whole control of marital matters over to religious bodies. This would have suited the Catholic Church well enough, because the Church stands for this type of control in Catholic nations; but when the 1937 Constitution was written, neither the Catholic hierarchy nor the De Valera government dared to go quite that far. Technically, the old English statutory law has been preserved, and any citizen, Catholic or non-Catholic, has the nominal right to marry in a registry office without a religious ceremony. But for Catholics this is an empty right which is almost never used, since it is hedged around with so much discrimination that it is virtually prohibited. Accordingly, nearly all baptized Catholics in the nation are married by their priests. The Irish people tend to take seriously the orthodox priestly view that any Catholic is an adulterer if he is married outside of his Church by a Protestant clergyman, by a Jewish rabbi, or by a public official. The Catholic who defies his Church in marriage matters is likely to suffer very severe social and economic penalties. Also, the marriage law is so rigged that an Irishman who wishes to have a civil marriage must wait about three times as long for the ceremony as the Irishman who goes to his priest. Only a few hardy souls in the Republic care to defy these taboos and marry without priests.

The refusal of the Church to recognize the divorce of *any* person, and the supplementary refusal to recognize Protestant or civil marriage for Catholics, lead to many interesting dilemmas. What is bigamy? Who is an illegitimate child? Should

Mary X and Patrick Y be known as Mr. and Mrs. Y after their marriage before a civil official? Should *any* Catholic be permitted to marry *any* Protestant or Jew in view of the pro-hibition against mixed marriages in Catholic canon law?

The bigamy question is embarrassing because it involves the possibility of defiance of the Church even by an Irish Catholic government. Under Catholic law a man may have had three or four civil "marriages," but when he comes to the altar before a priest for his first Catholic ceremony, he is not committing bigamy under Catholic law, even if two or three of his civilly-produced wives are still recognized by the newspapers and the neighbors as actual spouses. The Dublin *Standard* makes this anomaly clear in a priestly question-and-answer column for the faithful, from which I quote the significant phrases:

Q. A Catholic marries in a registry office and has a family. . . .
A. . . . the marriage of a Catholic in a registry office is not a valid mar-riage, and is, therefore, of itself, no obstacle to a subsequent marriage. The parties are not really married; they are single: the registry office made no difference to this single status.

The Church does not relax its opposition to non-Catholic marriage for Catholics even today, when the Protestant com-munity of the South is no longer a threat to its power. Some bishops have gone so far as to refuse to permit the marriage of any Catholic to any Protestant or Jew in their dioceses, even when the non-Catholic is willing to take the required pledge that all children of the marriage will be brought up as Catholics. In such circumstances the only way in which a non-Catholic can marry a Catholic and remain in Ireland is to renounce his religion and become a Catholic convert. The other alternative is to move out of the country altogether to escape from these economic and social pressures.

I did not learn of a single instance in the Republic in recent years where a Catholic defied his priest openly, married a non-Catholic without the usual pledges, and continued to live in the same community. On this issue the priests and the conservative Catholic laymen have created such an atmosphere of popular disapproval that the practice is virtually prohibited.

The pressure for Catholics, of course, is even greater against

Protestant marriage than against civil marriage, because of the penalties prescribed by canon law. When a Catholic is married by a Protestant clergyman, excommunication follows automatically — and in Ireland excommunication means social ostracism and economic boycott. The pressure against mixed marriage before a priest is less severe, but it is accompanied by many special types of discrimination and pressure. Even when a mixed marriage is permitted, a son of such a marriage who wishes to become a priest is not allowed to take orders in the Catholic Church until he has won over his non-Catholic parent to the faith.

In practice in the South, it is the Protestants who are yielding to the overwhelming Catholic pressure in all matters of mixed marriage. The Catholics almost never yield. This fact is in striking contrast to the American situation, since it is likely that more than 50 per cent of all the children of mixed marriages in the United States are lost to the Catholic faith. (See Chapter 11.) In Ireland the bishops permit mixed marriages only in those cases in which they feel sure that the pledge to raise the children as Catholics will be carried out. When such children grow old enough to attend school, their parents, if they show any signs of wavering, are put under relentless pressure to carry out their educational pledges.

Mixed marriages between Irish Catholics and Jews are regarded with special disfavor, and they almost never occur. The experience of Leopold and Molly Bloom in Joyce's *Ulysses* shows some of the problems involved. When a mixed marriage takes place, it is almost always a marriage between a Protestant man of the middle or upper classes and a younger Catholic girl of the people; rarely is the social situation reversed. The man, as he grows older finds himself isolated from the Protestant community and surrounded by a Catholic wife and Catholic children. Presently his whole family is absorbed into the Catholic life of Ireland, and the last traces of Protestantism disappear. There is no doubt that this traditional Catholic technique for bringing the children of mixed marriages to the faith is an important factor in the relative growth of Catholicism.

It should be said by way of extenuation of Catholic bigotry in matters of mixed marriage that for two centuries Irish bigotry in marriage relationships was primarily Protestant. For a long time, Protestants were prevented from marrying Catholics under any circumstances. Today the priests remind the Irish Catholic people of the former discrimination against Catholics, and thus help to justify their present intolerance. But when every explanation has been offered, the success of the Catholic policy on mixed marriage in Ireland is still difficult to understand. It runs counter to the whole trend of twentieth-century society toward mutual tolerance and freedom.

The Catholic use of mixed marriage as a device for proselyting unborn children has been strengthened by an Irish Supreme Court ruling in the famous Tilson case. Under this decision the written pledge of a Protestant in a mixed marriage to raise his children as Catholics can be enforced in the Irish courts. The pledge, of course, cannot be enforced if *both* parents decide to renounce it; but if the Protestant parent alone challenges the pledge, the courts will step in to enforce it against him, even when he is the father and nominal head of the household. The Tilson case is of immense significance to American and British non-Catholics because it shows how the traditions of the British common law — which underlie the domestic-relations law of both the United States and Great Britain — can be modified to establish Catholic marital principles.

Ernest Tilson, an Irish Protestant, married Mary Barnes before a Catholic priest, after signing the required pledges to bring up all their children as Catholics. Later, after a quarrel, the father took three of their four children to his parents' home to be brought up as Protestants. When the mother asked for their custody, the Supreme Court sent the children back to her because of the pre-nuptial mixed-marriage pledge — although English law would not have enforced such a pledge against the father in such circumstances. The Court held that the new Irish Constitution, with its special recognition of religion, made the Catholic mixed-marriage pledge enforceable.

Would a predominantly Catholic court in Ireland enforce a mixed-marriage pledge which ran in favor of the Protestant parent, calling for the education of the children as Protestants? In the Tilson case, the only non-Catholic member of the Irish Supreme Court, Justice Black, raised this question, and because he could not get an answer from his colleagues he registered a vote of dissent. He was quite justified in his skepticism. The Catholic Church denies the reality of Protestant marriage for Catholics, and no Catholic judge in Ireland would be permitted to enforce a promise which, in the Catholic view, arose out of immoral relationships. In fact, the Irish hierarchy, under its canon law, cannot admit that a non-Catholic home may be a good home for a Catholic child unless the final decisions concerning the education of the child are made by priests.

What happens in Ireland when a Catholic marriage becomes intolerable for a sensitive man or woman? The answers are largely guesswork, because no scientific study of the situation has been made. A number of social factors tend to prevent divorce. A middle-aged man is not so likely to choose the wrong mate if he takes ten years to make his choice — and frequently the Irish groom is middle-aged and has taken the full ten years. Moreover, Irish women, particularly in the country, do not have the freedom or independence of American women, and hence they are less likely to demand divorce even under circumstances which American women would consider intolerable. It is well known that the increase of divorce in many democratic countries in recent years is based primarily on the new freedom of modern women to part from philandering husbands and start over again. Women in Ireland lack opportunity for such rebellion, partly because of the shortage of available occupations outside of marriage.

When the marriages of the rich fail, there is the possibility of escape to British freedom, since divorce is obtainable either in England or in Northern Ireland, after establishment of a bona-fide residence for a short period. This possibility of escape relieves some of the worst tensions in Irish marital life. In fact, it would be interesting to compute all the special ways in which the propinquity of British civilization serves to make Irish Catholic civilization bearable. In matters of censorship, contraception, divorce and education, those Irish citizens who believe in Western concepts of freedom can cross the Irish Sea — or motor to Belfast — and find relief.

For the priests, officially at least, the "success" of Ireland's sexual code is self-evident. They point with pride to the elimination of divorce, and they gloat over the statistics of divorce in the "pagan" atmosphere of non-Catholic America. They ignore the agony of Catholic men and women who are held together in unhappy unions by clerical and social pressure, and they declare that the success of civilization is to be judged by its adherence to God's laws. They contend that the rescue of a Catholic soul in heaven is far more important than the rescue of a human being from the protracted agony of an unhappy home on earth. They argue, not without some justification, that almost any man can tolerate almost any woman in marriage if he makes up his mind that the union is indissoluble. If the assumptions of the priests are granted, their conclusions are inescapable. They are satisfied that Ireland is the world's great model of Christian family life.

8

Fanaticism and Moral Childhood

Bernard Shaw said fifty years ago that the Roman Catholic in Ireland "is content to regard knowledge as something not his business; he is a child before his Church." Shaw's generalization still applies to the Irish masses in all matters of faith and morals, but it should be remembered that this moral childhood is not a natural thing. It is an artificial product of clerical power; it is a logical consequence of the Catholic theory of controlled culture. Moral immaturity is systematically cultivated by the priests. From their point of view, the mature mind is often a disturbed and rebellious mind, while the childlike mind, if directed by the Church, finds happiness and security in obedience. For the purposes of an authoritarian church, perennial immaturity may be the key to heaven.

The Devices of Moral Childhood

The devices which the Catholic priests use to keep the Irish people in a state of moral childhood are not unlike the devices which priests use elsewhere; but in Ireland almost all the people take them seriously. The voices of doubt are not raised publicly. Even among the intellectuals one does not hear in Ireland the ridicule of relics, shrines, and indulgences heard in Italy or in the Latin American countries. When the alleged right arm of Saint Francis Xavier was flown from New York to Dublin in 1949 for exhibition, it was estimated that 100,000 persons headed by the President of the Republic crowded the church and highway to venerate it. Although Ireland has no shrine of its own comparable to Lourdes in France, or to Fatima in Portugal, it sends great hosts of Irish pilgrims to these shrines, and it sends even greater hosts — sometimes 25,000 at a time — to its own local shrine of Our Lady of Knock, in County Mayo. The Knock legend is not unlike that of Fatima; it is said that at Knock about seventy years ago an apparition of the Virgin Mary appeared.

The moral immaturity of the Irish people begins with the moral immaturity of their priests. We have seen how priests, young and old, are not permitted to read any systematic criticism of their faith. Irish Catholic culture tends to keep their minds wrapped in cotton wool. Under such circumstances the sermons of the priests are strikingly immature and conformist; they tend to be routine and elementary extensions of the catechisms used in the schools. The priestly articles in Irish ecclesiastical journals are timid, derived, and remote from the world of current values. I have waded through at least a hundred volumes of such priestly articles and sermons in a vain search for an original or advanced idea in the field of moral values. Even when the students for the priesthood become fairly mature young men at Maynooth, they may not retain a heretical book for more than eight days without sin — even if it is printed in a foreign language which they cannot read. Their Professor of Church History may not read to them in class any considerable part of Gibbon's *Decline and Fall of the Roman Empire* even for purposes of criticism. Nuns, of course, are more closely guarded from contamination than young priests; usually they must submit without protest to the opening and reading of their mail.

The moral decisions of the priests are almost always made on the basis of an appeal to clerical authority; they themselves are treated like children by their bishops and, in turn, they treat their parishioners in the same manner. "In the 1500 years during which the Gaelic nation has been Catholic," boasts one Catholic writer, "there has never been a native schism or heresy." There are many "spoiled priests" in Ireland — men who have started studying for the priesthood and then dropped out — but there are almost no ex-priests. Once a priest, always a priest — that is the Irish rule. This is largely because the Irish priest is not subjected to the strong modernist influences which take men out of the priesthood in other countries.

If a sign of theological liberalism appears in the mind of a priest it is quickly condemned. In 1951, an Irish priest questioned the Church's teaching that unbaptized infants cannot go to heaven because — as he pointed out — such a teaching unjustly excludes from bliss all but an "infinitesimal" percentage of the children born since the world began. He received an official rebuke: "It is Catholic teaching that God has provided a *limbus puerorum* as He has provided a hell for the damned. It is not credible that God should have made this provision and that the Church should enunciate the doctrine stated, if no one were ever to enter these places."

The moral world which the priests build for their parishioners is itself something of a *limbus puerorum,* rather like a house of blocks, neatly arranged in uniform and graded segments. All moral answers are supplied with great precision; nothing is left to the moral imagination. It is assumed that the Catholic mind craves definiteness and authority. Lying, the people are told, is not a mortal sin, but only "essentially evil" and a "venial offence." Such a formal classifying of sin inevitably leads to carelessness about those offenses which are graded as minor. A priest may win as much money as he pleases through the Irish Sweepstakes, but he may not — under Rule No. 47 of the Maynooth Statutes — attend a horse race or watch it from "a near-by place," without risking *ipso facto* suspension. Nor is he permitted to place a bet with a bookmaker — although bookmaking is a permissible profession for a Catholic. Apparently the question whether a priest may watch a horse race on television has not yet been decided.

The pattern of penance and forgiveness is similarly traced out in elementary fashion. Although the pattern is not peculiar to Ireland, it is more universally accepted in Ireland than in any other non-Latin country. The people are told that the dates and physical settings of their acts of contrition determine how effective those acts will be in heaven, and they are also told that the priests have exclusive power to set the dates and the places which will be so honored. In the whole process of forgiveness mechanical acts play a very vital part. A plenary indulgence remitting all the temporal punishment due to sin in purgatory is granted to any relative of a young priest who goes to the priest's first Mass after confession. A 50-day indulgence is granted for kissing the ring of a bishop. The use of rosary beads in prayer is assumed to secure extraordinary results: By using the rosary under rules laid down by the Dominican Order, a devout Irish Catholic through prayers, visits, and the counting of beads can gain in a single year — according to my reckoning — 434 plenary indulgences for sin, plus 557 years of remission in purgatory, plus 47,500 special days of remission, plus an indeterminate list of extra days, bringing the potential relief in purgatory to almost 700 years in one fruitful and repentant year in this world. The Irish Catholic people are encouraged by their priests to occupy their days in such repetitive exercises in order to escape the penalties of purgatory. The official booklet *How to Avoid Purgatory* says:

> Those who say the little ejaculation: "Sacred Heart of Jesus I place my trust in Thee" one hundred times a day gain 30,000 days Indulgence. Those who say it 1,000 times, as many do, gain 300,000 days Indulgence, each day. Nothing can be easier than to acquire the habit of saying this little prayer all day long, countless times each day.

Sin and Crime in a Moral Nursery

The system of morals by rote results in many priestly judgments about crime and sin which seem quite incomprehensible to non-Catholics. If an Irish public official accepts a bribe he may keep it under certain circumstances — but let Father Michael O'Donnell tell the story in his *Moral Questions,* a 1945 book bearing the Imprimatur of the present Archbishop of Dublin:

BRIBERY

Q. In an election for County Medical Officer, there are several candidates. A county councillor takes money (10 pounds) from each of three doctors. He votes for one, and the latter is successful. What are his obligations in regard to this doctor? What are his obligations in regard to the other two? Can he take money in such cases? And suppose he did not vote for any candidate, what then are his obligations in regard to the money he has taken?

A. County Councillors are appointed to do their best for the general welfare of the people that have put them in office. If they use their position for merely personal advantage, they are guilty of a gross abuse of trust.

If they accept bribes, they are guilty of injustice. The only question is: To whom are they obliged to make restitution?

If they vote for a qualified candidate and take a bribe, they are charging for what they are already obliged to do. They have no claim to additional recompense. They are bound in strict justice to restore that candidate the money he has given.

If they vote for a candidate who is not fit for the position, they are false to their trust. In common with all other non-bribed voters who support their cause, they are bound to repair all the injury that their action entails on the public. Possibly, they may return the bribe — as Judas, and every other traitor might in compensation for activities which they were not obliged to exercise. But that is a small compensation; and if Judas was the main traitor, he was at least decent enough to indicate the level on which the Catholic world was to range his imitators. In the case as given, we have no indications of the relative merits of the candidates. But:

1. If the Councillor votes for the qualified candidate, he is bound to restore the bribe.

2. If he votes for the unqualified candidate, he may, possibly, keep the bribe, but must answer for the sufferings that his action entails on the public.

3. If he does not vote, he is obliged to restore the money and is, possibly, bound for other consequences resulting from dereliction of duty.

Such formal casuistry in matters of morals extends into the whole field of stealing, which has been neatly subdivided by the priests into areas of sin and non-sin. The same Father O'Donnell — who is Professor of Theology at Maynooth — has this to say about a certain problem of theft and restitution:

Q. M steals from N a coin which he thinks is a sixpence, but which is really a half-a-sovereign. He loses it. When N complains he discovers the mistake he made. What is he obliged to N?

A. The situation depends on what is meant by the statement that M "thinks" the coin is a sixpence. If he had every reason for thinking so — if the probability of its being half-a-sovereign never crossed his mind — he may regard himself mainly as a blind, irresponsible agent of destruction, and his obligations will be over when he has paid N sixpence.

If he acted carelessly, imagining that the coin was a sixpence, but determined to have it no matter what it was, he is fully responsible for what happened objectively and he must pay N the ten shillings.

As an illustration of the first hypothesis, I might give something like this: N is a faddist — a collector of sixpences of various sizes, shapes and dates. He lets everyone know of his hobby, and keeps his treasures in a special box which he takes great pride in exhibiting to his friends

(M included). One day he falls from his high principles and adds half-a-sovereign to his collection. Not suspecting this lapse, M helps himself to a coin in the dark, and discovers the facts only when N raises his complaint. He is not bound to restore the larger sum.

Thus M is allowed to escape restitution of nineteen-twentieths of his theft because his victim committed a previous bit of harmless deception.

Quite a few non-Catholics in Ireland were somewhat shocked in May 1953 when a Catholic speaker on Radio Eireann announced that the falsification of income-tax returns was not an offense under Catholic canon law. In the *Irish Times* a Catholic layman explained the reasoning behind this charitable ruling:

> That a Catholic is not required under the moral law to make a complete income tax return is a commonplace of Catholic teaching. The reason lies in the realistic approach of the Church to all problems. Every Government knows that a considerable number of people who are liable will be able to avoid paying income tax either in whole or in part, and in consequence the rate is fixed at a higher figure than it would be if everybody paid his or her just share. The man who pays up is entitled in strict justice to take cognizance of this device; he should not be penalized for the evasion practiced by others, and he is morally entitled to hold back part of his income in fairness to himself. What part is a matter that will vary with individual cases, and it is here that the confessor must be consulted. People's circumstances differ so widely that no hard and fast rule can be laid down.
>
> To the objection that to sign an incompleted declaration of income is to sign to a lie and therefore to sin, the answer is quite simple. It is that the authorities do not expect the complete declaration. They know that in practice virtually every taxpayer who is in a position to suppress part of his income will do so. Consequently, they are not in the formal sense "deceived" by an incomplete return and the essence of a lie is deceit.

Perhaps this easy-going attitude toward tax obligations explains why only 1 in 7 of the working population of the Republic pays any income tax, whereas the corresponding proportion in the North is 1 in 3.

The crime pattern of the Irish Republic bears out the theory of moral immaturity. The felony rate is exceptionally low, but there are many crimes of juvenile irresponsibility. When an effort was made in July 1953 to show three-dimensional motion pictures in Dublin, more than $2,500 worth of polaroid viewing spectacles were carried off by the spectators in a single week, in spite of the most urgent appeals from stage and screen for their return. The number of thefts of spectacles in such exhibitions in Dublin exceeded the Belfast proportion of thefts by about 10 to 1, and the London proportion by about 700 to 1. Similar exhibitions of three-dimensional films in other Irish cities had to be abandoned.

In terms of total harm to the community, drunkenness is the most serious Irish crime — but few Irishmen think of it as a crime, and they tend to laugh pityingly when it is depicted on the stage. Perhaps drinking is the Irishman's confession that he is not mature enough to face life as a moral adult. "The Irishman," says Arland Ussher, "takes his drinking sadly; it is like a mournful symbol that even his beer is black. He drinks to attain forgetfulness of the whole human condition — that condition to which he feels so exceedingly ill-adapted." The Pioneer Total Abstinence Society of Ireland, with 400,000 members, is fighting valiantly against excessive drinking, but with little apparent effect. The nation's liquor bill is rising, and the average Irishman still spends his evenings in a pub in preference to his home.

Among the Irish, gambling is almost universal, and it is officially permitted by the Church. "We hold that betting is not wrong in itself. Gambling compared with other evils, is far less likely to lead to the breaking up of home life. . . . In the opinion of the Catholic moralist there is nothing essentially wrong in a man earning his livelihood as a gamester or a bookmaker." This quotation is from a memorandum on gambling submitted by the Catholic bishops of England and Wales to a British Royal Commission on Gambling in 1950. The Irish general hospitals — with the exception of one Protestant hospital — are supported by the Irish Sweepstakes, with priestly blessing, and gambling enterprises are operated openly by almost all Irish Catholic churches for their own benefit. On the front of Dublin's pro-cathedral is posted a notice headed "PRO-CATHEDRAL NON-STOP DRAW." Underneath, on the notice, worshipers are urged to pay one shilling a week to become a winner — £10 for first place and lesser amounts for lower prizes. Next to the notice is the calendar of prayers and saints' days for the week. Occasionally advertisements for rival "draws" sponsored by religious orders are printed in the newspapers side by side. "AUGUSTIAN NON-STOP DRAW" and "DOMINICAN NON-STOP DRAW" were two parallel advertisements on a certain day in December 1952 in the Limerick *Chronicle*. The customers could take their choice. The religious orders of Limerick were not content to allow the parish churches to get all the profits from gambling.

The Fanatic as Moral Hero

The priests teach nominally that a good citizen should serve humanity, and they themselves set a good example; but they tend to exalt above all other servants of humanity the apostle of Catholic ritual who spends endless hours in going through the forms of ecclesiastical contrition. Their latest national hero is the pathetic former drunkard Matt Talbot, who was regarded by many of his fellow-workingmen as mentally unbalanced. For twenty years the Dublin priests have been trying to make him into Ireland's first modern saint in order to use his memory and his relics in the fight against drinking — and against leftist tendencies in the labor movement. They are apparently about to succeed. The Sacred Congregation of Rites is now considering 1400 pages of evidence submitted to it by the Irish hierarchy concerning the saintly qualities of Talbot, and if the evidence is accepted at face value he will presently be beatified.

Talbot was a Dublin workingman who died at the age of 70 in 1925. He had had only a few years of schooling at a Christian Brothers' institution, and had started work as a porter at a bottling works. Later he went to a lumber-yard as a laborer. In his early life he was an inveterate drunkard, and after years of dissipation was approaching mental collapse. His friends gave him up in despair and refused any longer to lend him money for drink.

Then there came a turning point in his life which is shrouded in mystery. Some of his associates believe that the transformation was due to shock, and they say that he woke up one morning after a long spree to find a prostitute dead in his bed. Whatever may be the truth of this report, he suddenly realized that he was approaching disintegration. There was a sudden about-

face in his behavior. He stopped drinking and adopted a
schedule of ten hours a day of ritual and contrition. That
schedule — as described by a priest, Father Albert H. Dolan, in
his *Matt Talbot, Alcoholic* — follows:

> Returning in the evening at 10:30, he set his alarm for 2 A.M. From
> 2 to 4:30 he was on his knees in his room. . . . At 5 he was in church
> for Mass and Holy Communion. After a light and hasty breakfast he
> was at work promptly at 6. At the lunch hour he did not go home but
> ate a slice of bread and spent the rest of the time in scheduled prayer in
> a private place which his fellow laborers called "Matt's office." There
> he would return for prayer at slack moments during the day. At the close
> of the day's work at 5:30, he hastened to the church to make his visit
> to the Blessed Sacrament. Then he returned home for dinner, after which
> he spent the entire evening at home in prayer and in spiritual reading
> until 10:30 . . . his day consisted of ten hours of prayer, ten and a half
> hours of work, and three and one half hours of sleep. . . . [On Sunday] he
> remained in church from 5.30 A.M. until after Benediction following the
> last Mass, which usually ended about 1:30 P.M. He returned to his room
> about 2 o'clock, when he took the only meal of his day. Note that he had
> been without food from 6:30 P.M. on Saturday. During these eight hours
> in church on Sunday mornings he never rose from his knees except to go
> to the altar to receive Holy Communion. Eight hours kneeling erect.
> After his meal he spent the rest of the afternoon in spiritual reading
> and prayer, and in the evening he attended the Sodality devotions in
> church.

Although Matt Talbot lived during some of the most critical
years of the Irish labor struggle, he made no contribution to the
labor movement beyond the payment of union dues, and never
attempted to take a part in labor reforms. When he dropped
dead on a Dublin street in 1925, it was found that for fourteen
years he had been wearing around his body and legs, underneath
his clothing, heavy cart chains like the chains commonly used
by automobiles to prevent skidding, until the chains had become
imbedded in his flesh. Their apparent object was to prevent
sexual sin. Talbot has now been made by the Irish priesthood
in both Ireland and the United States the most important symbol
of man's conquest of alcohol by holiness. "There was packed
into Matt Talbot," says Father Dolan, "everything that was best
in Irish character."

Protestant-Catholic Separatism

The occupants of a moral nursery must be protected against wayward children. They are not capable of choosing their own associates wisely. In the eyes of the priests, all Protestants are at least potentially wayward, and their ideas are likely to contaminate pure faith. Accordingly, the hierarchy has developed a whole code of separatist conduct designed to protect its people from the contamination of heresy and to punish any Catholic who shows signs of defection. The separatism expresses itself in politics, in business, and in social life.

One element in this separatism is the natural reaction by Catholics against past Protestant discrimination. Professor Curtis has described the old Protestant Ascendancy of Ireland as "greedy, intolerant, and pampered." Even today there is in the final remnant of the Protestant Ascendancy a considerable strain of jealous pride. The Anglican Church of Ireland calls its prelates "Primate of All Ireland," "Primate of Ireland," and so forth, to the utter confusion of outsiders — for the church of 95 per cent of the Republic's people, the Roman Catholic Church, uses precisely the same titles for its own officials. Some members of the Church of Ireland even object when a newspaper inserts the word "Protestant" before the titles of their bishops to distinguish them from the Roman Catholic bishops. The Church of Ireland also objected in 1952 to being classed together with other Protestant churches in the determination of the religion of Irish children available for adoption; because of this objection, it was necessary to rewrite the government's Adoption Bill in order to separate the Church of Ireland from other Protestant groups.

Some of the Anglican snobbishness has an economic basis. The Church of Ireland in the towns of the South still represents the economic aristocracy, and this aristocracy tends to be slightly aloof and superior. *Our* people, runs the legend, are more responsible — not like *them*. (Each side calls the other "them.") Economic discrimination against Catholics occasionally breaks through in newspaper advertising. Want ads for "Housekeeper — Protestant" frequently appear; want ads for "Housekeeper — Catholic" would scarcely be necessary, since practically all housekeepers in the South *are* Catholic. Such advertisements may be justified in the hiring of employees for various religious and welfare organizations which have denominational functions, but when they are used for ordinary employment, they are hard to defend.

On the whole, however, the economic friction between Catholic and Protestant communities in the South is less than might be expected in view of the long history of religious bitterness. At present there is not much doubt that Protestants still hold more than their share of ownership power and executive direction of industry; some estimates give them 30 to 40 per cent of industrial supervisory posts and an even more favored position in the ownership of large farms. The great majority of the "fox-hunting squires" — and there are still some left in the Republic — are Church of Ireland men.

Protestants also have more than their proportionate share of posts in the civil service — but this is a result primarily of their superior education. The Catholic *Standard* in 1948 claimed that non-Catholics occupied 13 per cent of the senior posts in the Irish civil service, 8 to 10 per cent of other grades, at least 20 per cent of judicial posts, and 20 to 30 per cent of professional posts — certainly an achievement for a bloc that musters 5 per cent of the population. "There is no other country in the world," proclaimed the *Standard,* "in which such a small minority receives from such a majority such a remarkable position in the life of the community."

The word "receives" is slightly misleading. The Protestant minority in the Republic has received its power not from the Irish Catholic majority but from the old English Ascendancy in the days of the union. Now the Catholic majority is taking Ireland back into its own hands. The process of recapture is, for the time being, temperate and tactful, partly because of the still-great power of Protestant ownership, and partly because the Catholics are anxious to demonstrate their fairness to the world in order to bring the Protestant North under their control. Also, it should be added, the ordinary Irishman is at heart a liberal when his Church lets him alone.

In the South no Protestant can be elected to any political office if he becomes identified as a critic of Catholic policy. There are four elected Protestants in the Dail, and one in the cabinet of De Valera — the very able Minister for Posts and Telegraphs, Erskine Childers. But, in general, any Protestant political leader in the South would be doomed to oblivion if he appeared as an opponent of papal policy. The endorsement by a Protestant of any view which might be associated with "anti-Catholicism" means instant political extinction. The only exceptions to this rule are the three Protestant representatives from Trinity College in the Irish Senate, who are reasonably free to speak candidly about Catholic policies, because they are elected not by the general population but by Trinity alumni. It is fair to add that a fourth Trinity College Protestant has been nominated to the Senate by De Valera.

De Valera's dominant Fianna Fail shows conspicuous fairness to Protestants in its internal organization, putting at least three Protestant leaders, headed by Childers, on its controlling committee each year. For many years the De Valera regime maintained a general policy of appointing not less than two Protestants on each important commission and committee created by the government. But the Protestants who are given political positions in the Republic must never appear as champions of Partition, or friends of divorce and birth control, or critics of denominational education.

The hierarchy does not direct its people specifically to boycott non-Catholic candidates, particularly if they concede the validity of Catholic principles; but it constantly emphasizes the importance of electing "Christians," and the word "Christians" in priestly parlance means Roman Catholics. In an article in the *Irish Ecclesiastical Record* of October 1948, Father J. McCarthy discussed "The Morality of Voting for Non-Christians." "It is an agreed principle of theological and sociological teaching," he said "that Catholic citizens should not vote for leaders who are inimical to Christianity. This is not bigotry or unfair discrimination . . . there is simply an unwillingness to set up, in a position of trust, one who is an enemy of the Christian way of life. To act otherwise would prejudice the common good." But Father McCarthy left a loophole in his rule even for Jews by saying that under certain circumstances Catholics may voluntarily vote for them. Members of religious orders, however, may be *commanded* to vote for pro-Church candidates.

To avoid boycott and discrimination in business, most Protestant employers are careful to give some supervisory posts to Catholics, and they are especially careful not to discriminate against Catholics in mass employment. If they violate these principles, they are subject to reprisals from the Catholic community. A front-page barrage against the Singer Sewing Machine Company occurred in 1949 on the alleged ground that "all the leading people in the firm of Singers . . . in Ireland, are non-Catholics, although the overwhelming majority of the staff [are] Catholics. [Only one Catholic] holds an executive position of any consequence," although 95 per cent of the company's Irish employees were Catholic. The Singer Company denied the totals but did not dispute the details, and it kept silent as to future policy. Usually, under such Catholic pressure, Protestant employers make concessions.

Catholic pressure on Catholic employers is much more determined and bitter. "You are betraying your own people" — that is the fatal charge which every Catholic employer fears, and if he is branded with such an accusation, a boycott may destroy him. Here is a veiled appeal taken from the Dublin Catholic *Standard* of August 25, 1950, to boycott a Catholic manufacturer in Limerick because he employed a Mason:

> A Limerick reader proposes a dilemma for purchasers of a universally used commodity of which an Irish firm have had virtual monopoly previous to and during the war, but which is now being imported in great variety. A Protestant firm in this important provincial centre are the importing agents but, fairly enough, make no discrimination against Catholics in employment. The Irish manufacturers, on the other hand, recently appointed a district representative from amongst about thirty applicants and, in accordance with their tradition when good jobs are going, chose a non-Catholic who has a local reputation of being a leading Freemason. It is a pity that some firms which receive solid support on the grounds of being long established in Ireland still carry out a policy of discrimination.

The Punishment of Heresy

One of the most dreaded phrases in Irish life today is the phrase "lapsed Catholic." A lapsed Catholic is in much more danger of Catholic disapproval than an ardent Protestant. In an editorial on "The Principle of Toleration," the *Irish Rosary* of March 1951 made the Catholic policy on this type of retribution quite clear. "We owe it to ourselves to treat those who are in our power justly and fairly," said the editor. But he added this general rule of discrimination which puts the lapsed Catholic below the Protestant: "We allow no claim to good-will from those who have been brought up in the Catholic faith if they abandon it, but we can admire the good faith of those born outside the Church, even while we detest their errors."

All the power machinery of the Church and all the personal persuasiveness of the priests is immediately directed against any Catholic who shows tendencies of slipping away from the Church. At such a moment the wavering Church member is followed up with a persistence that would do credit to the American F.B.I. The priests call upon him at his home again and again, and attempt to enlist the support of all his relatives to keep him within the fold. If all other arguments fail, they threaten him both with the Catholic theological penalties for mortal sin, and with the Catholic social penalties for disloyalty to "your people and your faith." Almost no Catholic editor, businessman, banker, or merchant can resist such pressure, because resistance means the destruction of livelihood. Sometimes these tactics are combined with aggressive steps to win back or to hold for Catholicism persons who might otherwise become Protestant.

Here are a few examples of how Catholic pressure works, verified by personal observation, or taken from the approved Catholic press. For obvious reasons I must omit names in some cases.

(1) Dr. X and his wife, of Dublin, both baptized Catholics, have long ceased to believe in the major Catholic doctrines. In private conversation they express strong criticism of priestly policy. When Dr. X started to drift away from the Church openly by failing to attend Mass, he was warned by his priest. Now he attends Mass conspicuously with his wife. "I must live, you know," he says. "My practice would disappear if I were branded as a lapsed Catholic."

(2) Miss Y was a successful free-lance feature journalist who contributed frequently to Irish Catholic newspapers on subjects of feminine and family interest. A baptized Catholic,

she was the daughter of a mixed marriage. In maturity she began to veer away from the religion of her mother toward scientific humanism. She stopped going to Mass and confession. When her priest discovered her dereliction and confronted her with it, she told him frankly that she had ceased to believe in hell and in the teaching of the priests. She continued to rebuff him during several visits. He discovered her source of livelihood, and immediately all the Catholic papers in Ireland rejected her articles — and still reject them.

(3) In a famous Dublin institution, the Meath Hospital, which had been operated for generations by Quakers, many of the leading medical posts were held by non-Catholic graduates of Trinity College. The Knights of Columbanus became convinced that discrimination was being practiced against Catholic graduates of the National University. A group of Catholics took advantage of the open membership rules of the hospital society, joined in a body just before an annual meeting in April 1949, and captured the hospital with their votes. Some of Ireland's leading non-Catholic physicians were discharged or resigned. Fortunately the Dail recognized that such crude methods of conquest would serve as a boomerang, and passed legislation which brought the old officers back into control.

(4) A progressive critical journal of first-rate quality, *Ireland To-day,* was published in Dublin for a short time from 1936 to 1938. It was neither Communist nor Socialist, but genuinely independent in its progressive policies. It published some articles against Franco during the Spanish Civil War, and immediately priests went into the shops telling the proprietors to "take that red magazine out of the window." Gradually its friends and advertisers began to slip away, and it soon died.

(5) A meeting of distinguished Dubliners was called in the Hibernian Hotel to organize a much-needed Anti-T-B League for the care of the thousands of Irish persons suffering from tuberculosis. Unexpectedly, at the beginning of the meeting, a Catholic Monsignor stood up and read a brief letter from the Archbishop of Dublin saying that in his opinion this field of social welfare could more wisely be consigned to the Irish Red Cross than to a new and special organization. There was universal consternation. The Protestant chairman was unwilling

to have such an authoritative opinion challenged openly, and after one or two courageous protests from the hundreds who had been invited to attend, the meeting broke up. The suggestion of the archbishop was carried out without effective opposition.

(6) In 1936 the nation's only non-Catholic newspaper, the *Irish Times,* criticized Franco and presented facts from both sides of the Spanish Civil War. It was the only daily newspaper in the Republic to take this position consistently. In reprisal, virtually all Catholic educational advertising was withdrawn. In recent years some of this advertising has been resumed, but the financial loss to the *Times* has been substantial.

(7) A woman's co-operative guild in Dublin, failing to secure a Catholic hall, accepted for two years the low-rent hospitality of a Methodist schoolroom in the neighborhood, and prospered. The local priest, declaring that this use of a Protestant hall was improper for Catholic women, ordered the president of the guild, a Catholic, to transfer the meetings to an inferior Catholic hall. The members complied. When the guild, in the absence of the priest, passed a resolution endorsing the mother-and-child health scheme of Dr. Noel Browne, the priest, waving a newspaper which contained the offending resolution, walked into the next meeting of the organization and directed it to leave Church premises. The guild complied, and soon died.

(8) When the great Eucharistic Congress of world Catholicism was held in Dublin in 1932, a suggestion was made that Rotary International might be officially represented to help in welcoming visiting Catholic Rotarians. The *Catholic Mind* announced that "we will fight it with bared knuckles. . . . We are not unprotestingly going to allow any demonstration of pagan comradeship to be flaunted in the face of the Catholic world in the heart of Catholic Ireland's capital, on an occasion specially set apart for a great manifestation of the binding force of the charity of Christ. . . . The least that can be said against Rotary is that it is under the suspicion of the Apostolic See. That is enough for us." Later the *Catholic Mind* appealed to all Catholic Rotarians to leave the organization because a Rotary congress had been scheduled in Mexico where "the atheistical government of Mexico . . . persecutes all religions with intense bitterness."

(9) Mr. F, a Protestant farm owner in western Ireland, had promised, when he married a Catholic girl, to bring up their children as Catholics; but he later changed his mind, and his wife agreed with the change. In spite of priestly pressure, their first child was baptized as a Protestant. Immediately Mr. F's neighbors began to boycott him. In Tralee, owners of restaurants refused to serve him food. The local dairy declined to accept his milk. When he protested to the government against this discrimination, the dairy resumed trade with him for several weeks, but one night he was waylaid on a lonely road by strangers and beaten up. Soon he moved with his family to Northern Ireland.

(10) A native Irishman who went to America at the age of 18 and became a citizen returned sixteen years later to live in Leitrim for a while. He was asked by the village priest why he never attended Mass on Sunday. He replied that it would be hypocritical because he did not believe. He was visited again and again by the priest and a Jesuit leader. When he remained adamant in his attitude, he was reported to the Justice Department, and the next time he asked for a visa in New York to go to Ireland, it was refused by the Irish consul. The ban was not lifted until a threat was made to expose the incident on the floor of the Dail.

(11) Before the war an organization called the Mercier Society was formed by the Catholic Church to encourage "free discussion" of religious matters among cultured Catholics and Protestants. Its purpose was to answer common objections to Catholicism and to win educated Protestants to the faith. But it was discovered that the Protestants were not always getting the worst of the ethical and theological arguments. The Archbishop of Dublin promptly closed it down.

And so on. Such examples of separatism and discrimination could fill a book. Actually these incidents are relatively trivial compared to the reprisals and battles between Catholics and Protestants in Northern Ireland, where discrimination and partisanship are much more intense than in the South. The atmosphere of the South is rarely disturbed by any open conflict, partly because the disciplines and practices of separatism in social and cultural affairs are universally accepted. In the area of faith and morals the Protestants know that Catholic practices are dictated in Rome, and that no local pressure can change them. Irish Catholics, for example, are compelled to obey a Roman rule that Catholics must not, without special permission, attend the funeral services of Protestant friends. Although there are several Catholics on the teaching staff of Trinity College, they have not the right to attend the funeral service of a Provost of that institution in the (Protestant) Chapel. At the death of the late Provost of Trinity, Dr. Ernest H. Alton, in 1952, permission to attend such a service was denied to Catholic faculty members at Trinity by the Archbishop of Dublin. The Irish Catholic law on co-operation with Protestants is even more strict than this incident indicates. One of Ireland's famous priests, Father Michael O'Donnell, Professor of Theology at Maynooth, when asked about the limits of co-operation with Protestants, replied that Catholics may not even listen to Protestant broadcasts on the radio because this is "very objectionable," and that Catholics may not attend any Protestant service even for the purpose of acquiring understanding. As to the Church of England and its Irish offshoots, Father O'Donnell declared: "No human being has any authority to establish a body of that description or to claim that it shares in the prerogatives of the Church of Christ."

In Ireland this theological narrow-mindedness is accompanied by a whole pattern of separatist activity. The community is split into two permanent sections — with Catholic and Protestant schools, Catholic and Protestant churches, Catholic and Protestant athletic teams, Catholic and Protestant Boy Scouts, Catholic and Protestant newspapers, and so on. The avenues of friendly communication between the two segments are barricaded and policed by the priests. The "good" Catholic children must not be too friendly with naughty heretics. On the Protestant side the barriers against co-operation are much less formidable, because Protestants are not forbidden to attend Catholic services, read Catholic books, or marry Catholic mates. They are constantly warned of the disabilities of mixed marriages with Catholics but, as we have seen, they "cross the line" in spite of those warnings.

On both sides of the barrier the Catholic people and the

Protestant people may be inclined toward friendship, but co-operation is made difficult because the code of separatism has been included in the Catholic creed itself, and that creed is controlled in Rome.

The Papal Nuncio Incident

Under the separatist code, the most serious offense that can be committed by any critic of the Church is an affront to the Pope. Any Protestant or Catholic who is even remotely associated with an alleged gesture of disrespect to the Holy Father is likely to be punished with indiscriminate ferocity. The taboo against criticism of the Papacy applies even to the Papal Nuncio to Ireland, the Most Rev. Gerald Patrick O'Hara, who represents the Pope at all public functions in the Republic and who is dean of all the diplomats of foreign powers accredited to the government. In 1952, the operation of this taboo was dramatically revealed in an incident which came to be known as "The Papal Nuncio Incident."

It was on October 31, 1952, that the International Affairs Association of Ireland, an organization not unlike the Foreign Policy Association in the United States, held a meeting at the Shelbourne Hotel in Dublin; Peadar O'Curry, editor of the Dublin Catholic *Standard,* was chief speaker on the topic "Yugoslavia: The Pattern of Persecution." In the front row, in a special upholstered armchair, sat the Papal Nuncio, a burly man, looking somewhat like an enlarged edition of Cardinal Spellman. (At this meeting, I was sitting directly behind him.) At the end of the O'Curry address, a sober and routine affair which omitted any reference to forced conversions to Roman Catholicism under the Croatian Fuehrer, Ante Pavelitch, the problem arose whether there should be, as was the custom in these meetings, questions and discussion from the floor. The chairman of the meeting, John O'Brien, a Catholic businessman, revealed that he had agreed in advance with some of the officials of the organization that questions and discussion should not be permitted. This unusual ruling was challenged from the floor by several members as contrary to the society's usual practice, and a show of hands resulted in the overruling of the chair. The skirmish for free speech was led by the distinguished Irish liberal, Dr. Owen

Sheehy Skeffington of Trinity College, who had brought with him as a guest his friend Hubert Butler, of Kilkenny. Butler, an Irish Protestant and graduate of Oxford, is one of the few men in Ireland who knows Yugoslavia first-hand, since he has lived in the country, learned the language, and visited Archbishop Stepinac in prison. In 1935 and 1936, through the School of Slavonic Studies, he held a scholarship for study in Yugoslavia from the Belgrade Minister of Education.

Butler, in a quiet and courteous tone, opened the discussion period. He pointed out that there was a non-Catholic side to the Yugoslav story, that a published statement by the Orthodox Church of Yugoslavia (which he exhibited) had accused the Roman Catholic Church of initiating forced conversions of the Orthodox, that Episcopal Bishop Manning of New York had written a preface to an Orthodox book of evidence against the Croatian Church's policy, and that the Pavelitch government could be compared to the kind of government that might be expected in Ireland if the reactionary Irish organization Maria Duce came to power. The newspapers said that here Butler referred to Stepinac as "the dupe of a gang." At this point, the Papal Nuncio rose from his chair, bristling with anger, and walked out of the meeting in protest. The chairman, pale with apprehension, interrupted Butler and declared the meeting adjourned, "in view of the fact that a remark was made which was offensive to His Excellency and as a result of which he left the meeting." The Irish newspapers, naturally enough, featured the incident under large headlines: "PAPAL NUNCIO WALKS OUT."

It should be noted that there was not in Butler's discussion any attack on a Catholic doctrine; nor was there any mention of the Papal Nuncio. Neither Butler, who raised the issue, nor Skeffington, who had invited him to the meeting, knew that the Papal Nuncio was going to be present. Butler's approach to the problem was quite natural for any informed inquirer. In a diocesan letter on Yugoslavia four months later, the Anglican Archbishop of York, Dr. Cyril Garbett, was to express a point of view more unfavorable to the Catholics than Butler's by saying of Marshal Tito: "Popular anger and reasons of national security made it necessary for the Marshal's Government to take steps against those Roman Catholics who in the war collaborated with the invaders and who in some cases had been guilty of grave crimes against the non-Catholic population." It is true that diplomats do not usually attend meetings at which policies of their governments are criticized, and Butler's remarks by inference criticized Vatican policy. But Archbishop O'Hara did not sit on the platform or have any official role in the meeting, and the International Affairs Association had been traditionally an organization dedicated to free discussion.

Once the Irish newspapers had raised the issue of an "insult" to the Catholic Church, all possibility of free and fair discussion was forgotten. A press campaign began which made Butler a national villain and the Papal Nuncio, conversely, a symbol of insulted faith. The officers of the International Affairs Association surrendered to public pressure, made an official call upon the Papal Nuncio in his palatial residence in Phoenix Park, and offered their humble apologies. No regrets or apologies were expressed to Butler, to the diplomats of other nations who had attended the meeting, or to the members of the society whose traditional right of free discussion had been abruptly terminated by the chairman. Butler himself politely expressed personal regret in a letter to the Nuncio for "any embarrassment or pain I may have caused you" — but even this gesture did not protect him from reprisals.

Then began a series of events which can be taken as typical of the fate of any Irish citizen who directly challenges Catholic power. A special meeting of the Kilkenny Corporation was called to rebuke Butler; the motion to condemn him was passed unanimously. The chairman of the Corporation explained that the people of Kilkenny were "predominantly Catholic" and "excessively tolerant." (Presumably if they had been less tolerant, they would not have stopped with resolutions.) Next the Kilkenny County Council demanded the resignation of Butler from its Monuments Committee. Then the Kilkenny Vocational Education Committee, a public body, passed and publicized a resolution against Butler, denouncing "the affront" to the Papal Nuncio. The Kilkenny Archeological Society, which Butler had nurtured and guided through seven years as honorary secretary, turned on him under pressure, and he resigned in order to save it from disintegration. In the meantime the Kilmanagh Co-operative Dairy Association and the Catholic Young Men's Society of Kilmanagh passed resolutions condemning him. And, although many letters were written to the local press on behalf of Butler, none of them was printed.

Finally the wave of public attacks reached Skeffington. Catholic Action leaders decided that it was inappropriate to have any individual speak at public meetings in Dublin who had been even indirectly associated with an alleged insult to the Holy Mother Church. In August — three months before the controversial meeting of the International Affairs Association — Skeffington had been asked to appear in November as one of the principal speakers at a large inaugural meeting of the Technical Students Literary and Debating Society, at the Rathmines Town Hall in Dublin. Printed programs bearing his name, together with that of a cabinet minister who was also to speak, had already been sent out to guests. Suddenly Skeffington received a brief apologetic note from the students who had invited him to speak, saying that the publicly elected Vocational Education Committee (which is in charge of the technical schools in Dublin) had forced them to withdraw the invitation. "We ourselves," they declared, "have not been furnished with a reason."

Skeffington, son of one of the great national martyrs of 1916, refused to accept the rebuff in silence. He carried the issue to the press and wrote a personal letter to every one of the fourteen members of the Vocational Education Committee. He discovered that the Committee had never met to vote on the issue of his speaking and that their executive officer had acted against him — after consulting with the clerical chairman of the Committee but without formal sanction of the Committee — on the basis of unverified rumor. The "reason" for the rebuff had been, in the words of a very frank letter sent in reply to Skeffington by the Committee's priest-chairman, Canon John Fitzpatrick, that "rightly or wrongly, the citizens have associated your name with an incident at which the Apostolic Nuncio was forced to protest." Evidently no member on the Committee felt it necessary to investigate Skeffington's side of the story; it was enough that a Papal Nuncio had *thought* himself insulted, and that "rightly or wrongly" Skeffington's name had been "associated" with the incident.

In the Republic only one newspaper, the *Irish Times,* and three organizations — the Irish Association of Civil Liberties, the Dublin Trades Council, and a local branch of the Irish Labor Party — came to Skeffington's defense. No organizations or committees came to the defense of Butler — not even any Protestant organization or any outstanding Protestant leader. The public meeting at the Rathmines Town Hall, from whose platform Skeffington had been excluded, was "stacked" against his student admirers by a ruse: the Catholic educational manager invited his friends and supporters to the hall thirty minutes early, and when the students and their official guests arrived, they found most of the seats occupied. But in spite of this ruse the Rathmines meeting became a great protest meeting against the suppression of free speech. Christopher Gore-Grimes of the Irish Civil Liberties Association made an eloquent appeal for fair play and the rights of free criticism, and the overwhelming majority of the audience agreed with him. But neither the students nor the public could alter the Vocational Education Committee's repressive ban of Skeffington from the platform.

"Irish nationalism," said the *Irish Times* in deploring the incident, "has never assumed an authoritarian tinge." This was true enough — but it was not Irish nationalism in this instance which persecuted Butler and barred Skeffington from a large public meeting. It was Catholic power which had stepped in to punish any person even indirectly associated with criticism of any representatives of the Papacy.

The incident dramatized the fact that freedom of speech in Ireland is in actual practice limited by clerical power. This was clearly revealed by the final decision of the Vocational Education Committee. When the Committee was at last allowed by its executive officer and its priest-chairman — two weeks *after* the Rathmines meeting — to consider the matter, it voted retroactive unanimous approval of all the actions taken in its name without its previous authority. The Committee members — elected by the citizens of Dublin — did not venture to utter a syllable of criticism, for they knew that opposition to their clerical chairman meant political suicide.

One interesting feature of this Papal Nuncio incident escaped public notice at the time. Archbishop O'Hara is an American

citizen, and he had come to Ireland with both a Vatican passport and a United States passport. In which capacity was he
attending the October meeting of the International Affairs Association — as a citizen of the United States or as a citizen of the
Vatican? He would probably say that he attended as a diplomatic representative of the Holy See — and certainly he was
accorded at the meeting all the honors of his position as dean
of the diplomatic corps in Dublin. He took conspicuous precedence over the other diplomats present, who crossed the room
to greet him and to bow low over his hand.

But can an American citizen divest himself at will of his
responsibility to stand for American principles? Can he properly
use Catholic power for the punishment of critics of Vatican
policy — as he did in this instance — and at the same time
retain citizenship in a nation which stands for freedom of speech?
Certainly the United States did not come out of the Papal
Nuncio incident with enhanced prestige as a symbol of freedom. Archbishop O'Hara did not lift a finger to prevent a wave
of bigotry from sweeping across Ireland. He bluntly refused, in
a curt letter, to give Butler any support in the face of persecution by Kilkenny Catholics.

It was partly because of this conduct on the part of the
Nuncio that I later brought to the United States Embassy in
Dublin, and to the State Department in Washington, a petition
asking for the revocation of Archbishop O'Hara's American
citizenship under the McCarran Act. I felt that it was not appropriate for a man who represented a foreign state, the Vatican,
in the capacity of Ambassador — taking precedence over the
United States Ambassador — to retain American citizenship
at the same time. My petition and its fate are not part of this
narrative, but they are summarized in the Appendix (page 335).

The Shadow of Fascism

In such an atmosphere it is not surprising that a movement
toward fascism and the narrow anti-Semitic and anti-Masonic
Catholicism of Spain should develop. Indeed, Irish Catholicism
has always acknowledged a great debt to Spain and a great
affinity with its outlook. The present-day Irish Catholic press is
full of flattering allusions to Franco, and during the Spanish

Civil War it was almost hysterically pro-Franco. In recent years expressions of sympathy with fascism have become less popular, and pro-fascist comment is buried in such a mountain of anti-Communist propaganda that it is scarcely discernible.

There is a strong and sincere anti-fascist element in Irish Catholicism, and it is probable that the great majority of Catholics in the Republic sincerely despise the memory of Hitler and Mussolini. In 1936 De Valera successfully resisted right-wing political pressure to embroil Ireland in the Spanish Civil War, and in fighting the pro-Franco bloc in the Dail he courageously denounced the rising fascist spirit in Ireland at that time. Also at the time of the Ethiopian war he successfully resisted an attempt by his political opponents to use Catholic feeling to defeat the League of Nations' sanctions against Italy. For these two assertions of democratic independence, he deserves the gratitude of all progressives — especially because it meant opposing the pro-fascist drift of Vatican policy.

The Irish bishops and priests still reveal many pro-fascist tendencies, and many high Irish clerics praise Spanish and Portuguese dictatorship in extravagant terms. Salazar's "Christian dictatorship" is still held up as a model for Irish Catholics. The present Bishop of Cork, Dr. Cornelius Lucey, wrote in the *Irish Ecclesiastical Record* of March 1944: "Salazar is frankly a dictator. But he is a dictator with a difference. His regime is authoritarian but not totalitarian; his outlook is Christian, not materialistic or pagan . . . he acknowledges that the Government (of which he is the embodiment) is as subject to the moral law in its conduct of affairs as the individual is in his private life. . . . He is the perfect dictator if there ever was one." Then Bishop Lucey described Salazar's corporate state in glowing terms and concluded: "There is nothing very original, nothing very spectacular in all this, you may say; it is but a way of translating our Catholic social principles into practice along authoritarian lines."

Bishop Lucey's championship of Portugal has been echoed by many other Irish Catholic leaders. The late Irish Jesuit leader Father R. S. Devane, writing on "The Religious Revival Under Salazar" in the *Irish Ecclesiastical Record*, concluded: "May one respectfully suggest that the leaders of our Irish political parties would be well advised to watch closely and study carefully the political and economic development of Portugal, which, though it is not stated explicitly, yet sets before itself, as does the Irish Free State through its new Constitution, the idea of establishing a truly Christian State."

This use of Portugal as a Catholic model is common among priests in many nations, but the use of Spain as a model has met with some resistance even in Catholic Ireland. Irish Catholics contributed perhaps a thousand soldiers to Franco's forces in the Spanish Civil War, but they also contributed some brave fighters to the anti-Franco side. Of course, the Irish hierarchy itself, following the lead of the Vatican, has always been outspokenly pro-Franco. It has consistently condoned the suppression of free speech and of Protestantism in the Spanish state. When, during the Spanish Civil War, the Spanish hierarchy sent a letter of appeal to world Catholicism, the Irish bishops replied with fulsome praise for the rebellion, and spoke of "a people who like our own, are already convinced of the justice of your cause." They attacked the "unspeakable outrages" of the government forces and "the mendacious propaganda of your enemies."

The priests of Ireland had been prepared for this friendly attitude toward Spain by their leading journal, the *Irish Ecclesiastical Record*, when an article on the Spanish Republican "revolution" appeared in December 1933, describing that movement as "a perfect Masonic masterpiece," and branding the Republican Constitution as a document "framed by Jews, atheists, Freemasons, and Socialists." Today the partial suppression of Protestant sects by Franco is openly defended in the Irish Catholic press. When the Dublin *Standard* in 1948 described this suppression and pointed out that only one person in every thousand in Spain is Protestant, it quoted with approval this Spanish defense: "This microscopic minority does not constitute a juridical or religious problem sufficiently important to warrant a change in our existing legislation concerning public worship, education or the press." In January 1953 the same newspaper featured without unfavorable comment the story of the attack on Spanish Protestants by Cardinal Segura, Archbishop of Seville, in which the cardinal appealed to the Spanish Charter as authority for forbidding "Protestant sects to carry on activities outside their churches."

"Italian fascism," said the Rome correspondent of the Dublin *Catholic Bulletin* in 1937, when Mussolini was at the height of his power, "is fundamentally a sane and natural thing even if to the unsympathetic eye it may appear to have suffered from exaggeration and misdirection." Two months later this journal, published by Ireland's most orthodox publishing house, printed a 5-page eulogy of the activities of fascist organizations, written by a Jesuit priest. The editors were less enthusiastic about Nazism, calling it "that other development of the Protestant revolt."

Today two very substantial Catholic forces are pushing the nation to the right. One is a fanatical Catholic propaganda organization called Maria Duce, which is not very important in itself but which represents a great reservoir of potential fascist tendencies; the other is a more conventional reactionary movement against the welfare state by prominent Catholic priests who distrust both democracy and socialism. These two forces dovetail and strengthen each other in such a way that it is not possible in practice to disentangle one from the other.

Maria Duce

Maria Duce is an exclusively Irish organization led by a Dublin priest of the Holy Ghost Order, Father Denis Fahey, who resembles in many ways the famous American reactionary priest, Father Charles Coughlin. In fact, Father Coughlin in his anti-Semitic campaign on the American radio in the 1930's cited the publications of Father Fahey as "authority" for some of his grossest misrepresentations of Jews. Father Fahey's Maria Duce is now under a cloud because of its extreme dogmatism, but it is still able to hold great pro-fascist mass meetings in Dublin, with prominent priests on its platform. Its own leaders claim that at least one-half of the Irish Catholic people are sympathetic to its purposes. Whether this claim is true or not is impossible to say.

Maria Duce's particular target is the Irish Constitution, and its main charge against that Constitution is that it is not Catholic enough. The organization proposes to rewrite the famous religious clauses of Article 44 to eliminate all official recognition of Protestant sects by name and to acknowledge more specifically Ireland's allegiance to the Holy Catholic, Apostolic, and Roman Church "as the guardian and interpreter of the moral law." Maria Duce is violently pro-Franco, pro-monarchist, anti-Semitic, and anti-democratic. Its greatest mass meetings open as thousands of the faithful kneel to recite the Rosary in unison with Father Fahey. Usually the speeches end with bitter attacks on Jews, Masons, Socialists, Communists, and atheists as enemies of God and Ireland. (After I had attended a number of Maria Duce meetings and asked for an interview with Father Fahey, a committee of officers of the organization waited upon me, denied the request, and delivered a written warning that I ought to be "immediately expelled from this country." However, the committee accepted a cordial invitation for coffee and sandwiches, we debated the matter quite fruitfully for three hours, and I remained in the country. I found the Maria Duce leaders earnest, sincere, frustrated, provincial, and profoundly uncultured — resembling the least literate super-fundamentalist leaders in the southern states of the United States.)

To non-Catholics, Article 44 of the Irish Constitution seems to treat the Catholic Church very handsomely, with its grant of a "special position" as guardian of the faith of the majority; to the leaders of Maria Duce the Constitution seems to betray "the oft-repeated teaching of successive Pontiffs," because it "extends equal recognition to all cults and thereby expresses religious indifferentism." Actually, the Irish Constitution does not extend equal recognition to all cults, since it specifically grants a "special position" to the Roman Catholic Church. Maria Duce and its right-wing friends firmly believe that the Constitution has betrayed Catholicism in not discriminating more definitely against opposition cults. They want the Constitution rewritten in the Spanish pattern. In a statement in the *Irish Times* of March 7, 1950, Maria Duce's secretary, J. P. Ryan, summed up with great candor his organization's theory about Catholic tolerance in Ireland:

For a Catholic, religion is a matter of dogmatic certitude. For him there is only one true religion. In consequence, all non-Catholic sects, as such, are false and evil, irrevocably so. While a Catholic must always respect the non-Catholics' personal rights and liberty of conscience, he may never regard their beliefs as other than false, "may never connive in any way at false opinions, never withstand them less zealously than truth allows" (Leo XIII). For a Protestant, on the other hand, religion is a matter of private judgment, a question of opinion. Moreover, since no Protestant claims the prerogative of personal infallibility (as Catholics do for the Pope in matters of faith and morals), it is evident that for a Protestant, thus deprived of dogmatic certainty, the only sane attitude towards those who disagree with his religious opinions is to regard such opinions with a certain respectful deference. Hence the Protestant notion of "religious toleration," the "one-religion-is-as-good-as-another" philosophy which is the logical outcome of private judgment. Toleration for a Catholic always implies that what is tolerated is an evil, and that the toleration of this evil is itself justified only when such toleration is necessary to avoid a greater evil — that is, it is justified by the application of the principle of the double effect. Religious toleration for the Protestant, on the contrary, has no such implications. It is merely the "broadminded," "liberal" admission that people are entitled to their opinions.

What then must be the attitude of Catholic States, such as Spain and Ireland, towards Protestantism and non-Catholic sects in general? The ideal (as outlined in the Syllabus of Pius XI, *Ubi Arcano* and *Quas Primas* of Pius XI) is that the Catholic State, while extending full liberty and official recognition to the Catholic Church alone, should not only not connive at the proselytism of non-Catholic sects, but should suppress them as inimical to the common good. This attitude is quite logical, since for a Catholic State the vitality of Catholic life is the chief good of society. Such intolerance of error is the privilege of truth. Nor does it entail any violence to the liberty of the individual conscience, for "the Church is wont to take earnest care that no one shall be forced to embrace the Catholic Faith against his will." (Leo XIII — *Immortale Dei*).

Nowadays, however, the ideal, such as was realised in Catholic Spain under Ferdinand and Isabella, is not encountered in practice. In many countries predominantly Catholic, the Church, while never abdicating one iota of her sacred rights, is, nevertheless, obliged to be content with an imperfect recognition. In such circumstances the suppression by the State of falsehood and false sects, however desirable, is not feasible. The principle of toleration (in the Catholic sense already explained) may then be invoked as a temporary expedient, a concession to adverse circumstances, by no means a compromise with error itself. The principle is explicitly laid down by Leo XIII in *Immortale Dei*. There it is clear that this toleration is justified only when the Catholic State in question, while extending official recognition to the Catholic Church alone, has a proportionately grave reason for permitting the evil of heresy to survive within its borders.

We proceeded to point out that the liberalism of Article 44 of the Constitution stands unequivocally condemned for giving equal recognition to all forms of religious belief, since it is contrary to reason and revelation alike that error and truth should have equal rights (Leo XIII). From repeated Papal pronouncements, it is abundantly clear that the Catholic Church not only does not condone, but vigorously condemns, the much-vaunted "toleration" of most modern constitutions.

In fairness to Maria Duce, it should be said that Ryan's summary of the papal attitude toward tolerance and the separation of church and state has the overwhelming weight of Church authority behind it. In fact, Ryan's statement is quite a model of Catholic doctrinal correctness. But it was extremely embarrassing for the Irish hierarchy to have a Catholic leader bring such notions into the open in a democratic nation, and to suggest that Catholic toleration is only a "temporary expedient." Northern Ireland was listening carefully. Was this the kind of "religious freedom" which the Northern Irish would get if they united with the South? When would Catholic power begin, in the Spanish manner, to suppress Protestantism in Ireland as "inimical to the common good"? If Maria Duce did not represent the Irish majority, why were its leaders permitted to express such ideas without rebuke from the Catholic hierarchy?

Liberal Catholics in Ireland rushed to deny that Irish Catholicism had any intention of curtailing the nation's basic liberties, but the Catholic hierarchy, which had the power to silence Maria Duce overnight, remained silent. Father Fahey, a member of the same religious order as the Archbishop of Dublin, continued to hold large meetings for at least three years after the publication of the statement by Ryan which I have quoted, and his books, reissued frequently under official Imprimatur, became the best sellers in Ireland. His pamphlets are still distributed by the Catholic Truth Society of Ireland, the most official of the propaganda agencies of the Church. One of his books, *The Mystical Body of Christ in the Modern World,* still carries in its ninth (1952) printing, under official Imprimatur, the famous anti-Semitic forgery, "The Protocols of the Learned Elders of Zion," with the accompanying statement that the charges of forgery "do not carry conviction to many serious minds." The book attempts to prove in great detail that the Communist Revolution in Russia was the work of Jews; it ascribes the Republican movement in Spain to "Judeo-Communist Agents"; it bewails the fact that the "Vicar of Christ was excluded from the Masonic League of Nations"; it suggests that "Marxism is simply one of the weapons of Jewish nationalism"; it charges that "citizenship of the Irish State can be for the Jews only a means for the attainment of their own national ideal." In condoning Hitler, it cites the statement of an American Catholic leader: "If the Jews find themselves beneath the same heel that has set out to crush Communism, who is to blame?" This kind of anti-Semitism has been attacked by the Dublin *Standard,* but its authors have not been publicly disciplined or even rebuked by the Irish hierarchy.

The Counter-Revolutionary Reserve

Father Fahey's right-wing movement is important for a number of reasons. It is paralleled by similar movements within the Catholic Church in the United States and in Latin America. It is building up in Ireland a reservoir of fanatical hatred of anything that can be labeled anti-Catholic, and some leaders of the Church are already dipping into that reservoir in their campaign against "secular" democracy. They are skillfully combining bigotry with anti-Communism, anti-atheism, and opposition to the welfare state. They are denouncing the United Nations as a symbol of pagan internationalism. The whole process is familiar to any student of the diocesan Catholic press in the United States. The aim of the movement is to create such a fanatical loyalty to Catholic authority that if the Irish democratic state should attempt to shake off clerical control, the Catholic masses would rise against it. The aim of the Church is to control and use those masses as a kind of counter-revolutionary reserve.

The Irish bishops correctly reason that the one great force in the modern world which can successfully challenge Catholic power — and supplant them in their control of community life — is the modern democratic state. Accordingly, they use their power over the people to teach that the state as such is not a good society. It is, they say, worthy of support only as it follows the moral directives of the bishops. The people owe to it a certain loyalty, but that loyalty must be limited and conditional or it will come in conflict with the higher authority of the Church. In Ireland the bishops constantly implant in the minds of their people a fear of the state. This is done partly by using the word "state" as if it described a power alien to the people which is threatening to deprive them of family and personal rights. In this type of clerical propaganda the Church is represented as the defender of the rights of the individual, and the state is represented as a political machine ruling over the people against their will.

"The Irish," says Dr. James Devane proudly, in describing, in the *Irish Rosary,* Ireland's achievement in winning independence "did not believe in the primacy of the nation or of the state. The Irish did not believe that power or sovereignty ultimately resides in the people, or that the peoples' will is the ultimate sanction of law. The Irish did not believe that the nation-state was self-sufficient or that it was the supreme political unit." This line of reasoning in a Catholic magazine leads inevitably to the conclusion that any form of government is worthy of support only to the extent that it is Catholic.

Since monarchy is the form of government adopted by the Church itself, and since monarchy can be kept under Catholic influence more easily than democracy, many Irish Catholic leaders have openly announced their preference for monarchy. "Any detached student of history," says Devane, "must recognize that monarchy, in some shape or other, confronts us everywhere. It is an element in a polity that is the most enduring, best-beloved and most universal. That is to be found among the greatest peoples and states in history in their greatest days. It was with us for a few thousand years. We might almost say the idea of monarchy is embedded in the natural constitution of human society." And he concludes his cynical analysis of the present democratic church-state alliance in Ireland by asking: "Does anyone in his senses think that the political constitution of society symbolised by 'the Republic' will last anywhere for two thousand years? We might ask for a hundred years?"

A great many right-wing Catholic propagandists of the same type as Devane are at work in Ireland undermining the people's faith in democracy, and the Church seems quite willing to permit them to spread their propaganda without rebuke. In November 1952, Maria Duce brought to Ireland, for an address in Dublin's leading hotel, the Austrian Catholic monarchist Erik von Kuehnelt-Leddihn, who proceeded to ridicule democracy and the welfare state in language akin to the slogans of continental fascism. Von Kuehnelt-Leddihn has made his reactionary position on democracy quite clear in his 1952 work *Liberty and Equality.* Of the European nations he wrote that "the only possible hope they have is a monarchical restoration," and he contended that the monarchical form of government is the "one and only form of government that harmonises with the Catholic temper and promises a minimum of sanity, balance and peace." He declared that "it is virtually certain that Catholic nations, with their love for personal liberty, their earthy pessimism, their pride and scepticism, will never in their hearts accept parliamentary democracy."

If such "earthy pessimism" about democracy seems out of place in Ireland, it should be remembered that the Irish hierarchy has never favored an Irish republic as such; nor has the Vatican ever favored democracy as such. The Irish hierarchy constantly attempted to win Catholic rights from the English throne without disputing the divine right of that throne, and its leaders became nationalists only when they believed that the throne stood between them and the achievement of a Catholic nation. The present Bishop of Cork, writing as a priest and professor in 1933, attacked a Jesuit critic of monarchy sharply and said: "The system of absolute monarchy or dictatorship is condemned as 'incompatible with right reason or the principles of Christianity.' As a matter of fact all philosophers maintain it to be the ideal system, *if a suitable dictator is at hand."* When one of Ireland's leading priests, Dr. Lucey, makes such a statement in Ireland's leading Catholic magazine, and is thereafter appointed Bishop of Cork, his notions of democracy cannot be dismissed as unrepresentative.

If a "suitable dictator" should appear in Ireland, what kind of Catholic state would he establish? The prevailing answer of the Irish priests today might be summarized as follows: It would be a peaceful and formally democratic state, if the people did not abuse their privileges by denying to the Church any of its present rights; it would be controlled by a benevolent and wise Catholic statesman who would permit the Church to supervise not only the nation's schools but also, to a considerable extent, the nation's social services.

In the meantime the Irish Catholic Church is sanctioning a continuous campaign against "the party system" and the welfare state; and much of the propaganda bears all the earmarks of fascist theory. It naturally centers attention upon the fear of Communism, and it combines this fear of Communism with reactionary propaganda against extensions of democratic government. God is represented as an earnest conservative who, of course, belongs to the Catholic Church. He is also represented as being deeply concerned to defeat the Communist menace in the Republic, and to respect the Catholic Church as the only real bulwark against Communism. In nearly all Catholic propaganda in Ireland the horrors of Communism are carefully confused with the horrors of an "all powerful" democratic state.

"The Silken Tyranny" was the typical appellation given to the alleged menace of the state in a series of articles in November 1952 in Ireland's largest daily newspaper, the *Irish Independent,* by one of Ireland's leading Catholic theologians, the Rev. Felim O Briain. The articles in question pictured the welfare state as "a variant of the cruder methods of Nazism, Fascism, Communism," and spoke of "welfare totalitarianism" and "the dehumanization that State paternalism is bound to achieve." The State, Father O Briain argued, has "no primary goal of its own; it is a subsidiary instrument to be used by citizens in achieving their common goals." The Church, on the other hand must not be so confined in its field of authority. "It is consequently a mistake to think, as some of our politicians have been thinking, that the moral law must be corralled into a partitioned area from which all social norms must be excluded. The distinction set up between the moral and the social teaching of the Church is an artificial and false teaching. Social teaching is no more than the application of moral principles to human social relations, all of which form part of God's plan."

Nine months later, in an important address at a Catholic college, Father O Briain revealed that it was contrary to "God's plan" for Irish Catholics to have as president of the largest Irish trade union a Protestant who "could not profess the principles of the Encyclicals" and who "made it a point to teach his members that trade unionism must not be sectarian."

Such a philosophy, coming from so authoritative a source, makes it clear that the pattern of moral childhood produced by the Irish priests has more than religious significance. A submissive population, trained in the ways of moral and religious immaturity, is the natural prey of authoritarian rule in politics and economics. The Church makes effective use of submissiveness now; fascism could tap the same fund. Although the Irish people are genuine believers in freedom, democracy is always bound to be on the defensive in a genuinely Catholic country because the Vatican rejects democracy for itself and thus makes the denial of self-government respectable. Bernard Shaw saw this point when, in continuing the comment on Irish moral childhood with which I began this chapter, he said that if the Irishman "dared to claim a voice in the selection of his parish priest, or a representative at the Vatican, he would be denounced from the altar as an incredible blasphemer. . . . It is the aim of his priest to make him and keep him a submissive conservative."

9

Northern Ireland and Partition

Everyone in Ireland admits that Northern Ireland is not a nation; it is *part* of a nation. But *which* nation? Two-thirds of the people of Northern Ireland say: Great Britain. One-third say: Ireland. That makes a 2-to-1 vote for Union. But this method of counting Northern noses arouses apoplectic wrath among the Irish Catholics. "You must count the votes in the *whole* of the island of Ireland," they say, "and by that test almost 80 per cent of the Irish people want Ireland united under Republican rule." To which the majority of Northern Irelanders reply: "If you are going to include all of Ireland in the count, why not be even more logical and include all of Great Britain also? That is the most natural unit for a test, and if a fair poll could be held in that unit, the overwhelming majority of the people of the British Isles would favor one government for these British islands."

So the deadlock continues, and neither side is prepared to yield. Nominally the Partition war is a cold war, but it would break out into a shooting war if the Southern Irish saw any prospect of success by physical violence. In fact, the border dispute is constantly breaking out into small-scale violence in the form of skirmishes and demonstrations which fail to attract world-wide attention only because of more serious disturbances elsewhere.

The Border Question

On both sides of this dispute nationalism and religion are inextricably mixed into one amalgam. Every Catholic baby born in the North is a potential soldier or helper for the enemy;

every Protestant baby is a potential defender of freedom and loyalty to the British throne. Virtually all Catholics of the North are nationalists, and virtually all Protestants are Unionists. Almost the whole population on both sides of the border is committed by tradition, friendship, or blood connection to one emotional grouping or the other. The "border question," as everybody calls it, is as pervasive a factor in the life of the people as death and the weather.

Both sides in this dispute are fond of appealing to history, and by proper selection of fact each side can use history as a club with which to belabor the other side. For a non-Irishman it is an exceedingly difficult and embarrassing task to determine where the truth lies, but if strict logic is followed the Unionists and Protestants seem to have the better of the argument. The island of Ireland, in spite of oceans of propaganda to the contrary, has never been a united, independent nation with a centralized Irish government ruling over the whole territory. The High Kings of the golden age of the ninth century were only nominal rulers of all Ireland, and until the English unified the land by conquest the country was a collection of political fragments. The concept of all-Ireland nationhood arose as a defensive dream, a natural and compelling dream, but nevertheless a dream, manufactured by the Irish rebels in their fight against English misrule, and historically never more than an aspiration and a hope.

It is doubtful whether a majority of the people of the North ever accepted the dream even in the days when the Northern Presbyterians stood for independence. Certainly the Northern Presbyterians never accepted the concept of an all-island *Catholic* state. "Ireland was naturally, or at least originally, divided," says the British Catholic writer Christopher Hollis, in the London *Tablet*. "The partition of Ireland into North and South has behind it far more ancient tradition than any notion of Irish unity. . . . Up to A.D. 1000, the High Kingship was always held alternately by a King for the North and a King for the South, in recognition of Ireland's natural division. . . . It was the English, at and after the Reformation, who first conceived of the notion of treating Ireland as a unity; and they did so, of course, in order to impose on it their penal system."

Ulster has always been sturdily independent in spirit, and its present defiance of the South in claiming local self-determination has centuries of precedent behind it. Many of the Northern people — perhaps the majority of them —have what one critic has called "a united, well-defined and entirely self-conscious provincial nationality." The North's anti-Romanism dates back to the sixteenth century, and its hostility to Dublin rule even farther. The Battle of the Boyne in 1690 was partly a victory of the Protestant North against Catholic power in Dublin, as well as against the English Catholic monarch, James II; and later Ulster became a loyal part of a British Protestant commonwealth. The people have learned to think of themselves as British and Scotch as well as Irish, and their primary loyalties run to themselves and to Britain.

Such arguments, of course, are open to question and counterattack. Many contrary facts can be marshaled on the other side. All the Catholic children in the North are given a very different story in their Catholic schools; they virtually all attend Catholic denominational schools, where Irish nationalist history is fed to them unofficially, and sometimes surreptitiously. Their loyalty to the North is tempered with doubt, and their loyalty to the South as their "real" country is consistently cultivated. For them the detachment of Northern Ireland from the rest of the island is a monstrous wrong, which should be corrected by "Irish unity." All Ireland was once united, they are told, but now it is divided by the wicked British.

To this, one Northern historian replies that "there were no such people as the Irish, that the island was inhabited by no one homogeneous race and had no one language or culture destined to be distinctively its own. . . . Even Gaelic was a language imposed by a conquering minority, as English was later imposed; and it is meaningless to call the inhabitants of the country 'Gaels' or 'Celts.' . . . Early as was the emergence of Ireland in the cloudy myths of the European dawn, the division of the island and its people into two parts was already there." Such is the verdict of Hugh Shearman, Northern Irish scholar, in his biography of Lord Craigavon, *Not an Inch*. Shearman's interpretations of Northern history — disputed by the South, in some instances — have been made virtually official by the Northern government. In non-Catholic schools the fact is emphasized that "over two thousand years ago the geological frontiers of Ulster had been frontiers also of human sentiment."

The English and the Scots conquered Ulster more completely than they conquered any other section of Ireland, and they preserved their identity and their point of view more successfully in the North than in the South. This was partly the result of the systematic displacement of Ulster Catholics by the British Protestant population in the early seventeenth century under James I, through the establishment of great plantations of English and Scotch settlers. Six whole counties of Ulster were confiscated at that time and given, for the most part, to Protestant settlers — Tyrone, Derry, Armagh, Fermanagh, Donegal, and Cavan. (Many parts of Antrim and Down had already been parceled out to English and Scotch settlers.) On these plantations a policy of English and Scotch separatism kept the conquerors, as far as possible, aloof from the Catholic "natives." Today the descendants of those Protestant settlers still rule the North, proud of their heritage and still slightly contemptuous of the Irish Catholic "lower classes."

To an outsider the appeal to ancient history in the dispute over Irish Partition is as dated as would be a claim to the ownership of Florida by a tribe of Seminole Indians. The appeal to recent history is more relevant, but even in this appeal there are sharply varying interpretations of the facts. The North emphasizes the fact that the present boundary line between North and South was accepted by the Free State parliament in 1925 by a vote of 55 to 14. The South declares that this acceptance was not a free acceptance but a choice of the lesser of two evils — made necessary by the threat of an even more unfair arrangement of boundaries; and Southerners recall that De Valera's supporters boycotted the Free State parliament until 1927.

The present reality is that both sides have now reached the point where impartiality in any statement and analysis of facts concerning the border question is difficult. On the whole, the Unionists are more balanced and accurate in their propaganda than the nationalists, but on some issues both sides resort to very partisan interpretations. All Northern Ireland is a battle zone, and the Partition fight is in progress on three fronts simultaneously — political, economic and educational.

The Political Struggle

The political battle over Partition is taking place on three electoral levels. The level which is most immediately vital for the settlement of the issue is the middle level, that of the regional parliament at Stormont, which meets at the capacious new government building in Belfast. On the top, imperial level of the British Parliament, Northern Ireland sends twelve members to the House of Commons, elected by universal suffrage from constituencies carved out by a committee of the British House of Commons itself, whose methods of redistribution have never been challenged or assailed. Nine of these representatives are Unionists, loyal to the queen and the present status of Northern Ireland within the United Kingdom; the other three, two Nationalists and one Irish Labor, favor unity with Dublin. On the middle level the same voters send 52 regional representatives to the Stormont House of Commons, of whom only 13 are nationalists. On the lower level, some of these voters elect councils for the control of the local affairs of cities and country districts, but the right to vote for these local officers is sharply curtailed by property qualifications. On this level the Catholic nationalists suffer their primary grievance, since they hold considerably less than their proportionate one-third of the seats, and in several districts they must submit to local government by a Unionist minority.

All electoral levels are important for the Partition issue — representation at Westminster helps each faction to influence world opinion, and representation in local councils means control of local jobs. But the regional parliament at Stormont is the most important instrument of power in Northern Ireland because it has the authority under the Ireland Act of 1949, passed by the British Parliament, to say whether the North will stay with Britain or will join Southern Ireland.

Stormont is safely British by a margin of about 2 to 1 — and by a perfectly honest count. There is no more chance that this regional parliament will vote for merger with the South than there is that the Ottawa parliament will vote for the annexation of Canada to the United States. Occasionally a political meeting is banned under circumstances of threatened disorder; but it is fair to say that coercion does not determine Northern Ireland's choice in favor of the British connection. The choice is a free choice, made deliberately after discussion of all the issues involved. But the South will not admit that the choice is free.

The tension between the two factions is greatly increased by the open militancy of the Southern regime. The Republic officially denies the right of Stormont to rule any part of Ireland, and its propaganda on this subject describes the North as "occupied Ireland." Many anti-Partitionists even advocate a system of representation of the North *in the Southern parliament,* regardless of the attitude of the Northern majority, thus ignoring the existence of the Northern regime and by-passing its authority. Some of the Southern leaders agree with them. Sean MacBride has declared: "I believe that the time has come when we should begin to organize our parliament as the parliament of the whole of Ireland: the first step in that direction obviously is to open the door of our Dail to the representatives from the occupied portion of Ireland." For a time the Southern government dramatized this idea by appointing a senator from the North who sat in the Dublin Senate.

The Constitution of the Irish Republic calmly declares: "The national territory consists of the whole island of Ireland, its islands and the territorial seas." Although it refrains from asserting total jurisdiction at the present time, "pending the reintegration of the national territory," its thesis is unmistakable: Northern Ireland does not exist as a legitimate regime, and all good patriots should disregard its existence if possible. Meanwhile, they should so employ their energies that the Northern regime will be captured from within. At election time in the North, anti-Partition money (raised by national collections in the South) and anti-Partition oratory cross the border in large quantities, in support of the Northern nationalist parties. These parties are treated as if they were parties of the Republic. The Irish Labor Party, in fact, is officially an all-island party, operating on both sides of the border without respect to the national boundary line. The Catholic nationalists do not consider such a policy as interference with Northern affairs, since they claim that the North really belongs to the Republic by moral right and that the only foreign intervention to be condemned in Ulster is that of Great Britain.

For a parallel to such a situation one would have to imagine the Constitution of the United States asserting an official claim to Canada, regardless of the majority vote of the Canadian people, and announcing that Canada's independence would be acknowledged only for the time being, pending final and legal absorption by the United States. Add to this hypothetical parallel the assumption that one-third of the people of Canada were organized into a pro-American political party functioning on Canadian soil and proclaiming exclusive and complete loyalty to the United States, and you have the reason for Northern bitterness on the border issue.

Because of the fear of conquest by the South, all Northern economic factions, social classes, and religious groups opposed to Catholic absorption bury their differences at election time in order to make sure that the nationalists are defeated. Leaders who do not agree with one another on any other issue consider this issue so overwhelmingly vital that they temporarily lay aside their differences. So, for over thirty years, the Unionists have ruled Stormont and dominated every department of Stormont activity. They have become by force of circumstance the accepted champions of non-Catholic supremacy in Northern Ireland. They are officially a conservative party, but they have in their ranks a most varied collection of political types, ranging from complete Toryism to socialism. They are affiliated loosely with the British Conservative party, and their representatives at Westminster usually take the Tory whip in the House of Commons. But because of the border issue the Unionists have become a kind of "umbrella party," embracing thousands of liberals and laborites who, if they lived in England or Scotland, might be loyal members of the British Labor Party. In Northern Ireland they stand with Lord Brookeborough and his Unionist party not so much because of their loyalty to political and economic conservatism as because of their fear of clerical conquest from the South. For these non-conservative Unionists, it is a choice between two evils, and they choose to be ruled by a conservative party in the North rather than by what they often describe as the "Dublin-Rome axis." The great majority of the working-class votes in the Belfast area — as well as virtually all the Protestant votes from all classes — go to Unionists or their allies in spite of the fact that the top leaders of the Unionist Party are anti-socialist.

Ironically enough, the Northern workers, who would normally support a labor party, have not had to pay any substantial price for aligning themselves with a nominally anti-socialist party. They have achieved the welfare state vicariously, largely because of the strength of the British labor movement across the Irish Sea. Northern Ireland's workers fortunately have the same unemployment insurance, old-age pensions, and health insurance that the English and Scotch workers have, because Ulster is part of Britain. Under such circumstances, they are inclined to reason: "Why should we weaken our tenure as British citizens by dividing the Unionist vote when we can get the benefits of British socialism without the risks of surrendering our country to Catholic power?"

This thoroughly opportunistic approach would have dismayed Marx, Engels, and Lenin, all of whom attempted to fit Ireland into a conventional capitalist-socialist pattern in which the British master class was on one side and the Irish working class was on the other. Marx seriously underestimated both nationalism and religion as factors in the Irish struggle. He could scarcely have anticipated the day when his most confident prophecies would be reversed by the rise of a British government more socialist than any government chosen by the "oppressed" people in Ireland. In a sense, the Northern workers who vote Unionist are more astute Marxists than Marx, because, in this case, they are protecting their gains under British socialism by voting for an anti-socialist regime. They realize that if they were absorbed into the South, they would be cut off eventually from the forward march of the British labor movement.

British Labor Vacillates

One reason for this emphatic rejection of the British Labor Party is that it has played its hand very clumsily in Northern Irish politics. Its leaders have created the impression that they are less concerned than the British Conservatives about the absorption of the North into a Catholic nation. When the British House of Commons passed the Government of Ireland Act in 1920, conceding Northern Ireland the right to stay inside the British Commonwealth, the British Labor Party opposed the Partition clause. This created the fear in the North that if British Labor should ever get a clear majority in the British House of Commons, it might turn over Northern Ireland to Dublin rule in spite of past commitments. The alarm was increased by the fact that the Catholic voters of Britain — nearly all Irish in extraction — vote Labor by a considerable majority.

The Northern fears of a sell-out by British Labor were partly dispelled when the Labor Party under Clement Attlee came into power at Westminster after World War II. At that time Attlee assured the Northern Irish people that the Labor Party and the British government had no intention of changing the status of the North without the consent of their Northern parliament. It was the Attlee government, in fact, which in 1949 passed the law acknowledging the Republic in the South, at the same time assuring the North of its continued British status as long as the regional Northern parliament desired it. But the effect of this assurance was partly canceled by the fact that, when the law came to a vote in the House of Commons, at least sixty Labor members passively opposed it. By inference, at least, they took their place with the movement for a united Ireland under Republican rule.

This wavering on the Partition issue created a near-panic among Northern Irish voters, both labor and conservative. Their apprehensions about British Labor had been strengthened by the creation of a branch of the party in Northern Ireland, called the Northern Ireland Labor Party, which attempted for a time to treat the whole Partition problem in terms of formal economic classes. The working class, it was said, must not co-operate with the reactionaries of the Unionist movement; the entire Irish working class, North and South, should unite behind a socialist program, and the Partition bridge would be crossed later. It was not until 1948 that the Northern Ireland Labor Party saw the incongruity of a democratic socialist movement turning over the North to a Southern Catholic regime which was opposed to the welfare state. Then the party changed its front and about-faced on the Partition issue. But by that time its reputation for wavering on this issue had doomed it in Northern Irish politics. Today it does not have a single representative at Westminster or at Stormont.

Meanwhile, the Northern labor nationalists have developed their own branch of the all-island Irish Labor Party. In the North it is a kind of proletarian half-sister of the Nationalist Party, with elected representatives in five county government bodies. It also dominates the nationalist movement in Belfast. In practice it is even more nationalist than the Nationalists. In fact, nationalism in the North tends to be distinctly pro-labor because the Catholic nationalists are, for the most part, members of an underprivileged economic group, living in the poorest houses in the cities, and occupying the workers' cottages on the farms. One writer has called them a "pariah population." Their psychology is the psychology of the oppressed and the disinherited, and it is even reflected in the kind of clothes they wear and the kind of residential sections they live in.

"I will take you down *X* Street," said a Derry businessman to me, "and let you tell *me* where the Protestant houses stop and the Catholic houses begin. I will even walk down the street with you and ask you to pick out the Catholics and the Protestants as they go by. You won't make many mistakes." I did not accept his challenge because it was unnecessary. The night before, in Belfast, a professor had said: "We have a sentence in common use here which sums up the situation pretty well. When a Protestant mother wants her boy to look neat as he is going away to school in the morning, she says: 'Smarten yourself up, son, and be a bit more Protestant-looking!'"

Ulster and the War

In the dark days of World War II, when Ulster's aid in the battle against German submarines may well have saved the Allied cause from defeat by Hitler, the Unionist Party came to symbolize loyal support for Britain. Even although many Catholic nationals volunteered on the British side, the majority of them were heartily and sincerely disloyal. The combination of Churchill and loyalty on one side, and Hitler and Catholic nationalism on the other, hardened the support of the Northern people behind the Unionist Party. The great shipyards of Belfast went to work furiously to defeat the German campaign of destruction on the seas — a campaign doubly effective because the Allies could not use the ports of the South in their counterattack. If, in those days, some of the Catholic nationalist workers were discharged from the Belfast shipyards as security risks without substantial proof of treason, what else could be expected? They belonged to a section of the community which opposed the government en bloc, and denied its right to exist. Feeling against Catholics in these shipyards had existed long before the war. A bloody riot, beginning in the yards in June 1935, had swept into the business sections of the city. Before it ended, hundreds of Catholic families were driven from their homes.

In retrospect the most severe critic of De Valera must concede that his policy of neutrality in the war was not wholly unreasonable. Certainly it was supported by the majority of his people, who not only resented the Partition of Ireland but also disbelieved in Baldwin and Chamberlain as champions of the liberty of small nations on the Continent. But the passions of war do not usually permit a balanced appraisal of issues, and the British people were in actual, acute danger of conquest by the Nazis. Also, the De Valera policy as it applied to the North did not deserve the description of "neutrality," since the Irish Prime Minister declared in the Dail that the Republic would consider the application of conscription to Ulster "an act of aggression." Four months before the war began, the Derry nationalists asked De Valera to mobilize "the Irish race at home and abroad immediately to resist the conscription of Irishmen." When Churchill at the end of the war declared that "we left the De Valera government to frolic with the Germans and later with the Japanese representatives to their heart's content," after "the approaches which the Southern Irish ports and airfields could so easily have guarded were closed by hostile air-craft and U boats," he echoed the bitterness in many Northern Irish hearts. De Valera replied that "in our circumstances, with our history and our experience after the last war, and with a part of our country still unjustly severed from us, no other policy was possible"; but his answer did not satisfy the Northerners. Their bitterness was increased when De Valera censored all news of the war and would not even permit the Republic's newspapers to print any stories of the heroic deeds of the more than 100,000 Irishmen who volunteered on the Allied side. Of De Valera the Unionists said:

> The latter, sheltered from the errors of modern war by the umbrella of the armed forces of Great Britain and Northern Ireland, and of the many Allied Powers — in particular the U.S.A. — was able to declare a policy of neutrality at all costs. The real costs, of course, were not Eire's, but borne by the Allied nations in the severe toll of human life and war material in the form of ship and plane, because Eire, unlike loyal Ulster, would not offer her ports, aerodromes and training centres to those battling for the future of all mankind.

Of course the liberal critics of the Northern Unionists pointed out that they were not similarly concerned with the fate of "those battling for the future of all mankind" against Franco in the Spanish Civil War, and that this lack of concern everywhere had made World War II possible. But Spain was some distance away. In Northern Ireland, Unionism stood for the defense of freedom against tyranny. Politically speaking, the South's refusal to join Britain in the war, supported as it was by the Catholic nationalists in the North, guaranteed Unionist control of Ulster for another generation.

The Catholic Church in the North emerged from the war period with impaired moral standing. Its leaders did everything except advocate open insurrection to keep Ireland out of an alliance with Great Britain. (Curiously enough, this was the exact line of the Communist Party up to June 1941.) It should be remembered that in 1939 and 1940 the Vatican was just completing a long and uncertain period of alternating negotiation and collaboration with fascism. Its sympathies were not wholly fascist at any time, and it was definitely hostile to Hitler's anti-religious program, but its world policy was much closer to the Rome-Berlin axis than to the London-Paris axis. Its leaders in the United States at that time were the most determined isolationists in the nation.

Its leaders in Dublin were equally hostile to Britain's war effort even after war was declared, and its leaders in the North were only slightly less open in their hostility. The Dublin *Catholic Bulletin* in 1939, just before the outbreak of World

War II, revealed the dual pro-Germanism and anti-British sentiment of the Irish hierarchy by charging that "the English Government has been at work to encircle Germany and Italy," and
by stating that "Germany is not guilty on the Continent of any
act of aggression comparable to the British occupation of Northern Ireland or the Partition of Palestine, the seizure of the Sudan
or the subjection of India." The journal upbraided the Catholic
press of England for opposing the German proposals about
Danzig "merely because that justice conflicts with the selfish
interest of English, or shall we say Anglo-Jewish finance."

When the war finally came and Ireland declared its neutrality,
the *Catholic Bulletin* virtually asked for British defeat by saying:
". . . we could live on much better terms with a tamer England.
. . . The humanity in us makes us sorry for the suffering on
which the English are entering (whether they win, lose or draw
the war), but we believe that the chastened England of the future
will be happier, healthier, and Providentially likelier to recover
a Christian faith: and that it ought to be a better neighbour
than we have known during the centuries of English world
domination."

The Irish hierarchy in its first meeting after the outbreak of
the war cautiously expressed specific sympathy for only one
nation — "One great Catholic people, the Polish nation." The
bishops did not venture any direct condemnation of Hitler and
his policy. It is clear from all the Irish Catholic discussions of
European affairs during this period that Catholic opposition to
Ireland's entrance into the war was based not merely on a sincere
desire for peace, but also on a fundamental preference for the
Axis cause. Czechoslovakia, according to the *Catholic Bulletin,*
was not worth fighting for because it was "a Masonic conglom-
erate," and "the ulcer of Europe." "It is almost superfluous to
say," continued the *Bulletin,* "that war or no war, this country
whose sons for centuries have been driven by British oppression
to fight as mercenaries the world over, has no concern whatever
with France's undertaking to fight for composite Czechoslovakia,
and so facilitate the westerly expansion of Godless Russia, which,
in turn is secretly allied with communist France against Catholic
and Nationalist Spain, under General Franco."

It was such utterances that convinced many Northern Irishmen that in opposing consolidation with the South they were opposing the alignment of their government with a reactionary, pro-fascist power. Their support of Partition gained new moral force, and the Unionist Party, as the symbol of loyalty to Britain in the struggle for survival, gained new strength also.

The Church and Partition

The Irish Catholic hierarchy has been boldly political in its stand on Partition since 1921 in both the North and the South, and this commitment has helped to make the political contest in the North a clean-cut Protestant-Catholic struggle. The Protestants have been almost as partisan on the issue as the Catholics, but their partisanship has not been so conspicuous because the Catholic Church has been the church of rebellion. Successive cardinals have refused to give the Stormont regime official recognition by appointing a Catholic chaplain for Catholic members of parliament; and in 1921 the Irish cardinal announced that he was opposed to the new Northern parliament "root and branch." In that year Cardinal Logue and his bishops announced that "our countrymen spurn . . . the sham settlement [Partition] devised by the British government." Cardinal Mac-Rory was just as openly partisan on the Partition issue, describing Ireland as "an ancient land made one by God, partitioned by a foreign power against the vehement protests of her people." When Archbishop John D'Alton was made a cardinal in 1952, and gave his first broadcast to the Irish people as their new Catholic leader, he calmly coupled an appeal against Partition with an appeal for Christian faith. At the time of the division of Ireland, the Church officially described Partition as illegal conquest. "By the acceptance of partition," said the *Catholic Encyclopedia Supplement* of 1922, ". . . the Catholics in Northeast Ulster, without being consulted or given any guarantee of civil or religious liberty, have been handed over to the mercy of fanatical Orangemen, over 20,000 of whom in Belfast alone have been armed to crush Catholicism."

When the Northern Prime Minister, Lord Craigavon, offered in 1939 to adopt conscription in Northern Ireland, and was backed by Northern Ireland's representatives at Westminster, the British government did not dare to accept the offer — largely

because of the threat of an insurrection on the combined Parti-
tion-conscription issues by Northern Catholics under the leadership of their bishops. The bishops, headed by Cardinal MacRory,
said in a meeting at Armagh:

> We are convinced that any attempt to impose Conscription here would
> be disastrous. Our people have been already subjected to the gravest
> injustice in being cut off from one of the oldest nations in Europe and in
> being deprived of their fundamental rights as citizens in their own land.
> In such circumstances, to compel them to fight for their oppressor would
> be likely to rouse them to indignation and resistance. It would be re-
> garded by Irishmen not only in the Six Counties, but in Eire and through-
> out the world, wherever they are found, as an outrage on the national
> feeling and an aggression upon our national rights.

Priests throughout the North use their pulpits for nationalist
propaganda, thinly disguised as an assertion of Catholic rights,
and frequently appear as delegates and local chairmen at nationalist conventions. Sometimes they even appear as watchers
and directors of nationalist activity near the polls, urging their
people to vote for those who represent the Church's interests.
Under such circumstances it is not surprising that every Catholic
is considered a nationalist until proved otherwise. But in such
a situation it is not fair to speak of loyalty and treason without
realizing that the partisans of each side have some claim to the
terms. One man's loyalty may be another man's treason, if they
disagree concerning the identity of their true government.

The Catholic nationalists do not ease the tension in Northern
Ireland when they use the fact of Partition to excuse themselves
from all responsibility toward a Western anti-Communist military alliance. Most Northerners think that the Southerners, if
they are as ardent in opposing Communism as they say they are,
should join the North Atlantic Treaty Organization unconditionally. "To suggest that Ulster is an obstacle in the way is a
transparent pretence," says a widely distributed Unionist pamphlet. But De Valera is firm in his determination to treat the
Partition issue and Ireland's support of NATO as parts of the
same problem. At the Strasbourg Assembly of the Council of
Europe in 1950, he summed up the South's rejoinder to the
charge of welshing on its anti-Communist commitments: "It is

a mockery in Ireland," he said, "to talk about defense against aggression when part of the country is living against its will under foreign domination. The liberty of Ireland is as precious to the Irish as the liberty of France to the French or of England to the English."

Is Northern Ireland Suppressed?

Such an assertion raises the question: What part of Northern Ireland is "living against its will under foreign domination"? Certainly, Northern Ireland as a whole is not living under a government which can be honestly described as "foreign domination," since its people prefer their present regime by a margin of 2 to 1, and it is not any more foreign to them than the government at Washington is foreign to the people of New York. Do the Catholic nationalists have a moral claim to some *part* of Northern Ireland, even if their moral claim to the *whole* is unsound?

If the answer is given in terms of counties, two of the Six Counties of the North are Catholic and nationalist by a narrow margin — Fermanagh and Tyrone. The Catholic-Protestant ratio in these two counties is about 53 to 47, and the nationalists there have held a majority in every general election since 1920. Could the Partition issue be solved if these two counties were carved out of the North and ceded to the South? Some reasonable men favor such a compromise — but the leaders of the South reject the concession as too little, while the leaders of the North declare that it is too much. Both sides privately admit that such a dissection and readjustment of boundaries would probably not settle anything. The cession of the two counties would leave unsolved the problem of the North's second city, Derry, which is predominantly nationalist though located in a Unionist county. Derry is only a few miles from the Republic's County Donegal, to which it belongs in spirit. If Northern Ireland were to be carved up according to a pattern of local allegiance to Dublin or Stormont, the South would get not only the counties of Tyrone and Fermanagh, but also the city of Derry and the sections known as South Armagh and South Down. The Dublin *Irish Catholic* has advocated the right of these sections "to secede from the Stormont-ruled Statelet" because of their nationalist majorities. If they did, there would be almost nothing left of Northern Ireland except Belfast and its environs.

That is one reason why the Unionists are standing pat on the present boundaries. They feel that if they yield an inch they will be compelled ultimately to surrender everything. They do not hesitate to state their case with great firmness and moral conviction. To the question "Is there an insuperable obstacle to the union of the two areas?" Lord Brookeborough replies:

> Yes. The border between Northern Ireland and Eire exists because of the ideological gulf which divides the two people. There are differences of racial origins, of religion and political allegiance, and the three combined have made the separation of the two areas inevitable. Therefore there must be two Governments in Ireland. There are two Governments today and each has worked well in its own area. Ulster's allegiance to the Crown is fixed and unalterable. Although Ulster and Eire cannot unite, they can be good neighbors — on this condition, that each recognizes the right of the other to shape its destiny in its own way without interference. That is true democracy; it is also sound statesmanship.

Much of the language used by the Southern patriots and by the Northern nationalists in reply to a statement like Lord Brookeborough's is too sulphurous for this printed page. "Fascist Tory" is one of the milder epithets applied to him. The leaders of the nationalists in those areas which are claimed by the opposition carry on a verbal crusade against the government which comes at times very close to civil war. Even in Unionist Belfast, the opponents of Partition use every opportunity to dramatize their grievances by public protests. The Stormont parliament's nationalists refuse to recognize the British Governor and absent themselves from all ceremonies in which he is involved. Their assaults on "British tyranny" often throw the parliamentary debates into an uproar. Here, for example, are a few sentences from a debate on December 9, 1952, on the question of whether tenants occupying Housing Trust homes should be encouraged to fly the British Union Jack; the report is from the Belfast Catholic daily, the *Irish News:*

> Mr. J. Stewart (A.P.) asked if the Minister was aware that 50 per cent of the people of the Six Counties resented the flying of the Union Jack. (*Cries of "It's a lie" from the Unionist benches.*)

MR. STEWART — The Union Jack is steeped red in the blood of Irish martyrs.

Mr. CAHIR HEALY — Is the Minister aware that the Union Jack is not the flag of this country?

The Speaker intervened to say that the Union Jack was the flag of the country the hon. member was in. . . .

Mr. DIAMOND [Irish Labor] — Do I understand that the tenants who fly the [Irish] Tricolor will be granted permission to do so?

UNIONIST MEMBERS — Certainly not.

Mr. MINFORD — I think it is the duty of the Minister to see that the red, white and blue flag is flown everywhere in Northern Ireland.

Mr. Stewart asked if the Minister would see that a flag pole was erected and that a flag was put on it to please the member for Antrim, bearing the inscription, "To hell with the Pope."

The nationalists refused to recognize the coronation of George VI; and they began mobilizing against his daughter as soon as her coronation was announced. They were supported by the highest dignitaries of the Southern regime: De Valera refused to attend a coronation celebration at the British Embassy in Dublin, and Frank Aiken, his Minister for External Affairs, said of the inclusion of Northern Ireland in the young queen's titles: "It is an outrage on Irish sentiment to describe Queen Elizabeth as Queen of any part of Ireland." The Anti-Partition Association called for a complete boycott of the coronation throughout Ireland, and the Newry Urban Council, in County Down, forbade all public expenditures in that city for the coronation festival. When Elizabeth and Philip paid their coronation visit to Northern Ireland in July 1953, nationalist saboteurs blew up a bridge on the main railway line between Dublin and Belfast, and the nationalist members of the Stormont parliament issued a proclamation which was pasted on the walls, pavements, and shop windows throughout the North proclaiming that "these presents hereby repudiate all claims now made or to be made in the future by, or on behalf of, the British Crown and Government to jurisdiction over any portion of the land of Ireland or her territorial seas."

In a meeting of the Belfast Corporation, the leader of the Irish Labor Party fought so fiercely against an appropriation for coronation bunting for the parks that, after the noisy intervention of a citizens' gallery of nationalist sympathizers, the meeting was forced to adjourn. One of the ablest and most sincere of the anti-Partitionists, Mrs. Mary O'Malley of the Belfast Corporation, climaxed her attack on coronation expenditures with the charge, addressed to her opponents: "Your loyalty should be as ours is, always has been and always will be — to Ireland and not to any foreign power." It is a striking fact that this reference to foreign power is never today applied by any Catholic leader in the North or the South to the power of the Vatican in Ireland — although Daniel O'Connell once proudly declared: "We take our religion from Rome, not our politics."

Derry — the Irish Powder-Keg

In a sense the city of Derry — called Londonderry by the British — is the emotional center of nationalist-Unionist conflict in the North. It is the shirt-manufacturing capital of the British Commonwealth, and the world capital of Protestant-Catholic tensions. It frequently produces riots on Saint Patrick's Day, when Republican demonstrators try to carry the Irish tricolor in the presence of Orangemen. Its 1952 Saint Patrick's Day riot, centering around a tricolor, was so bloody that the Northern Home Minister banned the 1953 parade to prevent a hostile demonstration by those "who want to bring down the Constitution by force." This city of 50,000 is held by the Unionists in the face of a nationalist majority. It has a legal Unionist mayor, and a "pretender" mayor, Alderman Eddie McAteer, who leads the anti-Partition forces. "This is the Danzig of Ireland," he told me earnestly. "There is no place in the world where two white communities are so rigorously kept apart by mutual agreement. . . . I call this oil-and-water country. The people appear to be together, but they are actually separate. . . . The British have preserved much of the master-race psychology of white colonists who secretly think of their votes as equal to twenty colored ones."

McAteer is aggressive and deeply convinced of the righteousness of his own cause; and he gains courage for aggressive behavior from the clear nationalist majority in the city precincts. When he was defeated for mayor of Derry in May 1952 by a vote of 11 to 7 in the Corporation, and his victorious opponent was about to take the mayoral chair, McAteer walked to the rostrum and declared: "I shall take the seat to which I am rightfully entitled. I declare Alderman Orr's election is invalid in the name of the people of Derry."

But McAteer had no troops to back him up; the seat of the mayor remained in the possession of the Unionists, and Derry's new Unionist mayor was quietly installed at a later date when the nationalists were feeling less obstreperous. McAteer that night telegraphed his loyalty to President O'Kelly of the Irish Republic; he had received a special invitation to the Southern inaugural. "As the rightful mayor," he wired, "I extend to you congratulations from this Republican city on your unopposed return as President. With my colleagues, I pray the blessing of God on your term of office, and we pledge, through you, our loyalty to the Thirty-Two County nation." When Northern Ireland's new Governor, Lord Wakehurst, first paid an official visit to Derry in February 1953, the eight anti-Partition members of the Corporation sat through the six courses of an official luncheon with folded arms, refusing to eat or to stand for "God Save the Queen." When Lord Wakehurst rose to speak, McAteer also rose and spoke simultaneously in Irish. When Queen Elizabeth II spent two hours in Derry during her post-coronation tour in July 1953, and conferred a knighthood on the Unionist mayor, 1,300 police were assigned to duty in the city.

McAteer's program for achieving the annexation of Derry and ultimately the absorption of Northern Ireland into the Republic is quite similar to the original Sinn Fein program. The program officially disclaims violence and bloodshed — in a rather subdued and unconvincing voice — placing its reliance upon sabotage and disturbance. McAteer, in an amazingly frank pamphlet called *Irish Action*, has outlined his plans for sabotage.

> Most Irish people who are active in seeking freedom used to believe that it would come to us by force of either constitutional agitation or by violence. Then the mighty spirit of the late Mahatma Gandhi pointed a third road — non-cooperation, non-violence. . . .
>
> Each individual must constitute a complete action cell. If you resolve within yourself each morning that you will do something during the day to render the British occupation of Ireland more troublesome or more expensive you may rest assured that your enlivened imagination and more active thought will suggest a means. . . . The success of a pin-pricking campaign lies not in the actual size of the pin-pricks but in their number and frequency.

The old boycott idea springs to mind at once and it must be practiced to the maximum degree by each individual. Those who support the enemies of our freedom are guilty of a small act of treason. . . . All pro-British functions must be shunned like the plague. However fond you are of music or the arts you must avoid concerts, etc., where they insist that an artistic feast must be digested with the help of the British National Anthem. . . . Our attitude must be the attitude of the French to the Germans whilst France was under German occupation. . . .

Nowadays, governmental machinery works largely through the agency of myriads of forms which are showered on the helpless citizens. . . . All such forms must be lost and if needs be — under threat of active compulsion for example — you can cause the department concerned to issue a duplicate. . . . If it pays you to fill a form, fill it. If it doesn't, throw the form in the fire. Increased cost and difficulty in administration here will quickly make itself felt in Whitehall. Should it happen that you have the leisure to go to the Department, act stupid, demand explanations, object, anything at all that will clog the Departmental machinery.

When such a program of continuing sabotage is being advocated by one of the North's leading political figures — McAteer is also a member of the Stormont parliament — the Northern government is not willing to dispense with the Special Powers Act under which civil liberties can be suspended quickly for an emergency. Originally passed for a one-year term during the stormy period of 1922, this Special Powers Act makes it possible for the Ulster Constabulary to search nationalist headquarters and hold persons on suspicion, and even suspend the right of assembly and jury trial for a time. It has been a chief target of nationalist attack for several years, and because of it the nationalists have represented the whole North as a land of illegal suppression. It is true that for a time after the chief danger of civil war was past the special provisions designed to suppress insurrection were continued in force, and the continuance rightly drew the criticism of the British National Council for Civil Liberties. Now the most obnoxious provisions of this law have been suspended, but the government still retains the right to bring them back into force in an emergency and to round up persons on suspicion and hold them without immediate trial in case of a threatened uprising. Parallel powers were invoked by the De Valera government in the South during World War II.

If American officials in a parallel situation were confronted with such open defiance by a political opposition which professed allegiance to a neighboring country, they would probably take even more specific measures against such an opposition. The situation is a war situation in fact if not in name. The South itself was torn by violence and insurrection until recently, instigated by the same movement which now threatens the Northern regime, and military tribunals in the Republic were not abandoned until 1947. The threat of armed conquest is implicit in nearly all the propaganda of the nationalist movement, even when force is nominally repudiated for political reasons. The Derry *Journal,* leading Catholic paper of that city, as late as June 1951 advocated the taking over of the North by a Dublin constituent assembly.

The Orangemen

The counterpart of McAteer's forces and the backbone of Unionism in the North is the Orange Lodge of Ireland, one of the most powerful and certainly the most militant Protestant organization in the world. Estimates of its membership run as high as 200,000, and its Orange halls are scattered through the whole Northern region, serving as "centers of loyalty," centers of Protestant civic and social activity, and potential fortresses of military defense against the South. Each year, on July 12, anniversary of the Battle of the Boyne, the members of the Orange hosts march through the streets of the Northern cities with bright banners flying, draped in their brilliant-colored sashes, and whipped into a fine patriotic fervor by the ominous tom-tom boom of their lambegs — those special Orange drums which are carried by a single drummer and beaten with rattan canes until the heavens reverberate. The drums are often beaten so ardently by champion drummers that blood from wounded wrists flows over the surface. No one who has seen the grim and determined hosts of loyal Orangemen marching on July 12 doubts that a Southern Irish army would meet with stout resistance if it ever attempted a direct conquest of the North.

Although the Orange Order is not officially a military organization, it supplies the chief strength for the "B Specials" of the Ulster Constabulary — the reserve military force of about 10,-000 on which the Northern government would rely to suppress a nationalist insurrection. In political life the Order is virtually coextensive with the Unionist Party, serving as a kind of hard inner core for that organization and giving the movement an almost religious flavor. Almost all Unionist leaders are simultaneously leaders of the Orangemen. The organization is officially Protestant, a zealous denominational counterpart to Catholic Action. It enlists in its ranks not only laymen but many of the leading Presbyterian and Anglican clergymen of the North, who march in its parades and echo its policies from their pulpits.

When Queen Elizabeth II was crowned, the Orangemen sent resolutions of loyalty to her, declaring: "The very thought of entering an All-Ireland Republic is repugnant to every loyal Orangeman. . . . Year after year we have, alas, evidence that is indisputable, that the real power in Eire is the Roman Catholic Hierarchy, and to that authority we will never submit. We cannot accept any doctrine unless it can be proved from Holy Scripture, which is the basis of our Order."

The Orange Order's rules of denominational exclusion are as strict as Catholic rules on mixed marriage. No Catholic and no Jew may belong; if any Orangeman marries a Catholic, he is immediately dropped from membership. Children of Catholic parents may become members, but only if they receive special permission from the Imperial Grand Lodge. For a time, Orangemen were not even allowed to frequent a public house operated by a Catholic. If an Orangeman today sells his property to a Catholic convent or school, he is considered a traitor to his country and his Order. In some districts Orange lodges have banded together to buy up old estates in order to prevent their acquisition by Catholic organizations.

When Orange leaders are criticized for this policy of separatism, they simply refer to the parallel policy of the Catholic Church, and point out that that policy is officially promoted and directed by the priests. As evidence of their point, they circulate by the thousands a little card headed "Roman Catholic Policy in Northern Ireland," with the following passage from the *Irish Times* of May 4, 1951:

Speaking in St. Patrick's Church, Killenagh, Donemana, yesterday, after he had administered Confirmation, Most Rev. Dr. Farren, Bishop of Derry, expressed appreciation of the high religious standard in their parish, but issued a solemn warning in regard to two grave matters. One was the danger to young people who sought amusement in non-Catholic halls, and the other was the abuse of drink at wakes.

Bishop Farren said that if their young people went into dangerous surroundings, if they had to seek their amusement among non-Catholics in non-Catholic halls, where the standard of purity was not as high as it was among Catholics, could they expect their young people to come out of those halls as good as they went into them?

"If you allow your children to be contaminated by those who are not of the fold, then you can expect nothing but disaster, and surely the disasters that have happened should be warning for you."

In such an atmosphere it would be astonishing if there were *not* charges of discrimination and political manipulation by both sides, and it would be still more astonishing if some of the charges were not true. It should be remembered that both sides in the Partition dispute are fighting for what they consider their country, and that when treason is involved most men do not feel an obligation to give their enemies equal treatment with their friends. The fear of an actual physical conflict with the South is constantly in Northern minds, and it shapes the North's political program even in local affairs. If, for example, Alderman Eddie McAteer's nationalist forces should capture the city of Derry, there are many Unionists who believe that martial law in the area would be a necessity, since the nationalist forces in the local government would be, in effect, legions of the Southern government. They could be expected to sponsor an attempt at physical conquest.

Gerrymandering in Fact and Fancy

The chief charge made by the nationalists against the Unionists is that the nationalists are being deprived of political power by gerrymandering, the rearrangement of electoral boundaries to benefit the party in power. The Catholic nationalists of both Southern and Northern Ireland picture Unionist gerrymandering in the North as a major crime. I have met responsible persons in the South who believed that an actual nationalist majority in the North is being gerrymandered out of existence.

This claim is wholly unfounded. An analysis of all the confusing and bitter claims in the anti-Partition literature on this subject shows that there is some basis for nationalist complaints; but it is impossible to argue that gerrymandering has changed the electoral result except in some local councils. Some gerry-mandering *does* exist, but it is a much less important evil than the nationalist propaganda would indicate.

Gerrymandering does not substantially affect the control of the Stormont legislature or the representation of Northern Ireland in the British Parliament. The nationalists are somewhat under-represented at Westminster — they have only 3 out of 12 seats in the House of Commons, whereas their mathematical proportion in the population would entitle them to about 4. But such under-representation of a minority is not unusual in a democracy under the single-candidate method of voting. There are many places in the world where a dominant political party captures disproportionate representation through the ability to win large numbers of districts by a narrow margin, and frequently the ability to win districts by a narrow margin is based upon a favorable arrangement of boundary lines. In the United States, Republican plans to redistrict Massachusetts in order to gain a congressional seat were publicized in June 1953, after it became known that the Democrats would have done likewise if they had won in the 1952 election. There was a period in New York City in the 1930's when the Republican Party had only 1 representative of 65 on the Board of Aldermen, although it polled 26 per cent of the popular vote. A partisan analyst could have said that it took 339,000 votes to elect a Republican and 13,300 votes to elect a Democrat in New York City in 1931 — and the statement would have been literally true.

Ulster does not now use the voting method of proportional representation, but it did so in the election of 1921 for the Stormont parliament. In that election the result was almost the same as the Northern Ireland parliamentary result in 1949 — 40 members for Unionism in 1921, and 39 in 1949, out of a total of 52 seats. Today the Catholic nationalist proportion in the Northern population is about one-third, and its proportion in the Stormont House of Commons is about 23 per cent. Year after year in the elections for Stormont the proportionate vote of Unionists and anti-Partitionists has remained substantially the same; the floating vote is almost nil. If a national plebiscite were taken in Northern Ireland tomorrow, under the auspices of some neutral body like the United Nations, on the question of London or Dublin affiliation, there is no reason to believe that the balance of power would shift in any way.

The Belfast area itself seems to be free of gerrymandering; but some gerrymandering has taken place in behalf of the Unionists in the "danger zones" of west Ulster, where Unionists and nationalists are about equal in strength. Unfortunately, the nationalist propaganda on this subject is confusing because it intermingles evidence of actual gerrymandering with evidence of under-representation due to other factors. I have before me as I write the most famous of the pamphlets of the Anti-Partition Association on this subject, *Ireland's Right to Unity*. It lists six star cases of what it calls the new "democracy" and charges: "By a systematic manipulation of electoral boundaries and by an unequal franchise minorities are enabled to secure majority representation." But only one of these six instances concerns Stormont representation, and that instance is disputed by the Unionists. The other instances are all in the area of local representation, and the nationalists fail to point out that in many cases the under-representation is caused by property qualifications for local voting which existed first in Britain and have been retained by the Northern Ireland government. These limitations do not affect the choice of the Northern people in favor of separation from the South because they do not apply to the Stormont parliament.

The evidence seems to indicate some clear gerrymandering in Derry, with some probable gerrymandering in the counties of Tyrone and Fermanagh, but the total representation of these two counties in the Stormont parliament, taken together, is almost proportional. The Unionists poll 45 per cent of the vote and get 50 per cent of the eight representatives; if the nationalists were given one more than half, they would be getting 62 per cent of the representation with 52 per cent of the vote — which would, technically, be an even greater injustice. The independent *Leader* of Dublin expressed a temperate and honest judgment on the whole question of Northern gerrymandering when it said: "In local affairs gerrymandering did certainly produce some grotesque results, but in the Stormont constituencies it can hardly have deprived the Nationalists of more than a seat or two."

If I were a liberal citizen of Northern Ireland, I would be more embarrassed by property qualifications for voting than by gerrymandering. The total effect of gerrymandering seems hardly worthy of the turmoil it has created, while the property qualifications for voting in local elections run counter to all modern trends in democracy, and tend to perpetuate class divisions in society. These qualifications were dropped in Britain in 1946 and in Southern Ireland in 1935, but to this day in Northern Ireland the voting rules for local councils favor those residents who have property, and exclude from the local franchise the lodger and the man without possessions. A few businessmen have been given plural votes in proportion to their property holdings under a clumsy plan of corporation representation — which makes the local franchise look like a rich man's privilege. The total effect of the property restrictions is to reduce the parliament voting list in all of Northern Ireland by about 34 per cent for local government elections. The reduction affects the Catholic sections much more than the Protestant sections because the Catholic people of the North are poorer than the Protestants.

In practice, it is doubtful whether this system of property limitations on voting has justified itself even as a defensive measure. By penalizing the Protestant poor as well as the Catholic poor, it tends to make them hostile to Unionism. It gives the nationalists an opportunity to describe the Unionist government as an instrument of the British upper classes against the Irish masses. A special provision which permits banks and stock companies to get as many as six votes for their officers in local elections has created an outcry against "class privilege." Actually it has added to Unionist strength fewer than 5,000 votes — less than one per cent of the total vote — and if it were abandoned the Unionists probably would not lose a single seat.

Jobs for Protestants — and Catholics

The economic discrimination practiced by both sides in the North is more disturbing than the political discrimination. In some industrial plants an unofficial religious test for employment is taken for granted, although the test is usually not applied openly. In Derry, for example, it is assumed that when an employer advertises for help in a Protestant paper, he wants Protestant employees; in a Catholic paper, Catholic employees. In general, all Catholic employers in the North hire Catholics only, but this discrimination does not receive much public attention because at least 80 per cent of the large employers in the North are Protestants. Even the Orangemen among these large Protestant employers do not usually draw a hard-and-fast line against the employment of Catholics; if they did, they would destroy their own economic position, since that position is often based upon the employment of Catholic labor. But the Catholic employees themselves often enforce Catholic penalties upon any "renegade." In a Derry shirt factory in 1951, the Catholic employees went on strike against a Catholic forelady because she had been married to a Protestant husband in a Protestant ceremony. They refused to accept work from her, and she was ultimately transferred to another post in the industry.

The most important discrimination against Catholics occurs in the field of promotion and placement, since the tendency in Protestant firms is to give the important and well-paid posts to Protestants. It is not always possible to say how much of this favoritism is based on religious discrimination; education is often the determining factor. The young men and women from Protestant homes are likely to be better educated and better trained for supervisory positions because of their tradition and their greater wealth. In this respect the forces of separatism work in a deadly circle. Personal friendships are carried over into the world of business and the world of politics, and the separatism of social life extends itself automatically. The whole society of the North is divided up into Protestant and Catholic segments, and the two segments do not mix socially, from youth to old age. The more menial and subordinate positions in industry, in society, and in government are usually taken by the Catholics; the more responsible and better-paid posts usually go to the Protestants. When the Catholics gain control of a Northern industry or a Northern political body, they tend to reverse the rules with gusto.

The same tendency toward discrimination exists in the erection and assignment of new houses by local political bodies. The great Northern Ireland Housing Trust, supported from government funds and directed by public-spirited appointees, has set an example of non-discrimination in the erection of more than five thousand dwellings. But in the political no-man's-land of Tyrone and Fermanagh, the *local* housing authorities which are Catholic tend to erect houses for Catholics, and the *local* Protestant councils tend to favor houses for Protestants. In this battle for supremacy the Protestants have the advantage because they control more local councils.

In public employment those government departments controlled by Britain are more scrupulously fair than those controlled by Stormont. By tradition, one-third of the Ulster Constabulary may be Catholic, but in the chief departments of the regional government almost all the higher posts are held by Protestant Unionists, and there is no attempt to distribute them to Catholics. In some cases the selection for higher posts is nominally based upon competitive tests, but in many others the discriminatory exclusion of Catholic nationalists is all too apparent. And this discrimination in promotions runs through the entire government structure, in Belfast and elsewhere. The policy of exclusion of nationalists from key posts is frankly defended by the Unionists — in private — as a necessity for national survival. "If we didn't do it, we wouldn't be here," said one of them to me when I raised the question of discrimination. "It is our country or theirs — and if we relax, it will be theirs."

The Birth Rate as a Weapon of Conquest

For a time the Unionist majority in the North feared that it would be overcome by a wave of Catholic migration from the South; then the Northern government stopped the flow of Southern workers by requiring work permits for those who wished to stay in the North. Since there is considerable unemployment in peacetime in the North, very few immigrants from the South are now able to find both work and residence. The real fear of the North today is that the South will defeat the loyal majority by a higher Catholic birth rate. The Catholics themselves are convinced that they will ultimately conquer the North by this means, and that, as Dr. James Devane predicts in the *Irish Rosary,* "the dominant party in the six counties cannot hold out for any great length of time against a sovereign Irish state on their border, and the virile minority, which will soon be half the population within the six counties."

It is claimed that the Catholic birth rate in the North was double the Protestant rate in the 1940's. The North's educational statistics show that 41 per cent of the primary-school children are Catholic, whereas the Catholic proportion of the total population is about 34 per cent. If this superiority in the rate of reproduction should continue, Northern Ireland *might* be absorbed into the Republic within a few decades. The conditional tense should be emphasized. There are some indications that, in a final test, Catholic voters would not vote to move Ulster into the Republic. Unionists claim that a substantial percentage would balk at the surrender of an advantageous economic position, since even the Catholic nationalists, much as they like to rail at British rule, might prefer it to the lower standard of social services of the Southern regime. It should be pointed out, moreover, that the actual Catholic proportion in the Northern population has not changed appreciably since 1911. It was 34.4 per cent in 1911; 33.5 per cent in 1926; 33.5 per cent in 1937; and 34.4 per cent in 1951. Northern Catholics are certainly producing babies faster than Protestants, but apparently not all of them are staying in Northern Ireland.

The nationalists charge that the Unionists encourage emigration to Canada and elsewhere by nationalists — but not by their own people — in order to counteract the effect of the superior Catholic birth rate. Whatever may be the truth of this charge, the fact is that most Irish Catholics consider Northern Ireland a superior place to live — if they can find work. Migration within Ireland is virtually all from the South to the North, and not vice versa. "Surely," says the *Irish Times,* "if one tenth of the Nationalist propaganda were true, the immigrant's boot would be on the other foot." The situation today is about the same as it was in 1936 when a Protestant deputy from Monaghan — in the South — said in the Dublin Dail: "I have never succeeded in inducing a Northern Nationalist to buy land in the Free State, although we can offer them better land than they have . . . they would no more dream of coming to take up land in our country than they would of going to Spain at the moment." Since 1926 the rural population of the South has declined 13 per cent, while the rural population of the North has increased 2 per cent.

The Religious War

Religious antagonism in the North is out in the open — a debatable subject that does not need to be discussed in whispers. "To hell with the Pope" is more than an insult to be scrawled on walls by impish schoolboys; it is the underlying defensive thesis of thousands of respectable citizens who regard the Pope as an alien dictator. The Catholic people, in their turn, are particularly touchy about their own sacred symbols and alert to interpret any slight as an insult. When the Enniskillen Borough Council Emergency Committee dismissed thirteen Catholic relief workers for attending a 10 A.M. Mass without permission on New Year's Day of 1953, a priest wrote to the Catholic *Standard* that the incident "gives us just one more proof that freedom of worship is not recognized by the Protestant bigots who control the jobs in North-east Ulster." Said the Belfast *Irish News,* the chief Catholic paper of the North:

Had the Enniskillen workmen who were dismissed because they left an unemployment relief scheme to go to Mass on New Year's Day been worshippers of the Kremlin, we presume they would still have their jobs. They would regard Mass as unnecessary, perhaps in the Marxist phrase as part of the opium of the people. But because they were Catholics and determined to fulfil their obligation to be present at Mass on a Catholic Feast Day, they went to Church without leave, and were dismissed. . . . Had the work on which these men were engaged been held up for hours by Orange demonstrations, the Council would have ignored the time lost.

The churches themselves, Protestant and Catholic, are outspoken enemies, using language that would be considered much too frank for courtesy in the United States or even in Southern Ireland. The favorite hero of the Catholics is Blessed Oliver Plunkett, seventeenth-century Archbishop of Armagh, who was accused of taking part in a "Popish plot" and, on the flimsiest of evidence, hanged, drawn and quartered at Tyburn. The Catholic press keeps partisan animosities at white heat. The Belfast *Irish News* frequently carries long and exceedingly partisan sermons by Catholic priests who are conducting missions to Protestants, pointing out the imperfections in Protestant doctrine. The Protestant newspapers are slightly less dogmatic — but unmistakably non-Catholic. The General Assembly of the Presbyterian Church, the largest Protestant body in the North, asserts its loyalty to the British throne as conspicuously as the Catholic Church does not. The Church of Ireland, of course, because of its Anglican origin and connection, is equally loyal. Its leaders blessed the banners of Carson's men in 1912 when they threatened to fight against absorption into a Catholic Ireland, and it has been on the Northern side in the continuing struggle ever since. Some of its bishops imitate the Catholic policy — refusing to marry the members of their denomination to Roman Catholics.

"The N.U.P.," says a circular issued by the vigorous propaganda body, the National Union of Protestants (Ireland),

. . . is out to meet the challenge of Rome. . . . Roman Catholics in Ireland are demanding a United Irish Roman Catholic Republic. Roman Catholics in Northern Ireland are buying up Protestant farms, houses, land and property, in their efforts to establish the Papacy in Ulster. . . . The N.U.P. has helped Protestant employers to obtain Protestant employees. . . . The N.U.P. has pledged its determination to maintain its allegiance to the Protestant Throne and Constitution of England. The N.U.P. has united thousands of Protestants, and has opened the door to a Protestant way of life for every true loyalist who wants to see in Northern Ireland a Protestant country for a Protestant people.

One effect of the denominational tension is the absence of any large body of neutral citizens who might act as a cushion between Catholicism and Protestantism. Another effect is the creation of intense and almost fanatical dogmatism on both sides of the religious chasm. Northern Ireland is much more religious, officially and personally, than England — and one of the reasons is that religion is a weapon in the border war.

The Cultural Battle

In the cultural struggle in the North, the schools are the front-line trenches. As in the South, Catholic and Protestant school children are completely segregated, and there is continuing hostility between the Catholics and non-Catholic educational leaders. Protestant public officials openly describe the struggle between Roman Catholic education and public education as a struggle between foreign dictatorship and intellectual freedom, and the Catholic press replies with its usual charge that public schools are "godless" breeders of crime and Communism. This verbal struggle is continuous and bitter.

The Unionist government has in its colorful Minister of Education, Harry Midgley, one of the most outspoken critics of Catholic educational policy in Ireland. A veteran labor leader and opponent of Franco's Spain, he does not hesitate to cross swords with any priest. He has the sagacity to attack the weakest feature of the Catholic system — the theological coercion used by the Church in maintaining that system. He contends that thousands of Catholic parents would like to send their children to schools with the children of other faiths in order that they should learn tolerance and co-operation, but that the Catholic hierarchy prevents this *rapprochement*. "In Northern Ireland," he says, "over 70,000 Roman Catholic children are being compelled to segregate and separate themselves from the other children throughout the community at the dictates of the Hierarchy of their Church. We respect the right of every person in the community to worship in whatever way they like, or not to worship. But, on the other hand, we want to point out that the bulk of the people in Ireland are enslaved spiritually, mentally and philosophically by those who control their organization."

The Northern hierarchy counter-attacks vigorously. It goes to great lengths to maintain its policy of educational segregation, refusing to accept any individual as a teacher in a Catholic school, no matter how devoutly Catholic he may be, if he has obtained his teaching certificate from a non-Catholic institution. As a result, Catholic and non-Catholic teachers are almost completely segregated in two leading teacher-training institutions. In Derry, shortly before World War II, the hierarchy would not even permit a public nurse who had left the Church to enter a parochial school for routine medical work — although Protestant nurses were considered acceptable.

In spite of this antagonism, the Northern government has treated Catholic schools with great consideration, both financially and in matters of curriculum control. These schools receive from the public treasury all the salaries of all their teachers, lay and religious, their equipment costs, and 65 per cent of their building and repair costs, as well as 65 per cent of their lighting and heating bills. The teachers receive

Both Catholic and non-Catholic children suffer from the all-Ireland rule that children are required to go to school only until they are 14. After their fourteenth birthday, they may be turned loose in a world for which they are poorly prepared. Child labor at 14 is accepted and legal in Belfast, as in Dublin. Only 40 to 45 per cent of the children get *any* secondary education, as against 85 per cent who get *some* in England and Wales. But this low percentage in Northern Ireland is still much higher than the corresponding ratio in the Irish Republic.

The division of the children into Protestant and Catholic groups during their formative years tends to perpetuate the chasm between them. Segregation is accompanied by economic class stratification, and the total psychological effect is not unlike that of the effect of color segregation in the United States. In Belfast, even the heights, the weights, and the intelligence quotients of the children in the Catholic schools are lower than in the non-Catholic schools; and the children from the Catholic schools are much less likely to complete the higher grades. In the non-Catholic schools English history is stressed and the British outlook is fostered; in the Catholic schools, those history textbooks which emphasize British values are often thrown into the wastebasket, and Irish history is surreptitiously or openly taught. It is a notorious fact that the Catholic schools in the North are essentially schools of the Irish Republic, paid for by Northern Ireland taxpayers but oriented toward Dublin.

The separation between Catholic and Protestant in the North extends even into the medical field. The Catholic people have welcomed a new Northern Ireland health service which is similar to Britain's national service, but the bishops will not permit any Catholic hospitals to participate officially in the scheme. They have taken the great Mater Hospital of Belfast, the only large Catholic hospital in the North, out of the Northern health service because they will not accept the amount of government control which the Protestant hospitals are willing to accept. When the new health scheme was inaugurated, the majority of Catholic doctors in the Mater Hospital favored a compromise with the government on the issue of co-operation, but their hierarchy would not make the necessary adjustments. As a result, Catholic doctors have suffered the loss of many professional opportunities.

A Federated Irish Nation?

Could the bitter struggle over Partition be settled by the creation of a united federal administration for the whole island? De Valera believes it could, and that the North and the South could work together in one nation if the North had a large measure of local self-government. He would follow the general line of demarcation now established between Stormont and London, and simply replace London with Dublin authority, giving Dublin control over Northern Ireland's foreign relations, foreign trade, armed services, post office, and national-welfare services. Today Stormont controls its own education, police and local government within limits. De Valera would continue such powers, and transfer the rest to a democratically elected all-Ireland parliament convening in Dublin.

There are some sincere Protestants in the South who think that this is the proper solution for the Irish problem. They point to the fact that the presence in a Dublin parliament of a large and militant Protestant party, representing about one-fourth of the people of the island, would force all the Catholic-dominated parties to be more progressive, as well as less Catholic. They believe that the present one-party Protestant domination in the North is bad for the North, and that the all-Catholic party ascendancy in the South is just as detrimental to Southern progress.

Of course, the most serious obstacle to such a solution is not political but religious. In an all-Ireland nation, what would happen to denominational control of education, censorship, marriage, divorce, and birth control? When I asked De Valera, MacBride, and Norton such questions, their faces clouded over. They began immediately to talk in conditional terms. They are not themselves Catholic extremists, but it is obvious that they fear clerical reprisals if they deviate from Catholic policy by one iota. Their approach to all areas of clerical authority is one of extreme caution.

Their general attitude might be paraphrased in a few significant generalizations: *The Church represents the great majority of the people, and it has a right to speak on moral issues and be heard; Catholic beliefs should not be subject to political inter-*

ference. We believe in certain moral laws; you cannot expect us to violate the principles of our Church.

In a federated Ireland, would the right of divorce be granted to everyone? *Probably not; that involves Catholic principle.*

Would birth control be permitted? *No; that is a question of moral law, and besides there are many people in the North who do not want it.*

What about denominational control of schools? *Well, that might be allowed to remain as it is now, since Stormont controls its own education, but there must be no discrimination in giving out money in a united Ireland. Catholic schools should be treated on the same basis as other schools.* (Neither De Valera, nor MacBride, nor Norton sees anything undemocratic in the system under which a church controlled by foreign-appointed bishops operates the schools of 97 per cent of the Irish children.)

What about censorship? Censorship is the only distinctively Catholic feature of Southern rule which the Southern leaders seem to be willing to modify. They are ready to concede that its unpopularity is partly justified and that extreme standards have helped to make it ridiculous.

On the Northern side there is no inclination whatever to yield an inch to any suggestions of an all-Ireland federation. "The only federation we are interested in," says Lord Brookeborough, "is that of the British Commonwealth. There is no problem as far as Northern Ireland is concerned, because we have always been part of the United Kingdom and always intend to remain part." It is not only the Catholic policy on birth control, divorce, censorship, and denominational education which is regarded by the North as an obstacle to federation. The Northern Protestants do not trust any Catholic regime in a Catholic Ireland to keep its promises to observe non-Catholic rights. "They agreed to the present border in a solemn treaty with us and Great Britain in 1925," say the Northerners, "and see how their agreement with us has been kept!" Moreover, they say, since Catholic policies are controlled in Rome, any compromise agreement with Irish Catholic statesmen could be over-ridden in Rome when it suited Roman leaders to adopt a change of front. The present regime in the South, they point out, is on its good behavior temporarily because the Republicans want to entice the North into their country. "But wait and see," they say. "When we are in, we will find ourselves in a country like Spain."

The Unionist Party circulates a pamphlet *The Problem of Partition,* which sums up this fear in very frank language:

> The Protestants of the North certainly have very profound fears of being subjected to hostile discrimination as regards their professions and occupations if they were turned compulsorily into citizens of Eire. . . . However friendly and tolerant the great majority of Roman Catholic Irishmen may be personally towards Protestants, the last word as regards the toleration their Government would show towards adherents of other faiths rests with the hierarchy of the Roman Catholic Church, which maintains that non-Roman Catholics even in good faith have no natural right to practice a false religion. . . . Many Northern Protestants sincerely believe that if an all-Ireland Republic came into existence, the reduction in the Protestant population in the South would extend to the North. . . . In this connection, the cases of Spain and other Continental countries are mentioned. In Spain, it is almost impossible for Protestants to carry on evangelistic work, Protestant chapels and churches are often closed, and the importation of Bibles is stopped by the Spanish Customs.

So the deadlock continues, and the prospects of a settlement are today farther off than ever. There are a few co-operative North-South ventures — such as the management of the Great Northern Railway, the supervision of joint fishing territory, and a new hydro-electric scheme — which bring the two governments together to a certain extent; but in almost every other aspect of Irish life North and South are aligned as bitter antagonists. Smuggling across the obnoxious customs barrier aggravates the ill feeling on both sides.

The anti-Partition propaganda of the South is one of the major factors in keeping bitterness alive. Almost wholly unrealistic, it pictures the North as a police state under "Orange Terror" in which almost all civil liberties are denied to the minority. Some Southern voices have been raised against such hysterical propaganda. A leading Protestant nationalist, Ernest Blythe, director of the Abbey Theatre and formerly a minister in the Free State government, has deplored the Southern "smear campaign" and the propaganda which "compares a respectable force like the Royal Ulster Constabulary with the Gestapo." He has suggested that the South ought to "frankly acknowledge the Six Counties Parliament, despite its subordinate character, and despite a slight temporary lack of balance, due to some gerry-mandering, as being, nevertheless, a decent democratically chosen Irish assembly . . . and entitled, together with the Government chosen by it, to a measure of respect." Such wisdom is very rare in the South. The Southern politicians, in order to gain votes, vie with each other in calling for "action" against Partition, and the more bitter their language becomes, the more determined are the Unionists of the North to fight to the death for their country. Both Northern and Southern politicians now have a vested interest in Partition, and their exploitation of the issue is one of the most serious obstacles to compromise.

Comparative Freedom

Not the least obstacle to a settlement is the type of "comparison" made in anti-Partition propaganda between the amount of religious freedom and discrimination in the North and in the South. The Southern legend on this subject runs somewhat as follows: In the South, the Protestants are not persecuted at all, and there is practically no job discrimination; they are given their full proportionate share of school funds, and their civil liberties are completely protected; their treatment is a magnificent demonstration of Catholic good faith. But in the North — this thesis continues — the Catholic minority is persecuted by means of a Special Powers Act which permits jailing without trial and suppression of public meetings; there is widespread discrimination in government appointments, and financial discrimination against Catholic schools.

This type of propaganda omits the most important aspect of the comparative story. The Protestants of the South are not disloyal to the Southern regime, whereas the Northern Catholics are open and enthusiastic traitors to the Northern regime, who have never ceased, since the birth of the government in 1921, to organize and agitate for its transfer to Dublin rule. These Catholic dissenters are suffering some discrimination in the North, but the discrimination primarily exists not because they are Catholics but because, being Catholics, they are affiliated with a movement which is specifically treasonable and which has behind it a long history of violence and insurrection. When Northern Catholics are penalized for this treason, they plead that they are being subjected to "religious persecution." This "religious persecution," when looked at from another angle, is self-defense by a non-Catholic government determined to maintain self-determination against alien aggression. It is no more fair to describe the total Partition situation in terms of exclusively religious persecution than it is to epitomize in such terms the battle between Israel and the Arabs, or between Pakistan and India. Religion lies at the base of the struggle in each case, but the battle has gone far beyond the stage of mere religious discrimination and become a struggle for survival between bona-fide nations.

Actually, there is no religious persecution as such by the Northern regime today, and there are no restrictions on full religious activity. Catholic churches, Catholic schools, Catholic social organizations, and Catholic newspapers are guaranteed the full privileges of British freedom. But when Catholic citizens with the backing of their Church deny the jurisdiction of the government that maintains this freedom, and openly attempt to overthrow it, they are sometimes treated as enemy aliens. This treatment is quite conventional and would be adopted by any democratic majority in parallel circumstances.

It should also be pointed out that, while there is complete freedom for Protestants in the South, that freedom is conditional on Protestant passivity. Those Protestants who hold office are co-operators with the Southern regime, not basic opponents. It is unthinkable that the present civil liberty for Protestant activity would continue if a strong Protestant party, with the official sanction of Protestant church bodies, challenged the Republic's life and continuously agitated for a return to British rule. Such a disloyal political movement would undoubtedly be suppressed either by the Southern government itself or by mob violence.

The month of the coronation of Queen Elizabeth, June 1953, afforded a striking contrast in degree of civil liberty in the North and in the South. When it was announced that coronation films were to be exhibited in Dublin, theater owners were swamped with threats of violence. Although the government nominally protested against these threats, the Commissioner of the Civic Guards declared that it was probable that the exhibition of the films would cause organized protests which would result in damage to theaters and create panic. The coronation films were never shown except in Protestant private halls, and even the televised coronation ceremony was blocked by threats of violence. The editor of the *Irish Times* asked mournfully: "Are we living in a civilized country, where the law protects everybody or are we not? It is a grim and sorry prospect. Great men have died for Irish freedom; they did not die for the blackguardism that battens on poltroonery."

In Belfast, meanwhile, on June 14, 1953, 25,000 Irish nationalists assembled to dedicate a Roger Casement Gaelic Park and stadium, and to hear eulogies of the nationalist patriot who was hanged for treason in 1916 after his efforts to bring German troops into Ireland. The roads approaching the stadium were decorated with Irish tricolors and papal flags, and Cardinal D'Alton, in dedicating the park, declared that Roger Casement "was one of Ireland's noblest sons, who willingly made the supreme sacrifice for his country." The ceremonies were not disturbed. Later Prime Minister De Valera crossed the border and attended other ceremonies at the park without being molested in any way.

No parallel parade or demonstration, displaying the Union Jack, could proceed for a single block in any city of the South without bloodshed. South of the border today, there is, in fact, no church, no newspaper, no political party, no labor organization, no fraternal order, no language movement which challenges the right of the victorious Irish nationalists to rule. Relative peace exists there because Protestant power has accepted Catholic rule. Relative peace does not exist in the North because the Northern Catholics continue to defy Protestant rule.

This brings us back to the thesis we mentioned earlier in the chapter — that one man's patriotism is often another man's treason. It all depends on the definition of the object of loyalty. The majority of the people in Northern Ireland have decided that their country is Great Britain and not the Irish Republic. The majority of the people of Great Britain, on their side, have decided that these Northern Irish people should not be ejected from the British Commonwealth as long as they prefer to remain British. The majority of the people in the Irish Republic have decided that the issue can be settled only by an all-island vote in Ireland. All three decisions have been reached by a reasonable democratic process, if the limits of territorial jurisdiction of each contender are accepted — but this fact does not bring anybody nearer to a solution.

In such a situation the inertia of history favors the *status quo.* Also, there are certain important special factors favoring the Northern Irish. The preference of the Northern Irish people for Great Britain is a choice in favor of a more democratic society. Whatever may be said about the merits of the Irish Republic — and they are considerable — no one can say that Southern Irish democracy is as advanced or complete or mature as that of the British welfare state. In choosing affiliation with that modern welfare state in preference to a Catholic clerical state in the South, the people of Northern Ireland are acting as the great majority of the American people would act under similar circumstances. If, they argue, we are surrendering control of some aspects of our government to Great Britain, we are the gainers, since we participate in the British government as full citizens and members, and our representatives share in every important decision concerning the British future. If, they argue, we joined the South, many of the most important decisions concerning government policy would be made in Rome without our participation — and that would be far worse than British rule. On this point, the judgment of Bernard Shaw, made fifty years ago in his preface to *John Bull's Other Island,* is still sound — that, when the Irishman cares to choose between the British government and the Vatican, "of the two, the British government allows him the more liberty."

On one aspect of the situation, all observers are agreed — that there is no hope of an immediate solution of the border question. In a certain sense, there is not even any hope for an ultimate solution so long as the problem of freedom and authority is unresolved. Even if the political border were wiped out, the religious border would continue. A "united" Ireland with the continuance of the present animosities between faiths would be united in name only. In fact, the struggle between faiths in one Dublin parliament might in the end do Ireland more damage than the continuance of the present geographical division between North and South.

10

The Irish Catholic Empire in America

In the United States today, Irish-Americans of Protestant descent are rarely referred to as "Irish." There are no Irish Protestant blocs in our society, no Irish Protestant newspapers, no Irish Protestant residential sections. The Irish spirit appears to be a Catholic monopoly. The explanation for this distinction is not altogether flattering to Irish Catholics. After a century of development and progress, they are still not completely adjusted to the American community. They still do not quite "belong" in the sense that Irish Protestants "belong."

The first reason for this separateness is purely historical. The English Protestants, arriving first in the main colonizing areas of the new continent, made America predominantly Protestant. Many of them were quite militant Protestants, tinged with the philosophy of the Orange Order. Having fought "Popery" in Europe, they had no intention of allowing Irish Catholics to feel at home in *their* new country. Almost all of the original Irish immigrants who came to the thirteen colonies in the seventeenth and eighteenth centuries were from Ulster — a fact which Catholic historians are likely to overlook when they discuss the Irish contribution to America's beginnings. Irish Catholicism, in fact, made almost no contribution to the political foundation of the American nation. In 1790 there were only about 25,000 Irish Catholics in the whole United States — less than seven-tenths of 1 per cent of the American people, and less than 5 per cent of the Irish-American population. The rest of the 555,000 Irishmen in the United States were chiefly Protestants of Presbyterian persuasion.

By the time of the Revolution, these Irish Protestants found themselves well placed in American society. They owned many of the largest farms; they stood high in the professions; they prospered in trade. When the War of Independence began, their position in American society and their opposition to both the Church of England and the Pope made them natural revolutionary leaders. When the new nation was established, they supported it wholeheartedly, and from their numbers came many of the nation's greatest statesmen. Enthusiasts of the Ulster tradition like to point out that although fourteen Presidents, from Washington to Eisenhower, have had Ulster ancestry, there has never been an Irish Catholic President.

The Anti-Catholicism of the Pioneers

The whole atmosphere of colonial America was hostile to Catholicism largely because the founding fathers brought their hostility with them to American shores. The Puritans who landed on Plymouth Rock and the Anglicans who settled in Virginia had at least one thing in common — distrust of the Pope. They came from an England where men were still fighting and dying for religion, and where Catholic power challenged the government in battle. Irish Catholicism for them represented something popish as well as foreign, something alien to the English way of life as well as to the American way of life.

In many colonies the attitude toward Catholics was strikingly similar to the present-day American attitude toward Communists: "Papists" were considered criminals to be hounded and suppressed. Massachusetts required of its residents an oath of allegiance denouncing the Pope, and for a time it halted all immigration of Irishmen to the colony. New York disarmed every Catholic resident and demanded from him a bond guaranteeing good behavior. North Carolina and New Hampshire specifically denied religious freedom to Catholics. In fact, the whole concept of religious freedom was not generally accepted until the nation had been well established. Professor Billington has pointed out that in 1700 a Catholic could enjoy full civil and religious rights in only one spot in America, Rhode Island. Even in Maryland the Protestant majority soon banished the Catholic leader, Lord Baltimore, and withdrew all protection from those "who profess to exercise the Popish religion." These Maryland Protestants even required the Catholics to pay tithes to Protestant preachers.

The hostility toward Catholicism continued to be so bitter among the American colonists that in 1774, when England granted French Catholics a refuge in Quebec, the Continental Congress denounced the British for protecting "a religion which had deluged their Island in blood, and diffused impiety, bigotry, persecution, murder, and rebellion through every part of the world." This "Rome-manipulated coup to establish Popery" in Quebec was one of the basic factors in bringing on the American Revolution. As one versifier wrote:

> If Gaelic Papists have a right
> To worship their own way
> Then farewell to the Liberties
> Of poor America.

After the Revolution a gradual transformation took place in the American attitude about religious freedom and religious discrimination. The animosities born of European religious feuds cooled off. Jefferson and Madison, with their broad tolerance and their opposition to all established churches, led the nation toward a new day of charity and co-operation among faiths. The Constitution abolished religious tests for federal office, and an implied guarantee of equality as well as disestablishment was written into the First Amendment. All the great Protestant churches severed their ties with Europe and became American churches, controlled by American members in more or less democratic fashion.

The various states, however, were very slow to accept the new philosophy of church-state separation and to abandon their discriminatory measures. Nine of the thirteen colonies had established churches, and the transition from legalized favoritism to legalized equality was neither rapid nor painless. Connecticut did not put the Congregational Church on an equal plane with other churches until 1818. Anti-Catholic laws continued on the statute books of many of the states until the 1820's. Massachusetts did not abolish its religious tests for public office until 1833.

Nevertheless, the years between 1790 and 1820 were good

years for the development of broad-mindedness and charity in matters of religion. Americans began to appreciate the almost miraculous uniqueness of the American policy of church-state separation, and they thanked God that they were no longer involved in European religious wars. In some places there appeared the first modest beginnings of a non-sectarian school system free from church control. Horace Mann began his fight in Massachusetts to eliminate dogmatism from classrooms and textbooks. His chief opponents at first were the dogmatic Protestants, partly because the country was so overwhelmingly Protestant. The Pope was still considered a menace to faith and democracy, but his shadow did not loom very large over America. In 1807 there was only one Catholic see in the whole country. The few French priests in America were fading into the background; the German Catholics were beginning to come in, but not in very large numbers.

Then after 1830, came the first waves of the Irish Catholic deluge, which was destined to create the present-day Catholic problem in America. It was a kind of second colonization of America, representing a culture distinctly different from the first colonization. There were, of course, no bars against immigration in those days, and anybody with passage money and a spirit of adventure could come to the United States. It was not until 1917 that European white immigration was restricted, and not before 1921 was there a complete quota system with its nationality pattern. Even then, the limitations worked no hardship upon the Irish, since they were favored by the new laws.

In the 1830's, Irish farm laborers were welcome because the new country needed unskilled labor at low wages, and the Irish, coming from desperate poverty, were glad to accept low wages and long hours of work in return for the privilege of keeping alive in the new world. Their knowledge of English gave them an important advantage over other immigrants. They dug the Erie Canal, and their Church followed the line of the Canal with a row of fast-growing parishes. Later on, in construction gangs, they built the American railroads, and their young women became America's most famous housemaids and nurses.

In general, those who came were the poorest and the least

educated. Not many of them bought farms, because they were too poor; moreover, they disliked the loneliness of American farm life, preferring to cluster together in the great cities with other Irish immigrants. "The Irish are a social people," said the *Irish American* in 1853, "and require great self-denial to induce them to forsake the society of their kindred and kind, and take up their abode in less thickly settled locations, even though sure of becoming prosperous by so doing." That is the main reason why Irish Catholicism has never been an important phenomenon in rural America, and why the priests who believe in farm life for large Catholic families have never been able to persuade many Irish Americans to leave the cities and go to the land.

America and the Potato Famine

Even before the great Irish potato famine, the Irish Catholics had become the No. 1 immigrant group in the United States, and they outnumbered any other Catholic group of the period by a wide margin. Then, in 1845, when the Irish potato crop failed partially, and in 1846, when it failed completely, and when half a million people died at home and more than four million were driven out of the country, the Irish fortuitously clinched their hold upon Catholic power in America. They captured the Church by sheer numbers and took over its control from top to bottom.

Many of the Irish famine victims were so emaciated and feeble when they embarked for America that they either died on shipboard or failed to survive the rigors of the first months in America. Some of the "coffin ships" which brought them to America were operated, with almost no government supervision, by economic speculators who exploited the poor and the ignorant with appalling cruelty. (The cost of steerage passage was sometimes as low as £2.) The steerage passengers — and nearly all Irish immigrants were steerage passengers — usually cooked their own food and brought their own supplies for the 35-day voyage to New York or Boston. They were fortunate if they did not starve to death or die of disease on the way. "It was no unusual occurrence," says John Francis Maguire, "for the survivor of a family of 10 or 12 to land alone, bewildered and broken-hearted, on the wharf at New York; the rest of the family — parents and children — had been swallowed in the sea, their bodies marking the course of the ship to the New World." When the immigrants landed, they often fell victims to unscrupulous "runners" and pickpockets. At one immigrant shelter near Quebec, ten thousand died from disease and neglect in a single year.

For decades the Irish poor overcrowded the slums and hospitals of New York and Boston. Between 1849 and 1859, 85 per cent of all the foreign-born patients at Bellevue, and about half of New York's criminals and paupers, were Irish. New York's Irish Catholic juvenile delinquents outnumbered the Protestant and Jewish delinquents combined, and in 1858 there were almost as many Irish as native-born prostitutes on the streets of the city. "It is a melancholy fact," said the Catholic bishops of the United States, at their Second Plenary Council of Baltimore in 1866, "and a very humiliating avowal for us to make, that a very large proportion of the idle and vicious youth of our principal cities are the children of Catholic parents." It should also have been a humiliating avowal for the dominant non-Catholic elements in American society, whose indifference to Irish poverty and suffering had created the soil from which Irish Catholic delinquency developed.

Irish paupers continued to outnumber paupers from all other foreign groups until well into the twentieth century. This was not very surprising, because so many Irish came to the new world. About one million and a half came in the twenty years ending in 1861; by 1930 the Irish immigrants in the United States exceeded in numbers the present population of all Ireland. The overwhelming majority were Catholics. Because of their poverty and lack of education, they did not take their rightful places in the middle and upper classes until after 1900, and even then the Irish proportion of paupers was three times the Irish proportion in the general population. In Massachusetts the proportion was 4 to 1.

These millions of desperately poor Irish Catholic people, dumped unceremoniously at American ports without screening or plan, aroused in native American workers a violent wave of reaction and hostility. American capitalists wanted the cheap Irish labor; but American non-Catholic workers, fearing their competition, resented their arrival, their religion, and their poverty. It was in those days that the term "shanty Irish" became a part of the American language. The Americans who criticized and fought these "shanty Irish" were the workers who were nearest their economic level, the workers whose jobs were at stake in the fight for survival. From this group of the underprivileged came the first organized anti-Irish movement of our history.

In 1834 the first great convent-burning occurred in Charlestown, Massachusetts, when a convent school operated by Ursuline nuns from Limerick was destroyed by a Boston mob. An unfounded rumor had circulated through the area that an escaped nun had been recaptured and was being held in a dungeon cellar underneath the convent. The anti-Catholic sentiment was so strong in Boston that, after a one-sided trial, the leaders of the mob were acquitted, with public jubilation. About the same time many Irish laborers were attacked in the Boston area, and their shanties burned. About this time, also, Maria Monk's notorious book, *Awful Disclosures of the Hotel Dieu Nunnery of Montreal,* was published and became a national best seller. It pictured convents as centers of licentiousness and drunkenness where illegitimate babies were murdered by the hundreds. It was totally fraudulent — but millions of Americans believed it.

In 1844 in the Philadelphia area, after a nativist meeting had been stopped by the Irish Catholics, a three-day riot broke out between Irish laborers and native Americans. Before the fighting was finished, whole blocks of Irish homes and churches were burned by a furious mob of citizens who had been inflamed by the declaration of their nativist newspaper: "Another St. Bartholomew's day is begun on the streets of Philadelphia. The bloody hand of the Pope has stretched itself forth to our destruction."

Even before the great Irish famine, an anti-immigration party had started in America, the Native American Party, which polled more than one-third of the votes in New York in 1835. At first it was not particularly anti-Irish or anti-Catholic; but it soon became so.

In the 1850's the most famous of the anti-Catholic parties of American history, the Know-Nothing Party, made Irish Catholicism one of its primary targets. The party grew out of a secret patriotic organization, the Order of the Star-Spangled Banner, which had restrictive rules against Catholics. It pledged its members not to marry Catholics or to vote for any foreigner for any public office. "No Popery" became the central plank of its platform — the only plank on which the Northern and Southern nativists could agree. The Know-Nothing Party had a quick success in the 1850's, sent seventy-five congressmen to Washington, and captured nearly all of New England. But it rapidly collapsed because of its fanatically negative program and because the greater issues of the Civil War turned men's minds away from the shadow of the Pope.

But the Know-Nothing movement left a trail of bitterness and prejudice behind it, and after the Civil War, as the immigrant flood continued, there was much anti-Irish and anti-Catholic sentiment in American life. In the 1880's, political anti-Catholicism reached the national level again in the notorious American Protective Association, led by the semi-paranoiac Iowa lawyer Henry F. Bowers. It repeated all the familiar attacks on the "immorality" of convents, opposed the use of Catholics in the armed forces, and — quite justifiably — criticized the new alliance of Irish Catholicism with corrupt city bosses. It reached its high-water mark in 1893 with a million members, seventy weekly newspapers, and powerful branches in more than twenty states; then it rapidly declined.

By this time, the Irish Catholics, moving out of the pick-and-shovel caste, had begun to compete with the merchants and lawyers of the older American ascendancy. In the eastern cities they had also made great headway in politics. In moving up the social ladder, they had left the lower rungs to the new hordes of Italians and Slavs who flooded the country after 1890. After 1900, the "Mick" was not quite so low as the "Wop," the "Hunkie," and the "Polack." The Irish had arrived; and instead of denouncing them in the name of American nativism, most politicians were inclined to stick a shamrock in their buttonholes and join the Saint Patrick's Day parades. The Orangemen, who came to New York, Boston, and Philadelphia, originally had their parades also; but the Irish Catholics broke up these parades with the connivance of Irish Catholic policemen. When an Orange parade in New York on July 12, 1870, was attacked

by an Irish Catholic mob, eight persons were killed. The toll
in a similar episode on July 12, 1871, was 33 dead and 101
wounded.

How the Irish Bishops Provoked Anti-Catholicism

Was there anything in Irish Catholicism to deserve the bitter
hostility of so many native Americans? Some historians of bigotry in the United States have passed over that question rather
lightly. Too often they have assumed that the native opposition
to Catholicism was based entirely on narrow-mindedness and economic self-interest, inflamed by Protestant yellow journalism.
A study of the actual principles of Irish Catholic power and the
tactics of Irish Catholic bishops in the nineteenth century shows
that a great deal of the opposition to the Irish proceeded from
the refusal of their priests and bishops, in dealing with Americans, to accept a co-operative and tolerant way of life. They not
only did not accept, but peremptorily rejected, the new American
gospel of the separation of church and state. The Irish immigrants, as Thomas Sugrue has pointed out, "carried chips on their
shoulders eight feet high — chips placed there by four hundred
years of Irish hardship under Protestant English rule."

The chips were assiduously propped up by the priests. The
immigrants themselves would soon have abandoned their group
aggressiveness, if their priests had suggested a more co-operative
way of life. The Irish peasants were likable and eager to please;
they deeply desired to adjust themselves to the new culture; but
their priests and bishops stood for certain separatist and non-
American practices which immediately inflamed the opposition
and put the whole Irish Catholic community on the defensive.
These Irish priests were much more aggressive than the German
or French priests, and the Irish immigrants were correspondingly
much more submissive to them than the immigrants of other
nationalities. "In a sense," says Professor John J. Kane, of
Notre Dame's Department of Sociology, "Irish Catholics tended
to project onto all priests a sort of infallibility, and unlike papal
infallibility, it extended to all matters, sacred and profane." "It
is true," said Bishop Verot at the Vatican Council in 1870, "that
the Irish believe in the Pope's infallibility; but they also believe

in their priest's infallibility — and not only do they believe it, but they beat with sticks any who deny it."

The early opponents of Catholic power in America were well aware of this difference between Irish Catholicism and other brands of immigrant Catholicism, and they made the Irish Catholic churches their primary targets. Professor Kane points out that "at the height of the Philadelphia riots when Irish Catholic churches were burned to the ground, even though guarded by militia, a German Catholic church remained unguarded and unattacked although within a few blocks of the actual rioting." The Irish priests and bishops had little to lose by separatist tactics — for they were living and fighting in a non-Catholic nation, and the more thoroughly they could keep their people isolated from the main stream of American culture, the greater their own power as group leaders. The Irish Catholic bishops, incidentally, had become so powerful even before the Civil War that, to all intents and purposes, they *were* the hierarchy of the American Church. The Germans had been eclipsed; the French had been forgotten; and the Italians had not yet arrived. Almost all the recruits to the priesthood in the new country were Irish. "The American youth," said John Francis Maguire in 1873, "have an almost invincible repugnance to the ecclesiastical state." Of the 464 bishops appointed between 1789 and 1935, 268 were of Irish ancestry. "The American episcopate," says one French observer, "has been — and still is — a sort of Irish closed shop." "From the time of the first Bishop, John Carroll to the See of Baltimore," says the *Catholic Encyclopedia,* "to the present day, there is hardly a diocese or archdiocese in continental United States but has been governed by prelates of Irish birth or descent."

The first big controversy in which the Irish bishops took the non-American point of view was the struggle over the ownership of American churches. The members of all the non-Catholic churches in the new America took it for granted that the people owned the church buildings which their money had built. This was part of the Protestant tradition, and it was in keeping with the American belief in self-determination. Many Catholic churches in Baltimore, New Orleans, Philadelphia, Buffalo, and elsewhere adopted a form of church ownership called "trusteeism," which gave the titles of church buildings to boards of trustees representing the Catholic laymen instead of the bishops. As early as 1785, a New York City board of trustees had actually asserted the right of the Catholic people to appoint and dismiss pastors at will. To the Catholic Church, however, this was heresy, and Bishop Carroll administered a stiff rebuke: "If ever such principles should become predominant, the unity and catholicity of our church would be at an end; and it would be formed into distinct and independent societies, nearly in the same manner as the Congregational Presbyterians." Nevertheless there were a great many American Catholics who thought the people should own their own churches, and some German Catholic trustees in Philadelphia defied Carroll, went to court, and branded the authority of the Pope "as of foreign jurisdiction."

A series of dramatic public disputes and schisms followed, which only became more bitter after the American hierarchy had officially condemned trusteeism in 1829 and adopted a policy which delivered the titles of all American churches to the bishops. Under that policy, American Catholic bishops could not consecrate a church until they had received a deed of the property from the trustees. In Philadelphia, Bishop Kenrick defeated the trustees of Saint Mary's Cathedral, known as "the Irish church," only after a ten-year fight during which he placed the church under an interdict. This, said the *Philadelphian,* was a "singular specimen of papal authority exercised over the people of a free country." In New York State, the famous Archbishop John Hughes, born in County Tyrone, brought about the excommunication of the trustees of the Saint Louis church in Buffalo because they insisted on asserting their rights under New York law to control their own church.

In this whole struggle over trusteeism the Irish hierarchy was victorious not only because it was backed by Rome but also because the great mass of newly arrived Irish peasants had been accustomed to leave the entire direction of their Church to their bishops and priests. They had never learned to think of democracy as a necessary feature of religious organization. In this respect they differed sharply from most Americans, and the disagreement was an important factor in branding them as "un-American." They seemed so dominated by the priests that their submissiveness gave the Know-Nothings a substantial talking point in the drive against "Popery."

The trusteeship controversy was soon overshadowed by two other great controversies in which the Irish bishops were arrayed against the American majority: the fight for public money for Catholic schools, and the opposition to Bible-reading in the public schools. These struggles came at a time when American public schools were in their infancy and when the Fourteenth Amendment to the Constitution, extending the First Amendment to the states, had not yet made it illegal to use local tax funds for religious purposes. The chief Catholic protagonist in both controversies was again the Irish-born prelate Archbishop Hughes. He was the Cardinal Spellman of his era — aggressive, narrow, and ambitious. Of course, the Irish Catholics who came to the United States in such large numbers at this time had no conception of a publicly operated school system; they had learned to regard the priests as the natural rulers of both churches and schools, and when their priests told them to stay away from public schools they obeyed. The American Protestants of the period were, on the whole, more co-operative. They advocated general religious instruction as a basic part of any school curriculum, but most of them were willing to forgo any strictly denominational teaching in common schools.

The Beginning of the School Battle

The first public schools in New York were charity schools for the poor, supported by a Free School Society which obtained some of its funds from the state legislature. Later this society became the Public School Society of New York, authorized to educate all children and to operate schools which included a broad interdenominational program of religious instruction. Archbishop Hughes denounced such instruction as essentially Protestant, and demanded either that it cease or that the state give funds to the Catholic Church for its own schools. Some of his objections to the anti-Catholic bias in the public-school textbooks of the day were quite justified — such words as "Popery" and "Papists" were in common use. But even after the Public School Society promised to revise the textbooks, and after a policy was adopted of giving public money to non-denomina-

In Ireland the Protestant religion has been legally established for centuries; what is the success of that experiment? Let the desolating wars of religion, and the more horrible desolations of perennial famine and pestilence, and the national death that now broods over a land so fair and fertile, answer the question, and refute the theory that the establishment of "a true Christian pulpit," or of any Christian pulpit at all, is "the germ of national life." It is the germ of national perdition unfolded in a hot-bed of hell, and transplanted by the hand of the devil into this upper world for the ruin of human happiness. Here the arch-fiend is not yet successful, and we trust never will be, though he has many active agents at work.

It is some consolation to the friends of freedom in the old country to know that the extremes of Protestantism and Catholicism which meet here in the new are repudiated by the good sense and the patriotism of the great body of the people, and that the experiment of the American Republic without any establishment of religion is not a failure; but, on the contrary, that it is now, more than it ever was, the hope of oppressed humanity to the ends of the earth.

Mitchel even went so far as to defend the right of Protestant fanatics to preach about "the abominations of the Church of Rome, and the scandals of convents and nunneries" when the Catholics of Brooklyn attacked some of these Protestant fanatics in a riotous march. "Those Know-nothings (or whatever their preposterous name may be)," said the editors, "have a right to walk through the streets to escort a street preacher, or a tumbler, or juggler, or any public buffoon . . . to bawl and rant there against anything in heaven or on earth."

This was religious tolerance at its best, and if the Irish Catholics in America had listened to Mitchel instead of their bishops, the future might have been a happier one. As it was, the Young Irelander movement soon declined, and no anti-clerical leaders among the laity rose to replace John Mitchel. Among the Irish priests in America, however, several advanced liberals with a thoroughly American point of view attempted during the latter part of the nineteenth century to wean the Church from its cultural isolationism; and a bitter conflict broke out between the dogmatists and the co-operationists. The group favoring co-operation with public schools was led by Archbishop John Ireland of Minnesota, but his schemes were soon defeated by the dogmatists. In New York a courageous Irish priest, Father Edward McGlynn, who had been a supporter of Henry George, defied the order to establish a parochial school in his parish, declared that "the teaching in the parochial schools is altogether inferior to that of the public schools" — and was excommunicated. He was later readmitted to the Church, but his point of view was overwhelmed by the power of the separatists. The Irish bishops looked upon the segregated Catholic school as the foundation stone of their power, the instrument for keeping the Irish people in a subject status under their control, and they especially feared the biological effect of public education. Bishop McQuaid of Buffalo, one of the most reactionary Irish bishops, denounced public schools because they were "favorable to mixed marriages which arise from the intimacy of Catholic young men with Protestant girls."

After 1895 the bishops in America were almost unchallenged in their championship of a separatist policy for the Irish. They nurtured the Irish Catholic people as an insulated bloc in the American population, with separate churches, schools, residential districts, and social organizations — all sponsored, inspired, or directed by the priests. By emphasizing the Church's rule against marriage with Protestants and Jews, they helped to make the Irish a biologically isolated and inbred segment in American society. They developed a network of Catholic organizations and a network of Irish nationalist organizations. The two networks, with heavily overlapping memberships, fed each other and nourished Irish Catholic separatism. By 1953, the Church had become by far the largest and most powerful church in America, and in almost every important aspect of its life it was led by the Irish.

The Italians and Irish Power

Many observers have wondered why the great Italian Catholic community in the United States has never challenged Irish power and why such a host of believers from the Pope's own country have accepted with such docility a subordinate role in the American Church. Some of the reasons are purely historical. The Irish, who arrived first, took the posts of command almost by default. The Italian immigrant flood did not reach American shores until most of the Irish had been here for a generation, and by 1890 already almost all the bishops of the

American Church were Irish. The Italians fought the Irish parish by parish, and lost. (Oscar Handlin has told part of the story in his book *The Uprooted*.) The Italians of the first generation had to stumble along with their native language, while the Irish priests spoke English. Today, although the Italian bloc in the American Church is estimated at one-sixth of its membership, the Italians do not have a single representative among the Church's 26 archbishops; and only 3 of its 163 bishops have Italian names.

Probably the decisive factor in the Irish ascendancy over Italian Catholics in America was psychological. The Irish Catholic mind had been prepared for combat in a non-Catholic environment by the long struggle against odds in Ireland and by the fight against prejudice in the United States. Irish Catholicism in America developed as a fighting faith because it had never been anything else but a fighting faith. Its militant opposition to Protestantism in America was as natural as its militant opposition to the devil. It did not know how to be passive or placid or secure because it had been conditioned for group militancy by the Protestant Ascendancy in Ireland.

Many Catholic writers have pointed out the striking contrast between this Irish Catholic outlook and the Italian Catholic outlook. Thomas Sugrue contrasts "the relaxed and affectionate Catholicism of Italy" with the "fiercely Puritanical Catholicism of Ireland." Sean O'Faolain finds modern Ireland "painfully aggressive, touchy, fearful about its religion" while Catholicism in Italy is "like the joy of breathing." Erik von Kuehnelt-Leddihn thinks that the Irish Catholics "emphatically do not have the flippancy, sensuousness and largesse which characterizes the Catholics of the Continent." Irish religious pugnacity is a characteristic of the minority mind — the persecuted, watchful mind, alert against enveloping Protestant power. The Italians, as I discovered while living in Rome, regard such restless Catholicism as slightly gauche, a survival of the uncivilized frontiers of the faith. In America, they resent Irish aggressiveness; many of them have left the Church because of its Irish leadership and have sent their children to public schools. Some of them, as Evelyn Waugh has pointed out, succumb to the "temptation to identify the Church with their inferior station; to associate it with the smell of garlic and olive oil and grandfather muttering over the foreign-language newspaper; to think of it as something to be discarded, as they rise in the social scale, as they discard their accents and surnames."

Undoubtedly one of the reasons for the relative weakness of Catholicism among Italians is that Italian nationalism was identified for half a century with anti-clerical sentiment. Italy was free from Church control from 1870 to 1922, and during that period it had a chance to develop its own secular culture. The Italian struggle for freedom was anti-papal; the Irish was not. The hero of Italy's war of liberation was not the Pope but Garibaldi — and the Church penalized with excommunication the founders of the new Italian nation. The clash between the Italian clerical and anti-clerical forces even spread to America, where Irish-American as well as Italian-American prelates condemned Garibaldi and Mazzini. (Earlier, in 1851, they had condemned Louis Kossuth when he fought for the liberation of Hungary.)

The Scope of Irish Conquest

Because the United States does not have a regular religious census or official church statistics by nationalities, it is difficult to measure the extent of Irish power within American Catholicism. At the beginning of 1953 there were perhaps 15 to 16 million Catholics of Irish extraction, making up more than half of the 30 million nominal Catholics in the nation and numbering about five times the total Catholic population of Ireland. Every cardinal in the United States was of Irish extraction — Spellman in New York, Mooney in Detroit, Stritch in Chicago, and McIntyre in Los Angeles. (Moreover, every other cardinal in the English-speaking world was of Irish stock — McGuigan in Toronto, Griffin in London, and Gilroy in Sydney.)

The editorial mastheads indicated that every important Catholic newspaper and magazine in the United States was edited by priests and laymen of Irish stock. Many of them were militant Irish patriots who tended to accept Irish Republican rights along with God and the Pope as fixed values — *Our Sunday Visitor,* the Denver *Register,* the Brooklyn *Tablet,* the Boston *Pilot,* the *American Ecclesiastical Review, America,* and *Commonweal.* Most of the Catholic universities and colleges in America were dominated and directed by Irish-American priests; Irish-American nuns played the major role among the thousands of educational Religious who held more than 90 per cent of the teaching posts in the Catholic elementary schools. Largely because of this influx of Irish devotees, the United States has become quantitatively the greatest source of supply for convents and monasteries throughout the world. It contributes 198,000 Religious to the Church — 15 to 20 per cent of the world's nuns, monks, and brothers — although the nation does not have more than 8 per cent of the world's Catholic population.

Wherever the Irish have clustered together in America, there the Church has become strong — Boston, New York, Philadelphia, Chicago, Cleveland, Buffalo, Providence, Jersey City, and so on. As Bishop Timothy Manning of Los Angeles has put it, "the strength and health of the Church in America is correlative to the flow and well-being of the Irish." And wherever the Church has become strong, the Irish Catholic bloc, under the direction of the priests, has continued to operate as a kind of Roman-Irish enclave on American soil, defending its separatism with religious zeal. Its philosophy was perfectly summarized in a sentence on Catholic education in a 1919 pastoral letter of the Catholic Bishops of the United States: "The Church in our country is obliged, for the sake of principle, to maintain a system of education distinct and separate from other systems." The bishops calmly assumed that the Catholic principle of segregation was more sacred than the American principle of community in education, and that when there was a conflict the Catholic principle should rule the minds of their people.

The Irish-American people, of course, have had no part in this decision in favor of separatism. They have never been responsible for that Catholicism which Thomas Sugrue has called "a sort of counter-Americanism — with an Irish flavor." They have always been ready and anxious for complete American assimilation, and they are, on the whole, eagerly and sincerely patriotic. Probably they are more deeply and emotionally attached to America than any other national group in American society, and their remarkable record as volunteers in American wars would bear this out.

America and Irish Independence

During the long struggle for Irish independence, the Irish-Americans have played a role almost as important as that of the revolutionists at home. Even today the movement against Partition is as much an Irish-American movement as a home-country movement. Irish-American money has kept Irish nationalism alive through many of its most serious crises, and it has also kept millions of Irish people from starvation. Immigrants' remittances in 1950, for example, totaled more than £10,000,000; and much of this came from America.

From the day when Benjamin Franklin, during the American Revolution, sent an "Address to the Good People in Ireland" condemning the "rapine, treachery and violence" of English rule, Americans and Irishmen have found common cause in opposing "British imperialism." Throughout the nineteenth century, leaders of the Irish revolts came to America for money and recruits; they usually received a cordial reception from the American public, both Catholic and non-Catholic. Even earlier than the nineteenth century, Wolfe Tone, when he was building the United Irishmen, won much support in the United States. The Fenian movement against Canada was launched from American bases in 1866, and every anti-British cause in American history has been fostered and encouraged by the Irish-American priests. Said the *Irish World* in 1874:

This country is Ireland's base of operations. Here in this Republic — whose flag first flashed on the breeze in defiance of England — whose first national hosts rained an iron hail of destruction upon England's power — here in this land to whose shores English oppression exiled our race — we are free to express the sentiments and to declare the hopes of Ireland.

Naturally enough, American support for Irish rebels has been one of the major sources of friction and ill-feeling between Britain and the United States. "It is in America," said Winston Churchill in 1922, "that Ireland and England can always help and hurt each other most." In June 1919, De Valera as President of the unofficial Irish republic, after escaping from an English prison, arrived in the United States. He came as a stowaway, in clothing which had been partially gnawed away by rats.

He was welcomed by the whole nation as a hero, with great mass meetings from coast to coast, and official receptions by city governments and state legislatures. In the midst of the wave of sentimental enthusiasm he floated an Irish loan of $5,000,000. Throughout the long campaign which followed, "Dev" made the United States his financial base.

Since then America has bristled with Irish patriotic societies, usually led by men of political ambition. Although these societies have been divided for many years into bitterly hostile factions, with De Valera worshipers on one side and De Valera haters on the other, they have presented a common front against the English enemy, and they have found a common cause in their Church. The Irish priests have held the quarreling factions together, and the ancient faith has been the underlying cohesive force in the whole combination. The Irish-American press is exclusively a Catholic press, and the American Catholic press is automatically a pro-Irish press. The American branches of the Ancient Order of Hibernians, the Holy Name Society, and the Catholic War Veterans may carry different banners, but the faces in their parades are very often the same.

Aside from Catholicism, the masses of Irish Catholics in the United States are united on only one issue — the ending of Irish Partition. They cultivate this issue with desperate earnestness, equating it with the world-wide struggle against Communism and the survival of Western democracy. Their propaganda on the subject is even less accurate than the corresponding propaganda in the home country. It is compounded of indiscriminate hatred of England and uninformed loyalty to Catholic Ireland. It professes supreme confidence in the triumph of Irish righteousness over English villainy, proclaiming, in the words of the *Irish World*, that "the ghost of John Bull rattles in the dungeons of Stormont, and a few of his puppets hang on to a certain area in Northeast Ulster, but their fate is inevitable. Soon these parasites will go back to the gutter of their own iniquity."

The anti-Partition movements in America have a national coordinating organization, the American League for an Undivided Ireland, as well as countless local committees and associations of Irish patriots. The local organizations range all the way from the Bronx Branch of Fianna Fail, the Sligo Association, and the Cork Ladies Auxiliary to the more inclusive United Irish-American Societies and the United Irish Counties Association. It is quite possible that altogether these societies do not represent more than 100,000 Irish-Americans — but because they have no substantial opposition in the Irish community, they seem to speak with the voice of twenty million. The relatively dignified Ulster voices are drowned out by the din of the Irish Catholic chorus.

The anti-Partitionists succeed in keeping up a constant two-way flow of misinformation between the United States and the home country — which deceives part of the American public concerning the actual situation in Northern Ireland, and deceives nearly all of the Irish Catholic audience at home concerning the force of anti-Partition sentiment in the United States. They have produced a situation in Ireland which would be ludicrous if it were not also tragic, a situation in which a great many serious and earnest citizens actually expect the United States government to intervene in Ireland to "drive the British out" — if not by armed force, then by some kind of financial ultimatum in which Irish freedom will be bought by American gold. The tacit assumption behind most of this anti-Partition propaganda is that if the leaders of the movement talk long enough and loud enough the United States will use its power to end Partition. The militants point out that Irish propaganda in the United States in the 1920's earned large dividends in political pressure, and they argue that the formula may be successful if used again.

There is some superficial evidence to support this theory. John W. McCormack of Massachusetts, then majority leader of the House of Representatives and still the leading Irish Catholic spokesman in Congress, declared in 1950 that President Roosevelt had had a plan for an Irish plebiscite prepared in 1943, and that Roosevelt thought the plebiscite would result in three or four of the six Northern counties breaking away and joining the South. "He expected Belfast would resist in the plebiscite or referendum," said McCormack, "in which case, satisfactory plans could be devised to meet the situation. . . . The late President realized that the Partition of Ireland could not in the long run and should not stand." McCormack did not say what "satisfactory plans" could be devised for American intervention.

Roosevelt was by no means unique in his superficial approach to the Partition problem. In recent years many American political and labor leaders have endorsed Irish unity with greater or less sincerity. Usually their statements about Ireland are vague and general, expressing nothing more specific than a sentimental desire for co-operation among all faiths and peoples. But the anti-Partitionists seize upon these vague statements with avidity as proof of American sympathy, and exploit them endlessly in the Irish Catholic press at home and abroad. Unfortunately, the Catholic people of Ireland are not always aware that statements in behalf of American pressure groups can be easily and painlessly produced in political campaigns — and forgotten immediately. During the 1952 presidential campaign, future Vice President Nixon gave the Irish News Agency a highly improper interview, advocating support for the Irish nationalists by "putting pressure on the British when it comes to handing out American money"; and it received large headlines in the Irish press. The principal leader of the Northern Irish nationalists attributed Stevenson's defeat largely to the fact that Nixon had spoken out for a united Ireland whereas Stevenson had entertained a Minister from the Northern Ireland regime when that Minister was traveling in the United States.

Even responsible political leaders commonly exaggerate the amount of American support for the abolition of Partition. Sean MacBride declared in a 1951 address that "most of the legislatures of the United States and the two largest labor federations in the United States have actually espoused our cause. The House of Representatives of the Congress of the United States went so far as to cut off all financial aid to Britain temporarily to mark its attitude on the matter." This extraordinary claim referred to a legislative coup effected in 1950 by some Irish Catholic Congressmen in the House Committee of the Whole, at a time when most House members were absent; the full House promptly reversed the "decision." In May 1953 the pro-Irish Congressmen rallied only 73 members — less than 17 per cent of the House — to support a petition for a hearing on the Irish border issue. The Eisenhower administration had already, in April 1953, announced that it had no intention of interfering in the Partition question.

MacBride was correct in stating that both the American Federation of Labor and the Congress of Industrial Organizations — with their powerful Irish Catholic blocs — have endorsed the movement for a general all-Ireland plebiscite on the border question, but no branch or session of the United States Congress has taken anti-Partition very seriously since the 1925 border settlement by Britain, Eire, and Northern Ireland. In spite of much pressure at political conventions, no major political party in the United States has committed itself against Partition. A famous resolution in favor of the cause of Irish unity was passed by the American House of Representatives in March 1919 by a vote of 216 to 45, but it was primarily an expression of the American desire for permanent peace, and merely asked that the Peace Conference "favorably consider the claims of Ireland to the right of self-determination."

The Super-Irish Patriots

But the Irish-American politicians, particularly from eastern states like Rhode Island, New York, and Massachusetts, have continued to hold Washington congressional hearings on Partition almost every year, and the Irish press has gleefully reported their verbal assaults on "British tyranny." At these Partition hearings, the friends of Northern Ireland usually permit the Irish Catholics to monopolize the testimony — and the results are frequently bizarre. With no competition in matters of fact, the testimony of the nationalists is often spectacular. Northern Ireland is pictured as a downtrodden British colony ruled by a virtual Gestapo. At a 1950 Washington hearing, a local secretary of the American League for an Undivided Ireland testified that in Northern Ireland "the vote is restricted to landowners." The president of the Brian Boru Club of New York stated that in the Ulster election of 1949 the nationalists had "received a majority of votes in all except the county of Antrim" but that the Unionists won because of "shameless gerrymandering." This statistical tour de force was achieved by omitting the fact that 20 of the 48 constituencies were not contested; the Unionists, as we have pointed out above, in fact have a clear majority in four of the six counties.

The Ulster Irish Liberty Legion of Chicago asserted that, while it was opposed to "the menace of godless communism," it could not countenance any alliance with a Britain whose armed occupation of the North was "an act of aggression equaled only by Hitler's seizure of Austria." The secretary of the Philadelphia chapter of the American League for an Undivided Ireland asserted: "This gerrymandering has been carried out to such an extent that the whole idea of elections is just as much a mockery there as it is in the equally infamous dictatorship of the Communist Party in Russia. . . . In essence there is no difference between the dictatorship in Northern Ireland and the dictatorship of the Kremlin, and the crimes committed by the puppet junta in Belfast are no less than the crimes committed in the Lubianka prison." Paul O'Dwyer, brother of New York's former mayor and now national co-ordinator of the American League for an Undivided Ireland, opposed aid to Britain on the ground that "our money is being used to pay 17,000 secret police that at the present time maintain a reign of terror in that portion of the globe." In 1952 O'Dwyer visited Ireland for a ten-day "investigation" of the Northern Irish terror — without once attempting to get at first hand the government's side of the story.

Probably the two most vociferous of the anti-Partitionist groups in America are the American Irish Minute Men, headed by a minor-court judge in New York City, Matthew Troy, and the National Hibernian Anti-Partition Committee, headed by Father Edward Lodge Curran, who is also head of the International Catholic Truth Society. The Irish Minute Men, carrying inflammatory signs, frequently picket visiting British celebrities when they come to the United States. They created much disturbance when Lord Brookeborough visited the United States. In 1948, in protest against Partition, they attempted a national picketing campaign against the sale of British goods in American department stores.

Their most fanatical journalistic ally is the New York weekly *Irish Echo,* which now claims the largest circulation of any Irish-American newspaper. It refuses to carry British steamship advertising, describes the British Empire as the "root of all evil," and specializes in suggesting violence against England — without using those specific words which would make it liable to the prohibitions of law. On January 3, 1953, when Winston

Churchill was about to visit the United States, the *Irish Echo* carried a typical editorial by Matthew Troy calling for mass picketing:

The American Irish Minute Men will give Winnie Churchill a real workout when he arrives on the Queen Mary. . . . The Pickets want to keep reminding the American people that there are 50,000 British troops in Ireland, and that they are there solely because United States money keeps them there. . . .

The Gold Star Parents of the more than 20,000 American boys killed in Korea should hound Churchill when he comes. They have a real grievance because the lives of their sons were bartered for British trade. The war in Korea has been a trade war — a British trade war as usual — with the stupid Truman administration fighting for John Bull.

When Churchill finally arrived, he was greeted by signs reading "BLOODY CHURCHILL IS HERE AGAIN." A cartoon in the *Irish Echo* pictured Uncle Sam as shouting — to "Black and Tan Bloody Churchill" — "Beat it and don't come back." In an editorial, the *Echo* declared that "Churchill and Stalin have very much in common," and that among their parallel traits is "hatred of the Roman Catholic Church, the greatest institution which exists in the civilized world today."

The *Irish Echo* hails with satisfaction the frequent reports of violence in Northern Ireland, and calls for action in place of words. In its issue of July 11, 1953, it described the explosion of a planted bomb in a Newry theater after a coronation film had been announced, and commented:

Last week, after receiving warning after warning from Nationalist leaders in Ulster, about the danger that threatened in letting the queen be used as a Partition symbol, the British Government stubbornly went on with its program. The Poles, now strenuously trying to drive the Russians out of their country, had hardly as much reason as the Irish would have had for starting, during the queen's visit, to drive the English out of their country.

Troy and his allies are considered too extreme even by the anti-Partitionists at home: when he toured Ireland in April 1953, his meetings were boycotted by Dail members of all parties. On his return to America he accused the De Valera government of preparing a "sellout on the Border question," and he attacked the regime for treachery in permitting an Irish ambassador in London to attend the coronation of Elizabeth II.

Censoring the News From Ireland

The two-way flow of misinformation between Ireland and the United States is maintained partly by censorship and pressure against any author or publisher who speaks with candor about unpleasant aspects of Irish life. In a sense it is a censorship by vilification — vilification directed against any writer, either at home or in America, who publishes unflattering conclusions about the Irish Catholic way of life. In the United States the center of this kind of censorship is Boston, in the old country Dublin.

Probably the Boston Irish are the most thin-skinned inhabitants of the new world; they protest against even an inference if it can be interpreted as anti-Irish or anti-Catholic. Having risen from the shanties of 1830 to wealth and political power, with a near majority in the city's population, they like to think of their conquest of Boston as a triumph of culture and morality over godlessness and bigotry. Their interpretation of Boston's origins was summed up by J. J. O'Kelly in *Ireland's Spiritual Empire,* published in 1952 under the Imprimatur of the Archbishop of Dublin:

> . . . the "Pilgrim Fathers," a group of about a hundred Puritans fleeing from England, sailed from Plymouth, settled in Massachusetts, where they affected to colonise "New England" and, for a time, contrived to get the name of "the Puritan City" for Boston. Their outlook is symbolised in the notorious Blue Laws of Connecticut; but the steady immigration from Ireland generally into Boston and neighboring ports, the growing contact of Western and Southern Ireland with Maine and Newfoundland with its gradual overflow southwards, so overshadowed the Puritan nucleus that Boston duly became one of the most Irish cities outside the motherland.

On January 15, 1945, in connection with a story about Saint Patrick's Day in Boston, *Life* published some unflattering pictures of Boston's slums and certain underprivileged children, including a picture of "Knocko" McCormack, saloonkeeper brother of Representative John W. McCormack. Under one picture was this text:

> Irish kids in South Boston are aggressive and venturesome. The world they live in is a tough place, very far removed from polite Beacon

Hill. For generations the immigrant Irish were herded into Boston slums and held down by the dominant Yankees. But now they out-number all other groups and are pretty much on top as far as city politics are concerned.

There did not seem to be anything inaccurate in this statement, but Mayor John Kerrigan called the *Life* feature "an atrocity against our city." Massachusetts House Democratic Floor Leader John E. Flaherty declared that *"Life* Magazine has reached a new low for cheap circulation tactics in a futile attempt to ridicule the Irish people of Boston." State Senator Joseph Murphy demanded that the sale of the magazine be banned as "derogatory, bigoted, un-American." But the magazine was already sold out.

In January 1949, *Time* was subjected to a similar barrage because a writer had placed under the picture of a public demonstration in India the caption: "Congress Party Parade in Jaipur Like St. Patrick's Day Without Liquor." The matter was investigated by the Committee on Public Exhibitions and Caricatures of the United Irish American Societies of New York, and *Time* was solemnly rebuked for its "evident anti-Irish bias."

Such protests almost always start with Catholic organizations like the Ancient Order of Hibernians, whose members act as volunteer thought police for Irish nationalism. Father Edward Lodge Curran of Brooklyn is the organization's chief spokesman on Irish issues. The A.O.H. has been so persistent that in 1953 even Frank Aiken, the Irish Republic's foreign minister, classed it with the Orange Order as one of the two organizations "which has bedeviled Irish history over a long number of years." In Chicago the A.O.H. protested against the inclusion of "America" in the public-school songbooks — because the tune was identical with "God Save the King." When the play *Suds in Your Eye* was produced in a Pasadena playhouse, the Los Angeles branch took umbrage at one of the characters, Mrs. Feeley. "The setting of the play," said the A.O.H., "with a fence constructed with tiers of empty beer bottles surrounding the Feeley house is vulgar enough, but the boast of Mrs. Feeley that she consumed the contents of all the bottles herself is a gross lampoon on Irish American womanhood. Her cremating of her Irish husband, and burying him 'in his own bottle' in his own backyard is most repulsive to anybody with the Irish conception of the dignity of the human body."

Such comments are mild compared to the attack upon writers who question Irish Catholic ways in Ireland itself. Sean O'Faolain was bitterly denounced in the American Catholic press for his article "Love Among the Irish," which appeared in *Life*. There he dared to criticize the Irish censorship and to say that an anti-sexual attitude is being unconsciously fostered by the Irish Church when it "thunders against the dangers of sex." He quoted a young Irishman as saying, "We Irishmen have been conditioned into a state of sexual frigidity and repression because for generations we have clothed the sublimity of love in shrouds of taboo, false prudery and an attitude of Victorian Puritanism that has given to the act of sexual union the blasphemous nature of something offensive." In retaliation O'Faolain was called "an active propagandist for the worst evils of modern paganism"; before 3,300 policemen at a New York communion breakfast he was denounced by a Washington priest as "advocating more impurity in Ireland." In the *Irish Echo*, Father Curran declared that as a penalty for such impertinence, *"Life* should be barred from every Irish home."

When the magazine *Holiday*, in December 1949, carried a brilliant analysis of modern Ireland by the famous Irish author Frank O'Connor, who was once a supervising librarian for the Irish government, he was subjected to a barrage of criticism in both the Irish and the American Catholic press. A plan for the widespread distribution of the magazine by the Irish government was quickly cancelled. O'Connor had been indiscreet enough to say that Ireland "contains slums you have not seen the like of elsewhere in Europe"; that there is a "scandalous decline in general standards of literacy" as a result of the concentration on the Irish language in the schools; that the priests are "all powerful"; and that 289 of 535 Galway school children examined at school had dirty heads.

Misinformation About America

In Ireland itself the misinformation about American life is more negative than positive. In the Irish press a heavy emphasis is placed upon news from abroad which exalts the importance of Catholicism. I met many Irishmen who were astonished when they discovered that only about 19 per cent of the American people were Catholic; they had assumed a much larger proportion because of the constant emphasis in the Irish press on Catholic achievement. In that press, news of Irish-American cardinals and bishops is continually featured and inflated. When Archbishop Cushing of Boston visited Ireland in 1949 and recruited a group of Irish nuns for service in America, his reception, which lasted a week, rivaled that of a visiting monarch. The lord mayor of Cork presented him with a silver replica of Saint Patrick's bell, the city of Dublin made him a Freeman, and the national government carried him off on an Irish ship of war. When, on the other hand, Cardinal Spellman engaged in his famous controversy with Mrs. Roosevelt in June 1949 on the question of American public money for Catholic schools, and it became evident that the overwhelming weight of American opinion was against the cardinal, the news was carefully played down for Irish consumption. On the day the story became public, the *Irish Press,* the De Valera organ, carried a quarter-column, heavily weighted in favor of Cardinal Spellman. Later it printed another brief story about the controversy, carefully withholding Mrs. Roosevelt's arguments, and including a reference to her by the Right Rev. John Cartwright of Washington as "a little more than tolerant toward Reds and Communists." The leading Catholic weekly, the Dublin *Standard,* did not print a sentence of Mrs. Roosevelt's letters or newspaper columns, but it carried a wholly partisan story under the heading "CARDINAL REBUKES 'ELEANOR THE GREAT.' "

In Ireland the conventional attitude toward American culture is built upon the Catholic assumption that all non-Catholic philosophy is amoral or pagan. The glories of the American public school system are completely ignored, because the American schools are considered "godless." American philosophy is called superficial because it fails to honor Thomas Aquinas. In 1949, analyzing a book about America in the *Irish Ecclesiastical Record* a reviewer calmly announced: "It would be reasonably accurate to say that up to the present, the contribution from thinkers in the United States of America to the development of philosophy has been of little importance."

On both sides of the Atlantic, the Irish Catholics are constantly fed exaggerated tales of the role of Ireland and of Catholicism in the foundation and growth of the United States, while a running attack is made against the alleged tendency to belittle Irish Catholic accomplishments. America, according to a claim published by the *Irish News* in 1952, was discovered in the ninth century by an Irish Catholic missionary bishop, Saint Brendan, who called it Ireland the Great. In a typical editorial entitled "Lest We Forget," the *Irish World* of New York — which in 1946 claimed "the greatest circulation of any Irish-American newspaper" — charged that Irish achievements in the founding of America were being ignored in American public schools because of "influences which are foreign and Godless . . . which have one and only one mission in life, namely to overthrow organized government, to eliminate God, to teach false philosophies and to substitute their perverted, idiotic and satanic theories in place of all that is high and holy in our land." Then the editor marshaled his arguments:

From a careful study of our public school textbooks we find the following facts omitted or deliberately distorted: That Commodore John Barry is the Father of the American Navy. That forty per cent of Washington's soldiers in the War of Revolution were Irish. That among the 56 who signed the Declaration of Independence were Smith, Taylor and Thornton, of Irish birth, McKean and Rutledge of Irish parentage, that Hancock and Whipple were of Irish descent on their maternal side. . . . That George Washington's private secretary was a native born Irishman; that the first secretary of the Continental Congress was Charles Thompson, who was born in County Derry, Ireland. That 30.2 per cent of the entire United States forces in the World War were of Irish descent. That of the 100,000 men who laid down their lives on the battlefields of France and Belgium during the conflict, one third were of Irish descent.

That the best schools, colleges and universities were either established by native born Irishmen or men of Irish lineage, and that the highest phases of education were introduced and taught by Irish men and women throughout the length and breadth of America. That the Irish have contributed infinitely more than any other race toward the making and stabilization of the United States.

Probably most of the *Irish World's* readers did not notice the sleight-of-hand performance by which the accomplishments of Scotch-Irish Protestants in United States history were used to glorify the Irish Catholic outlook — although they had been informed in an earlier issue that less than 1 per cent of the American people were Catholic at the time the Constitution was adopted.

Such partisanship in the interpretation of history is an accepted element of the whole Catholic system of instruction in the United States. The English Protestant contribution is almost ignored; the Irish Catholic contribution is over-emphasized. The Catholic Church is represented as a pro-democratic force in Western civilization and as the primary fountainhead of American democracy. "The doctrine of inalienable rights, the basis of the Constitution," according to Father Paul Hallett, chief columnist of the Catholic *Register* chain of diocesan papers, "is the gift of Catholic civilization." "The fundamental documents of Amercian liberty," says the *National Catholic Almanac* of 1953 — in a discussion of "Catholic Aid in the Founding of the Republic" — "derived from traditional Catholic thought and philosophy. The culture of our fathers was predominantly that of Western Europe, which for more than a thousand years had been Catholic. It had produced the doctrine of the fundamental equality of all souls; and this, in turn, produced the democratic ideal that all citizens have equal rights." The fact is carefully suppressed that almost all the founders of America's original institutions were men who had repudiated Catholicism as hostile to democracy. Two pages later the *Almanac* affirms: "The Constitution is more to Catholic Americans than a guarantee of our religious liberties. It is a re-statement for our own nation of the Catholic basis of all human liberties."

Censorship and Separatism

Irish-American censorship cannot be separated from the official censorship of the Catholic Church: the two phenomena are facets of the same system of power. Nearly all the leading figures in American Catholic film and magazine censorship in recent years have been of Irish stock — Joseph I. Breen of the Production Code Administration, who was brought to Hollywood by the industry as a good Irish Catholic to appease the hierarchy; Fathers John J. Devlin and Patrick J. Masterson of the Legion of Decency, who have been engaged in sifting out material unfavorable to the Church in the films; Monsignor John F. McClafferty, executive secretary of the Legion; and Archbishop John Noll of Fort Wayne, chairman of the National Organization for Decent Literature. In the film world this Irish Catholic censorship group uses the coercive methods of a political machine quite openly, acting on the assumption that every Catholic must obey the judgment of his priest loyally. When, for example, the Legion of Decency and Cardinal Spellman condemned *The Moon Is Blue* in 1953, no Catholic in America had the moral right thereafter to see the film and judge its merits for himself. Although its racy dialogue, as *Life* described it, was "100 per cent on the side of conventional morality," and Chicago audiences "thought it charming and inoffensive," all Catholics were directed to participate in a punitive boycott, not only against the film itself, and the future releases of any film company which distributed it, but also against the future attractions shown by any theater which exhibited it. W. H. Mooring, leading Catholic convert and film critic whose reviews are syndicated in most Catholic weeklies, called for this nation-wide, coercive boycott in the following words:

Catholic organizations everywhere should immediately implement the terms of our annual Legion of Decency pledge by: (1) Causing all theater owners to know that as Catholics and members of the Legion of Decency they are under solemn pledge to "stay away *altogether* from theaters which show immoral films as a matter of policy." Whoever books "The Moon is Blue" indicates anti-Code, anti-Legion policy. (2) By refusing to patronize any of the films released by the company distributing or offering "The Moon is Blue" in line with the Legion of Decency's pledge "to . . . strengthen public opinion against the production of indecent and immoral films and to unite with all those who protest against them."

Within the Irish-American community itself, all the leading advocates of group boycott and discrimination are vociferous Catholics, and the non-Catholic point of view has no agency, organization, or newspaper to challenge the priests. Accordingly, all thinking about social policy in this community tends to follow a circular pattern, traced out by the priests. Biological separatism is added to cultural separatism by two rules of Catholic canon law — that Catholics must not marry non-Catholics, and that, if Catholics persist in marrying outside of the Catholic community, the non-Catholic bride or groom must sign over the religion of all future children. In a sense this is a kind of biological censorship practiced against all Protestants and Jews.

The priests also attempt to preserve their people from moral contamination by prohibiting association with Protestants and Jews in any organization which might represent a point of view hostile to priestly policy. It was the Irish-American prelates of New York City, acting under the directives of Cardinal Spellman, who in May 1953 ordered all the Catholic charitable agencies of the city to withdraw from the Welfare and Health Council of New York if the Mother's Health Center of the Planned Parenthood Federation continued as a member. This boycott, of course, was purely a decision of the Irish Catholic hierarchy and not of the Catholic people in New York. The majority of the city's welfare organizations, accepting the ultimatum as a challenge to American freedom, defeated it by a vote of 317 to 259. Thereupon the Catholic agencies of the city withdrew from the Welfare and Health Council — charging that it was not the Catholic Church which was refusing co-operation, but the welfare leaders who would not banish one of their own organizations for disagreeing with the priests on birth control.

Usually the boycott and censorship policies of the Irish priests are tragically effective in separating the Irish people from the rest of America. The tragedy is most acute in those small American communities where a few Irish Catholics are isolated from a Protestant majority by priestly pressure. The ways of separatism and intolerance are imposed upon the priests by the hierarchy, and upon the people by the priests. No priest dares to be too friendly with Protestants for fear of being branded as disloyal to his Church. This gospel of enforced separatism, sanctioned by Roman canon law, is peculiarly Irish in operation because it comes directly from Ireland. The thousands of young Irish priests and nuns who come to America to take posts in churches and schools bring with them from the old country a tradition that any formal co-operation with Protestants is sinful. One Irish-American priest in 1944 wrote back from a small

American town to the question-and-answer editor of the *Irish Ecclesiastical Record* of Dublin a question which, with the answer, does more to illuminate the whole position of Irish priestly separatism in America than any lengthy treatise could possibly do. I quote the significant sentences:

Question: In a small [American] town, after an antiprejudice meeting which was addressed by a Catholic priest, a Protestant minister and a Jewish rabbi, the Protestant minister wishes to hold a religious service in the Episcopalian church. He discovers, however that there are no breads or wine for a communion service. May the priest, if requested to do so, give to this Protestant minister (old) breads and wine?

Answer: . . . he may not. . . . It does not matter whether the breads are old or fresh . . . there is a question of a very serious sin — the sin of idolatry. Many of the participants in the Protestant communion service will doubtless regard the matter as validly consecrated, and may . . . adore it as such. . . . As a result of the priest's action many might be led to think that the different religious services were not so different after all. Thus once again indifferentism would raise its ugly and pernicious head.

The Political Machines

Irish Catholic separatism has developed in the big American cities in the form of political machines which have dominated civic affairs in many states for almost a century. In every part of America except the old South the most famous and most powerful city organizations have been Irish in personnel, with an Irish Catholic boss in supreme command. Officially, of course, no political party in the United States ever represents a foreign nation or a religious sect; all parties have at least a formal façade of inter-group co-operation and religious neutrality. City political bosses usually select conspicuously Protestant and conspicuously Jewish candidates to "balance" the Catholic names on any municipal slate. But the most successful machines almost always have an inner group of dependable leaders who are Irish and Catholic. These leaders are not necessarily "good" Catholics, but they must never be "bad" Catholics, i.e., they must never be renegades or critics of clerical policy.

The history of American municipal politics shows that the Irish Catholic group of voters is the one group which can be counted on most consistently to hold together and obey the orders of a boss. The Irish have learned to think of themselves as one cohesive racial and religious community, and that community spirit is carried over into machine politics. It makes for party regularity and effective bargaining power. Also it makes for Irish and Catholic supremacy over all other racial and religious factions. The Irish have demonstrated a certain genius for this kind of conquest by manipulation and adjustment. "The Irishman," according to John R. Commons, "has above all races the mixture of ingenuity, firmness, human sympathy, comradeship, and daring that makes him the amalgamator of all races. He conciliates them all by nominating a ticket on which the offices are shrewdly distributed; and out of the Babel his slate gets the majority."

That has been the political story in New York, Boston, Jersey City, Philadelphia, Hoboken, Chicago, and almost all large American cities where the Irish Catholic bloc is substantial. It is not possible to prove Irish Catholic power by statistics, because the statistics do not exist; but the claims of the official Catholic publications concerning Catholic proportions in the population indicate the source of the power. Boston claims a Catholic proportion of 45 to 75 per cent, depending upon the areas included in the designation "Boston"; Providence and Buffalo claim about 64, Cleveland 46, Chicago 41, San Francisco 34, and so on. These estimates include non-Irish Catholics, but until the recent emergence of Italian blocs, the Irish have monopolized the Catholic high command in nearly all local machines. The *United States News,* in a 1951 analysis of the influence of the Catholic vote in American politics, pointed out that that vote may be decisive in controlling the results in nine large cities, which in turn may swing their respective states. The key cities are New York, Boston, Chicago, Philadelphia, Detroit, Cleveland, Milwaukee, St. Louis, and Los Angeles. The nine states in which these big cities are located cast 222 votes for President in the electoral college; only 266 votes are needed to win.

Even when they are in a distinct minority, the Irish Catholics usually swing the balance of political power in city machines by manipulation. They have never approached a majority in New York City, but Tammany operated as a predominantly Irish Catholic machine continuously from 1858 to 1947. Tammany's most famous bosses and front men have generally been Irish Catholics — Richard Croker, Charles F. Murphy, "Honest

John" Kelly, James J. Walker. Murphy, Kelly, and Walker were
buried from St. Patrick's; Croker would have been buried from
that cathedral if he had not taken his shady millions to Ireland,
where he died in 1912 after contributing heavily to the cause
of Irish independence. Boss William Marcy Tweed was not
Irish Catholic, but his two chief lieutenants — Richard B.
Connolly and Peter Barr Sweeney — were; and for a time he was
backed by all three of New York's Irish newspapers: the *Irish
American,* the *Irish Citizen,* and the *Irish World.* When Tweed
finally went to prison for his activities as head of a ring which
plundered at least $75,000,000 from the city, he recorded him-
self as of "no religion." Conspicuous Irish Catholics among
recent metropolitan political figures have been John H. McCooey
and William O'Dwyer in Brooklyn; Frank Hague, who ruled
Jersey City for thirty years; and James Michael Curley, who as
mayor, governor, and congressman bossed the Boston area for
forty years, in and out of jail.

In general, the Irish Catholic political machines in the United
States have been notoriously and flamboyantly corrupt — a disgrace to Catholicism, to American democracy, and to the Irish
people. Their government of American cities has been rightly
described by Professor Edward Alsworth Ross as a "planetary
scandal." But it would be an oversimplification to say that the
corruption has been Catholic, or that the priests have systematically condoned corruption. They *have* condoned corruption
too often — but the explanation for their leniency is not altogether religious. The Irish, being Catholics in a non-Catholic
country, and belonging to an underprivileged group, were thrown
back upon themselves and acquired a political morality in
which group loyalty assumed a disproportionate place. This
loyalty happened to fit in with the moral code of priestly teaching
which winks at minor sins by a special type of casuistry. "The
Irish," says Professor Ross, "detest the merit system, for they
make politics a matter of friendship and favor. In their willingness to serve a friend they are apt to lose sight of the importance
of preparation, fitness and efficiency in the public servant."

The Irish Catholic political boss originally appeared in American history as a kind of lay priest, a local secular shepherd for
the bewildered immigrants, a shepherd who guided them through

the labyrinths of city life as the priests purported to guide them through the tortuous ways of purgatory. The Irish at home had learned to obey their priests blindly, and this habit of obedience had prepared them intellectually to obey their political bosses in the new world. The "good" political boss helped them to find lodging and work; when they were hungry and cold he told them how to get free food and coal. They repaid him by voting in droves as he directed.

The boss, in his own judgment, performed a highly moral service in getting his people onto the city payroll, and he naturally gave precedence to those Irishmen who belonged to his political club. When the Irish Catholic bosses were kind to their people, the priests appreciated the kindness partly because the priests and the bosses were the same kind of people. The Church benefited from the increase of Irish Catholic power secured by the bosses, and the Church's treasury gained money from the Irish jobholders on the public payroll. For the priests it was not too difficult to condone a little favoritism and corruption if it was accompanied by a great deal of kindness to their people. A conspicuously devout Catholic politician who took only minor graft from the city treasury could partially cancel out his sins by ritual and by Catholic loyalty and service.

The Church itself was not entirely unwilling to receive from the public treasury favors which, in the light of present-day ethics, seem questionable. M. R. Werner in his *Tammany Hall* has pointed out that the land which is the present site of Saint Patrick's Cathedral in New York, some of the most valuable land in America today, was given to the church by the city in 1852 by a lease which cost $83.33; and that this lease, which gave the church complete title, was used as a basis for profiteering by the church. Although the city had virtually given the church the land, it had to pay the church $24,000 for permission to extend Madison Avenue through the property, and it also paid all the taxes on the increased value of the property arising from the extension.

The priests did not seriously protest when there emerged in American city politics a figure who became stereotyped as the Irish Catholic boss. He was warmhearted, generous to his friends, fairly decent in sexual morals, shrewd, utterly unscrupulous in collecting "honest graft" from the public, uncultured, loyal to Irish nationalism, and capacious of liquor. The stereotype was dramatically portrayed in the Seabury investigation into New York corruption in 1931, when a whole row of Irish Catholic politicians who had milked the public treasury in one way or another passed across the witness stand and failed to explain their mysterious bank accounts except in terms of racing bets and "dependent" relatives. They became known as the Tin Box Brigade, from the "wonderful tin box" used by Sheriff Thomas M. Farley, who was removed from office after admitting that much of an unexplained $270,000 came from such a magic repository. The public was alternately convulsed with laughter and consumed with rage by the spectacle. It was evident that, whatever their religion, the political morality of Tammany's bosses was like the conscience of an easy woman.

The Bishops and the Bosses

The story of Irish Catholic corruption in American politics is too long for these pages, but two facts stand out in that story. The Irish Catholic machines have been the most notoriously corrupt in American life, and the Irish Catholic bishops have never taken the primary initiative in exposing and breaking up those machines. Sometimes the bishops have joined in a dutiful chorus of disapproval after an Irish machine boss has been exposed by others; but in every case the original exposure has been accomplished by independent newspapers, non-Catholic civic groups, or Protestant and Jewish spokesmen. The agitation in New York City in 1892 which led to the Lexow inquiry was headed by a Presbyterian, Dr. Charles H. Parkhurst, who thundered from his pulpit against "the polluted barflies that under the pretense of governing this city, are feeding day and night on its quivering vitals." The agitation which culminated in the Seabury inquiry and the resignation of Mayor James J. Walker in 1932 was nurtured and led by independent newspapers, by Socialists like Norman Thomas, and by non-Catholic religious leaders like John Haynes Holmes and Rabbi Stephen S. Wise.

The agitation which finally unseated James M. Curley as

mayor of Boston was the result not of any Catholic drive to clean house but of Curley's conviction by a federal court for mail fraud, and his service for a term in Danbury penitentiary. Cardinal O'Connell was personally critical of Curley, but he never unleashed his tongue in public in such a way as to make his condemnation official or mandatory. The Irish Catholics of Boston, without rebuke from the hierarchy, treated Curley as a young hero when he went to jail for impersonating a friend in a civil-service examination in 1903; they elected him to a minor office on the strength of the campaign he waged from jail; and forty-five years later, having elected him mayor of Boston for the fourth time *after* his indictment for mail fraud, they gave him a rousing welcome when he emerged from a federal penitentiary.

At any time in the notorious history of the Tammany machines in New York, or the Kelly-Nash machine in Chicago, or the Curley machine in Boston, the power of the Irish Catholic bosses could have been broken if the Irish hierarchy had cared to speak out as strongly against corruption as it later spoke out against Communism. But the Irish cardinals, archbishops, and bishops did not choose to speak in this fashion. They had learned as Irishmen to regard Irish Catholic political power as part of the Irish Catholic empire in America — and they refused to be disloyal to that empire.

Frequently the Irish Catholic press in the United States has either openly supported corrupt politicians or fought the only forces capable of reform. In 1937, when Mayor LaGuardia was running for re-election, the *Irish World* featured scurrilous attacks upon his administration by an irresponsible Irish Catholic Tammany candidate, Jeremiah Mahoney. In 1945 the *Irish World* openly called for the election of William O'Dwyer: "We can help swell his majority if each and every one of us go to the polls and pull down the lever in his favor." In 1939 this paper had described with approval the award to O'Dwyer, by the Cathedral Club, of the title of "outstanding Catholic layman of Brooklyn." Even after the Kefauver committee had exposed O'Dwyer as a mayor who had "contributed to the growth of organized crime, racketeering and gangsterism in New York

City," and after his closest political aid, James J. Moran, had been convicted of participating in a racket which "shook down" millions of dollars in fire-department graft, the Irish Catholic press continued to condone his conduct. An ecstatically complimentary article in the *Catholic World* of November 1952, calling O'Dwyer "perhaps the only resounding success in the history of modern United States-Mexican diplomacy," described his attendance at Mass and his approval by the Archbishop of Mexico; it failed to mention that American crime investigators had traced enormous sums of graft to his closest subordinates.

A Boston Irish Catholic woman, Katherine Loughlin, writing in the Catholic magazine *Commonweal,* put her finger on many of the basic factors in Irish Catholic charity toward corrupt government by blaming the priests for keeping the laity in a condition of moral childhood. She pointed out that both Curley and Jimmy Walker "were tolerated under a low standard of public morality, a myopia shared by large portions of laity and clergy. When the saintly Archbishop of New York [later Cardinal Hayes] threw his arms about Jimmy Walker in affectionate embrace, no wonder Protestants were shocked and baffled. They concluded logically that Catholics did not demand the same kind of integrity for good standing in their religious and social circles." And she pointed out that the Catholic standard is likely to be higher where Catholics are less segregated; in "an excess of goodness, docility, almost infantilism, they [the Boston Catholic laity] respond to every dictum of the clergy . . . lay leaders are not to be looked for in a regimented society where every Catholic association is ruled over and lectured to by a priest. . . . Without these monitors, we might learn to use our own mental and moral muscles."

To support her charge that the rule of the priests produces docility in the area of political morals, Miss Loughlin might have cited an exchange of questions and answers in the *Irish Ecclesiastical Record* about the moral right of an American law officer to keep liquor captured in a raid during the days of prohibition. The answer — given by Father P. O'Neill, D.D., O.C.L., Professor of Theology at Maynooth — might be termed the Irish Catholic theological sanction for the Jimmy Walker code of political morals:

Q. During the day of Prohibition in America, an officer of the law chases an automobile which he regards as suspect. The occupants flee, abandoning the car, which is filled with liquor worth approximately $200. If the officer turned in the liquor to the authorities it would be destroyed, according to law. Knowing this, he appropriates the liquor, and divides it generously among his many friends, with no monetary recompense. He makes no report whatever on the case. What are his obligations in justice if any?

A. It seems to us that the law officer in question, however illegal or reprehensible his action may have been, has no obligations in strict justice. He is not the possessor of another's property. He has not been enriched by transferring it to others. He has not caused injury by the destruction or consumption of another's property. We have, therefore, no *radix restitutionis* whereon to base an obligation . . . the officer of the law in distributing the liquor among friends, may be said to have usurped the ownership of the State. At the same time he has inflicted no *effective* injury on the State, seeing that the property was in any case doomed to destruction.

Oddly enough, the factor which is most likely to weaken the Irish Catholic control of American cities is not the civic conscience of the people but the rise of Italian-American political power. The Italian bloc is already successfully challenging the Irish in cities like New York, Providence, and Boston. The Italian vote in New York City is said to be 80 per cent as large as the Irish vote. Tammany has had a leader of Italian stock for several years; Rhode Island, the only Catholic state in the Union, has a Senator of Italian ancestry; New York has had two Italian-American mayors in the last decade. Because the Italians are less priest-ridden than the Irish, they are more loyal to the public school and more ready to accept the American policy of separating church and state. They rarely follow the clerical demagogues in Catholic campaigns of censorship and boycott. They tend to be charitable toward Protestantism — more charitable, at least, than the Irish — and in cities like New York Protestantism has a considerable Italian-American following. Professor Handlin estimates that by 1918 there were 25,000 Italian converts to Protestantism in New York City alone. La-Guardia, a Protestant, was able to win majority support from the Italian-American community of his city. It is unthinkable that an Irish Protestant could gain similar political support among Irish Catholics.

Irish Catholic Power at Washington

In national politics the separatism of the Irish Catholics has not been so noticeable or so unfortunate in its results — although, as we shall see in the next chapter, it has had a very serious effect on the financial position of the public school. The Catholic Church in the United States has never organized a national party of its own — as it has done so successfully in many European countries — nor has the Irish Catholic bloc at Washington ever approached the importance of the Catholic city machines. The absence of a national Catholic party is due not so much to a lack of ambition on the part of the Irish bishops as to the strategic policy of the Vatican. According to this policy, Catholic parties should not be organized in non-Catholic countries unless they are reasonably sure of substantial success. A Catholic party is permissible in Holland, where the Catholic people comprise 39 per cent of the population, and the opposition is divided; or in West Germany, where the Catholics are 45 per cent; or in Italy, where the Church is fighting for its life against a growing Communist movement. In the United States, with 19 per cent Catholic strength, or Australia, with 17 per cent, or Great Britain, with less than 7 per cent, the Vatican wisely avoids direct tests of political power.

This policy does not prevent the Irish-American Catholics from using their group solidarity for their own benefit at Washington, nor does it prevent Irish Catholic scandals in national politics. When Attorney General Howard McGrath, an outstanding Irish Catholic layman and former chairman of the Democratic National Committee, was removed by President Truman in 1952 after national scandals had disclosed a whole nest of "friendly" Irish Catholic politicians in the Bureau of Internal Revenue, the phenomenon was generally considered a matter of personal sin; but it was in fact largely a matter of easy-going accommodation. The genial Irish tax collectors had rated co-operation above integrity, and as a result the morale and the morals of a national department had virtually collapsed.

In this matter of over-friendly influence, the Democratic Party has suffered much more than the Republican Party. The great body of Irish immigrants arrived in the United States when the party of Andrew Jackson had already taken its place in American life as the party of the underdog. They were underdogs; *ergo,* they were Democrats. Since then the overwhelming majority of Irish Catholics have been Democrats, and they are likely to remain so — although many of them must have "crossed the line" into the Republican fold in 1952 to vote for General Eisenhower. Since Al Smith first appointed the industrialist John J. Raskob as chairman of the Democratic National Committee, the Democratic Party has recognized the special place of the Irish Catholics in its direction by giving that post successively to Farley, Flynn, Hannegan, McGrath, Boyle, McKinney, and Mitchell.

One of the oddities of the situation is that the new Irish middle class, which has money to spare for financial contributions to party politics, might be expected to be more Republican than Democratic. Its outlook is more conservative than that of the New Deal or the Fair Deal, and it feels somewhat uneasy in Democratic harness. Also, the Vatican's continuing hostility to many aspects of the welfare state and its frequent alliances in Europe with reactionary parties make it a natural ally of the conservative forces in Western democracy, and in the United States those forces happen to be more closely connected with the Republican than the Democratic Party. But the original proletarian character of the Irish Catholic immigration into America has outbalanced all these factors. Tradition, for the time being at least, continues to keep the Irish Catholic bloc safely Democratic and somewhat pro-labor in economic policy. On the whole, Irish Catholicism in the United States tends to be left of center, and the voting record of its congressmen in Washington is generally progressive on every issue concerning which contrary orders have not come from Rome. Its racial policy is magnificently humane and liberal, partly because the papal policy on racial segregation is broadly equalitarian.

It is hard to escape the conviction that most Irish Catholics in the United States are politically progressive in spite of their priests and not because of them. There is a smattering of progressive discussion in the Catholic press, but most of the literature of the priesthood is consummately reactionary. The American diocesan press, edited and managed by Irish Catholic priests, which represents more than nine-tenths of Irish Catholic literature in this country, reads like a denominational version of the Hearst press. The *Irish Echo* in two recent editorials used two phrases which might be combined as the registered trade mark of Irish clerical culture in the United States. It said that Franco was "one of our best friends," and it conferred upon "the late revered" William Randolph Hearst its accolade as "America's journalistic genius."

The striking success of the separatist policy of Irish Catholicism in American politics was demonstrated during the 1952 presidential campaign when both leading candidates, Dwight Eisenhower and Adlai Stevenson, paused in their crowded campaign schedules long enough to pay conspicuous personal visits to the leader of Catholicism in this country, Cardinal Spellman. By such a gesture they recognized the power of the Catholic Church in American politics to deliver votes as a religious bloc. The candidates did not feel obliged to pay corresponding homage to the heads of other religious organizations. About one mile from the place where Eisenhower and Stevenson visited Cardinal Spellman was the headquarters of the largest religious organization in America, the National Council of the Churches of Christ in the United States, which unites 35,000,000 Americans under the Protestant banner. Although Stevenson is a Unitarian and Eisenhower has described himself as an "almost fanatic Protestant," neither candidate thought it necessary to visit the man who was then the official leader of American Protestantism, Bishop Henry Knox Sherrill.

The Super-American Agitators

In the segregated cultural world of Irish-American Catholicism, it is very easy for religious and political fanaticism to develop. The enemies of Catholicism and the enemies of Ireland are natural targets for hatred, and the Irish-American agitator, whether priest or layman, often embodies and expresses both the ideals of his people and their inner sense of insecurity. He helps them to compensate for their cultural isolation from the main stream of American life by fierce and extreme forms of "Americanism." A psychologist might say, with some semblance of truth, that the agitator helps them to lessen their secret sense of guilt for belonging to a Church which is neither American nor democratic. Since Communism is the favorite enemy of both Catholicism and the American people, Irish Catholic anti-Communism is at once an emotional catharsis and an assertion of loyalty to America and the Church. It is a kind of anti-anti-Catholicism which serves a double purpose in opposing the Enemy and in demonstrating the super-Americanism of the Church.

The great Irish Catholic champion of super-Americanism in the 1930's was Father Charles Coughlin of Detroit, avowed enemy of alleged "international Jewish finance," who argued that the Russian Revolution was a Jewish product, and whose teaching nourished the powerful reactionary organization, the Christian Front. In 1939 the Institute of Public Opinion estimated the number of his Sunday radio listeners at 3,500,000. He was finally quieted down and removed from the spotlight not by Irish Catholic opinion in America but by Vatican pressure on Irish-American bishops — since the Vatican recognized that his open assault on government authority was dangerous to its prestige. Until the Vatican frowned upon him, his own bishop said that he was "an outstanding churchman and his voice . . . is the voice of God."

The great Irish Catholic hero-agitator of the present decade is Senator Joseph McCarthy of Wisconsin. In the case of McCarthy, as in the case of Father Coughlin, there are sober and constructive elements in the Irish Catholic world opposed to his methods — but they are in a distinct minority. The overwhelming weight of Irish Catholic opinion in America supports McCarthy heartily. He has described himself in the Jesuit magazine *America* as an "ardent Catholic." He came from Irish stock, having been born in 1908, the fifth child of Timothy and Bridget McCarthy, in a rural section of Wisconsin known as "The Irish Settlement." In Wisconsin, which is 29 per cent Catholic, the nucleus of his political strength has always been in the strong Catholic population pockets. The Catholic hierarchy in the state has backed him enthusiastically, and many priests have thrown their support to him, even from the pulpit. (See Anderson and May, *McCarthy: The Man, the Senator, the "Ism."*)

McCarthy has received the warmest and most undiscriminating praise from the most powerful figures of the Irish-American Catholic world. He has been guest of honor at innumerable official banquets of Catholic organizations. In May 1953, Father Edward Lodge Curran, as president of the International Catholic Truth Society, told 1,800 Brooklyn firemen at a communion breakfast that McCarthy was "a great American" and that he was a "controversial figure only in the minds of Communists and fellow travellers that he has on the run." Elsewhere Father Curran hailed McCarthy as "one of the greatest living Americans in the United States today," and said: "He is not afraid to attack England, as well as Soviet Russia, as the enemy of the United States of America. We hope that other Representatives and Senators of Irish ancestry are going to follow his leadership." The *Irish Echo* in May 1953 hailed McCarthy as "another Patrick Henry heralding the glad tidings to the world that Americans are ready for ACTION." Two months later it said: "Our trusted secret service head, F.B.I. Director J. Edgar Hoover, has paid a priceless compliment to the Irish race when he said: 'Senator McCarthy is Irish.' Thank God for your brand of Americanism, Senator McCarthy." Archbishop John F. Noll of Fort Wayne, the most important Catholic publicist in America, has thrown the support of his great chain of *Our Sunday Visitor* weeklies to McCarthy; and the most widely syndicated Catholic columnist, Father James M. Gillis, former editor of the *Catholic World,* supports McCarthy with an almost continuous stream of favorable comment. The present editor of the *Catholic World,* Father John B. Sheerin, defended the Wisconsin senator as a victim of slanderers in a lecture entitled "Who Is Guilty of McCarthyism?" In November 1952, in an editorial, his magazine declared that "the American people are for McCarthyism." In the same issue McCarthy was praised in a special article as "a deeply religious man." In June and July of 1953, Father Richard Ginder, editor of the influential magazine, the *Priest* — which is owned and published by *Our Sunday Visitor* —declared: "I think McCarthy has done and is doing a grand job. Many people will say: 'I like McCarthy but not his methods.' I can see nothing wrong with his methods. . . . We should cheer for Senator Joe McCarthy."

This pro-McCarthy chorus almost drowns the restrained and dignified voices of the two Catholic magazines which have consistently criticized McCarthy, *Commonweal* and *America*. In view of the prevailing Catholic opinion, it took courage for *Commonweal* to declare in July 1953:

> No man on the current political scene can obscure an issue quite as quickly or as effectively as Senator McCarthy can, and he has an almost unmatched talent for the logically ridiculous, but politically invaluable, *non-sequitur*. On this structure he has built his whole political career.

But, speaking in terms of circulation, it is conservative to say that 95 per cent of the American Catholic press supports McCarthy ardently, and that the support engendered by this press is the backbone of his political strength. (Catholic weeklies and monthlies claim a circulation of nearly 16,000,000. The combined circulation of *America* and *Commonweal* is less than 50,000.) Although educated Catholics realize that McCarthy belongs to an underworld of Irish Catholic culture and that he taps the same reservoirs of fanaticism from which Father Coughlin drew his strength, they can do little to change the picture as long as they do not control the Catholic press.

An underlying hostility to liberal Protestantism is an organic part of McCarthyism, and this hostility feeds on the propaganda in the Catholic press which labels liberal Protestantism "godless" and "pink." When J. B. Matthews, the leading anti-Communist investigator of the Hearst newspapers (a Protestant), declared in July 1953 that the "largest single group supporting the Communist apparatus in the United States today is composed of Protestant clergymen," he was only reflecting two commonplace assumptions of Irish Catholicism: (1) that conservative religious faith, particularly Catholic faith, is per se the best natural bulwark against Communism, and (2) that liberal Protestantism with its gospel of the open mind is an easy prey to Communism. After Matthews had published his charge against Protestant clergymen in the *American Mercury*, McCarthy employed him as chief investigator for the Senate subcommittee on investigations, with the enthusiastic support of the Irish Catholic press. Matthews was not forced out of the position until President Eisenhower intervened against him.

It is not an accident that the two most vociferous Irish Catholic leaders in the United States today, Father Edward Lodge Curran and Judge Matthew Troy, are both ardent supporters of McCarthy, and that Father Curran was an equally ardent supporter of Father Coughlin in the 1930's. Father Curran still uses many of the Coughlin tactics and the Coughlin ideas in his propaganda, attempting to create distrust of all forms of international cooperation which do not fit the Vatican pattern. He unites denunciations of Communism and British policy with denunciations of almost everything that is progressive and free in Western culture. In 1947 he filed a complaint with the New York State Supreme Court attempting to force the United Nations headquarters to leave New York City on the ground that the city had no legal right to convey land to a "foreign sovereignty."

Two dominant facts emerge from the story of Irish Catholicism in America. In the early years of the great Irish Catholic immigration, the American people were often harsh and indifferent to the sufferings of their new fellow citizens, and they permitted the growth of an American anti-Catholic nativism which was a disgrace to the American spirit of tolerance and good will. The second and equally important fact is that the Irish, under the guidance of their priests, have developed a powerful nativism of their own which is only a little less obnoxious than the anti-Catholic nativism of the nineteenth century. Too often the Irish Catholics in America have lived, thought, voted, played, married, and gone to school as Irish Catholics rather than as citizens of the United States. In the beginning this establishment of a partisan and bitterly sectarian Irish community within the American state may have been justified as a defensive measure against prejudice; but today it is an anachronism in a free society. We shall see in the last chapter that it is also a significant challenge to that institution which, more than any other, must shape America's future — the American public school.

11

The Future of Irish Catholic Power

It seems appropriate to return to that 1951 challenge in the Irish Jesuit magazine, mentioned in the Foreword, and ask: How good is the Irish Republic as a pilot model for a future Catholic America? What lessons does the Irish experiment suggest for American democracy?

It must be clear from the foregoing analysis that the Irish experiment provides the United States not with a model but with a warning — a warning against a solution of the church-state issue which at least 80 per cent of the American people would find utterly repugnant. Ireland has not produced cither in the South or in the North the kind of society described in the first chapter of this book as the American ideal — a society of tolerance and good will where men of different faiths can live together as equals, educate their children together, marry across religious boundaries without discrimination, and refuse to use sectarian advantage for political power. On the contrary, the Irish Catholic policy on church and state has produced a society of deep religious divisions characterized by conflict and suspicion. Far worse, it has produced in Southern Ireland a society where cultural freedom and, to a certain extent, genuine political freedom have been sacrificed to clerical dictatorship. Without laboring our points at great length, it seems fair to make certain inductions from the evidence.

(1) In a nation in which the Catholic hierarchy controls the organs of public opinion, formal political democracy is not an adequate defense against clerical dictatorship. The Irish Republic has complete political democracy, but democracy cannot rise higher than its source, and its source is public opinion. When

295

the priests control all elementary education and indirectly almost all of the press, they exercise a veto power over the whole national life. Because of this condition, the Irish Republic is an exhibit of mutilated democracy.

(2) A state which once accepts the partial union of church and state finds it almost impossible thereafter to free itself. Religious partisanship becomes part of the warp and woof of the national tradition. This is the condition today in both the Irish Republic and Northern Ireland. The vested interests of established religion are so powerful that a political leader who advocated the clean-cut separation of church and state would be victimized by all religious groups as an enemy of faith.

(3) A segregated denominational school system is the worst obstacle to national unity and inter-faith co-operation, particularly when it is used, as the Catholic system is used in Ireland, to indoctrinate its pupils with narrow dogmatism and distrust of the moral precepts of other faiths. In the Irish Republic segregated education has destroyed the possibility of public nonpartisan education; in Northern Ireland also it has helped to create a great cultural cleavage between the Protestant and Catholic sections of the community.

(4) An unrealistic sexual code, such as that of the Irish priests, when rigidly interpreted and dogmatically enforced, may do more to destroy family happiness or the family itself than the most "pagan" forms of living. In the Irish Republic, family life under the coercive control of the priests has gone sour. Ireland's young people are escaping in such large numbers from clerical coercion to the comparative liberty and realism of non-Catholic society that today Ireland's population policy can be fairly described as a complete sociological failure.

(5) A religious hierarchy strong enough to enforce the rule which prohibits mixed marriages unless the children are reared in the faith can conquer a minority sect by attrition. The Irish Republic with its fading Protestant fragment of 5 per cent is the world's most dramatic example of the success of this clerical strategy.

(6) In a tolerant democratic society, a tightly organized and well-disciplined sectarian and nationalist pressure group can, by using the hold-up principle, double its proportionate power in

politics and culture. This has been the story of Irish Catholic power in American society. The strategy has been especially effective in America because of the prevailing taboos against any candid criticism of religious organizations.

The Irish Republic as a Crystal Ball

Perhaps the full force of these inductions can best be appreciated if we take the Irish Republic as a kind of crystal ball for a brief and tentative prophecy. Prophecy concerning Ireland should be left to Irishmen; and among Irish soothsayers the young George Bernard Shaw was the most provocative and inspiring, even though his time-schedule has gone awry. He predicted that, when Ireland won political freedom, "the Roman Catholic Church . . . would meet the one force on earth that can cope with it victoriously. That force is Democracy, a thing far more Catholic than itself. . . . When it is let loose, the Catholic laity will make as short work of sacerdotal tyranny in Ireland as it has done in France and Italy. . . . The Holy Roman Empire, like the other Empires, has no future except as a Federation of national Catholic Churches."

It would be rash to make any such definite prophecy concerning the future of Irish Catholic power in America. The most that can be done is to explore certain basic factors. What would happen to America if the Irish Catholic church-state pattern were applied to the United States as systematically as it has been applied to the Irish Republic itself? In trying to answer this question, it is impossible to divorce Irish from non-Irish Catholicism, since the whole program of Catholicism in America is dominated, administered, and promoted by the Irish priests.

In one sense the Irish experience is reassuring, and the Jesuit scholar who asked me to take Ireland instead of Spain as a pilot model for a future Catholic America is justified by the facts. If the Vatican permitted a Catholic America to follow the Irish instead of the Spanish pattern, there would be complete political democracy in the United States, with the right of non-Catholics to hold office and proselyte freely. No church would receive public revenue for the purely devotional phases of its work, and even the Catholic Church would not be given official status as a state church. It should be pointed out, of course, that no one can guarantee that this kind of freedom will endure permanently in any Catholic nation, since the Pope, supreme in authority over all aspects of Catholic activity, can alter any policy of tolerance by fiat. A Spanish-minded Pope could prescribe a Maria Duce program for a Catholic America, and he could find more than enough authority for this policy in past papal utterances, which have always defended the policy of suppressing non-Catholic activity in a Catholic society. But we have a right to assume a little elementary wisdom even in a dictator, and it is not likely that any Pope would try to force Irish Catholic policy — either in Ireland or in the United States — into a Spanish mold.

We have a right also to assume normal ambition in any priestly group — particularly in a group like the Irish priesthood which has been nurtured on the belief that the extension of its own power is a means for the salvation of the human race. If the Irish priests had the same power over their people in the United States that they now possess in Ireland, they could and would make America Catholic in a few generations by the exploitation of one device: the Catholic rule in mixed marriage. It is exceedingly difficult to make scientific guesses as to the speed with which this transformation could be accomplished, since there are several uncertain factors in any prophetic equation. Probably it is fair to assume that, for a long time to come, there will be at least 150,000 marriages each year in the United States between Catholics and non-Catholics. If all the resultant families were held within the Catholic fold, it would mean the transference each year to Catholicism of the equivalent of a city about the size of Toledo. It would be conservative to say that the United States would be one-third Catholic in a century, and one-half Catholic in two centuries; it is more probable that the nation would have a Catholic majority by the year 2125. (The statistical basis for this guess is given in the Notes.)

If America followed the Irish Catholic pattern in education, the present public elementary-school system would be succeeded by multiple denominational-school systems, controlled in each case by Catholic priests, Protestant clergymen, or Jewish rabbis. All these systems would be entirely supported from public revenue. Free high schools would be abolished and succeeded by private fee-charging schools, chiefly under religious control. The Catholic elementary-school system would start with about one-fifth of America's children, and in many localities would recruit more pupils than all other denominations combined. This condition would result from two facts — that the Catholic Church is the largest church in America, and that other churches are so fragmented that maintenance of separate school systems would be difficult. The Catholic system would grow more rapidly than other systems because of the superior coercive power of the priests over their people, because of the increase in Catholic population through mixed marriage, because of the concentration of Catholic people in cities, and because the teaching nuns on the public payroll would turn over about half their government salaries to religious orders for denominational expansion.

If America followed the Irish Catholic pattern in censorship, a national board of review for all printed literature would be established in Washington, headed by a Catholic official, and empowered to suppress any book or magazine which advocated birth control or which, in the opinion of the board, was indecent or obscene. If the record of suppressions in the Irish Republic is used as a basis for prophecy, it is safe to predict that millions of copies of important literary works would be kept out of circulation each year by this censorship.

If America followed the Irish Catholic pattern in birth control and divorce, all divorce and all birth control, except the rhythm method, would be completely outlawed. All advocates of planned parenthood by contraception would be subject to prosecution as criminals, and physicians would not be permitted to give birth control supplies or material to their patients even in case of acute danger to life and health. Divorce obtained outside the United States would not be recognized as valid within the United States. All therapeutic abortion, even when required to save the life of a mother, would be outlawed as sinful interference with the laws of nature.

How much of this woeful vision in the Irish crystal ball has any serious significance for America? A short answer must be arbitrary: Divorce — very little. Censorship — little. Birth control — somewhat serious. Mixed marriage — very serious. Education — critically serious.

In the field of American divorce the Church has met with no affirmative success; its policy has nuisance value only. It has been able to block intelligent reform in many states by negative action, particularly in New York, where divorce racketeering has become a national scandal and where the hierarchy prevents even a study of the scandalous condition by the legislature. The Church may be expected to continue its obstruction in the field of divorce legislation, but probably it will make no attempt to abolish divorce in the near future. Recently a Catholic legislator's bill to abolish divorce in Massachusetts was quickly defeated. There is only one state in the Union today, Rhode Island, where the Irish priests appear to be strong enough to abolish divorce — and they have not yet attempted its abolition in that state. The whole force of American public opinion is against them. Every state in the Union now permits divorce.

In the field of censorship, there is no more chance of the establishment of a national board of review for the priestly extermination of modern books than there is of the election of Senator Joseph McCarthy as President of the United States — and the two contingencies are not unrelated. Already a large part of the American public is angrily resentful of Catholic film censorship, and even Hollywood is showing some signs of independence. Most American Catholics, Irish and non-Irish, are too thoroughly American in their belief in freedom of speech to follow the Irish priests in any program of repression.

The Catholic campaign against birth control in the United States has been a farcical failure except in Massachusetts and Connecticut, where the Irish Catholic bloc holds the balance of power. All available evidence indicates that only the most naïve and uneducated of the Irish Catholic people entirely abjure birth control; the rest resort to contraceptives in spite of their priests. In Massachusetts and Connecticut they go along with their priests only as "public" Catholics in order to preserve the prestige of their Church. In private they buy as much contraceptive material as the citizens of other states.

Massachusetts and Connecticut, however, afford a very interesting preview of the hypothetical Irish Catholic conquest of America — a preview which is quite horrifying to most spectators. In these states a political reign of terror on the subject of birth control has been established by the Irish priests, a reign of terror based on gross misrepresentation of the medical aspects of contraception and threats of political extermination for any legislator who dares to vote against "the laws of God." At each session when the state legislatures have an opportunity to bring their laws into line with the laws of other states, the Irish Catholic blocs defeat the proposed reforms by treating them as insults to "holy faith." The legislators are well aware of the fraudulent character of the Catholic representations of birth control, but they dare not defy the Irish lobby.

The challenges of mixed marriage and education are much more serious, for the Catholic policy on these two subjects is probably the most fertile source of intolerance in American life today. In both cases Catholic policy is based on cultural and biological separatism, ordained by a foreign agency which is outside the effective range of American opinion. No matter how valiantly Americans may work with liberal Catholics to overcome the divisive effects of these two policies, they can hardly hope that their labors will alter the policies directly. The final power lies with the Vatican, and the Vatican, if its top officials choose to be intransigent, is no more amenable to democratic pressure than the Kremlin. In the execution of both of these policies, the Irish priests and bishops are spearheading the drive against traditional American practice. They have transferred two components of the Irish way to American shores, and they defend them vigorously as necessary bulwarks between priestly power and "pagan" democracy.

The Present Challenge to the Public School

Of these two components, the educational policy is by far the greater challenge. Irish Catholic power is today the greatest single threat to the prosperity and expansion of the American public school. Perhaps the most ominous fact about this threat is that in most parts of America public officials dare not discuss it openly because of the fear of the hierarchy's political power.

In the area of education the Irish bishops and the American majority hold diametrically opposite conceptions. The American majority believe that education is one of the primary functions of government and that no one is better able to establish, to develop, and to control the schools than the citizens through their government. The Irish bishops, taking their theories of education from medieval times when the Church ruled all schools, hold that the business of education belongs primarily to organized religion. They believe that a special authoritarian class — the class of priests — should dominate popular culture. They teach that their God-given authority over education includes not only the right to educate Catholic children in Catholic schools at public expense, but also the right to supervise and censor the education of Catholic children in all public schools.

Here is a conflict which goes to the very roots of our democracy. It involves both the right of men to think freely and their duty to tolerate those who do not think as they do. It also involves the fundamental question whether a society like ours, divided as it is by a great Protestant-Catholic cleavage, can ever attain even a moderately unified culture.

The history of Catholic education in the United States shows that the present narrow and punitive rule of the Church against the attendance of Catholic children at public schools, which was incorporated in the canon law in 1918, was largely the result of a victory of the reactionary Irish-American bishops over the more liberal bishops of the Church in the 1880's and 1890's. In 1892, Leo XIII was willing to compromise with the American public school in several particulars, and the liberal wing of American Catholicism, headed by the great liberal archbishop, John Ireland, was about to triumph. Then the more reactionary Irish leaders, headed by Bishop McQuaid of Rochester, won the Pope over to a narrowly separatist policy. Archbishop Ireland never received his cardinal's hat, although he was the most logical leader of a truly American Catholicism. Since then, Catholic policy in America has been dogmatically separatist in fact as well as in theory, a replica of the Irish Catholic policy at home. When Cardinal Spellman, in his famous attack on Mrs. Roosevelt in 1949, accused her of anti-Catholicism and prejudice because she opposed the use of public funds for denominational schools, he was simply renewing and redramatizing the conflict of Ireland versus America which had broken out in New York in 1841, when Archbishop Hughes championed the Irish Catholic point of view. Both conflicts centered around public funds for church schools, and both reflected the larger struggles over church-state relations and philosophies of culture.

Since 1841 the local strategy of the Irish hierarchy has varied according to the militancy of particular bishops, archbishops, or cardinals, but the official and underlying educational policy has remained unchanged. The Church wants in America the same right to operate established denominational schools that it possesses in Ireland. In 1952 the *National Catholic Almanac* headed its section on "Federal Aid and State Aid to Education" with a declaration which might have come word for word from Archbishop Hughes in 1841 — or from Archbishop McQuaid of Dublin today:

> In the United States the use of local, state or federal tax funds to support denominational schools is prohibited by law. State constitutions and laws explicitly forbid state tax aid to any school giving sectarian instruction. The United States Supreme Court has ruled that the First Amendment to the United States Constitution prohibits federal aid to sectarian schools.
>
> Catholic authorities maintain that these laws are unjust and discriminatory because they arbitrarily deny tax aid to schools, which, like the public schools, prepare for the responsibilities of American citizenship. They see no reason why the inclusion of religious instruction in a school's curriculum should deprive it of tax support as long as the school complies fully with all the requirements of compulsory education laws.

Such a pronouncement, supported by an even more official expression of the same sentiment by Pius XII himself (given in the Notes), should dispel any notion that the Catholic Church in America intends ultimately to limit its financial demands for schools to textbooks, buses, and school lunches. It demands an established denominational school system as a moral right, in spite of the Constitution. The Irish priests recognize that the achievement of this demand is for them all-important. The Irish experience has demonstrated that financial support by taxpayers for Catholic schools is more vital in preserving and extending clerical power than the direct establishment of the Church itself. If the Irish Catholic school policy should be transferred to the United States, it would mean the end of the American policy of church-state separation.

Thus far the United States Supreme Court has not surrendered the American tradition of secular public schools. The Court has declared, in the Everson case in 1947, that the First Amendment — "Congress shall make no law respecting an establishment of religion" — has "erected a wall between church and state. That wall must be kept high and impregnable." In its decision, the Court permitted a state to use public funds for Catholic school buses, but it indicated that expenditures for such bus transportation represent the extreme limit of concessions to Catholic demands. In the McCollum case in 1948, the Court prohibited religious instruction under public auspices in public-school buildings. In the Zorach case in 1952, the Court permitted "released time" religious education outside the classroom, but it did not waver in its basic contention that public money may not be used directly for the central purposes of a denominational school system. The Court's decision in this case reiterated the basic philosophy of the Constitution: "Government may not finance religious groups or undertake religious instruction nor blend secular and sectarian education nor use secular institutions to force one or some religion on any person."

Can this clear and unequivocal doctrine of the separation of church and state be defended against Catholic power? I do not know. The pressure against that doctrine has been great and persistent since November 1948, when the Catholic bishops officially challenged what they called the "doctrinaire secularism" of the Supreme Court's interpretation of it. Partly because of that pressure, the Supreme Court in the Zorach case, by a vote of 6 to 3, made a slight breach in the wall of church-state separation by permitting religious education for public-school pupils on released time outside public-school buildings. It permitted the use of the public machinery of American compulsory education to bolster up denominational enterprises. Justice Jackson in his dissent in this case rightly warned that the wall of separation between church and state was becoming "warped and twisted." The Catholic hierarchy hailed the Zorach decision as a victory, even describing it as a reversal of principle. It was not a definite reversal of the major principle involved, but time alone can tell whether it was the beginning of a process of appeasement and surrender which will end in permitting denominational agencies to levy their costs upon the American taxpayer.

It is quite possible that under Catholic pressure American policy on the separation of church and state will go the way of educational policies in Europe, and that even the courts will succumb to the plea that denominational schools have a natural claim upon the public treasury. The propaganda in favor of this latter view is subtle and engaging. It exploits, in behalf of a separatist and segregated educational enterprise, all the traditional sentiments about tolerance and fair play. In 1953, in the preliminary stages of a legislative battle in Washington over the use of the federal share of the income from off-shore oil resources, this propaganda was successful. The Senate passed a bill which left the door open for the use of such funds for denominational schools. The House defeated the measure without specifically repudiating the concept behind it. The funds at stake in this battle are estimated at many billions of dollars. The Catholic campaign for the use of a part of this golden treasury by the parochial schools began in 1952, when Father Paul Hallett announced, in the *Register* chain of diocesan papers: "We believe that the revenues from the nation's estimated $50,000,000,000 in coastal oil reserves should be marked off for school relief — for all schools."

Even more portentous than the direct drive for public money for Catholic schools is the ingenious propaganda for some modification of the American system. The Canadian scheme for tax exemption of those parents who pay tuition to private schools offers one possibility for defeating the Supreme Court's interpretation of the Constitution. The French schemes for giving "scholarships" and other welfare grants to Catholic parents might be developed in the United States in such a way as to bypass the First Amendment. The Irish bishops are relying heavily on the large Catholic blocs in the labor unions to win their battle for school funds, and their confidence seems to be justified. The American Federation of Labor, where Irish Catholic leaders are particularly powerful, has actually sponsored a law in Washington, the Mead-Aiken bill, which would have made it mandatory to include money for Catholic school buses in federal appropriations for education. Neither the C.I.O. nor the A. F. of L. has taken a militant stand against the program of the Catholic bishops.

Australia and Canada Too

The never-to-be-forgotten fact about Catholic church-state policy is that the demand for public money for segregated schools is the key to the whole Vatican program of expansion. The hierarchy is already permitted to receive such funds in Britain, Ireland, and most parts of Canada. It now looks to the two other English-speaking countries, Australia and the United States, as the next logical fields of conquest. In Australia a modified form of the American policy still prevails, but many political bodies, including branches of the Australian Labor Party, have swung over to the Catholic position on this question. The Australian struggle is strikingly similar to the struggle which is going on in the United States, because the Catholic proportion of the Australian population is almost as great as the proportion in the United States — 17 per cent as against 19 per cent. In Australia, as in the United States, the Catholic hierarchy is almost entirely Irish; hence a policy which has been made in Rome is being executed by militant bishops who have been nurtured in an atmosphere of denominational partisanship.

Neither Australia nor Canada has any constitutional prohibition against the use of public funds for religious schools. Accordingly, all Australian and Canadian legislative bodies, local and national, are open to continuous pressure by denominational groups for public money. The pressure is particularly strong in Canada, because the Canadian school system began in the days when churches controlled virtually all schools, and because Catholics now comprise nearly 44 per cent of the national population. Australia is still holding the line against government support of religious schools, but Canada long ago conceded the point to the churches in its chief provinces. Quebec has the same educational pattern as Ireland: not public schools, but Catholic and Protestant systems supported by the public treasury. Newfoundland has four denominational school systems — for the Catholic, the Anglican, and the United (Protestant) churches, and for the Salvation Army. Ontario, Saskatchewan, and Alberta grant public funds to separate denominational schools; Manitoba, Nova Scotia, New Brunswick and British Columbia do not. Everywhere in Canada the Catholic priests are increasingly successful in segregating the Catholic children from the non-Catholic children; and they are confident that their educational policy will soon prevail in the whole country. Already in Ontario, 1 child in 4 is in a Catholic school. In all English-speaking Canada, the fight for segregation is led by the Irish priests, who control the Catholic Church as completely as they control it in the United States. "Outside of Quebec," says the *Irish World*, "nearly every priest and nun in Canada is Irish." This is an exaggeration, but it is close to the truth. The outside world has tended to think of Canadian Catholicism as exclusively French; it is time to realize that it is both French *and* Irish.

The Sabotage of Public Schools

Continuing sabotage of the public school is an organic and necessary part of Catholic policy. Usually the sabotage is indirect, and frequently it is camouflaged by protestations of great friendship for public education. In April 1952, the National Catholic Educational Association officially declared that "Catholics believe in the public school," that they recognize the "obligation to pay taxes for the support of the public schools," and that they will not "interfere with the justifiable expansion of the public school system." Such words should not deceive anyone. The Catholic canon law still prohibits Catholic children from attending public schools; when the Church declares that it believes in public schools, the honest Catholic expositor should add the phrase *for other people*. The very existence of Catholic schools depends upon the maintenance among the faithful of the belief that public schools are inferior; without that conviction the Catholic people could not be persuaded to contribute large sums of money to their own segregated schools. The priests continually remind them of the alleged godlessness, pro-Communism, and immorality of the public schools. Also the priests serve as permanent focal points of discontent in the community in regard to all phases of public education. While Catholic educators believe that they are sincere in favoring "justifiable expansion" of public schools, in practice they represent a competing institution whose survival depends upon distrust of the public school. The tendency of the Irish priests, therefore, is to find that public-school expansion is not justifiable wherever it may have an unfavorable effect upon the position of a Catholic school.

Among their own people, Irish Catholic leaders are sometimes quite frank in coupling their support of Catholic schools with opposition to public institutions. When the State University of New York in 1952 was starting a new medical school, State Senator Walter Mahoney told a Catholic dentist guild's communion breakfast in Buffalo that such expansion should be opposed — because if the public institution were allowed to grow it would "undermine and eventually extinguish many of our privately-endowed colleges and universities . . . including many of our Catholic colleges." The *Irish World,* in a 1937 editorial headed "Pope Lauds United States Parochial Schools," managed to include in a few sentences nearly all the basic prejudices of Catholic propaganda concerning public schools:

Atheistic doctrines are rife and rampant today in our American schools. Distorted teachings warp the minds of many of our young students, while alien dogmas are carefully propagated by not a few of our would-be American teachers and professors. . . . Communistic, irrational and radical philosophies are advocated and in no insignificant degree in many of our Public Schools, colleges and universities today, all of which tend to pervert and warp the mind. The Catholic school . . . has been at all times and shall continue to be the fountain of knowledge according to the Divine principles of Christ-like ethics.

The Catholic hierarchy is especially determined in America to defeat all public appropriations for public schools in those cases where a Catholic veto can be given the color of "distributive justice." This has been the situation for at least twenty-five years in respect to federal aid for public schools. I have told part of that story in *American Freedom and Catholic Power,* and the more recent portions of the story have been admirably summarized by Leo Pfeffer in his 1953 work, *Church, State, and Freedom.* Repeated efforts by the National Education Association and other organizations to secure an appropriation of $300,-000,000 for education in backward states have been defeated in the House of Representatives by the obstructive tactics of an Irish Catholic bloc, which has, as a condition of approval, held out for a guaranteed amount for Catholic school buses. Non-

Catholic legislators in Washington have refused to surrender to the Catholic ultimatum, because they fear that even a small appropriation for Catholic school buses may be used as the entering wedge for a larger program of financial demands in behalf of religious schools. The whole history of Catholic strategy in other countries warrants that apprehension. The result is a complete deadlock at Washington on all matters of general federal aid for education. American children, particularly in the poorer states, pay the price. Catholic intransigence on this issue has been supported by an Irish Catholic Attorney General of the United States, J. Howard McGrath; in an address before the National Catholic Educational Association in Cleveland in 1951, he attacked the Supreme Court for a "distorted" interpretation of Jefferson's doctrine of church-state separation.

On the local level, the policy of sabotage of public education in the United States frequently takes the form of opposition to local bond issues for public high schools, especially when the Church is attempting to raise funds simultaneously for a competing school. In hundreds of American communities where the Irish contingent in the population is substantial, the Catholic school becomes the divisive factor in the community, and the propaganda of the Irish priests in favor of that school becomes a major cause of group hostility and mutual bigotry. German, Italian, and French priests rarely equal the zeal of the Irish priests in this guerrilla warfare of sabotage and separatism.

Conant Versus Cushing

The basic conflict between Catholic policy and American democracy in the field of education was dramatized in April 1952, when James B. Conant, then president of Harvard University, challenged the dogma of educational separatism as it is embodied in the private school. Before a meeting of the American Association of School Administrators in Boston, he declared that "a dual system serves and helps to maintain group cleavages" and class distinctions. "We do not have and have never had an established church," he said. "To my mind, our schools should serve all creeds. The greater the proportion of our youth who attend independent schools, the greater the threat to our democratic unity. Therefore, to use taxpayers' money to assist such a move is, for me, to suggest that American society use its own hand to destroy itself."

The torrent of abuse which descended upon the head of the leading educator for this assertion of a fundamental American attitude poured from the Catholic press for weeks. In Boston, Archbishop Cushing, asking for "distributive justice" for "independent" schools, declared that Conant's philosophy was a "threat to our faith." Many Catholic writers pretended that Conant's clear plea for democratically controlled and non-sectarian public education was a plea for dictatorship. At the ensuing annual convention of the National Catholic Educational Association, the opening address, an attack on Conant, contained these words: "Government-controlled education for all children and youths is the necessary foundation for all dictatorships. . . . Totalitarians have to take over the education of the children in order to have grown people who will consent to live without freedom."

From that point forward, Conant was an almost continuous target for reactionary criticism. A year later, when he appeared before the Senate Foreign Relations Committee for confirmation as United States High Commissioner to Germany, the undercover opposition to him was based on Catholic pressure against "an enemy of parochial schools." The opposition was totally ineffective only because of Conant's unblemished record as an outstanding American. When Senator McCarthy later assailed Conant before a Senate committee investigating the "Voice of America," there was no doubt that Catholic animosity on the school question was behind the attempted smear.

Conant's judgment on the divisive effect of parochial education could not have been delivered in a more appropriate city than Boston. Boston is the Irish Catholic capital of the United States, the No. 1 exhibit in America of the defeat of American public education by Irish Catholic power. During the course of the century in which the Irish have risen to dominance in that city, its public schools have gone steadily down in their relative importance and prestige, while the Catholic schools have steadily risen. Today in Boston proper, the Catholic elementary schools enroll only about 29 per cent of the pupils — not an impressive total when the size of the Catholic proportion is considered. But the recent history of the two school systems makes the figures more significant. In the 7-year period from 1944 to 1951, attendance at the public schools declined about 8 per cent, while attendance at the Catholic schools increased 21 per cent. In many parts of the city the Catholic schools are larger and more modern than the public schools; and the public schools are slowly dying by attrition.

Since 1945, the Archbishop of Boston has bought eleven public schools, some of them at bargain prices, and transformed most of them into Catholic parochial schools. Here are the names and addresses of the schools, the dates of transfer, and the prices paid.

Name and address	Date of transfer	Price paid
Capen		
I St. at East 6th, South Boston	June 22, 1945	$1,250
Christopher Columbus		
Tileston St. near Hanover St., Boston	May 3, 1945	12,500
Comins		
1424 Tremont St., Boston	December 5, 1946	500
Damon		
Readville St., Hyde Park	July 15, 1947	3,000
Henry Vane		
234 Baker St., West Roxbury	January 15, 1953	4,500
Lawrence		
B St. at West 3rd, Boston	May 25, 1948	200
Nahum Chapin		
Commons, Charlestown	May 13, 1946	500
Paul Jones		
Horace St. at Byron St., East Boston	June 22, 1945	2,500
Sam G. Howe		
West 5th St., South Boston	June 22, 1945	2,250
Wait		
125 Shawmut Ave., Boston	May 3, 1945	3,200
Wells		
Blossom St., Boston	July 15, 1947	12,000

The story in near-by communities is almost as significant as in Boston. In Cambridge, public-school enrollment has been declining, while parochial-school enrollment has been increasing. But the story of the relative growth and decline of the two competing school systems in the Boston area is not nearly so important as the conquest of the *public* schools by Irish Catholic cultural and political power. To borrow a phrase from anti-Partition propaganda, the public-school system of the Boston area is "occupied territory."

It is an element of Catholic policy that Catholic school officials should at least share in the control of all public educational ventures, on the theory that the Church has an obligation (in the words of Pope Pius XI) "to watch over the entire education of her children, in all institutions, public or private." Today, in both Boston and Cambridge, the rulers of the public-school systems are almost wholly Irish Catholic, and the overwhelming majority of the teachers are Catholics of Irish extraction. In 1953, for example, the Boston School Committee, elected by the voters of the city to control all *public* schools, consisted of four Irish Catholics and one Jew. Six of the seven superintendents and assistant superintendents employed by this School Committee to operate the system were Catholics of Irish stock. Many of the teachers and supervising officials in the system send their own children to parochial schools, and some responsible administrators have had their entire training in Catholic schools. The superintendent of the system has two pictures conspicuously displayed in his office — one of the Madonna and Child, and a photograph of himself shaking hands with Archbishop Cushing.

In Cambridge it is generally recognized that a non-Catholic has virtually no prospect of promotion to a supervisory post in the system. When the public-school teachers of Cambridge recently listed the colleges they selected for refresher courses, their favorite was Boston College, a Catholic institution. Partly as a result of this Catholic training of public-school teachers, the system of educational regimentation used in the Catholic schools has spread to the public schools. They have become parochialized in spirit and techniques. The Cambridge school survey of 1947 found striking evidence of the mentally deadening effect of this spirit in the Catholic-dominated public schools of that city. It found that there was an alarming emphasis on "repetitive drill" by a teaching force which was "disconcertingly lethargic," a "rather complete rigidity and unusual traditionalism of methods, curricula, and administration of the system," and a tradition of extreme "localism" under which local residents were given almost all the jobs. The experts who made the survey were too polite to describe this condition as Irish Catholic machine politics in action.

A Test of Loyalty to Public Schools

Is it "prejudice" and "bigotry" to list these obvious facts about the Irish Catholic conquest of Boston's school system? Many Americans might say that it is, and they might well ask: Do not Irish Catholics, particularly when they are in the majority in a community, have as much right to rule the public schools as anyone else? I think the honest answer is this: As Americans, yes — as Irish Catholics, no. As Americans they should believe in the public school as the proper place for the education of the children of all faiths. This is the basic conception of tolerance and co-operation which is vital to the very life of the American school system. If they accept that conception as a premise, they have the same right to govern or operate the public schools as any other Americans. As Catholics, however, they belong to an organization which repudiates that ideal and which orders creedal isolation for Catholic children; and as Irish Catholics they belong to a nationalist group in the American community which uses Irish national spirit to promote that concept of isolation. Has a member of a group which incorporates this policy of isolation into its basic law a moral right to supervise *public* education while still adhering to this policy?

In 1951 that question was brought dramatically to public attention when Governor Paul Dever of Massachusetts — a popular Catholic political orator — made the Right Rev. Cornelius T. H. Sherlock, archdiocesan superintendent of Boston's Catholic schools, a member of the state Board of Education. As head of the parochial-school system of the region, Monsignor Sherlock was pledged to enforce to the utmost the Catholic rule that Catholic children should attend Catholic schools only. As a member of the state Board of Education, he was pledged to promote the interests of the public schools. Could a citizen pledged to a policy of keeping the majority of the city's children out of the public schools loyally serve those schools? It is evidence of Irish Catholic power in Massachusetts that no

Massachusetts newspaper raised this obvious question editorially.

My own answer to this question, and to certain related questions, was expressed in a "model" letter to a hypothetical Catholic candidate for an American school board, published early in 1953:

Dear Mr. Candidate:

I understand that you are a candidate for membership on our local school board. I understand also that you are a member of the Roman Catholic Church.

Ordinarily the fact that you are a Catholic would not influence my vote one way or another. This is a free country, and no Protestant, Catholic, Jew, or unbeliever should be rewarded or penalized at the polls for religious belief, or the lack of it. I respect your faith and I believe that the American Catholic people are on the whole loyal to our democratic way of life.

But there is a law on the statute books of your Church which disturbs me very much. It was not written by American Catholics, and it has never been ratified by the American Catholic people, but the priests of your Church tell you that it is binding on all Catholics everywhere. It reads:

Canon 1374

Catholic children must not attend non-Catholic, neutral, or mixed schools, that is, such as are open to non-Catholics. It is for the bishop of the place alone to decide, according to the instructions of the Apostolic See, in what circumstances and with what precautions attendance at such schools may be tolerated, without danger of perversion to the pupils.

This law, you will see, imposes a boycott on all public schools, because the public schools are open to the children of all faiths. The Holy Office of your Church has declared that the law applies to both the elementary schools and the high schools of the United States. (Bouscaren and Ellis, *Canon Law,* pp. 705-6.) The law takes away from you as a Catholic parent the moral right to choose a public school for your child's education, and it gives the final decision to a Catholic bishop. That bishop is not chosen by you or your fellow Catholics in the United States but appointed in Rome, and when he decides which school your child must attend, he cannot act as a free American citizen but he must follow "the instructions of the Apostolic See."

Do you support this law of your Church?

It seems to me that this is a fair question and that, before I vote for you as a member of our local school board, you should answer it directly and without evasion. The question has nothing to do with your personal religious faith. It concerns your Americanism and your obligation as an American official to support our public schools.

Although you may be a person of the highest personal merit, I cannot vote for you unless you are willing to stand up and be counted against the boycott-rule of your own Church.

New York and UNESCO

Although Irish Catholic power in public education is most conspicuous in the elementary and secondary schools of New England, it is also well defined in other geographical areas, and in the field of higher education. The Church maintains its own system of universities, and simultaneously exerts pressure on public colleges. In almost every instance in which Catholic pressure is used to control a public school or college, it is the Irish bloc which assumes the leadership.

Irish Catholic power in the public schools of New York may soon parallel such power in Boston. The Catholic hierarchy of New York is more successful than that of any other large city in the United States in keeping its children out of the public schools; and it is almost equally successful in exerting influence over the schools which it boycotts. Already about one-fourth (300,000) of the city's pre-college students are enrolled in Catholic schools — a proportion almost equal to the percentage of Catholics (27 per cent) in the total population. This means that New York has a higher percentage of Catholic children in Catholic schools than Boston itself. Brooklyn, the largest single diocese in America, has 188,000 children in its Catholic school system, more than one-third of all Brooklyn school children, as against a corresponding proportion of 29 per cent in Boston. In New York, the Irish Catholic political bloc — with some help from Italian Catholics — has become powerful enough to force a distribution of key positions in the city school system on a religious basis. In 1952 and 1953 the selection of a Protestant associate superintendent for New York's public schools was blocked in the Board of Education for eleven successive meetings on the ground that the "religious balance" of the school system would be upset by the selection of a Protestant. An Irish Catholic associate superintendent, Miss Regina Burke, had retired, and Superintendent Jansen wished to name as successor a Protestant, Miss Florence Beaumont. Because of an unofficial Catholic ultimatum, Miss Beaumont's appointment was held up until the New York State legislature had created a second associate superintendency, and the new post had been filled by an Irish Catholic, E. J. Gannon.

A Catholic drive for the control of New York's Board of Higher Education and the displacement of its non-Catholic chairman, Ordway Tead, ended in victory in 1953 with the selection as chairman of Joseph B. Cavallaro of Brooklyn, Knight of the Order of the Holy Sepulchre, who, shortly after his election, appeared at a Knights of Columbus mass meeting with the Rev. Edward Lodge Curran, announced his support of Senator Joseph McCarthy, and expressed regret that he himself had not been educated in parochial schools. In 1949, three years after Cavallaro's appointment to the Board of Higher Education of New York, the New York *Post* discovered that all four of his children of school age were attending Catholic schools. It was this same political bloc in New York's Board of Higher Education, backed by the Knights of Columbus, which in 1949 defeated a distinguished liberal, Dr. Bryn J. Hovde, for the presidency of New York's Queens College — on orders of Mayor O'Dwyer.

Frequently it is not possible to identify or document the expressions of Irish Catholic power in public education because in any given situation the Catholic bloc may work through an "economy" or "Americanism" group without disclosing its denominational character. Throughout the country in recent years, local campaigns have been waged against the United Nations Educational, Scientific, and Cultural Organization because of its generally progressive attitude toward modern thought and its past leadership by liberal scientists like Julian Huxley. In almost every case the nucleus of the opposition to UNESCO has been an Irish Catholic bloc. Usually the Catholic press has led the attack. In Los Angeles in July 1953, the Catholic archdiocesan weekly, *Tidings,* united with Hearst's Los Angeles *Herald-Express* and a local group of reactionaries to defeat a proposed $335,000 project for public-school teacher training. The project, which was to have been financed by the Ford Foundation, was defeated largely because it was alleged to have a "UNESCO taint." Because of Catholic and other reactionary pressure, the Los Angeles Board of Education banned from the city schools a pamphlet, *E in UNESCO,* which praised international co-operation in educational affairs; and *Tidings* gloated over the consignment "to the wastebasket of rejected global-conscious themes."

When, in 1952, Principal James P. McGeough of East High School, Pawtucket, Rhode Island, suspended the "UNESCO Thinkers Club" in his school on the ground that there had been "rumors of Communist infiltration and atheistic domination in UNESCO," he was simply carrying out in a Catholic state the general anti-UNESCO policy of his Church. When asked to defend his action, he referred inquirers to the front page of the local diocesan newspaper, the *Visitor,* which had supplied him with the misinformation on which he had acted. The Providence *Journal* had the courage to protest: "Rhode Island's future should be so precious to all of us as to fight suppression of thought and opinion and the imposition of dogma whenever and wherever they appear. We were born with a great cup of liberty and we shall die in the spirit and in the growth of the mind if that cup is smashed from our lips."

When Dr. George D. Stoddard, a former moderator of the American Unitarian Association, was removed as president of the University of Illinois in July 1953, his active friendship for UNESCO was one of the main charges against him; the attack upon him — originally launched by the Catholic Bishop of Springfield — was led in the university's board of trustees by a Catholic layman who said: "I never make a move without consulting my bishop."

The Non-Catholic Answer

Who will meet the challenge of Irish Catholic power to the American policy of church-state separation and to the American pattern of inter-faith co-operation? In a nation which is more than four-fifths non-Catholic, it should not be difficult to find defenders of the American tradition. Candid criticism of Irish Catholic policy might be expected from the non-Catholic press, from progressive political leaders, from the universities, and from leading Protestants and Jews. The most natural defenders of America's traditional policy are those independent liberals not committed to any form of denominational partisanship.

Unfortunately, the liberals — even the liberal social scientists in the non-Catholic universities — have revealed a marked reluctance to join issue with the Catholic hierarchy. In a sense, Irish Catholic separatism and the general Catholic assault on the American policy of church-state separation have been protected by a myth. Like most myths, it has some truth in it. The Catholic Church in America — runs this legend — represents a persecuted minority; and a true liberal should be the last one to add to the Catholic handicap. This must be a country in which the followers of every faith must be treated with absolute fairness. Since the Protestants are in the majority, and since the fundamentalist segments of Protestantism still reveal some anti-Catholic fanaticism, it is one's duty to refrain from any criticism which might increase hostility to the Catholic people. Furthermore, one has a special obligation to refrain from criticism of Irish-American ways of life, because the Irish immigrants have been an underprivileged group in our society.

This is obviously sound doctrine as far as it goes; but in a miasma of kindly sentiment many American liberals overlook the fact that the regulations of the Catholic hierarchy contradict the very principles of tolerance and co-operation to which an appeal is made. It is not the American people but the members of the Irish hierarchy who are chiefly responsible for placing the Irish Catholic segment of American society in a kind of cultural ghetto where their people are fed on denominational partisanship. When a church by its own rules promotes bigotry and partisanship in a free society, it has no claim to exemption from criticism, least of all from the liberals. There is in the United States, of course, no question of freedom for Catholics to teach, or to proselyte, or to develop as many separate institutions as the priests care to establish. Every church in a free society has the moral right to preach and to teach exactly as it pleases, in political as well as spiritual matters, however reactionary or idealistic or stupid or revolutionary it may be. But the *right* of a great foreign ecclesiastical dictatorship to promote separatist ways and to challenge the American policy of church-state separation does not imply the correctness of the policies so promoted or the wisdom of the liberals' silence on such matters.

Today, although most non-Catholic and many Catholic Americans appreciate the dangers of Irish Catholic policy when these dangers are pointed out, the issues cannot be candidly discussed in any standard magazine or newspaper, or even suggested in films, plays, or radio programs. Catholic power is sufficient to brand any such discussion as "bigotry" if it involves any realistic treatment of the hierarchy's policies.

A few non-Catholic organizations insist on facing the issues. A national organization, Protestants and Other Americans United for the Separation of Church and State, is doing valiant service in protecting the public schools from priestly sabotage. In the Jewish world, the American Jewish Congress, the American Jewish Committee, and the General Conference of American Rabbis speak out consistently for a policy of church-state separation. But even in these circles many voices of appeasement are being raised. It is fashionable — and easy — to define tolerance in such a way as to evade all responsibility for eliminating the intolerant features of any powerful religious group.

The largest organization in the United States dedicated to the promotion of understanding and tolerance, the National Conference of Christians and Jews, has surrendered its right to criticize Catholic policy by excluding from its program any discussion of such subjects as segregated education, inequality in mixed marriage, birth control, and denominational censorship. An astonishing number of good Americans accept this Munich-like policy. They do not realize that it grants absolution to the Catholic hierarchy for the most serious forms of religious bigotry in American life, and that simultaneously it shifts to other organizations the responsibility for fighting Catholic intolerance which should be borne by the NCCJ itself.

The Jewish and Protestant press in the United States is not consistent in resisting Catholic policy by advocating for itself a clear line of church-state separation. The *Christian Century* and the *Churchman* speak out fearlessly, but the excellent Jewish monthly *Commentary* pursues a hesitant and equivocal line, blowing hot and cold on the issue of religion in the public schools. Even the Protestant federation, the National Council of Churches of Christ in the United States, while consistently opposing the use of public funds for sectarian schools, has recently issued an ambiguous statement on religion in the schools which has been seized upon and exploited by opponents of church-state separation. In December 1952 the Council said:

We cannot . . . admit the proposition that in a public system of education the state should have the unchallenged right to monopolize all the
hours during which a boy or girl receives instruction five days a week.
In some constitutional way provision should be made for the inculcation
of the principles of religion, whether within or outside the precincts of
the school, but always within the regular schedule of a pupil's working
day.

The suggestion that, even after a Supreme Court decision to
the contrary, religious education should be given within the
precincts of an American public school in the regular schedule
of work plays into the hands of the enemies of church-state separation. The attempt to carry out such a policy might open the
door to endless denominational wrangling over the kind of religion to be taught. The United States has fifty different Christian
sects with a membership of more than ten thousand each, and at
least fifty different interpretations of what is "fundamental" in
Christian faith. If religion of any non-Catholic variety were offered to public-school children as part of the curriculum, the
Catholic bishops would be sure to use that modification of public-
school neutrality as their trump card in opposing the attendance
of Catholic children at schools where their "faith would be perverted." Ultimately they would use such a program as an argument for giving public funds to the only schools which Catholic
children could "in conscience" attend.

So the deadly conflict of church versus church in education
— the conflict which has poisoned the cultural and social life
of Ireland — might be renewed in America. The weakness in the
National Council's position on religion in the schools was revealed when a Protestant leader promptly used the statement
just quoted as partial justification for advocating the abandon-
ment of public schools and the establishment of four separate
creedal school systems — Protestant, Catholic, Jewish and
secular — in order "to assure democratic choice to all persons
as to the kind of education their children shall receive." The
Protestant leader involved, Dean James J. Malloch of the St.
James Episcopal Cathedral of Fresno, California, added: "In
areas where there were sufficient adherents of Eastern orthodoxy,
there would be a fifth school system." Dean Malloch's plan was
hailed with jubilation in the Catholic press.

Although few non-Catholics would go as far as Dean Malloch, there are too many who fail to see that the public school is, as Justice Frankfurter said in his opinion in the McCollum case, "the most powerful agency for promoting cohesion among a heterogeneous democratic people. . . . The public school is at once the symbol of our democracy and the most pervasive means for promoting our common destiny." How few leaders of American democracy would speak today with the frankness of Horace Greeley in 1869? (His statement is especially appropriate because it was addressed to an Irish audience.)

In New York we feel, as in Londonderry you do not, the pressure of Old-World prelacy in determined, though as yet quiet, efforts to break up our common schools into theological fragments, each under the control of the hierarchy of some sect or denomination. I deprecate the change thus sought as perilous, if not fatal, to republican institutions. When the time shall have come for apportioning our children to Catholic, Orthodox, Liberal, Baptist, Methodist and Unitarian primary schools, I shall apprehend that the last sands of the Republic are nearly run. When our common schools shall have perished we may still have a country; but it will not be the land of Liberty and Equality for which our fathers toiled and suffered, and poured out their blood.

The Irish Catholic Answer

If American non-Catholics show much vacillation and inconsistency in meeting the challenge of Irish Catholic power, what of the Irish Catholics themselves? Are there not enough Irish-American laymen who sincerely believe in democracy and who can be trusted to eliminate those policies of their Church which make for intolerance and separatism? I believe that there are. For the time being, however, they are in the grip of an exceedingly ingenious system of ecclesiastical feudalism under which their democratic impulses are all smothered in the name of religious faith. The code of separatist conduct imposed upon them by their priests has been made an organic part of the Catholic creed. It has been built into Catholicism itself. When Catholic laymen protest against the narrowness and anti-American character of that creed, they are told that its terms come from God Himself. If they ask how the priests know that the terms come from God, they are told that God has made the priests the sole, authorized agents of His voice. The reasoning is circular, and the circle cannot be broken if once the authoritarian premise is granted. The doctrine in its classical form was recently expressed in an official Catholic pamphlet. In reply to a question addressed to priests about a detail of Catholic procedure, the pamphlet stated: "The fact that the Catholic Church does so is sufficient proof that she is justified in doing so."

This closed-circle type of logic is one of the fundamental reasons why it is so difficult to bring about effective co-operation between Catholics and non-Catholics in the United States. The co-operative Catholic layman has no real authority in his own Church. He is not open to persuasion in the same sense as a sincere Protestant or Jew. He is told by his priest that he may not marry a non-Catholic, that his son and daughter may not attend a school with non-Catholic children, that he may never attend a Protestant religious service, and that he must not read books which are directly critical of Catholic doctrine and policy. All of these directives are supremely un-American and anti-democratic, and probably most Irish-American Catholics reject them in their hearts; but within the Catholic community they have no right to change such rules. A valiant and liberal Catholic, the late Thomas Sugrue, put his finger on the problem of co-operation with Protestants in his book *A Catholic Speaks His Mind*. "Nothing can be done about it," said Sugrue, "because action means co-operation and the Catholics cannot co-operate. Many among the laity — the younger folk especially — would like to, but they have neither power nor influence with their clergy."

Sugrue, however, was not as pessimistic as this statement might indicate. He believed that his own Church could be reformed from within, and that Irish Catholicism in America would someday redeem itself from clerical intolerance and separatism. Are there any signs that his hope was justified? I believe that there are — in the fields of marriage, of education, and of political philosophy.

In American Catholicism today, there is a distinct drift toward American equalitarian marriage, and the drift is in open defiance of the priests. On page 298 above, appeared a brief prophecy concerning what might happen to America if all Catholics who marry non-Catholics should obey the rigid and partisan directives of their priests. In practice the drift is not toward such obedience but away from it. It is not possible to say with accuracy how much of the drift is Irish, but undoubtedly the new tendency has a profound effect on the Irish-American community. It is significant that, almost alone among American dioceses, the archdiocese of Boston refuses to make public its statistics on mixed marriage. A recent study, "The Truth About Mixed Marriage," indicates that four out of every ten "mixed" couples in the United States are married by public officials or non-Catholic clergymen, thus by-passing the usual pledge to raise their children as Catholics. If we use the mixed-marriage statistics of the *Catholic Directory* as a base, and apply to them the conclusions of the new Catholic study of mixed marriages, it is probably safe to conclude that at least one-ninth of Catholic young people are now rejecting priestly marriage outright in favor of the more tolerant forms. If this ratio continues, it will produce in two or three decades in America a group of several million Catholics and ex-Catholics who, having rejected the separatism of their priests in marriage, will be psychologically prepared to reject similar priestly policy in the fields of education, censorship, and birth control.

A distinct drift is also noticeable among educated Catholic laymen toward a more tolerant attitude in education. In August 1953, two articles by an Irish Catholic layman, Joseph E. Cunneen, appeared in the liberal Catholic magazine *Commonweal;* they showed how the separatist philosophy of the priests is being questioned. Although the author paid lip service to all the standard Catholic theses on segregation, he questioned the spirit of separatism created by the policy of segregation, and he did not once appeal to the Church's canon law which makes attendance at public schools without episcopal permission a mortal sin. He declared that there would be a better attitude toward Catholic education "if attendance at Catholic schools had less of a compulsory character about it," and he pointed out that "in small towns the addition of a Catholic school may mean a duplication of facilities that in fact is uneconomical." In appealing for more sincere support of public schools by Catholics he said:

In our town there has been a conspicuous alliance between Catholics prominent in parish organizations and groups such as the Taxpayers'

Association, whose thinking emphasizes concern for the tax rate and property values. The common enemy of this alliance? The public school. In election after election, although most of their children are now attending the school, these Catholics have been active in seeking to defeat the appropriation of funds for a school library, for additional classrooms, or in seeking to elect to the school board those who would reflect their views. Inevitably, ill feeling has been stirred up. Although the word "divisive" is rightly considered a special contribution to jargon by professional anti-Catholics, the Catholic response to the problem of education in our town gives it some meaning. . . .

The fact is that in many cases the additional parochial school is a threat to the public school, in terms of both economic and moral support. Sometimes this threat is exaggerated, but it is made credible by what looks like Catholic cooperation with groups which, sometimes unintentionally, have served to undermine confidence in public schools from Pasadena to Scarsdale.

This analysis illustrates a growing sense of uneasiness among Irish-American Catholics concerning the sabotage of public schools by their priests, and an increasing opposition to "exaggerated separatism" — Cunneen's own phrase. He even dared to say that "New Catholic schools should not be started 'automatically' " — and that "Some non-Catholic neighbors who are better educated in history cannot help being aware, too, that clerical control of education in many European countries was a prize in a search for power, fought out with disastrous educational and national consequences which are still evident, and in which responsibility cannot be limited to the 'anti-religious forces.' They are right to wish to avoid such a struggle in America."

It is true that the relatively progressive *Commonweal* is not representative of Irish-American Catholicism — its editors are constantly dancing on a tight rope over the gulf of excommunication — but the fact that any Catholic journal could publish such frank comments on the divisive effects of Catholic educational policy is extremely hopeful. It should be remembered that the Irish Catholic community contains a very large proportion — possibly one-half — of persons who are graduates of the American public-school system and who have deep loyalties to that system. These public-school graduates form a permanent liberal force within the Irish community, pushing the priests toward co-operation and tolerance. Professor John Kane of Notre Dame (whose article "Catholic Separatism" was cited on page 254), after tracing the way in which this Catholic separatism was imported into America by the Irish priests, said: "In the past, separatism was an effective method of transmitting and preserving the faith. An Irish Catholic of the last century might well have lived his life and satisfied most of his needs within a Catholic ghetto." But things have changed. "Catholic separatism," continues Kane, "as reflected in a set of parallel institutions, has lost much of its effectiveness in the contemporary world. Its future appears even more dismal."

Most hopeful of the factors in Irish-American Catholicism today is the engagement of the Irish priests themselves in a great doctrinal war for and against the Spanish (and papal) theory that freedom may be denied to non-Catholics in a predominantly Catholic state. Thus far no leading defenders have appeared for non-Catholic freedom per se, but several priest-editors have cautiously · committed themselves to the doctrine that, in the special circumstances which prevail in Western democracies, a policy of tolerance may be as logical and permissible as a Spanish policy of suppression. In the struggle of words, all the leading contenders are of Irish stock. The Jesuit weekly *America,* the liberal Catholic *Commonweal,* and the important Jesuit monthly *Theological Studies* have lined up on the side of Western freedom. The chief priestly journal in the United States, the *American Ecclesiastical Review,* which is edited at the Catholic University of America, stands with the Vatican in favor of the more reactionary pro-Spanish view. Although the Vatican has openly supported the Spanish position, the Pope has not yet excommunicated or disciplined any American priests for deviation. Perhaps he realizes that the whole future of Catholic power in America is at stake in the controversy.

On the world scale, the doctrinal conflict — which is really a conflict between democratic tolerance and Catholic intolerance — came to a head in 1953, but it had begun much earlier and had received world-wide attention in 1952, when Cardinal Segura of Spain attacked even the limited toleration for Protestants in Franco's Spain as an abuse which "causes real pain." Some American Catholic leaders protested that such a gospel was not suitable for America, but in March 1953 the nascent liberalism of the more progressive Irish-American priests was sternly rebuked by Alfredo Cardinal Ottaviani, in an address at the Pontifical University in Rome. Speaking obviously for Pope Pius XII, the cardinal approved and reiterated the Catholic theory of the double standard of freedom — liberty for the Church in *any* society but denial of liberty to opponents of the Church in a *Catholic* society. He declared that this "two-standards" policy is not inconsistent, that Catholics as "individuals who find themselves in possession of the truth" may "appeal to the rights of man, to tolerance, to freedom of conscience" for themselves when living in non-Catholic countries, but that in principle "other individuals cannot demand the same rights by title of the error they profess." He condemned the Kremlin's parallel policy of favoring Communist institutions and restricting the freedom of all Christian churches while professing "liberty of faith."

The Vatican's endorsement of the Spanish philosophy of suppression produced a profound effect in American Catholicism. American liberal Catholics realized that they could not accept such doctrines and remain Americans. The editors of *Commonweal,* using an old phrase of Leo XIII as "authority," flatly condemned the "classical position" on the state as "out of date, and useless, and even harmful if applied in the twentieth century — and this whether it be applied in the United States or in Spain." "If cooperation between Church and State in the United States is to be effective," they said, "it must be along American lines and unquestionably in terms other than those acceptable in Spain."

My own conviction is that, because of these new fissures and liberal tendencies within Catholicism, the old-line dictatorship of the Irish priests in America is doomed. It is inconceivable that a spiritual and moral feudalism, living side by side with American democracy, can survive in its present form.

It is probably not too optimistic to say that there are two Irish Catholicisms emerging in the tolerant atmosphere of America: the medieval, Spanish, and old-Ireland type in which the priests are all-powerful and the people are moral serfs; and a new Irish-American Catholicism which seeks to apply to the Church the militant spirit of the Irish revolutionists who believed in genuine self-determination. For the members of this latter school of thought, self-determination in religion will ultimately seem as inevitable as self-determination in politics, and Roman dictatorship as anachronistic in the United States and Ireland in 1953 as British dictatorship was in Ireland in 1900 or in America in 1776.

For the time being, men and women who try to be Catholic, Irish, and American at the same time must develop a kind of moral schizophrenia in order to reconcile their real love of democracy with papal dictatorship. With the political portion of their personalities they must assert that they are good Americans who believe in self-government; with the religious portion of their personalities they must accept foreign authoritarian rule in one of its most antiquated and absolute forms. In the long run such an illogical combination must die from the sickness of inner conflict.

Michael Davitt, founder of the Irish Land League, son of an American mother, and one of the greatest of the Irish Catholic revolutionists, saw the issue clearly when he challenged the dictatorship of the Irish priests as well as British rule. In a famous controversy in 1906 with the Catholic bishops of his country, Davitt wrote: "The growing experience of progressive civilization is coming to see that the American system of universal and free secular education is the best all-round plan yet devised." When Bishop O'Dwyer of Limerick blasted him with five columns of pastoral rebuke in the *Freeman's Journal,* Davitt was not dismayed. He was conscious that the future belonged to those who believed in complete democracy and complete tolerance. In a letter to the press, he wrote a sentence which I have used as the epigraph of this book — a sentence which may well be applied to two present-day countries in which Irish Catholic power is struggling with modern conceptions of freedom and tolerance, Ireland and the United States: "Make no mistake about it, my Lord Bishop of Limerick, Democracy is going to rule in these countries."

APPENDIX

Map of
IRELAND
═══ Indicates Border
Between Northern Ireland
and The Irish Republic

IRISH FACT SHEET

THE IRISH REPUBLIC

Area	26,601 square miles
Population	2,959,000
Proportion of Roman Catholics	95 per cent

The Four Provinces (Twenty-six Counties)

LEINSTER: Carlow, Dublin, Kildare, Kilkenny, Laoighis, Longford, Louth, Meath, Offaly, Westmeath, Wexford, Wicklow

MUNSTER: Clare, Cork, Kerry, Limerick, Tipperary, Waterford

CONNACHT: Galway, Leitrim, Mayo, Roscommon, Sligo

ULSTER (part): Cavan, Donegal, Monaghan

Principal Cities

Dublin	521,000	Limerick	51,000
Cork	75,000	Dun Laoghaire	48,000
	Waterford	29,000	

The Decline in Population

1841	6,529,000	1901	3,222,000
1851	5,112,000	1911	3,140,000
1861	4,402,000	1926	2,972,000
1871	4,053,000	1936	2,968,000
1881	3,870,000	1946	2,955,000
1891	3,469,000	1951	2,959,000

NORTHERN IRELAND

Area	5,238 square miles
Population	1,370,933
Proportion of Roman Catholics	34 per cent
Proportion of Presbyterians	30 per cent
Proportion of Church of Ireland	26 per cent

The Six Counties

Antrim, Armagh, Derry, Down, Fermanagh, Tyrone

Principal Cities

Belfast	452,000	Derry	50,000

The data on the Irish Republic are taken from its 1946 and 1951 census reports and from the *Irish Times Review and Annual* (1953). The data on Northern Ireland are taken from its 1951 census report.

NAMES AND DATES IN IRISH HISTORY

1798	The United Irishmen, including many Protestants as well as Catholics, conduct a short rebellion against the English-dominated Irish parliament. Wolfe Tone, their leader, is captured and commits suicide in prison.
1801	England unites Ireland with Great Britain in the Act of Union. The Irish parliament is abandoned, and Irish non-Catholics "represent" Ireland in the British House of Commons.
1803	Young Robert Emmet, only 24, plans a hopeless and desperate attack on Dublin Castle, stronghold of British rule. He is tried, convicted, and hanged, after making a "Patrick Henry" speech from the dock.
1823	Daniel O'Connell (1775-1847), Dublin lawyer, organizes the Catholic Association of Ireland as a constitutional and clerical opposition to Protestant England, and becomes Ireland's foremost nationalist leader for twenty years.
1829	Catholic emancipation is granted by the British Parliament, when Peel and Wellington yield to O'Connell.
1842	Young Irelanders, led by Catholics and such Protestants as Thomas Davis and John Mitchel, launch revolutionary movement for self-government.
1845-47	Great potato famine.
1848	Rising of 1848, led by Mitchel and others, is quickly suppressed by British troops, and Mitchel is exiled.
1866-67	Fenian Brotherhood, led by James Stephens and others, stages small and short-lived rebellions in Ireland and Canada.
1869	Anglican Church in Ireland is disestablished by Gladstone government after a hundred-year campaign against compulsory tithes.
1870	Gladstone's First Land Act passed, protecting tenants against some abuses.
1875	Charles Stewart Parnell, Protestant landlord, enters British Parliament and soon becomes leader of Home Rule movement.
1879	Michael Davitt organizes the Irish Land League.
1881	Agitation in both Ireland and England leads to Gladstone's Second Land Act, bringing substantial relief to landless peasants.
1886	Gladstone's first Home Rule bill is defeated in British Parliament.
1891	Parnell dies, repudiated by the priests after a marital scandal, and is succeeded as nationalist leader by a Catholic, John Redmond.
1892	Douglas Hyde founds the Gaelic League for the revival of the Irish language.
1906	Sinn Fein, an outspoken revolutionary party, is founded by Arthur Griffith.
1912	Home Rule bill passed by House of Commons, to take effect in 1914. Ulster, under leadership of Sir Edward Carson, threatens armed revolt if North is put under Dublin rule.

1914	World War I intervenes; Home Rule indefinitely postponed.
1916	Easter rebellion in Dublin is quickly suppressed, and fifteen leaders are executed.
1918	Sinn Fein, advocating non-participation in British Parliament, wins 73 of 105 Irish seats, and creates a clandestine parliament of its own, naming Eamon de Valera as President.
1920 ff.	Long guerrilla war between Irish Republican Army and British forces keeps nation in turmoil. Government of Ireland Act is passed.
1921	Irish question is "settled" by treaty negotiated by Lloyd George, Arthur Griffith, and Michael Collins, recognizing an Irish Free State for the Twenty-Six Counties of the South with dominion status, and independent affiliation of the Six Counties of the North with Great Britain. But the settlement is repudiated by De Valera and his associates.
1922-23	The Irish Free State is established with a new Constitution, but it is immediately challenged by extremist Irish Republicans. The ensuing civil war leads to great bitterness, temporary defeat, and the execution of 77 rebels. The Free State government continues under William T. Cosgrave and his Cumann na nGhaedheal (later Fine Gael) for ten years. De Valera, with his Fianna Fail, leads the opposition, but refuses until 1927 to sit in the Free State parliament.
1925	Sir James Craig, Northern Ireland Prime Minister, leads the North in boundary dispute, which is temporarily settled along the present border when Britain makes financial concessions to the South.
1932	De Valera wins a majority in the Dail and becomes head of the government for sixteen years.
1937	A new Constitution, written largely by De Valera, is adopted by plebiscite, and Dr. Douglas Hyde becomes first President.
1939-45	Eire remains neutral during World War II, while Northern Ireland participates with British forces.
1946	Sean T. O'Kelly, a De Valera lieutenant, is elected President. (He is re-elected in 1952.)
1948	De Valera is defeated in February election by an Inter-Party coalition headed by Fine Gael, and J. A. Costello, Dublin barrister, becomes Prime Minister.
1948	Dail Eireann, under Costello, repeals the External Relations Act, severing last formal link with the British Commonwealth.
1949	Republic of Ireland is formally inaugurated on Easter Monday.
1951	De Valera and Fianna Fail return precariously to office, with the help of a small number of independent deputies, who hold the balance of power.

THE CASE OF THE PAPAL NUNCIO

(An article by Paul Blanshard, reprinted from the *Christian Century*, May 6, 1953.)

May an American citizen serve as a Vatican diplomat in a foreign country and still retain his American citizenship? That is the question brought to public attention by a petition which I filed with the United States embassy in Dublin calling for revocation of the American citizenship of Archbishop Gerald P. O'Hara, papal nuncio to the Irish Republic, on the ground that he has violated the McCarran act by serving a foreign state in a capacity which requires an oath of allegiance to its ruler.

The larger issue which lies behind this immediate question is significant: Is the Vatican above the level of American law? Will it be permitted to continue acting as a state within the American state, imposing upon its 29 million American followers by fiat certain undemocratic policies of citizenship, and at the same time avoiding the legal responsibilities of statehood?

Some aspects of this issue were discussed in 1951 when President Truman designated General Mark Clark as an ambassador to the Vatican, and met overwhelming opposition in the Senate. Then it became apparent that the Vatican wanted full political recognition from our government but was unwilling to accept the consequences of that recognition and register its bishops as agents of a foreign state under the Foreign Agents Registration law. Its defeat on the ambassador issue did not alter Vatican strategy. Recently American Catholic magazines have launched a second campaign to secure the appointment of a full American ambassador, and at the same time Catholic editors furiously deny that Vatican diplomats have any but a spiritual status.

The case against Archbishop O'Hara is quite simple. He was born in Pennsylvania of Irish stock, became Roman Catholic bishop of Savannah, and later archbishop of Savannah-Atlanta. After serving as a papal diplomat in Rumania, he was designated papal nuncio to the Irish Republic in 1951 and began his service in Dublin in March 1952 by presenting his "Letter of Credence" from Pope Pius XII to President Sean O'Kelly. In his travels abroad he uses both an American passport and a Vatican diplomatic passport.

The McCarran act says:

> Sec. 349 (a) From and after the effective date of this Act a person who is a national of the United States whether by birth or naturalization shall lose his nationality by —
>
> ....
>
> (2) taking an oath or making an affirmation or other formal declaration of allegiance to a foreign state or a political subdivision thereof; or
>
> ....
>
> (4) (B) accepting, serving in, or performing the duties of any office, post, or employment under the government of a foreign state or a political subdivision thereof, for which office, post, or employment an oath, affirmation, or declaration of allegiance is required;

The penalties of this section apply only to Americans who are living abroad. It came into force only on December 24, 1952, and so no American can be penalized under its terms *merely* for an act committed before that date. This means that if Dr. O'Hara is to be penalized under this law it is not for an oath of allegiance taken before December 24, 1952, but for continuing to serve today in a position which requires allegiance to a foreign state.

Has Dr. O'Hara actually taken an oath of allegiance to a foreign state within the meaning of this law? Yes, because (1) the Vatican is a foreign state; (2) his oath of allegiance as a bishop to the pope is complete and sufficient as a declaration of loyalty under the law. Both these propositions are easily proved.

The Vatican is a state by its own claim and admission. True, it is not much of a state, but size in this case is not legally conclusive. The Vatican has all the essential attributes of a state — an independent government, physical territory, courts, citizens, passports, a sovereign, diplomats, diplomatic immunity, treaties, a flag, a police force, postal status, etc., etc. Thirty-nine nations recognize its statehood by sending diplomats to its court. In turn it sends diplomats to their courts. The treaty of 1929 with Italy, which is in a sense the political charter of the modern papal state, "recognizes the sovereignty of the Holy See in the international field as an inherent attribute of its nature, in conformity with its tradition and the exigencies of its mission in the world." Cardinal Spellman said in March 1940, when the status of Myron Taylor was being debated: "The Holy Father is not alone the supreme head of the Catholic Church. He is also the head of a sovereign state."

Although we have refused to send an ambassador to the Vatican, because we rightly consider it a church-state combination whose recognition would violate our policy of the separation of church and state, our government has frequently acknowledged the legal existence of the Vatican as a state. Our American diplomats accepted asylum in the Vatican as a foreign state in World War II, and one of them, Harold H. Tittmann, was actually given full diplomatic status as a representative accredited to a foreign state by President Roosevelt on recommendation of Sumner Welles. In all the capitals of the world where papal nuncios serve as deans of the diplomatic corps, our ambassadors recognize them in that political capacity, thus acknowledging by implication that they represent a foreign state.

As to Dr. O'Hara's oath of loyalty as a bishop to the pope, it is a very comprehensive commitment and could not possibly be construed as being merely spiritual. It binds each bishop completely to serve every aspect of papal rule. It dates back many centuries to the time when it was used to bind Catholic dignitaries to the pope as monarch of a large European political territory. It commits each bishop to be "loyal and obedient" to "our Lord Pope," and to do nothing prejudicial to the "position and power" of the pope, and it compels each bishop to say: "Such orders as are given by the Apostolic See I will receive humbly and carry out diligently." It pledges each bishop to obey all "the decrees, ordinances or regulations, reservations, provisions and commands of the Apostolic See."

The only possible defense which the Vatican can make against these points is technical. Morally it has not a leg to stand on. Every person familiar with political history and tradition knows that the Vatican is a state, and that the diplomat of such a state occupies a post of intimate trust in relation to his sovereign, so intimate and vital that his complete allegiance must be presumed. By all the traditions of international law Archbishop O'Hara fits precisely into the pattern of an offender against the McCarran act. He is an American citizen serving a foreign state in a capacity which implies a bond of allegiance much stronger than that of the ordinary citizen.

The Vatican's first off-the-cuff reply, issued in Rome on February 18, was that my petition "does not take into account the special and singular task of the apostolic nuncio, which is exclusively in the religious and ecclesiastical field, and which therefore is outside the norms established by the McCarran act and its aims." This reply is both untrue and immaterial. It was temporarily adopted by the state department, evidently on the word of the Vatican, but it was promptly abandoned as untenable when the law and the facts were examined. The truth is that the McCarran act does not exempt religious officials from its penalties if they are serving abroad under an oath of allegiance to a foreign state. Moreover, a papal nuncio is not and never has been a purely religious official; he is a full-blown ambassador serving as the dean of the diplomatic corps, not as spiritual adviser or priest to that corps. He is defined by the *Catholic Encyclopedia* (Nuncio) as being "vested with both political and ecclesiastical powers." Purely religious legates are usually called apostolic delegates; Dr. O'Hara is *not* an apostolic delegate.

Moreover, if the Vatican seriously relies on this claim that its papal nuncios are exclusively religious, it will be hoist by its own petard when it faces the question of an American ambassador at the Vatican. Such an ambassador must be a political appointee or he is nothing. He could not, under our Constitution, be a religious envoy to a single church. And if his counterpart, the papal nuncio, is considered a purely religious envoy, we could not possibly receive him with political honors in Washington, as a return agent. The Vatican cannot have it both ways. It cannot use religion as a quickly removable mask to hide its political status whenever convenient, and at the same time gain for itself special privileges without the corresponding responsibilities of statehood.

A more important technicality, but one which is equally indefensible, is the claim that the Holy See and the Vatican City State can be split in two for the purposes of allegiance, and that even if the Vatican City State is a foreign state, it is distinct from the Holy See. This alleged double existence is considered relevant because it is argued that Archbishop O'Hara's oath of allegiance runs only to the Holy See and not to the Vatican City State. This casuistic explanation was actually offered to the public by the Vatican press office in Rome as one answer to my petition. The claim will not hold water for a number of reasons. Archbishop O'Hara serves under the Holy See, but the Holy See is an organic part of the Vatican aggregate, and it is just as much a state in its own right as the papal administrative agency known as Vatican City State. All the ambassadors accredited to the Vatican are accredited to the Holy See as the state with which Italy is dealing.

In any case such semantic jugglery is of no avail. The McCarran act, quite accidentally, by-passes the semi-imaginary distinction between the Vatican City State and the Holy See, and for the purposes of this case it makes no difference whether Archbishop O'Hara is serving under one or the other or both. The law penalizes an American who serves as ambassador under "the *government* of a foreign state." The government of both the Vatican City State and the Holy See is lodged completely in the pope, and the papal nuncio's oath of allegiance runs to the pope as the total and absolute sovereign of all branches of the church. The pope, as the *Catholic Encyclopedia* points out, "can legislate for the whole church, with or without the assistance of a general council" and "has authority over all appointments to its public offices."

The chief technicality on which the Vatican is relying to escape the penalties of American law is the contention that an oath is not "required" for the post of papal nuncio. It is possible that no *special* oath is required *exclusively* for this post — although that supposition should be carefully investigated by the state department before it is accepted — but the law does not speak of any *special* oath. Any formal commitment of loyalty is sufficient so long as it actually binds the citizen at the time of his service. In this case Dr. O'Hara is bound by his bishop's oath, and this oath binds all papal nuncios because every papal nuncio must be a bishop. In fact, the most official handbook of the Vatican, the *Annuario Pontificio* of 1952, says on page 869: "Today nuncios are always invested with the title of archbishop . . ." When nuncios are taken exclusively from an oath-bound episcopal class, the oath of that class binds them also.

Why should we, in a troubled world where there are more critical things to talk about, question the American citizenship of a Vatican diplomat? There are all too many Americans who seek refuge in the claim that the matter is not important and that in any case it is ungracious to "criticize another man's religion." On such polite timidity is Catholic aggression built. The long history of papal encroachments on democracy shows that the most important special privileges begin with almost insignificant concessions to "religious" feeling, and progress gradually to the point where vital areas of citizenship are surrendered to hierarchical control.

It is unfortunate that we are obliged to use so shabby an instrument as the McCarran act, and so crude a tool of controversy as "Americanism," to defeat this effort to evade the requirements of equal justice under law. But the end in this case justifies the means because the means are legitimate and the end is morally vital. No matter how internationally minded one may be, it is repugnant to our ideal of American citizenship that an American should serve a foreign authoritarian state in an exalted diplomatic capacity and still call himself an American.

We would not tolerate such dual loyalty if it involved a Communist state. Can anyone imagine the state department taking months to reply to a petition showing clear proof that, as the newspaper headlines might put it: "G. O'Hara Patrick Kremlin Envoy to France; McCarthy Charges Georgia Communist Forfeits American Citizenship"? Substitute Vatican for Kremlin and Catholic for Communist, change the names a little, and you have in a nutshell the legal case against Gerald Patrick O'Hara, citizen of a state which stands before the world for democracy and the separation of church and state, and simultaneously envoy extraordinary of a state which stands for the reverse.

STATE DEPARTMENT EVADES THE POINT

(An editorial reprinted from the *Christian Century,* July 8, 1953.)

After Paul Blanshard visited Ireland a few months ago, he reported in the *Christian Century* (May 6) that an American citizen serves as papal nuncio to the Irish Republic. At the same time Mr. Blanshard filed with the department of state a memorandum asking whether the American citizenship of Archbishop Gerald P. O'Hara should not be revoked. His point was that the

Roman Catholic cleric was representing a foreign state to another foreign state, that his representation had required him to take an oath of allegiance to the foreign state whose representative he was, and that taking such an oath violated the 1952 Immigration and Nationality act. Mr. Blanshard tells us that on May 18 he received a reply from Jack B. Tate, deputy legal adviser to the department of state. Mr. Tate denied Blanshard's petition on the ground that papal nuncios are not required to take an oath of allegiance to the state of Vatican City. This reply was true but irrelevant, since Blanshard's charge is that they take an oath to the Holy See and its sovereign, the pope, not to the local government of the state of Vatican City. In taking this "out," however, the department of state makes a concession which should prevent any President from ever again attempting to send an ambassador from the United States to the papal court. By holding that all political aspects of the Vatican, including all the attributes of statehood, are segregated in the local government unit called the Vatican City State, the state department says by implication that that portion of the Vatican aggregate which receives foreign diplomats is a strictly religious segment. In that case, an ambassador sent by the United States to the Holy See (which was the appointment President Truman tendered General Clark) would be an ambassador assigned to a *religious* organization. Tate's second point was that the drafters of the McCarran-Walter act did not intend to have it affect papal nuncios. This too is invalid, for the act, in outlawing the principle of dual nationality for American citizens, was laying down a sound principle which applies to everybody. We hope Mr. Blanshard is patient and that he will continue to press upon the department of state its obligation to apply the law without favoritism or evasion.

Notes

Books listed in the Bibliography are here referred to by the author's surname (and, when necessary, by his first name or the book title).

A few words are required about certain names and titles which are frequently used in Ireland as tools of partisanship. Nearly all Roman Catholics in Ireland, and elsewhere, call their Church the "Catholic Church." Many Protestants, particularly the adherents of the Church of Ireland, dispute the monopoly of the word "Catholic" by Roman Catholics, contending that *their* church has the best historical claim to the word. I think there is much to be said for the Anglican claim, and I would not care to dispute it; but it seems to me permissible in a book of this kind to use the shorthand of common speech and call the Roman Catholic Church the "Catholic Church."

Similarly, it seems to me permissible to use for the Southern and Northern regimes in Ireland those titles which each regime, in turn, prefers. There are many partisans in the North who dispute the right of Southern Irishmen to use the term "The Republic of Ireland"; and there are even more partisans in the South who would dispute the right of the Northerners to use the title "Northern Ireland." The descriptive term "Six Counties" is often used in the South for the North by those who are somewhat hostile to the Northern regime. It is quite accurate, but it implies a slight derogatory note which I would like to avoid. The title "Ulster" for present-day Northern Ireland is technically not quite accurate, since Northern Ireland does not include all of the old province of Ulster, but it has come into such common use as a descriptive term for the present Northern territory that I have occasionally used it. In most cases, I have referred to the Northern regime as "Northern Ireland."

The word "Eire," which was adopted by the Free State government as its title in 1937, is in an indeterminate stage of dignity at the present moment. It is the Irish word for Ireland and it is still perfectly correct to use it as the name for the Republic, since the national postage stamps still carry that title. But, in general, the most dignified and universally acceptable title for the Southern regime today in the South itself is "The Republic of Ireland"; and I have used that title in most places.

Although the official name of the second Northern city is "Londonderry," nearly all its residents of all faiths call it "Derry," and I have adopted that custom.

For the members of the nationalist movement, I have used the term "nationalists" or "Catholic nationalists," to indicate that the movement — which includes the Irish Labor Party — is larger than the Nationalist Party.

FOREWORD

Page ix. The Jesuit review was by Father Joseph Crehan, S.J., in *Studies* of June 1951.

CHAPTER 1

PERSPECTIVE AND PURPOSE

PAGE 3. The Sheen quotation is from the New York *Times* of April 21, 1952. The Gannon quotation is from the *Irish World* of June 15, 1946. The Cotter quotation is from that journal's issue of December 12, 1945.

Spain is the only country which might dispute Ireland's claim to being "the world's most devoutly Catholic country." Father Charles Mullaly, American Jesuit who had lived in Spain, estimated in the *Irish World*, July 3, 1937, that only 65 per cent of Spain was Catholic. Under Franco the percentage may be higher — but there is less freedom of choice. Most observers would probably agree that the people of the Irish Republic are at least 90 per cent Catholic.

The estimate of missionary priests is that of Bishop Michael Browne of Galway, in the Brooklyn *Tablet,* July 4, 1953: "Each year some 80 priests are ordained for the Irish dioceses, while more than 300 are ordained for foreign missions." Father J. T. Ellis of the Catholic University of America, in the London *Tablet* of January 24, 1953, gave statistics which indicated that there is 1 priest for every 426 Catholics in England and Wales; 1 for every 661 in the United States; and 1 for every 3,535 in Colombia. The corresponding ratio in the Irish Republic, according to the *Irish Catholic* of June 2, 1949, was 1 for every 600. This journal put Holland first as the "country of priests"; but its estimates did not include nuns, and it seems fair to credit Ireland with some of the very large number of "vocations" in Britain and the United States, since it is the Irish families which are producing many of the priests and nuns. Strauss (p. 210) cites figures to show that Irish priests, monks, and nuns increased in number 158 per cent from 1861 to 1911, while their flocks were declining by 28 per cent. The *Irish World* of June 8, 1946, pointed out: "Most of all the leaders of the Church in India are Irish. Ninety nine per cent of the Church leaders in Australia and New Zealand from the Cardinal to the latest priest are Irish. Most of the convents and all the parishes in British-dominated Africa are controlled by Irish women and men."

PAGE 4. The Devane quotation is from the *Irish Rosary,* December 1952. The 1951 *Catholic Year Book* for Great Britain claimed a grand total of 67,548,191 Catholics in the English-speaking world; this included 12,800,000 in the Philippines. Father George Stebbing in *The Position and Prospects of the Catholic Church in English Speaking Lands* gives 1930 estimates. The U. S. *Catholic Directory* for 1953 reports 30,425,015 Catholics in the United States — about 19 per cent in a population of 160,000,000. The *National Catholic Almanac* for 1953 (p. 188) gives the Catholic estimate of the Catholic population by American cities. There is no scientific measure of the "Irish Catholic stock" in America, but it is usually estimated by Catholic writers at half or more of the 30,000,000 Catholics. Freeman (p. 4) is especially conservative in saying that "there are three to four times as many people of Irish extraction on the west side of the Atlantic as at home." Bishop Shaughnessy has made the most detailed study of the problem; he estimates (p. 238) that the Irish stock in the United States in 1890 totaled 12,623,000, of whom 4,723,000 were Catholics.

PAGE 5. The *Irish World* quotation is from the issue of June 8, 1946.

PAGE 9. For a discussion of the hate merchants, see Ralph Lord Roy, *Apostles of Discord* (Boston: Beacon Press, 1953).

PAGE 10. The three rules are from Catholic canon law; here, the page numbers in parentheses refer to Bouscaren and Ellis, 1948 edition.

The public-school rule is Canon 1374 (p. 704): "Catholic children may not attend non-Catholic, neutral, or mixed schools, that is, those which are open also to non-Catholics, and it pertains exclusively to the Ordinary of the place to decide, in accordance with instructions of the Holy See, under what circumstances and with what precautions against the danger of perversion, attendance at such schools may be tolerated."

The marriage rule is spread over several canons. Canon 1060 (p. 458): "The Church everywhere most severely forbids the contracting of marriage between two baptized persons of whom one is a Catholic whereas the other is a member of a heretical or schismatical sect. . . ." Canon 1061 (p. 459): "The Church does not dispense from the impediment of mixed religion unless: (1) there are just and grave reasons therefor; (2) the non-Catholic party shall have given a guarantee to remove all danger of perversion from the Catholic party, and both parties shall have given guarantees to baptize and educate all the children in the Catholic faith alone; (3) there exists moral certainty that the guarantees will be fulfilled. The guarantees are as a rule to be required in writing." Canon 1070 (p. 476): "A marriage contracted by a nonbaptized person with a person who was baptized in the Catholic Church or who has been converted to it from heresy or schism, is null." Canon 1102 (p. 532): "In marriages between a Catholic and a non-Catholic party . . . all sacred rites are forbidden; in case it is foreseen that graver evils will result from this prohibition, the Ordinary may permit some of the usual ecclesiastical ceremonies, excluding always the celebration of Mass."

The censorship rule is in Canon 1399 (p. 729). It bans books which "propound heresy and schism," "attack religion or right morals," "attack or ridicule any of the Catholic dogmas," or "strive to overthrow ecclesiastical discipline."

CHAPTER 2

PAST AND PRESENT

PAGE 13. The Leslie quotation is from page 43. The Devane quotation is from the *Irish Rosary* of December 1952.

PAGE 15. The Curtis quotation is from page 1. The Shaw quotation is from page x. Beckett's summary is excellent for the general reader. W. G. Hanson supplies some interesting details in *The Early Monastic Schools of Ireland*.

PAGE 19. The Beckett quotation is from page 31.

PAGE 20. The Trevelyan quotation is from page 362.

PAGE 21. The Spenser quotation is from his *View of the State of Ireland*, cited by Curtis (p. 223).

PAGE 22. As to Cromwell, the New York *Irish Echo* announced on August 22, 1953: "A butcher named Cromwell, another protege of His Satanic Majesty, . . . brought brigades of mercenary cutthroats and butchers clothed in the garb of British hirelings into Ireland. Their mission was to destroy the deep-rooted love of God and country. . . . The butchery at Limerick has still to be avenged." Many of the Catholic disabilities are summarized in Curtis (Ch. 15).

PAGE 24. The Arnold quotation is from page 21 of his *Irish Essays* (1882).

PAGE 25. The Wolf Tone phrases are from an article by Frank McDermot in *Ireland Today*, January 1, 1938. The Parnell branch of the Anti-Partition

Association has proposed that Nelson's statue be replaced by a "suitable monument."

The Yeats charge against O'Connell was used in an Irish Senate debate; it is a very common one in Ireland. O'Faolain discusses the charge in his *King of the Beggars* (p. 200). He points out that there is only one published record of O'Connell's alleged philandering — that of Eleanor Courtenay, who claimed that her child was O'Connell's and referred to "ten or twelve wretched females whom he has seduced."

PAGE 26. The Smith and O'Connell quotations are from an article on "The Sacred Tenth" by Father E. J. Quigley in the *Irish Ecclesiastical Record* for December 1935. Quigley indicates that the resistance to tithes dated from 1785. Evans has an excellent discussion, with bibliography, of the whole question of tithes and disestablishment. She cites (p. 153) from *Hansard*, June 25-29, 1868, the opinion of Bishop Tait of London that "the great reason for the failure of the Irish [Anglican] Church was that it has become the meanest instrument of English misrule"; and from Archbishop Boulter's correspondence the suggestion that "if a clergyman lost his character in England, a place was provided for him in Ireland." In the parliamentary debates on disestablishment, Sir John Gray revealed that many pieces of church land were actually used by the Irish Anglican clergy for their relatives and friends.

PAGE 30. De Valera discussed this "last night" with me in person, displaying as much cool detachment as he showed on the night itself. To this day he does not know how much his American birth influenced the decision of the British government. The Carson story is told, in part by Shearman in *Not an Inch,* and more fully by Colvin.

PAGE 31. The 1918 election statistics are in Macardle (p. 1019). The Anglo-Irish negotiations are described at length by Macardle, O'Hegarty, Gwynn (*De Valera*), and Pakenham; and Shearman discusses the larger implications in his *Anglo-Irish Relations.* The Macardle account is favorable to De Valera, who wrote the preface to this book; O'Hegarty's work is pro-Irish but very critical of De Valera; and Gwynn is also somewhat critical. De Valera was angered when Pope Benedict XV telegraphed to King George V his best wishes for successful negotiations with Ireland; "Dev's" answering wire to the Pope was described by the London *Times* as "an act of impertinence." See Pakenham (pp. 165ff).

PAGE 33. In his conversation with me, De Valera defended his about-face on the oath, on the ground that the British authorities had finally required him not to swear allegiance verbally but only to "sign a book" — which he chose to consider a mere formality.

CHAPTER 3

PROGRESS AND POVERTY

PAGE 34. See my Irish Fact Sheet (p. 331). The 1946 census showed a proportion of 94.3 Catholic — 943 per 1,000 in the population, with 42 Protestant Episcopalians, 8 Presbyterians, 3 Methodists, and 4 "all others." The 1951 census did not record religions. Since it is universally admitted that the Catholic proportion in the population is increasing, I have used the round figures of 95 and 5 per cent, respectively, to represent the Catholic and Protestant proportions. Past religious census returns for both the North and the South are summarized in the 1953 *Irish Catholic Directory* beginning on page lvi.

PAGE 35. The quoted phrase is a summary of material on page 24 of *Industrial Potentials*.

PAGE 39. The Freeman quotation is from page 45. The Leslie quotation is from page 16. The facts on privies, etc., were summarized in the *Irish Times Review* of 1952 (p. 17). The nutrition estimate is from Part II of the *National Nutrition Survey*.

PAGE 40. The comparisons of income are based on *Industrial Potentials* (p. 8). The estimate of weekly earnings is that of the research department of the Irish Trade Union Congress, as published in the *Irish Times* of August 19, 1953. The statement of General Michael Costello is from the *Irish Times* of May 27, 1952, together with comparative production figures; the statement of De Valera is from the issue of January 23, 1953. See Johnston for a thorough discussion of agricultural problems and remedies.

PAGE 41. The "gate" quotation is from an article by Ann Binchy in the *Irish Times* of January 26, 1953. The *Irish Rosary* quotation is from the issue of November-December 1948. The Lucey statement is from the *Irish Times* of May 28, 1952.

PAGE 42. The Attlee quotation is from *Hansard*, May 11, 1949.

PAGE 43. The social services of North and South have been summarized by the Trade Union Congress. See the 1953 *Irish Times Review and Annual*, and the issue of November 10, 1952. Typical unemployment and sickness benefits for industrial workers are about 32s 6d per week in the North and 24s in the South. An important summary of Ireland's international position is that of Nicholas Mansergh in *International Affairs*, July 1952.

PAGE 44. The Leslie statement is from page 128. The statement on the Fenians is attributed to Bishop Moriarty of Kerry in the *New Statesman and Nation* of May 15, 1948. The Skeffington quotation is from page 258.

PAGE 46. The Davis statement is quoted by W. B. Stanford of Trinity College in a significant booklet, *A Recognized Church*.

CHAPTER 4
THE CLERICAL REPUBLIC

PAGE 48. The Portuguese Concordat of 1940 is reprinted in T. Lincoln Bouscaren, *Canon Law Digest* (Vol. II, p. 11). The Portuguese Law of Separation of 1911 was nullified by the opposition of the Church. The Dublin Jesuit magazine *Studies* in an article extolling Salazar (Vol. XXX, 1941, p. 260) quoted Pius XII's eulogy: "The Lord has given to Portugal a chief who has won for himself the love of his people, especially of his poorer people, and the respect of the whole world. All credit to him."

PAGE 49. The 1953 Concordat with Spain was partially summarized in the New York *Times* of August 28, 1953, but the text was not made public at that time. The general position of the Church in the Franco system of dictatorship is described by a Catholic writer, Emmett J. Hughes, in his *Report From Spain*. The Vasconcelos ultimatum was in the New York *Times* of August 18, 1953. The Salvador and other concordats are discussed by Thomas F. Doyle in *The Catholic Mind Through Fifty Years* (p. 432). The Boylan statement is from the *Irish World* of July 10, 1937.

PAGE 50. The quoted treaty section is the first part of Section 16. Macardle (p. 990) has the full text, dated December 6, 1921.

PAGE 52. Leo XIII's philosophy was stated in his encyclical *Christian Constitution of States*, where he reached the conclusion that "the origin of public power is to be sought for in God Himself and not in the multitude." He said also: "The sovereignty of the people, however, and this without any reference to God, is held to reside in the multitude; which is doubtless a doctrine exceedingly well calculated to flatter and to inflame many passions, but which lacks all reasonable proof, and all power of insuring public safety and preserving order."

PAGE 53. See *Constitution* for the complete text; the 1922 Constitution is also published as a pamphlet by the government. The religious clauses in the 1937 Constitution caused little discussion in the Dail, but other provisions were fiercely attacked as tending toward dictatorship, and the draft was carried by a vote of only 62 to 48; and the vote for adoption was only 686,042 to 528,296 in a plebiscite. The opposition carried Dublin by a wide margin.

PAGE 54. The Bates quotation is from page 513.

PAGE 56. Browne's figures on infant mortality were published in the *Irish Catholic* of June 10 and July 22, 1948. The United Nations *Demographic Yearbook* for 1949-50 (Table 29) gives the infant mortality in 1949 as 51.5 for Ireland, 45.2 for Northern Ireland, 34.1 for the United Kingdom, and 31.1 for the United States.

PAGE 57. The Catholic prohibition against contraception and therapeutic abortion is contained in Pius XI's encyclical *Christian Marriage;* it is amplified in all Catholic medical manuals, notably in Father Charles McFadden's *Medical Ethics for Nurses,* and Father Patrick Finney's *Moral Problems in Hospital Practice.*

PAGE 58. The hierarchy's letter and nearly all the other documents in this case were published in the *Irish Times,* after Browne had released them to the press at the time of his resignation; the issue of April 12, 1951, contained the most important items. The documents and the Dail debates were reprinted in a comprehensive report (*Southern Ireland — Church or State?*) by the Belfast *News-Letter,* obtainable from the Ulster Unionist Council, 3 Glengall Street, Belfast, Northern Ireland. The 1952 *Irish Catholic Directory* (pp. 657, 681, 692) contains the Church's further attacks on the Browne scheme, by Cardinal D'Alton and others. "The Catholic workingman," said the Bishop of Galway, "does not want to have his wife and children treated by a State official in accordance with bureaucratic instructions, as if they were the chattels of the State."

PAGE 60. The *Register* quotation is from the issue of May 20, 1951.

PAGE 61. The *Irish Times* comment was in the issue of April 12, 1951.

PAGE 63. In England, the overwhelming majority of Catholic hospital patients use the National Health Services, without apparent moral damage. The hierarchy does not oppose this co-operation, but it insists on keeping about two hundred small hospitals out of the scheme — mostly hospitals conducted by religious orders. Local health authorities sometimes contract with these hospitals for the care of individual patients.

Sean O'Faolain's article was in *The Bell* of April 1951.

PAGE 65. The revised health bill was finally passed in the Dail, July 30, 1953, by a vote of 79 to 40, with the concurrence of Browne, the support of the Labor Party, and the opposition of Fine Gael. The Irish Medical Association opposed the bill to the end.

PAGE 66. The O'Kelly statement is on page 737 of the 1951 *Irish Catholic Directory;* the Dublin Corporation's resolution is on page 724. The item about the Fermoy Council was in the *Irish Catholic,* May 11, 1950. The item about the armed forces was in the *Irish News,* November 18, 1952. I personally observed many of the acts of homage described.

PAGE 69. The quotation is from the *Irish Ecclesiastical Record,* May 1923.

PAGE 70. The McDonald quotation is from page 305.

PAGE 71. The press circulation figures were made public in the Dail by the Minister for Finance and Commerce, and published in the *Irish Times,* March 20, 1953.

CHAPTER 5
CENSORSHIP, OFFICIAL AND UNOFFICIAL

PAGE 72. The Yeats statement is in *Senate Debates* (January 7, 1923). The *Catholic Bulletin* of March 1939, just after Yeats's death, deplored his designation as "the supreme man of letters writing in English in our time"; it recalled his "quarrel with Christianity" and his "long war on sacred things." In July 1939, this journal said: "A curious effort was made quite recently to impose the 'study' of the pointless outpourings of William B. Yeats on all schools. . . . Why such things should be is a very real mystery. The sinister move was promptly met with resistance, to which, we are glad to say, more than one Irish literary review was enabled to give point and strength." As a substitute for the works of Yeats, the editors proposed "a good selection of high grade prose literary material, which will positively contribute to the study of our permanent Christian Philosophy."

PAGE 73. Brown's statement is in the *Irish Monthly,* January 1936. A Catholic senator, debating the censorship in the Irish Senate (November 18, 1942), proudly announced: "Our standards are not the standards of the modern world." Canon 1399 (already cited in the note to page 10, above) is fully set forth in Bouscaren and Ellis (pp. 726ff).

PAGE 74. The Protestant canon's statement is in *The Liberal Ethic* (p. 78). Bishop Lucey's article was in the *Irish Ecclesiastical Record* of December 1937. An equally striking summary of the Catholic doctrine of limited intellectual freedom was written in February 1948 by the editor of *Blackfriar's,* the English Dominican magazine. He said: "The Church, then, cannot leave stupid ignorant mankind to choose its own truth in the way that the Protestant attitude to the Sacrament of Confirmation indicates for the young Christians. The custodian of Truth cannot allow the weak-minded to listen to persuasive words of heresy, or to agree to dissemination of books which spread error undermining the salvation of men's souls. The freedom of the will does not mean its liberty to sin."

The 1952 *Irish Catholic Directory* (p. 673) gives major credit for both the 1923 Censorship of Films Act and the 1929 Censorship of Publications Act to the leading Jesuit, Father Richard S. Devane, who died in 1950. The De Valera statement was in the *Catholic Bulletin,* July 1937.

PAGE 77. According to Fergus Murphy's *Publish or Perish* (Mercier Press), Ireland averaged only about 56 titles a year in the ten-year period from 1938 to 1948. The number of titles published in 1950 increased to 174. The 1951 total in the United Kingdom was 17,800.

PAGE 79. The O'Connor statement was in the *Irish Times*, August 24, 1946. The description of the workings of the Censorship Board is based on conversations with past and present members and officials. The list of banned books is taken from the published *Register of Prohibited Publications* of December 31, 1950 (obtainable from the Government Publications Sales Office, Dublin), and from the unpublished bound register at the Censorship Board's Dublin headquarters.

PAGE 90. The Kiely statement was in the *Standard*, December 22, 1950. The O'Faolain letter was in the *Irish Times*, January 28, 1948. The London meeting was described in the London *Catholic Herald*, July 1, 1949. The attack on the "Nasty Document" was in the *Irish Catholic*, June 30, 1949.

PAGE 91. The *Irish Press* comment was reported in the *Irish Catholic*, October 27, 1949.

PAGE 92. The honor accorded Greene and others was listed in the 1952 *National Catholic Almanac* (p. 486). The *Standard's* comment was in the issue of August 20, 1948. The *Irish Ecclesiastical Record* comment was in the issue of January 1949.

PAGE 94. The Senate debate on *The Laws of Life* was on November 18, 1942. Dr. Sutherland's protest was in the London *Tablet*, September 20, 1952.

PAGE 96. Father Brown's statement is from page 112. The story of Miss Dunbar-Harrison was told in the *Irish Times* in January, 1931, especially in the issues of January 6, 7, 9, 12, 13, 16, 21, and 22.

PAGE 98. Archbishop Gilmartin's statement was in the *Irish Times*, February 16, 1931. De Valera straddled the issue in a meeting at Irishtown, reported in the *Irish Times*, January 7, 1931. The *Catholic Bulletin* editorial was in the issue of March 1931.

PAGE 99. Sean O'Faolain's statement was in the *Irish Times*, July 13, 1949.

PAGE 101. The complaint of the *Irish Times* was in the issue of July 14, 1949.

PAGE 103. The two Devane statements are from the *Standard*, December 1, 1950, and October 27, 1950. The statement of the president of the Gaelic League is from the issue of November 10, 1950. The *Standard* of April 21, 1950, supported the Devane plan for a "licensing system" for imported newspapers, saying: "This would give us a chance of allowing the importation of desirable newspapers and periodicals." Many Irish county and city councils passed resolutions favoring this plan. The recently established Society for Banning Foreign Publications, at a Dublin mass meeting in 1952, announced a plan for establishing committees in every parish in Ireland to develop a boycott of "foreign literature." It is impossible to measure the effects of such propaganda. The Irish Republic's distribution of newspapers per capita is about one-third that of the United Kingdom, and less than half that of Australia, Norway, Denmark, and Sweden (*Irish Times*, August 19, 1953).

PAGE 104. The *Irish Catholic's* statement is from the issue of February 3, 1949. Ireland has nation-wide licensed radio, with 400,000 license-holders out of 650,000 households; Radio Eireann, unlike the B.B.C., carries sponsored programs.

PAGE 105. Father Agnellus Andrew's statement is from the *Clergy Review* of April 1951. The film data are from annual reports of the Film Censor, and from personal interviews. The law is in the Censorship of Films Act, 1923, and amendments of 1925 and 1930.

PAGE 106. *The Miracle* decision of the United States Supreme Court was published in the New York *Times*, May 27, 1952.

PAGE 107. The film critic's statement is from the *Irish Catholic* of February 3, 1949. The charge against Arthur Miller was published in the *Irish Times*, September 26, 1952. The complaint of the priests is from the *Standard*, December 8, 1950.

PAGE 109. The Salazar statement was quoted in the *Catholic Bulletin*, March 1939.

CHAPTER 6
SEGREGATED EDUCATION

PAGE 111. The only part of the Irish elementary-school system which might be considered "public," in the American sense of that word, is the system of vocational schools for post-primary work, attended chiefly by part-time students who work in the daytime and attend classes at night; under public agencies, they now enroll almost 90,000 students. But they are not unde-nominational in the American sense. They include denominational religious instruction in the curriculum; the Dublin Technical Schools alone employ forty clerical teachers "to teach Christian doctrine"; and the chairman of the controlling committee for these schools is a priest.

Irish school estimates are based on the most recent available annual reports, and on the educational statistics in the 1951 *Statistical Abstract of Ireland* (pp. 163-70). American estimates are based on studies by the National Education Association. A mimeographed study of school retention rates by the Research Division of the N.E.A. (dated June 1953, and based on the 1948-50 *Biennial Survey of Education in the United States*) showed that of all the children in the fifth grade in the United States in 1942-43, 90.9 per cent later went beyond the sixth grade; 80.7 per cent entered a high school (ninth grade) in 1946-47; 50.5 per cent were graduated from high school in 1949-50; and 22.5 per cent entered college in 1950.

The figure of $226, from the N.E.A., is for 1949-50. It is broken down into 85 per cent for current costs and 15 per cent for capital expenses. The *Teachers' Work* quotation is from the spring issue of 1945.

PAGE 113. The Minister for Education's statement and Father Brennan's article were published in the *Irish Ecclesiastical Record*, September 1938 (p. 260).

PAGE 114. The Catholic Education Council statement from England was in its 1951 booklet, *The Case for Catholic Schools*, a valuable summary of facts as well as propaganda for the expansion of Catholic schools throughout the British Isles. The *Irish Times* headline was in the issue of April 19, 1952; the Sean Moylan statement was in the issue of April 8, 1953.

PAGE 116. The statement of the I.N.T.O. president is from the *Irish Catholic*, April 8, 1948.

PAGE 117. The Protestant canon's boast was in the *Irish World*, November 13, 1937.

PAGE 118. The estimate of $25,000,000 is based on the Ministry for Education's budget of £10,252,000, as reported in the *Irish Times*, May 7, 1952.

PAGE 120. The verse is from Shearman's *Anglo-Irish Relations* (p. 80).

PAGE 121. The O'Flaherty quotations are from pages 21 and 29.

PAGE 123. The Johnson article was in the *Irish Ecclesiastical Record*, February 1937.

PAGE 124. The review of the sociology work was in the *Irish Ecclesiastical Record* of December 1935.

PAGE 125. The quoted prose passage is from page 83, and the poems from page 97, of M. T. Marnane's *A Guide for Catholic Teachers*, obtainable from the publishers, M. H. Gill, 50 Upper O'Connell Street, Dublin.

PAGE 126. The Mahony quotation about Spain is from page 121.

PAGE 127. The Murphy statements are from Part III, pages 76 and 74 respectively. The Sheehan statements are from pages 200, 201, and 205.

PAGE 128. The McQuaid statement was in the *Irish Times*, February 16, 1953. The Kinane warning was in the 1952 *Irish Catholic Directory* (p. 675).

PAGE 129. The extract from the professors' oath was in the *Standard*, January 28, 1949.

PAGE 130. The comment on the program of night study is from the *Irish Catholic* of July 20, 1950. Further facts are contained in an article by Alfred O'Rahilly, president of University College Cork, in *Blackfriar's* for February 1951. The *Standard's* comment on the National University debate was in the issue of January 28, 1949. The student's letter was in the *Irish Times*, January 19, 1949. The chief story of the canceled debate appeared in the *Irish Times* of January 17. The Trevelyan quotation is from page 431.

PAGE 131. The Devane quotation is from the *Irish Rosary*, December 1952.

PAGE 134. The MacDermott statement is from *Dail Eireann Debates* (February 17, 1937). The *Irish Monthly* quotation is from the issue of January 1949. The Olden statement is from the *Irish Times* of March 24, 1953.

PAGE 135. The Ussher statement is from page 141.

PAGE 136. The results of the 1911 literacy test are summarized by Ervine (pp. 195, 613). No formal literacy test has been made since 1911; but the records of persons signing their marriage documents with a cross indicate that the illiteracy rate, though now very low, is much higher in the South than in the North.

PAGE 138. The *Register* statement was in the issue of August 19, 1951. Moylan's statement was in the *Irish Press*, November 5, 1952.

CHAPTER 7
SEX, CHASTITY, AND POPULATION

PAGE 140. The figure of 700 brothels in Italy was given by the Rome correspondent of the London (Catholic) *Tablet*, March 15, 1952 (p. 207).

PAGE 141. Devlin's article was in *Christus Rex*, July 1952. The comparative significance of the 1951 census was analyzed in the *Irish Times* of April 29, 1953. The United Nations *Demographic Yearbook* for 1949-50 shows that the Republic has the lowest crude marriage rate in post-war Europe; but the reported birth rate is about average — 21, in comparison with 23.4 for the United States, 23.3 for Australia, 18.6 for Denmark.

PAGE 142. The Sean de Cleir article was in *Christus Rex*, October 1952. The Irish cities are growing at the expense of the countryside; Dublin has grown 45 per cent since 1911, while the rest of Ireland has declined 15 per cent. Oddly enough, one of the criticisms leveled at Irish peasants before the great famine was that they married too young, and that the priests promoted such marriages because of the large fees involved. See Sydney Smith's *Posthumous Fragments,* and Thomas Campbell Foster's *Letters on the Condition of the People of Ireland* (1846).

PAGE 143. The Protestant age-level figures are from Freeman (p. 172). A fertility inquiry in conjunction with the 1951 census, summarized in the *Irish Times* of May 27, 1952, showed that Catholic families were larger than Protestant ones, and that the fertility of Irish married women was high. It is their late marriage and emigration which keep the Irish population down. The Waters quotation is from the *Irish Ecclesiastical Record* of October 1938.

PAGE 145. The latest government population figures were published in the *Irish Times* of May 7, 1953. The statistics of the "young active" age group appeared in the same journal on April 29, 1953. The 1950-51 *Irish Statistical Survey,* compiled by the Central Statistics Office of the government, shows (p. 34) that the average annual net emigration in 1946-51 was 24,326, and the average annual natural increase (births minus deaths) was 25,481. Before that, from 1926 onward, the emigration exceeded the natural increase. Young women constitute the bulk of the emigrants. Said Sean MacBride (*Irish Times,* August 17, 1953): "If emigration continues for another 30 years, this country will be left with only old people."

PAGE 146. The Ryan quotation is from page 78.

PAGE 147. Arensberg (p. 72) describes the marriage customs of the Irish countryside in detail, and says that marriage arranged by matchmaking "is the only respectable method of marriage and the usual method of inheritance." Archbishop McQuaid of Dublin, in his Lenten pastoral of 1952, said: "We take occasion to express our grave disapproval of the practice which has begun to show itself of permitting young women to compete in cycling and athletics in mixed public sports" (*Irish Press,* February 25, 1952).

PAGE 148. Freeman (p. 173) gives the numbers of Catholic religious professionals as more than 11,000 nuns, postulants, and lay sisters; 6,000 clergy and monks; and over 3,000 theological students. The Ussher quotation is from page 130. The Maguire statement is from the *Irish Ecclesiastical Record* of April 1935; the Barry article is from the issue of March 1922. Says Father Benoit Lavand, O.P., in his article "Perfect Chastity," in *Blackfriar's* for January 1949: "The married state is not the best one for obtaining intimate union with God. . . . The Council of Trent anathematized 'all who teach that the state of marriage is preferable to the state of virginity or celibacy'."

PAGE 149. Frank O'Connor has kindly granted permission to quote from this poem, which was originally published by Maurice Friedberg in Dublin in 1945, and suppressed by the censors.

PAGE 150. The ages of recruitment are taken from notices in the Dublin Catholic press and from the 1952 *Irish Catholic Directory.* The words of Father Cassilly are from his *What Shall I Be?* Cassilly points out that St. Thomas Aquinas was offered to the Benedictines when 5 years old and joined the Dominicans at 15 or 16; and that Saint Rose of Lima made a vow of chastity at 5. As to the recruitment of nuns in England, the difficulties are described by Father J. Bennett in an article in *Blackfriar's* of September 1952: "At the present time the Church is facing a critical situation with regard to religious manpower. Until comparatively recently most Catholic girls wishing to engage in charitable work almost automatically became religious because only thus could they fulfill their vocation. Today social work has become a recognized and respected profession with high standards and, in many cases, with its own sense of vocation. . . . Religious life has lost its attractiveness and the modern girl is satisfied that her basic Catholicity is adequate to meet the demands of her profession as a social worker."

PAGE 151. The D'Elbee story is from the *Standard* of October 17, 1952. The Browne statement is from the *Irish Times* of July 27, 1949.

PAGE 152. The articles on venereal disease were published in July 1949.

PAGE 153. Irish priestly marriage in the eighth century is mentioned by H. C. Lea in his *History of Sacerdotal Celibacy* (Vol. I, p. 78).

PAGE 154. The Kornitzer statement was quoted, and the facts deplored, by the Scottish *Catholic Herald* of June 6, 1952; the author also said: "Only in Roman Catholic adoption work are there more children than there are adopters willing to take them." Ordinarily an illegitimate boy may not be a priest but an illegitimate girl may be a nun (*Irish Ecclesiastical Record*, May 1922). Pius XII's statement on therapeutic abortion was made on October 29, 1951, and his supplementary explanation on November 28; *Time* (November 12 and 26) discussed the papal views. The *Church of England Newspaper* called the Pope's doctrine "inhuman, callous, and cruel." The Dean of St. Paul's said: "The Pope's teaching would be regarded by most normal people as inhuman. . . . It seems to us that the death of the mother means the loss of a valuable personality. . . . On the other hand, no one knows whether the child will live."

PAGE 156. The statement referring to rape is from Mahoney (Vol. II, p. 415). The McCarthy article was in the *Irish Ecclesiastical Record* of June 1949.

PAGE 157. The W. H. O. story was summarized in the London *Express* of May 16, 1952, and the New York *Times* of May 20, 1952. The American and British delegates played inglorious roles in the surrender to Catholic pressure, and their inconsistency was exposed on the floor of the House of Commons by a Labor member, Douglas Houghton (*Hansard,* July 18, 1952).

PAGE 158. The League of Nations episode was described in the London *News Chronicle* of October 5, 1932; it was revived in 1953 by Dr. Marie Stopes, in a pamphlet version of her evidence before the Royal Commission on the Press, with a preface by Bertrand Russell. The Cohalan statement is from the *Irish Catholic* of October 5, 1950.

PAGE 159. The suppression of the B.M.A. recommendations on divorce was described in the *Irish Times,* July 4, 1952. After the suppression, the London Catholic *Universe* of December 19, 1952, headlined the victory: "Doctors' Guild Killed B.M.A.'s Divorce Idea." The O'Callaghan statement was in the *Irish Times* of May 6, 1953.

PAGES 160-61. The O'Donnell, Finlay and Yeats quotations are all from Yeats's speech in the 1925 *Senate Debates* (pp. 437ff).

PAGE 163. The *Standard* quotation is from the issue of August 12, 1949.

PAGE 164. The Catholic rule on excommunication for marriage by a Protestant minister is in Canons 1063 and 2319 (Bouscaren and Ellis, pp. 462, 863); the offense is listed under "Crimes Connected with Marriage." The mixed-marriage impediment for a son who wishes to become a priest is in Canon 981, and it was restated in the *Irish Ecclesiastical Record* of December 1950.

PAGE 165. The texts of the two decisions of the Higher Court and the Supreme

Court in the Tilson case are in the *Irish Ecclesiastical Record* of June 1951. Non-Catholics in Ireland are quite justified in wondering whether any non-priestly marriage of a Catholic would be recognized as legal if the North were absorbed by the South. Father Felim O Briain, Professor of Philosophy at University College Galway, in the *Irish Times* of November 1, 1949, bitterly attacked the present power of the Irish state to "uphold as valid a union that the Church condemned as invalid."

CHAPTER 8

FANATICISM AND MORAL CHILDHOOD

PAGE 168. The Shaw passage with which I begin and end this chapter is from page xx of the preface to *John Bull's Other Island*. The story of the arm of Saint Francis Xavier was in the 1951 *Irish Catholic Directory* (p. 717).

PAGE 169. The rule of eight days for retention of a heretical book, under Canon 1398, was in the *Irish Ecclesiastical Record* of November 1921. Canon Mahoney (Vol. II, p. 250) advises mothers superior to return rejected letters to their senders. The boast on heresy was in the *Irish Rosary* of December 1952.

PAGE 170. The rebuke was in the *Irish Ecclesiastical Record* of May 1951. The verdict on lying is from O'Donnell (pp. 209, 211). The horse-race rule is from the *Irish Ecclesiastical Record* of June 1951, and the bookmaking rule from the issue of April 1950. Both priests and religious brothers are generally forbidden to attend theaters (*Irish Ecclesiastical Record,* January 1935).

PAGE 171. The rules about plenary indulgences for a priest's first Mass and for kissing a bishop's ring are in Mahoney (Vol. II, pp. 292, 180). The rosary indulgences are from *The Rosary and How to Say It,* published in 1950 by the Catholic Truth Society of Ireland. The bribery ruling is on page 174 of O'Donnell.

PAGE 172. The theft ruling is on page 153 of O'Donnell.

PAGE 173. The statement on income-tax evasion appeared in the *Irish Times* of May 23, 1953, and it has not been denied by any Catholic authority. The comparative numbers of income-tax payers in North and South were given in the Dail by the Minister for Finance and Commerce; they were published in the *Irish Times* of April 29, 1953. Irish crime figures show that there has been a great increase in indictable offenses in recent years, but Donat O'Donnell, a responsible critic, writing in *Commonweal* of January 20, 1953, claimed that Ireland's crime rate is "probably" the lowest in the world.

PAGE 174. The spectacle-theft story was told in the Dublin *Evening Mail* of June 17, 1953, and in the *Irish Times* of June 27, 1953. Although the Church still lists drunkenness as a mortal sin, the consumption of liquor in Ireland is on the increase. In the *Irish Catholic* of December 2, 1948, Father Dargan, assistant director of the Pioneers, estimated that the Irish spend more than twice as much on drink as on primary education, children's allowances, and old-age pensions combined. The bishops' memorandum on gambling was summarized in the Scottish *Catholic Herald* of March 10, 1950. The *Clergy Review* of August 1950 published the following comment: "Lotteries are allowed by the laws of this country and so long as they are honestly conducted do not appear to constitute any evil. Pools have become a national pastime, and we consider that in some ways they are quite beneficial, since in many homes happy evenings are spent by the family remaining together and filling up their coupons."

PAGE 175. The "Apostolic Process in the Cause of Matt Talbot" opened in Rome on March 5, 1947. More than ninety meetings were held in Ireland to take evidence, etc. His body was exhumed on June 29, 1952.

PAGE 177. The Church of Ireland adoption story was told in the *Irish Press* and the *Irish Times* of June 12, 1952.

PAGE 178. The *Standard's* figures on non-Catholic employment were in the issue of November 12, 1948; the general claim was in the issue of September 5, 1952.

PAGE 179. Mahoney (Vol. II, p. 251) outlines the circumstances under which the superior of a religious institute has the power, "through the vow of obedience, to force a subject to vote for a certain candidate at a general election, for instance for a conservative rather than a liberal." The answer is affirmative only if the issue is clearly religious or moral — and Mahoney cites as examples the Spanish Civil War and the attack of the Belgian bishops on the Rex movement.

PAGE 180. The Singer episode was in the *Standard* of October 14, 1949.

PAGE 182. The Meath Hospital story appears in part in *Senate Debates* (February 28, 1951); in *Dail Eireann Debates* (December 6, 1950); and in the *Irish Times* of April 4, 5, 16 and 26, 1949.

PAGE 183. The *Catholic Mind* statements on Rotary were in the issues of February 1932 and July 1935.

PAGE 185. The O'Donnell statement is from page 62; his comment on the Church of England is from page 301.

PAGE 186. Stories and letters on the Papal Nuncio incident appeared in the *Irish Times* on November 1, 1952, and on many succeeding dates. The Skeffington explanation appeared in the issue of December 20, and that of Butler in the London *Spectator* of February 27, 1953.

PAGE 187. The Garbett statement appeared in the New York *Times* of March 2, 1953.

PAGE 192. De Valera's position on the Spanish Civil War appeared in *Dail Eireann Debates* (November 27, 1936), in reply to a pro-Franco speech on an unsuccessful motion of censure by William T. Cosgrave. The Devane praise of Salazar was in the *Irish Ecclesiastical Record* of November 1937.

PAGE 193. The Irish bishops' comment on Spain was published in the *Catholic Bulletin* of November 1937. The *Standard* quotation was in the issue of September 24, 1948.

PAGE 194. The *Catholic Bulletin's* eulogies of Mussolini were in the issues of April 1937 and June 1937.

PAGE 195. The Ryan statement was also published in *The Liberal Ethic*.

PAGE 197. The newspaper *Fiat* (published at 11 Lower Abbey Street, Dublin) is distributed by Maria Duce as its unofficial organ. Issue No. 27, distributed early in 1953, devoted the entire first page to a reprint of a Spanish bishop's article headed: "Freemasonry, Communism and Zionist Judaism, the Allies and Advisers of the Beast of the Apocalypse." The second page carried pictures of Felix Frankfurter, Henry Morgenthau, Jr., and Herbert Lehman over the heading: "Secret Government of the U.S.A."

PAGE 199. The Devane statement was in the *Irish Rosary* of December 1952.

PAGE 200. The Von Kuehnelt-Leddihn statements are from pages 206 and 207. He is author, under the pseudonym of Francis S. Campbell, of another book worth reading, *The Menace of the Herd;* and he is a frequent contributor to the American liberal Catholic weekly *Commonweal.*

Bishop Lucey's statement appeared in the April 1933 issue of the *Irish Ecclesiastical Record.* The movement for a corporate Catholic "vocational" state has fallen rather flat in Ireland because of the anti-fascist sentiment. De Valera appointed a 25-man Commission on Vocational Organization in 1939, and it rendered an informative 539-page report in 1943. The report repudiated fascist doctrine and did not endorse a corporate state as such. Nothing has been done to implement its general recommendations for professional and vocational co-operation.

PAGE 201. The O Briain statement was in the *Irish Independent* of November 25, 1952. Irish Catholicism, of course, has always been officially opposed to socialism, and the *Decrees of the Synod of Maynooth for the Laity,* published by the Catholic Truth Society, says (p. 12): "Particular care should be paid to the working class lest, lured by the promises and deceived by the frauds of Socialists, it lose its ancestral faith." No labor group in Ireland today dares to use the word "socialist" in its propaganda.

CHAPTER 9
NORTHERN IRELAND AND PARTITION

PAGE 204. The Hollis statement was in an article — one of three — in the *Tablet* of November 5, 1949.

PAGE 205. The critic cited is D. Lindsay Keir, quoted by Shearman on page 171 of *Not an Inch;* the direct Shearman quotation is from page 14.

PAGE 208. The MacBride statement was made in a Dublin address to his party's Ard Fheis, June 30, 1951. The constitutional quotations are from Articles 2 and 3.

PAGE 210. Mansergh has an excellent chapter, "The Communist International and the Irish Question," quoting the Marx-Engels correspondence on Ireland. One reason for the weakness of the British Labor Party in Northern Ireland is the distribution, largely by the nationalists, of 65,000 copies of a British *Tribune* pamphlet, *John Bull's Other Ireland,* by the able left-wing leader Geoffrey Bing. Bing's anti-Unionist treatment of the problem is completely one-sided, omitting all mention of the anti-democratic features of clerical policy, and of the acts of violence by nationalists which have made special protective measures necessary. He also omits all the major reasons why Northern workers wish to remain within the United Kingdom.

PAGE 211. For British Labor's stand on the Government of Ireland Act, see *Hansard,* May 18, 1920; for Labor's stand in 1949, see an article by Griffin Barry in the *Nation,* August 13, 1949. Geoffrey Ashe, writing in *Commonweal* for May 22, 1953, estimates that, of 20 Catholic members of the House of Commons, 16 are Laborites and continues: "The Labor Party gets the votes of 70 per cent of the Catholic community, with little clerical opposition." At the present time the pro-nationalist Irish Labor Party in the North is split by a bitter feud, and sections of the party are running candidates against one another. If it were not for this split, it would be safe to predict that the Irish

Labor Party would gain increasing control of the nationalist movement, since this movement is distinctly pro-labor. The situation is confused partly by the continued existence of the old Sinn Fein party, which continues to advocate non-participation in the Stormont parliament.

PAGE 213. De Valera's statement and the plea of the Derry nationalists were published in the *Nation*, January 13, 1942. The Churchill broadcast was on May 13, 1945; De Valera's reply was on May 17.

PAGE 214. De Valera's censorship of war news was described by W. L. Chenery in *Collier's*, January 26, 1946. The Unionist criticism of De Valera is in a pamphlet, *Ulster Is British*, which also contains a valuable factual summary of the Unionist political case, and is obtainable from the Ulster Unionist Headquarters, 2 Glengall Street, Belfast. Other valuable booklets explaining the Northern point of view are *The Problem of the Partition of Ireland* by "Red Nib"; and the government booklet *How Northern Ireland Is Governed*. Three valuable anti-Partition pamphlets (obtainable from the All-Party Anti-Partition Conference, Mansion House, Dublin) are *One Vote Equals Two; Discrimination;* and *Ireland's Right to Unity*.

The Catholic hierarchy in the United States was particularly bitter in its opposition to American entrance into World War II after the Soviet Union's entrance. Archbishop Beckman of Dubuque, on the Columbia radio network, July 27, 1941, described the war as "a war to make the world and particularly this beloved America safe for the new Bolshevism . . . a war of one imperialism against the other in which godlessness is incidental to all belligerents" (Brooklyn *Tablet*, October 23, 1948). In Boston, Cardinal O'Connell was a particularly strong isolationist. His diocesan paper, the *Pilot*, expressed the hierarchy's point of view quite accurately in a statement on April 19, 1941: "Shall we feel ourselves morally bound to don shining armor and go knight-erranting again?"

PAGE 215. The *Catholic Bulletin's* first statements were in the issue of June 1939; its later ones were in the issue of December 1939. The statement on Czechoslovakia was in the issue of October 1938.

PAGE 216. The Logue statement was in the *Irish Ecclesiastical Record* of August 1921. The MacRory statement was in the *Nation*, January 31, 1942.

PAGE 217. The bishops' warning against conscription was published in the *Catholic Bulletin* of May 1939.

PAGE 218. The De Valera statement at Strasbourg was in the Glasgow *Observer* of August 18, 1950. The *Irish Catholic's* suggestion of secession was in the issue of February 17, 1949.

PAGE 219. The Brookeborough statement is from *Ulster Is British* (p. 24). The Irish-American Catholic press is even more sulphurous in its language in discussing Lord Brookeborough, having coined the word "Basilmander." The *Irish Echo* of August 29, 1953, called him "Churchill's choice to carry on His Satannic Majesty's regime in the Six North-East Ulster Counties of St. Patrick's Ireland." The Aiken statement was in the *Irish Times* of May 4, 1953; the Northern nationalist proclamation was in the issue of July 2, 1953.

PAGE 221. The O'Malley statement was in the *Irish News* of January 2, 1953. The defeat of McAteer was described in the *Irish Times* of May 30, 1952 and the Wakehurst incident in the issue of February 21.

PAGE 224. The Derry program of conquest was the subject of warm exchanges in the Derry *Journal,* beginning with the issue of June 20, 1951, and in the Londonderry *Sentinel,* beginning with the issue of June 21.

PAGE 225. The Orange resolution addressed to the queen was in the *Irish Times* of July 4, 1953.

PAGE 226. Butler presents a careful study of the 1951 Northern Ireland election, by Desmond G. Neill of Queen's University, Belfast. Some fraudulent personation of voters exists, and political parties are afraid to canvass the territory of their opponents; but in other respects the findings do not indicate a very unusual situation.

PAGE 227. The new Massachusetts plan for gerrymandering was described in the New York *Times* of September 13, 1953, under the heading: "Bay State Draws New Political Map; G.O.P. Is Expected to Improve '54 Chances by Realigning Congressional Districts." The story pointed out that gerrymandering had begun with the Democrats, who "so redistricted Essex County that the alignment somewhat resembled a dragon or salamander in contour." The statement from the *Leader* was in the issue of September 13, 1952.

PAGE 230. The story of the strike in the Derry shirt factory was in the Belfast *Telegraph* of October 5, 1951. The leading Nationalist, Cahir Healy, summarized his charges of job discrimination in the Northern Ireland *House of Commons Debates,* January 13, 1953.

PAGE 232. The Devane statement was in the *Irish Rosary* of December 1952. The claim concerning the Northern birth rate was made by W. F. McCoy in the Stormont House, and reported in the *Irish Times* of November 15, 1951. For religious proportions in population and education, see the 1950 *Ulster Year Book* (p. 41); the 1950-51 report of the Ministry of Education; and especially Freeman (p. 166). McDermott and Webb (p. 16) tell of a limited investigation of Catholic and Protestant fertility rates in the North, indicating a higher rate among Catholics. The net 1951 emigration from Northern Ireland was 40,000, but over the period between 1926 and 1951 the emigration *rate* of the South was almost twice that of the North.

The *Irish Times* statement was in the issue of November 8, 1951. The statement of the deputy from Monaghan, Alexander Haslett, is in *Dail Eireann Debates* (November 19, 1936). The figures on rural population were in the *Irish Times,* May 1, 1953.

PAGE 233. The *Irish News* editorial about Enniskillen was in the issue of January 6, 1953; the story was in the issues of January 3 and 8.

PAGE 235. The Midgley statement was in the *Irish Times* of February 18, 1953.

PAGE 236. The Northern Ireland Committee of the Board of Education of the Church of Ireland estimated (*Irish Times,* May 14, 1952) that eventually the drift to public schools would reduce the attendance at its own denominational schools from 51,553 in 1923 to "less than 3,400." Meanwhile the Catholic primary schools in the North have increased in attendance from 67,923 in 1923 to 77,653 in 1950.

PAGE 241. The Blythe statement was in the *Irish Times* of October 28, 1950.

PAGE 244. The *Irish Times* editorial comment was in the issue of June 4, 1953; the chief stories about the suppression of coronation activities were in the issues of May 30, June 9, and July 4. The story of Roger Casement

Park was told in the issues of June 15 and July 29, 1953, and in the *Irish Echo* of June 20, June 27, and August 15.

CHAPTER 10
THE IRISH CATHOLIC EMPIRE IN AMERICA

PAGE 246. The estimate of Irish Catholics in the United States in 1790 is from Shaughnessy (p. 43).

PAGE 247. For details of the religious status in the colonies and early states, see Billington (pp. 6ff); Pfeffer; and Stokes (Vol. I).

PAGE 248. The quoted words of the Continental Congress are from McGee (p. 76); the poem is from Billington (p. 16).

PAGE 250. The *Irish American* quotation is from the issue of September 7, 1853, as cited by Ernst (p. 63). The Maguire quotation is from page 181.

PAGE 251. Handlin tells of the Quebec fiasco in *The Uprooted* (p. 55). His *Boston's Immigrants* is an important contribution to the whole Irish story. In Volume II of *International Migrations*, compiled by the International Labor Office, D. A. E. Harkness of Queen's University, Belfast, has an excellent chapter on Irish migrations. The criminal and pauper figures of early New York are given in Ernst (pp. 56-58). The Irish juvenile-delinquency estimates are from Maguire (p. 514). The bishops' statement on delinquency is quoted by Maguire (p. 511).

PAGE 252. Accounts of the convent-burning are in Billington; Stokes (Vol. I); and Maguire. Fairchild also tells the important story of the Molly Maguires.

PAGE 253. An article on Bowers by John Higham appeared in the *American Quarterly* in the spring of 1953. The Orangemen's troubles are described in Gibson (p. 248).

PAGE 254. The Sugrue quotation is from page 39. The Kane statement is from *Commonweal*, June 26, 1953. The Verot statement is from Cuthbert Butler's *The Vatican Council* (Vol. II, p. 53).

PAGE 255. The figures on the number of Irish bishops are from James Hackett (p. 5). The statement of the French observer is cited in the *Standard*, February 10, 1950.

PAGE 256. The Carroll statement on trusteeship is from O'Gorman (p. 269). The *Philadelphian* quotation is from Billington (p. 40).

PAGE 257. Stokes, Pfeffer, Butts, and Billington all give some account of the Hughes battle involving public schools.

PAGE 258. A Catholic historian, J. A. Burns, is cited by Stokes (Vol. I, p. 823), from his *Catholic Education* (p. 15). The *Freeman's Journal* statement of January 21, 1843, is quoted by Billington (p. 158).

PAGE 259. The Plenary Council statement is summed up by De Courcy (p. 205). The Murray quotation is from page 438.

PAGE 260. The *Citizen* editorial is from the issue of May 13, 1854; and the appeal for tolerance in the issue of June 10, 1854. Shane Leslie has called Mitchel "the most brilliant, the most downright and the most dreamshot of the patriots of '48."

PAGE 261. The McGlynn and McQuaid quotations are from Moehlman (pp. 47, 146).

PAGE 263. Daniel Bell, in the *Antioch Review* (Summer 1953), estimates the Catholics of Irish descent at half of the 30,000,000 total in the United States, and those of Italian descent at one-sixth of the total. (See also note to page 4, above.) In the absence of a religious census in the United States, it is possible only to guess at the Italian and Irish totals; the figure of 16,000,000 for those of Irish stock seems to fit in with the studies of Shaughnessy most logically, but there is no agreement on a scientific definition of the phrase "Irish stock."

PAGE 264. The Manning statement, in an address at Maynooth on June 24, 1953, was reprinted in the Dublin *Furrow*. The 1919 pastoral letter was in the 1953 *National Catholic Almanac* (p. 354). Said the *Irish World* of July 4, 1953: "Perhaps the most thorough Americans today are the Irish element, and of this element perhaps the most intensely patriotic are the readers of the *Irish World*."

PAGE 265. The *Irish World* quotation is from the issue of September 19, 1874, cited by Gibson (p. 329). The Churchill statement is quoted by Leslie (p. 171). Good accounts of De Valera's life are in MacManus, O'Faolain, and Gwynn. O'Hegarty gives an account unfavorable to De Valera.

PAGE 266. The *Irish World's* attack was in the issue of December 18, 1937. The suggestion of a possible 100,000 fanatical minority in America was made by Cornelius Ryan in an excellent, if somewhat pro-Costello, article on "Ireland Today" in *Collier's* of March 1951.

PAGE 267. The McCormack claim is from *Hearing on Unification of Ireland* (House Committee on Foreign Affairs, April 28, 1950, p. 5).

PAGE 268. Nixon's statement, given to the Irish News Agency in Boston and published in the *Irish Catholic* of September 11, 1952, read: "One thing that occurs to me is the possibility of putting pressure on the British when it comes to handling our American money. Then it would be made clear we do not favor their policy in relation to Ireland. It can be said that there is a better chance of the Republican administration doing something about Partition than the Democrats. Democrats have talked about the problem but did nothing. The reason for that is that the Democrats believe they have the Irish vote in their pockets. We are more honestly concerned in meeting the demands for the settlement of the Partition problem than are the Democrats." The news story then continued: "Senator Nixon said that the United States could exercise considerable moral weight behind the demand for the ending of Partition and he would endeavor to see it did so."

The nationalist leader mentioned was Cahir Healy, and his statement was summarized in the *Irish News* of December 31, 1952. The 1953 figures on the Congressional petition are from the *Irish Times* of May 26, 1953. Alistair Cooke said of the 1950 resolution on Irish unity: "It was considered one of those jokes that provide a brief, hilarious interlude in the day's serious business." The House reversed the vote about 24 hours later by a vote of 260 to 60.

PAGE 269. All testimony is from the *Hearing on Unification of Ireland* (House Committee on Foreign Affairs, April 28, 1950).

PAGE 270. Another New York Irish weekly, the *Advocate*, is more sober than the *Irish Echo*.

PAGE 271. The Troy articles on Ireland were in the *Irish Echo* of May 16, 23, and 30, 1953; the cartoons were in the issue of January 10, 1953.

PAGE 272. The O'Kelly paragraph is from page 245.

PAGE 273. The uproar over the *Life* article was described in part in the *Irish World* of January 27, 1945. The *Time* picture, which appeared in the issue of January 3, 1949, was attacked in the New York *Catholic News* of February 5, 1949. The Aiken statement was published in the *Irish Times* of April 30, 1953. The Los Angeles A. O. H. protest was in the *Irish World* of December 15, 1945.

PAGE 274. The O'Faolain article was in *Life* of March 16, 1953. The quoted attacks upon him appeared in the Brooklyn *Tablet* of May 2, 1953, and in the New York *Times* of April 20, 1953.

PAGE 275. Archbishop Cushing's reception was described in the *Standard* of September 30, 1949. The *Irish Press* stories on the Roosevelt-Spellman controversy were published on July 23 and 26, 1949. The *Standard* story appeared on July 29, 1949. The book review was in the *Irish Ecclesiastical Record* of January 1949.

PAGE 276. The *Irish World* editorial was in the issue of October 2, 1937.

PAGE 277. The Hallett statement was in the *Register* of June 27, 1948; the 1953 *National Catholic Almanac* claims were on pages 191 and 193.

PAGE 278. The *Life* statements about *The Moon Is Blue* are from the issue of July 13, 1953. The Mooring directive is from the Brooklyn *Tablet* of June 20, 1953.

PAGE 279. The New York Planned Parenthood fight was described in the New York *Times* of January 15 and May 8, 9, 10, 19 and 30, 1953.

PAGE 280. The question and answer are from the *Irish Ecclesiastical Record* of January 1944.

PAGE 281. The Commons statement is from page 182 of his *Races and Immigrants in America*. The most detailed claims of the Catholic Church as to the Catholic population of American cities are in the 1953 *National Catholic Almanac* (p. 188); but Boston Catholic leaders frequently claim much more than the estimated 45 per cent given by the *Almanac* — sometimes as high as 75 per cent. The Boston *Pilot*, official organ of the archdiocese, in 1949 claimed the largest percentage of Catholics of any American city; this would imply a Catholic percentage of at least 65. The analysis of the *U. S. News and World Report* was in the issue of November 21, 1951.

PAGE 282. The early story of Irish bossism in New York is told in part in Myers; and Werner's excellent review brings the story to a later date. The Ross statements were made in his *The Old World in the New* (pp. 262, 42).

PAGE 283. The Werner item is from page 77. The manner in which the politicians woo the Irish Catholic vote was demonstrated in the *Irish Echo* of September 12, 1953, in an advertisement for the New York Democratic primary, which read in part as follows:

FOUR COUNTIES DOMINATE WAGNER TICKET

CORK — WESTMEATH — MAYO — FERMANAGH

VOTE FOR ROBERT F. WAGNER FOR MAYOR

A true son of Cork, and a member of the Knights of Columbus, the American Legion, Catholic War Veterans, and the Friendly Sons of St. Patrick

VOTE FOR A BITTER FOE OF THE PARTITION OF IRELAND

Vote American — Vote Wagner and His Entire Ticket

PAGE 285. The Curley story is told by Dineen; and by Frank Kluckhohn in an article in the *American Mercury* of April 1948. The *Irish World's* statement for O'Dwyer was in the issue of November 10, 1945.

PAGE 286. The *Commonweal* article was in the issue of March 15, 1946. Another interesting Catholic analysis of Catholic responsibility for corruption appeared in the New York Catholic journal *Integrity* in October 1948. Said Father Edward Lodge Curran in the *Irish Echo* of April 4, 1953: "It is particularly obnoxious when bigoted critics try to blame our entire race for the derelictions of a few in politics. No one despises a defaulting Irish politician more than the Irish themselves."

PAGE 287. The O'Neill answer was in the *Irish Ecclesiastical Record* of October 1935.

PAGE 289. *Time* of November 17, 1952, estimated that "U. S. Roman Catholics have been voting about 75 per cent Democratic," but that in the 1952 presidential election "the percentage was cut down at least to 60 per cent." Lubell has a general discussion of the Catholic vote in America. When Edward J. Flynn died, the New York *Times* of August 19, 1953 said: "A long-time personal friend of President Roosevelt, Mr. Flynn was picked by the President to succeed Mr. Farley as National Chairman because of the necessity of naming another Roman Catholic." When Stephen Mitchell was appointed by Adlai Stevenson in the campaign of 1952, *Time* said: "Mitchell is a Roman Catholic, which is almost a requirement for the job of Democratic national chairman."

PAGE 290. Eisenhower's description, as reported in the *Irish Times* of May 21, 1952, was: "Although I myself am an avowed and almost fanatic Protestant, I willingly give credit to the efforts of the Roman Catholic Church and its Pope in fighting the evil and venom of the Kremlin."

PAGE 291. The Coughlin story is told in part in Myers' *History of Bigotry*. Coughlin's connection with Fahey is mentioned on page 449. The quoted phrase from his bishop was in *Time*, September 14, 1936. McCarthy's claim was in *America* of December 13, 1952.

PAGE 292. Curran's praise of McCarthy was described in the New York *Times* of June 1, 1953. The *Irish Echo's* statement was in the issue of May 23, 1953. Father Ginder's statements were in the Brooklyn *Tablet* of June 27 and July 11, 1953. The *Register* supported McCarthy with cartoons.

PAGE 293. The *Commonweal* attack on McCarthy was in the issue of July 24, 1953. In the issue of August 28, the editors stated: "The side we have chosen has some disreputable fellow-travelers. (So did the anti-Hitler and the anti-Mussolini movements.) But we do not believe that they form the center or the 'hard core' of anti-McCarthyism. That center, that 'hard core,' is composed rather of many of the most patriotic and responsible people in American life — Democrats and Republicans, liberals and conservatives; educators, journalists, public servants. Most of these, like the active editors of this magazine, are anti-McCarthy primarily *because* they are anti-Communist. Some of them may indeed be antagonistic, in an ultimate sense, to the two cities which The Commonweal wants to help build: a tolerable city for civilized men, and the City of God. There are undoubtedly dogmatic secularists, materialists and opportunists among them. But The Commonweal is not associated with them in any ultimate task. It joins them, rather, in fighting an immediate threat to those minimal values of a decent and orderly America which we believe McCarthyism endangers. For unless this fight is won we see little chance of preserving whatever is decent in the city of man we have — much less of building a better city."

The Catholic Press Association, in a report summarized in the Brooklyn *Tablet* of August 27, 1953, claimed a total Catholic press circulation of 19,765,809 in the United States and Canada. The Catholic side of the Matthews story was told at great length in the Brooklyn *Tablet* of June 11, 18, and 25, and August 1, 1953.

PAGE 294. Curran's suit was described in the New York *Times* of November 22, 1947.

CHAPTER 11

THE FUTURE OF IRISH CATHOLIC POWER

PAGE 298. The annual *Catholic Directory* gives almost complete figures for *priestly* mixed marriage, which in three recent years averaged about 34 per cent in a total of 314,000 *priestly* marriages (303,444 in 1952). A study summarized in the Brooklyn *Tablet* of August 1, 1953, indicates that, for every 6 Catholics who marry non-Catholics before a priest, 4 others marry such mates without a priest. Applying these proportions, we get in round numbers about 150,000 total marriages to non-Catholics annually. If we assume that 2 persons are transferred from a non-Catholic bloc of 130,000.000 to a Catholic bloc of 30,000,000 by each such marriage, one-third of the population could become Catholic in 77 years, one-half in 170 years. Toledo's population is 303,616.

PAGE 300. The Catholic bill to abolish divorce in Massachusetts was introduced in the House in 1947 by Representative Edward J. Donlan, and supported editorially by the *Pilot* of February 8, 1947, which said: "The only method by which the divorce horror in the state of Massachusetts can be controlled is to destroy divorce in its entirety."

PAGE 302. The defeat of the liberal Catholic wing on the school question is described by Moehlman (p. 150).

PAGE 303. The *Almanac* quotation is from page 357. The popes do not use such specific language about any country, but they support such demands with general statements. Pius XII on September 15, 1951, in a speech before the first international congress of teaching nuns (reprinted in the Brooklyn *Tablet* of November 3, 1951), stated as a general principle: "for those who have a part in drawing up school legislation we must expect that determination for justice, that, so to speak, democratic sense which corresponds to the will of the parents in such a way that the schools founded and directed by religious institutes be not placed in a worse condition than the state schools." This philosophy is made clear by the Boston *Pilot's* statement of May 19, 1951, that "state funds should be made available to responsible private schools whenever this will be necessary or useful in enabling these schools to function efficiently."

PAGE 304. Pfeffer has an excellent discussion of these three cases.

PAGE 305. The off-shore oil story was in the New York *Times,* July 31, 1953. The Hallett statement was in the *Register* of April 20, 1942.

PAGE 306. Australia once had state aid for denominational schools, but discontinued it. The Church in 1936 launched a heavy campaign to get public funds for its schools — a campaign led by graduates of the National University of Dublin. The New South Wales branch of the Australian Labor Party endorsed the principle of state aid for denominational schools in 1950 (*Standard,* August 4, 1950), but the hierarchy has not thus far been victorious in its drive. In 1947, about 21 per cent of the pupils of Australia attended Catholic schools (1951 *Official Year Book* of the Commonwealth of Australia). In 1952, Archbishop Mannix of Melbourne advocated a universal capitation payment for all pupils by the government; this would allow the Catholic schools to receive the same revenues as public schools. The Australian hierarchy is now advocating more immigration, against a rising wave of opposition. Its policy of large Catholic families is increasing the Catholic proportion in the population at a rapid rate. At a Sydney anti-birth-control mass meeting in 1951 (as reported in the Brooklyn *Tablet* of January 5, 1952), a Catholic doctor declared: "The only really happy women are women with large families. The most unhappy are those who practice birth control."

Four valuable articles about Canada's school system in relation to religious instruction have appeared recently in the *Information Service Bulletin* of the National Council of Churches for October 2, 1951; the *Catholic Digest* of March 1953; *Liberty,* first quarter of 1953; and the *Churchman* of May 15, 1949.

PAGE 307. The statement of the N.C.E.A. appeared in the New York *Times* of April 17, 1953.

PAGE 308. The Mahoney statement was in the Buffalo *News* of February 18, 1952. The *Irish World* editorial was in the issue of July 28, 1937.

PAGE 309. The complete text of the Conant speech was in the *N.E.A. News* of the National Education Association, May 16, 1952. The Cushing reply appeared in the Brooklyn *Tablet* of April 19, 1952. Typical of the anti-Conant headlines in the Catholic press was that of the *Register* of February 1, 1953, when Conant was named United States High Commissioner to Germany: "Conant Appointment Seen Help to Anti-Christians."

PAGE 310. The statement from the N.C.E.A. convention was reported in the New York *Times* of April 16, 1952.

PAGE 311. The figures concerning Boston's schools are derived from the 1951 *Annual Statistics* of the Boston public schools.

PAGE 312. The Cambridge facts are mostly from Sections I-XII of *The Cambridge School Survey,* 1947 (pp. 334, 330, 15).

PAGE 314. My letter was published in *Church and State* (organ of Protestants and Others United for the Separation of Church and State), March 1953.

PAGE 315. Statistics on New York schools are from the New York *Times* of September 14, 1953; on Brooklyn schools, from the Brooklyn *Tablet* of August 15, 1953. The Board of Education story was in the New York *Times,* May 1, 1953.

PAGE 316. Portions of the Cavallaro story were in the New York *Post* of April 26, 1949; in the New York *Times* of May 19 and July 5, 1953; and in the Brooklyn *Tablet* of May 23, July 4, and July 11, 1953. The Hovde story was in the New York *Times* of February 18, 19, and 21, 1949, and in the Brooklyn *Tablet* of March 12, 1949. The *Tidings* statement on UNESCO was quoted in *Commonweal,* August 21, 1953. The anti-UNESCO side was given in the Brooklyn *Tablet* of July 18, 1953.

PAGE 317. The Providence *Journal* editorial was in the issue of January 13, 1952; the Pawtucket story appeared in the issues of January 4 to 13. Part of the Stoddard story appeared in the New York *Times* of July 30 and August 3, 1953.

PAGE 320. The National Council statement was in the New York *Times* of December 13, 1952. The Malloch plan, inspired by "a recent visit to the provinces of Ontario and Quebec," appeared in the April 1953 *Marianist*, was condensed in the *Catholic Digest* of May 1953, and was commented upon at length by the author in *Commonweal*, June 19, 1953.

PAGE 321. The Greeley statement is contained in a pamphlet by V. T. Thayer, *Religion and Our Public Schools*.

PAGE 322. The statement is from page 22 of *Eucharist Quizzes* (Radio Press). The Sugrue statement is from page 60.

PAGE 323. The study on mixed marriages was summarized in the Brooklyn *Tablet* of August 1, 1953. See also note to page 298, above. Actually, on the basis of available studies, almost 12 per cent of the marriages of American Catholics may be assumed to be non-priestly. Father Peter Bernardino in the *Homiletic and Pastoral Review* (Vol. XXXIV, p. 1267) indicates a loss to the public schools of 80 per cent of all children of non-priestly mixed marriages, and a loss of 55 to 70 per cent from priestly mixed marriages. See also *Acolyte*, July 11, 1928, and the *American Ecclesiastical Review*, July 1948.

The Cuneen quotation is from *Commonweal* of August 7, 1953.

PAGE 325. The doctrinal controversy came to a head in 1949 in a series of articles in the June and September issues of the Jesuit magazine *Theological Studies*, edited by John Courtney Murray, S.J. Murray praised certain aspects of the First Amendment, especially "its provision for religious liberty," and said that "the totalitarian threat has made it clear that the freedom of the Church is intimately linked to the freedom of the citizen; where one perishes, so does the other." In the *American Ecclesiastical Review* of May 1951, Murray carried his argument further, contending that the state church "does not represent a permanent and unalterable exigence of Catholic principles." Murray's position was condemned by the editor of that journal in the issue of June 1952, in an article, containing a detailed bibliography of the whole controversy, which argued that civil society itself should "worship God according to the rites of the Church." When the Spanish hierarchy attacked the more liberal American view (New York *Times*, May 21, 1952), Father Hartnett of *America* replied. Cardinal Ottaviani expressed the Vatican's reactionary position by deploring liberalism and supporting Spanish intolerance; the New York *Times* of July 23, 1953, contains a summary, and the *American Ecclesiastical Review* of May 1953 the full text, of Ottaviani's statement. The *Commonweal* attacks on the more conservative position were in the issues of August 7 and September 18, 1953.

PAGE 327. The Michael Davitt quotations are from Skeffington's important work (pp. 236, 269).

Bibliography

Books

Anderson, Jack, and May, Ronald W. *McCarthy: The Man, the Senator, the "Ism."* Boston: Beacon Press, 1952.

Arensberg, Conrad M. *The Irish Countryman.* New York: Macmillan, 1937.

Arensberg, Conrad M., and Kimball, Solon T. *Family and Community in Ireland.* Cambridge: Harvard University Press, 1940.

Beckett, J. C. *A Short History of Ireland.* London and New York: Hutchinson & Co., 1952.

Billington, R. A. *The Protestant Crusade.* New York: Macmillan, 1938.

Bing, Geoffrey. *John Bull's Other Ireland.* London: *Tribune,* 1950.

Blanshard, Paul. *American Freedom and Catholic Power.* Boston: Beacon Press, 1949.

Bouscaren, T. Lincoln, and Ellis, Adam C. *Canon Law: Text and Commentary.* Milwaukee: Bruce Publishing Co., 1946.

Butler, D. E. *The British General Election of 1951.* London: Macmillan, 1952.

Butts, R. Freeman. *The American Tradition in Religion and Education.* Boston: Beacon Press, 1950.

Chauvier, Roger. *History of Ireland.* Dublin: Clonmore and Reynolds, 1952.

Colvin, Ian. *The Life of Lord Carson.* 3 vols. London: Macmillan, 1937.

Constitution of Ireland (1937). Dublin: Government Publications Sale Office, 1951.

Curtis, Edmund. *A History of Ireland.* London: Methuen, 1945.

Davitt, Michael. *The Fall of Feudalism in Ireland.* London and New York: Harper, 1904.

De Courcy, Henry. *The Catholic Church in the United States.* Ed. Dunigan, 1857.

Devane, Richard S. *The Failure of Individualism.* Dublin: Browne and Nolan, 1948.

Dineen, Joseph F. *The Purple Shamrock.* New York: Norton, 1949.

Duff, Charles. *Ireland and the Irish.* London and New York: T. V. Boardman and Company, 1952.

Ernst, Robert. *Immigrant Life in New York City, 1825-1863.* New York: King's Crown Press, 1949.

Ervine, St. John G. *Craigavon, Ulsterman.* London: Allen and Unwin, 1949.

Evans, Anna L. *The Disestablishment of the Church of Ireland in 1869.* Lancaster, Pa., 1929.

Fahey, Denis. *The Mystical Body of Christ in the Modern World.* Dublin: Browne and Nolan, 1952.

Fairchild, Henry Pratt. *Immigration.* New York: Macmillan, 1913.

Freeman, T. W. *Ireland.* New York: Dutton, 1950.

Gallagher, Sister Anthony Marie. *Education in Ireland.* Washington: Catholic University of America, 1948.

Gibson, Florence E. *The Attitudes of the New York Irish Toward State and National Affairs, 1848-1892.* New York: Columbia University Press, 1951.

Gwynn, Denis. *The History of Partition*. Dublin: Browne and Nolan, 1950.
.... *De Valera*. London: Jarrolds, 1933.
Hackett, Francis. *Ireland: A Study in Nationalism*. New York: B. W. Huebsch, 1918.
.... *The Story of the Irish Nation*. New York: Century, 1922.
Hackett, James D. *Bishops of the United States of Irish Birth or Descent (1789-1935)*. American Irish Historical Society, 1936.
Handlin, Oscar. *Boston Immigrants, 1790-1865*. Cambridge: Harvard University Press, 1941.
.... *The Uprooted*. Boston: Little, Brown, 1951.
Industrial Potentials of Ireland. New York: Ibec Technical Services Corporation, 1952.
Irish Catholic Directory and Almanac. Dublin: James Duffy and Company, 1953.
Irish Times Review and Annual for 1952. Dublin, 1953.
Johnston, Joseph. *Irish Agriculture in Transition*. Dublin: Hodges, Figgis, 1951.
Kiely, Benedict. *Counties of Contention*. Dublin: Mercier, 1945.
Lecky, W. E. H. *A History of Ireland in the Eighteenth Century*. 5 vols. London: Longmans, Green, 1892.
Leslie, Shane. *The Irish Tangle*. London: MacDonald and Company, n.d.
The Liberal Ethic. (A symposium of letters.) Dublin: Irish Times, 1950.
Lubell, Samuel. *The Future of American Politics*. New York: Harper, 1952.
Macardle, Dorothy. *The Irish Republic*. London: Victor Gollancz, 1937.
McCarthy, Michael J. F. *Irish Land and Irish Liberty*. London: Robert Scott, 1911.
McDermott, R. P., and Webb, D. A. *Irish Protestantism Today and Tomorrow*. Dublin: Association for Promoting Christian Knowledge, 1945.
McDonald, Walter. *Reminiscences of a Maynooth Professor*. London: Jonathan Cape, 1925.
McGee, Thomas D'Arcy. *A History of the Irish Settlers in North America*. Boston: Patrick Donahoe, 1852.
McKnight, John P. *The Papacy*. New York: Rinehart, 1952.
MacManus, M. J. *Eamon De Valera*. London: Victor Gollancz, 1944.
Maguire, John Francis. *The Irish in America*. London: Longmans, Green, 1868.
Mahoney, Canon E. J. *Questions and Answers*. London: Burns Oates, 1947.
Mansergh, Nicholas. *Ireland in the Age of Reform and Revolution*. London: Allen and Unwin, 1940.
Maynard, Theodore. *The Story of American Catholicism*. New York: Macmillan, 1941.
Moehlman, Conrad H. *The Wall of Separation Between Church and State*. Boston: Beacon Press, 1951.
Murray, John O'K. *Popular History of the Catholic Church in the U.S.* D. and J. Sadlier, 1879.
Myers, Gustavus. *History of Bigotry in the United States*. New York: Random House, 1943.
.... *The History of Tammany Hall*. Published by the author, 1901.
National Council for Civil Liberties. *Report of a Commission of Inquiry*. (Special Powers Act, Northern Ireland.) London, 1936.
Nichols, James Hastings. *Democracy and the Churches*. Philadelphia: Westminster Press, 1951.

O'Casey, Sean. *Inishfallen Fare Thee Well.* New York: Macmillan, 1949.

O'Donnell, Michael. *Moral Questions.* Dublin: Standard House, 1945.

O'Faolain, Sean. *The Irish.* London: Penguin, 1947.

———————— *King of the Beggars: A Life of Daniel O'Connell.* New York: Viking, 1938.

———————— *The Life Story of Eamon De Valera.* Dublin: Talbot, 1933.

O'Flaherty, Liam. *Tourists Guide to Ireland.* London: Mandrake Press, 1929.

O'Gorman, Thomas. *A History of the Roman Catholic Church in the United States.* Vol. IX in "American Church History Series." New York: Scribner's, 1916.

O'Hegarty, P. S. *A History of Ireland Under the Union, 1801 to 1922.* London: Methuen, 1952.

O'Nuallain, L. *Ireland: Finances of Partition.* Dublin: Clonmore and Reynolds, 1952.

Pakenham, Frank. *Peace by Ordeal.* London: Jonathan Cape, 1935.

Pfeffer, Leo. *Church, State, and Freedom.* Boston: Beacon Press, 1953.

Register of Prohibited Publications. Dublin: Stationery Office, 1951.

Report of Commission on Vocational Organization. Dublin: Stationery Office, 1943.

Ryan, W. P. *The Pope's Green Island.* London: Nisbet, 1912.

Shaughnessy, Gerald. *Has the Immigrant Kept the Faith?* New York: Macmillan, 1925.

Shaw, Bernard. *John Bull's Other Island.* London: Constable, 1927.

Shearman, Hugh. *Anglo-Irish Relations.* London: Faber and Faber, 1948.

———————— *Not an Inch.* London: Faber and Faber, 1942.

Sheehan, Archbishop M. *Apologetics and Christian Doctrine.* Dublin: M. H. Gill, 1951.

Skeffington, Francis Sheehy. *Michael Davitt: Revolutionary Agitator and Labor Leader.* London: T. Fisher Unwin, 1908.

Statistical Abstract of Ireland, 1951. Dublin: Stationery Office, 1951.

Stokes, Anson Phelps. *Church and State in the United States.* New York: Harper, 1950.

Strauss, E. *Irish Nationalism and British Democracy.* London: Methuen, 1951.

Sugrue, Thomas. *A Catholic Speaks His Mind.* New York: Harper, 1952.

Thayer, V. T. *The Attack Upon the American Secular School.* Boston: Beacon Press, 1951.

Trevelyan, George M. *History of England.* London and New York: Longmans, Green, 1945.

Ulster Year Book, 1950. Belfast: H. M. Stationery Office, 1950.

Ussher, Arland. *The Face and Mind of Ireland.* London: Victor Gollancz, 1950.

Werner, M. R. *Tammany Hall.* New York: Doubleday, Doran, 1928.

PERIODICALS

For a study of this nature, periodicals are even more useful than books. Among Irish periodicals, the *Irish Times* is the most important because of the volume and reliability of its information. Among Catholic weeklies in Ireland, the *Standard* comes first, the *Irish Catholic* second. Among Catholic monthlies and quarterlies, the *Irish Ecclesiastical Record* is the most essential. Other important journals are the Dublin Jesuit magazine *Studies;* the *Irish Rosary;*

Christus Rex; and a Dublin journal that is now defunct, the *Catholic Bulletin.* The annual *Irish Catholic Directory and Almanac* is indispensable.

In Northern Ireland, the one important source of Catholic information is the *Irish News* of Belfast. The leading non-Catholic dailies are the Belfast *Telegraph,* the *Northern Whig,* and the Belfast *News Letter.*

In the United States, the most partisan of the Irish Catholic weeklies is the *Irish Echo* of New York; the *Irish World* and the *Advocate* are more sober. More important than the exclusively Irish journals for an understanding of the total situation are the large standard Catholic weeklies. Among these, the Brooklyn *Tablet* is the most important, the Boston *Pilot* less voluminous, the *Register* and *Our Sunday Visitor* about equally revealing. The annual *National Catholic Almanac* is the richest mine of contemporary facts about American Catholicism.

Index

Supplement to

THE IRISH
AND CATHOLIC POWER

by Paul Blanshard

THE BEACON PRESS • BOSTON

1. *Corrections*

On the jacket of *The Irish and Catholic Power* by Paul Blanshard, issued by the Beacon Press in 1953, the author and the publishers promised that they would issue a supplement, to be distributed free of charge on request, to correct any substantive errors discovered in the text of the first printing. A few minor substantive errors have been found and will be corrected as follows in all subsequent printings:

PAGE 115. Although the Waterford teacher who was discharged for his liberalism by the school's priest-manager served later in the International Brigade in Spain, he was discharged not for this reason but earlier (in 1935) on the ground that he had participated in an Irish Republican Congress meeting in Dublin, which had displayed some socialist tendencies.

PAGE 155. The case against the Massachusetts birth-control law was somewhat overstated. The law provides penalties for a doctor's conduct at a birth-control consultation if he implements his advice in any way by exhibiting or furnishing a contraceptive or by giving certain information in writing. For example, a doctor who shows a diaphragm to a woman patient, or gives her a fitting, or directs to a specific druggist a prescription for a contraceptive device violates the law. This makes birth-control clinics impossible, but technically it does not prevent oral advice if such advice stands alone. (Mass. General Laws, Chap. 272, Secs. 20 and 21.)

PAGE 236. In the last paragraph the inference about the Scottish system of controlling Catholic school buildings is not quite accurate. Under the complicated Scottish system of dual control, the title of the school buildings passes to the government, but the buildings are leased back to the Catholic authorities — rather than the other way around.

PAGE 247. The phrase "Puritans who landed on Plymouth Rock" should read "Pilgrims who landed on Plymouth Rock."

PAGE 296. The phrase "all elementary education" should read "nearly all elementary education."

PAGE 332. Under the date of 1315, "King of Ulster" should read "King of Ireland."

2. *Interpretations and Typographical Errors*

In addition to the substantive errors just discussed, several matters of interpretation or omission, slips in citation, and typographical errors will be corrected as follows in subsequent printings:

PAGE 22. Cromwell had not only a general but also a particular motive for his harsh treatment of the Irish Catholics in 1649: he was avenging the terrible slaughter of Protestants in Ireland in 1641.

Copyright 1954 by Paul Blanshard. Printed in U.S.A.

PAGE 130. In the quotation from Trevelyan, "questioning orthodoxy" should read "unquestioning orthodoxy."

PAGE 248. In the poem, "Gaelic Papists" should read "Gallic Papists."

PAGE 276. One Irish scholar has privately — and quite properly — chided the author for mentioning the *Irish News* story about St. Brendan without pointing out (a) that St. Brendan, according to the legend, is supposed to have discovered America in the sixth instead of the ninth century, and (b) that the name "Ireland the Great" was supposedly used by the missionaries of the ninth instead of the sixth century. It should also have been pointed out that there is some serious literature supporting these claims.

PAGE 320. "Dean James J. Malloch" should read "Dean James M. Malloch."

PAGE 324. The editors of the *Commonweal* have objected to the statement that they are not representative of Irish-American Catholicism and that they "are constantly dancing on a tight rope over the gulf of excommunication. . . ." Although the author believes that the statement is both justifiable comment and substantially true, he has no desire to question either the sincerity of the editors' faith or their actual loyalty to Catholic law. In fact, he regards the *Commonweal* as the most hopeful and intelligent force in American Catholicism today. He has therefore agreed to change the offending metaphor in future printings to read: ". . . its editors are far in the vanguard in their social and economic liberalism. . . . " However, the view that the *Commonweal* is not representative of American Catholicism has been officially sustained by Cardinal Spellman's Chancery Office in a letter dated December 10, 1953, and published in the Brooklyn *Tablet* of March 27, 1954. The letter, which confirms the fact that the magazine "does not have any ecclesiastical approval," concludes: "It is unfortunate that the *Commonweal* is described as a 'Catholic' magazine, for actually such is not the case."

PAGES 351-352. In the last sentence of the note to page 164, "Canon 981" should read "Canon 987." In the first sentence of the note to page 169, the issue of the *Irish Ecclesiastical Record* cited should be April 1924 instead of November 1921. The November 1921 issue covers the reading matter of nuns, referred to elsewhere on page 169.

Although these last two errors of citation did not in any way affect the accuracy of the main text, they were made the chief occasion for complaint in a smashing editorial in the St. Louis Catholic *Register,* in which the editorial writer pretended that Catholic law had been seriously misrepresented. By checking the sources as corrected above, readers may see for themselves that the principles cited — the rule about sons of non-Catholics becoming priests and the rule about the retention of heretical books — are squarely based on Canons 987 and 1398 respectively. Canon 987 provides: "Simply excluded from receiving orders are (1) Children of non-Catholics so long as the parents remain in their error. . . ." (*Codex Juris Canonici,* Vatican Polyglot Press, 1947, p. 274). Canon 1398 specifically lists retention of forbidden books as a sin (*Ibid.,* p. 380). Of course, dispensations from these rules are sometimes granted.

PAGE 361. In the note to page 298, the mixed-marriage study mentioned is *The Truth About Mixed Marriages* by Father John A. O'Brien (Our Sunday Visitor Press, 1953). It is neither comprehensive nor up-to-date.

3. Supplementary Facts

Because of the importance of several events that took place in Ireland after the book went to press, the author wishes to add here some supplementary facts, which he will include in later editions of the book:

(1) In the Irish Republic's general election on May 18, 1954, DeValera's Fianna Fail was defeated, although it remained the largest single party in the state. John A. Costello (pronounced with the accent on the first syllable), leader of the opposition, became prime minister again by putting together his shaky and incongruous coalition of conservatives and labor. The election result had little significance for matters of Catholic power and policy, since all Irish parties are about equally submissive to the Church. Dr. Noel Browne, who had challenged the bishops in 1951 with his mother-and-child health scheme, was defeated for re-election.

(2) In the October 1953 election of the parliament of Northern Ireland (Stormont), the nationalist and unionist forces were returned in exactly the same proportions as before — 39 for continued association with Great Britain and 13 for union with Dublin. The most striking event during the campaign was the election of a young nationalist, Liam Kelly, as Republican Abstentionist from mid-Tyrone, after he had openly championed "force, the more the better," against the Northern government. He was tried in a Belfast court (whose authority he refused to acknowledge), was found guilty of sedition on December 5, 1953, and chose to go to jail for a year rather than pay a fine.

(3) Father Denis Fahey, leader of the right-wing organization Maria Duce, died in Dublin in January, 1954, and Prime Minister DeValera attended the obsequies.

(4) Among several hundred books added to the banned list by the Irish Censorship Board after mid-1953 were Kinsey's *Sexual Behavior of the Human Female; The Second Happiest Day* by John Phillips; *Too Late the Phalarope* by Alan Paton; *The Fires of Spring* by James A. Michener; and *The Second Sex* by Simone de Beauvoir.

(5) In June 1954 the Vatican announced the transfer of Archbishop O'Hara from Dublin to London, to serve as Apostolic Delegate to Great Britain — a post without diplomatic status which is, technically at least, outside the range of the McCarran act.

7498 4